YOU CAN'T SERVE TWO MASTERS

Undivided Allegiance To Christ In An Age of Cultural Compromise

Drew Reitzel

Published 2026

Undivided Allegiance Press

ISBN: 979-8-9964176-0-5

Printed in the United States of America

For information about bulk orders, speaking engagements, or ministry partnerships, visit UndividedAllegiance.com

Dedication

To God, whose mercy endures beyond every failure and whose grace made this book possible—not because I deserved it, but because He is faithful.

To my mother, whose prayers outlasted my wandering and whose life was the first sermon I ever heard. You showed me what it looks like to love God with your whole life, not just your words. This book exists because you never stopped believing.

And to the godly men God has placed in my path—you know who you are. Iron sharpens iron, and you have sharpened me. I am grateful beyond what words can hold.

Contents

Chapter 1: The Rise of Cultural Christianity

Section I: The Hollowing of Holiness

The crisis of the American church did not arrive like a sudden storm. It emerged like a slow leak beneath the floorboards, unnoticed at first, tolerated next, and eventually treated as normal.[1] The landscape of modern Christianity is now littered not with the fruit of repentance but with the debris of compromise, shaped less by persecution pressing in from without than by corrosion rising from within. This is not chiefly the age of open rebellion against God but of gradual drift, quiet accommodation, and dignified apostasy. The tragedy is not that the world has rejected truth; the tragedy is that the Church has grown comfortable without it.

The vocabulary of faith remains familiar: grace, repentance, holiness, obedience. But the meaning of these words has been drained, reshaped, and repurposed to satisfy a culture that elevates affirmation above surrender and self-expression above submission. If one can claim salvation without submission, faith without faithfulness, or belief without obedience, then Christianity becomes a label rather than a life, an affiliation rather than a rebirth. And when faith is reduced to self-identification, it becomes indistinguishable from the culture it was meant to confront. Scripture does not recognize such a faith. It declares plainly, *"Having the appearance of godliness, but denying its power."* (2 Timothy 3:5).[2] Appearance without power is not weakness; it is deception.

The unraveling of spiritual conviction began when the Church traded the fear of the Lord for the approval of men.

Reverence was quietly replaced with relevance, and the pulpit, once a furnace that refined the saints, cooled into a stage that entertains spectators.[3]

The call to holiness, once thundered with apostolic authority, was softened into suggestions for self-improvement. Pastors once trained to rightly divide the Word of truth became managers of religious sentiment, shaping their messages to avoid offense, preserve attendance, and maintain institutional peace. A Church that no longer trembles before God will inevitably tremble before culture, donors, critics, and the shifting winds of ideology. Grace becomes a blanket for rebellion rather than the power to overcome it. Faith becomes an accessory rather than a summons to allegiance. Sin becomes a misstep instead of spiritual treason. Christ becomes a consultant instead of a King.

This collapse was not accidental. Thomas Watson warned centuries ago that when a people lose their reverence for God, they lose everything that flows from it—wisdom, moral clarity, and the courage to stand against the tide of their age.[4] When the fear of the Lord evaporates, so does wisdom, discernment, and conviction. Scripture declares without apology, *"The fear of the Lord is the beginning of wisdom."* (Proverbs 9:10).[5]

The fear of the Lord is the foundation of everything else. When it collapses, wisdom goes with it, and when wisdom goes, moral clarity follows. The most basic tenets of Christian morality become negotiable; sexuality, marriage, gender, justice, truth, and holiness are treated as matters of personal interpretation rather than divine decree. The Church begins to mirror the culture rather than confront it. But Scripture has never granted permission to adjust righteousness to the temperature of the times.

The American church's descent into sentimentalism accelerated as her understanding of God Himself shifted. The biblical portrait of the Almighty, holy, sovereign, righteous, and consuming was domesticated into a deity whose primary attribute is therapeutic comfort.[6] God's holiness became a footnote. His justice became an embarrassment. His sovereignty became a philosophical inconvenience. What remained was a god fashioned in the image of Western sentimentality: affirming, indulgent, and harmless. Sproul understood this with prophetic clarity: a god who makes no demands produces worshipers who have no convictions, and a Christ stripped of holiness cannot save anyone from sin.[7] He offends no one, transforms no one, and judges no one. And a Christ without judgment inevitably produces a Christianity without conviction.

Every era has its idols, but today's idol is autonomy, the enthronement of the self as ultimate authority. The Church, desperate not to appear outdated or oppressive, subtly sanctified this idol. Rather than calling sinners to bow before Christ, she began suggesting that Christ bends toward their preferences. The gospel was reframed not as rescue from sin but as validation of identity. The Church stopped asking, "What does God require?" and began asking, "What will people tolerate?" This inversion was not theological evolution; it was theological surrender. As Tertullian warned the early church, when God is treated as weightless, sin grows bold, and the conscience dulls.[8]

The modern believer often seeks the benefits of the cross without the burden of it, the comfort of God's promises without the confrontation of His authority, and the warmth of

His compassion without the weight of His commandments. It is not ignorance alone that produces a hollow Christianity, but a willful refusal to yield. Cloaked in religious language and Christian sentiment, this refusal has produced a faith that outwardly honors Christ while inwardly dethroning Him.

Even secular observers recognize what the Church has refused to confront. Jordan Peterson, analyzing Western cultural collapse from outside the faith, has warned that modern people "confuse feelings with convictions," treating emotional resonance as moral legitimacy.[9]

When this framework infiltrates the Church, repentance becomes psychologically destabilizing, holiness becomes oppressive, and obedience becomes optional. Douglas Murray, another voice from beyond the church walls, notes that modern Western societies now operate under the assumption that "hurt feelings carry the weight of moral claims."[10] Churches, eager to appear compassionate, have quietly absorbed this expectation. But compassion divorced from truth is neither love nor mercy; it is surrender. A Church that affirms what God condemns cannot claim to represent Him.

The consequences of this shift are visible everywhere. Churches swell in attendance but shrink in holiness. Worship is loud, but lives are unchanged. The metrics of success, attendance, giving, and engagement replace the biblical metrics of fruitfulness, repentance, and righteousness.[11] Programs expand while prayer meetings disappear. The crisis is not that the world is dark; the crisis is that the Church has grown dim. The lampstand meant to shine has been smothered by compromise. The salt meant to preserve has lost its distinctiveness. A compromised church cannot confront a corrupt culture; she can only mirror it.

At the root of this collapse lies a catastrophic misunderstanding of the gospel itself. The gospel is not an invitation to self-fulfillment but a declaration of spiritual bankruptcy. It does not affirm the old life; it demands its death. It does not coexist with sin; it conquers it. It does not negotiate with rebellion; it crucifies it. *"I have been crucified with Christ. It is no longer I who live, but Christ who lives in me."* (Galatians 2:20).[12] These are not poetic metaphors for sentimental reflection; they are declarations of death. When the gospel is reframed as inspirational messaging rather than divine intervention, sin becomes a habit to manage rather than a master to overthrow. Repentance becomes optional instead of essential. Discipleship becomes recommended rather than required. Holiness becomes extreme instead of expected.

The Church forgot that salvation is not a transaction but a transformation, not the mere removal of guilt but the remaking of the soul. It is the supernatural invasion of divine life into the dead heart of a sinner. When Christ becomes Lord, regeneration produces evidence. Grace produces godliness. Where these are absent, salvation is absent—not weakened but absent. Jonathan Edwards understood this with surgical precision: religious emotion without holiness is not conversion but self-deception.[13] The crowds that filled American churches for generations may have possessed religious fervor, but fervor without fruit is not faith.

This truth has been obscured by leaders who fear that preaching holiness will repel crowds. Yet the crowds Jesus drew were the ones who left when He spoke plainly. When He declared, *"Whoever does not take his cross and follow me is not worthy of me."* (Matthew 10:38),[14] the crowds thinned. The true Jesus offends flesh, confronts pride, and exposes hypocrisy. He is not safe, manageable, or available as a mascot for political or cultural identity. He is Lord, and His lordship demands surrender.

The modern church's aversion to confrontation has left a spiritual vacuum where conviction should dwell. People confess Jesus with their mouths while denying Him with their lives. Services are attended without pursuing sanctification. Crosses are worn by people who refuse crucifixion. Yet the gospel declares that only those who die with Christ will rise with Him. Anything less is counterfeit Christianity, an emotional experience without spiritual rebirth, a cultural identity without eternal transformation.[15]

Charles Spurgeon captured the eternal stakes with chilling clarity: hell will be filled not only with rebels but also with the "almost persuaded," those who were close to truth but never surrendered to it.

Jesus' words remain eternally confronting: *"Why do you call me 'Lord, Lord' and not do what I tell you?"* (Luke 6:46).[16]

He does not ask this question to condemn but to expose; calling Him Lord without treating Him as Lord is a contradiction heaven will not recognize. It is spiritual lip service, religious performance, and moral pretense. True lordship is not declared; it is demonstrated, not by enthusiasm in worship but by obedience in private, not by emotional fervor but by moral surrender, not by doctrinal agreement but by transformed desires. The Church lost this clarity when she began measuring faith by expressions rather than fruit.

The confusion deepens because many assume that fruit refers only to visible works, acts of service, charity, prayer, ministry involvement, or spiritual activity. But the fruit Scripture emphasizes is internal: humility, holiness, self-denial, purity, love of righteousness, hatred of sin, perseverance in truth, and conformity to Christ. These fruits cannot be manufactured through discipline or personality; the Spirit produces them in those who have truly died to themselves. This is why Jesus warns that *"every tree that does not bear good fruit is cut down and thrown into the fire."* (Matthew 7:19).[17]

The absence of fruit is not evidence of immaturity but evidence of unbelief. No branch connected to the Vine remains barren. No soul indwelt by the Spirit remains untransformed. No heart surrendered to Christ remains unchanged.

The calamity now confronting the American Church cannot be understood as institutional decline or moral drift; it must be recognized as the logical consequence of abandoning the God of Scripture. When a people redefine God, they inevitably redefine themselves; and when they redefine themselves, they inevitably redefine righteousness. The result is a Church that speaks in Christian terms while thinking in secular categories, a Church fluent in spiritual talk but foreign to spiritual power. Such religion can imitate devotion but cannot produce transformation. It can stir emotion but cannot raise the dead.

Survey data confirms what Scripture already declares. Among self-identified Christians, 65% attend church less than monthly, and 72% report that faith has "no significant impact" on daily decisions.[18] Among Protestant churchgoers, only 35% believe the Bible is literally true, while 52% say it contains "helpful moral teachings" but should not be taken literally in all areas.[19] These are not statistics; they are symptoms of spiritual death masquerading as religious life. When Scripture loses authority, Christ loses lordship. When Christ loses lordship, the Church loses identity.

Yet even in this crisis, hope is not lost. God has always preserved a remnant, not a remnant of perfect people, but of surrendered people. And in our time, God is raising a remnant again: men and women who feel the weight of His holiness, who tremble at His Word, who refuse to bow to cultural idols, who seek revival not through innovation but through repentance. These are the ones who understand that awakening does not begin in the world but in the Church. God Himself identifies them:

"This is the one to whom I will look: he who is humble and contrite in spirit and trembles at my word." (Isaiah 66:2).[20]

This is the call of this chapter: not to diagnose the crisis but to awaken the conscience. The Church must rediscover the God of Scripture: the God who is holy, sovereign, and uncompromising; the God who calls sinners not to adjustment but to death; the God who demands allegiance, obedience, and repentance; the God who will not bless a Church that refuses to bow. Christianity without lordship is not Christianity. Faith without fruit is not faith. Identity without obedience is not discipleship. And a Church without holiness is not the Bride of Christ.

The line is drawn. The hour is late. The crisis is real. But so is the promise of renewal. For the God who judges also restores, and the God who exposes also revives. *"For the time has come for judgment to begin at the household of God."* (1 Peter 4:17).[21] If His people will bow, He will heal. If His Church will repent, He will return with power. And if the remnant will rise, the darkness of our age will not have the final word.

Section II: The Death of Discipleship

Discipleship did not die because the Church stopped speaking Jesus' name. It died because the Church stopped obeying His commands. The vocabulary survived conversion, commitment, and following Christ, but the meaning was gutted from within. What was once understood as total surrender became rebranded as personal enhancement. The cost of entry, which Scripture presents as absolute, was softened into an "advanced track" for the unusually committed.[22] Modern Christianity did not reject discipleship outright; it redefined it until nothing remained but the word itself.

Jesus did not call people to improvement. He commanded death.

"If anyone would come after me, let him deny himself and take up his cross daily and follow me." (Luke 9:23).[23] The cross in the first century was not a symbol of inspiration; it was an instrument of execution, the most brutal and humiliating death Rome could devise. To take up one's cross meant to walk publicly toward one's own annihilation. Jesus did not soften this image or qualify His demand. He meant exactly what He said: the life you have must end so that the life I give can begin. Modern Christianity has reversed this order entirely, promising comfort before commitment, resurrection before death, and victory without surrender.[24]

This inversion did not happen suddenly. It emerged as Western culture began to catechize the Church into a new moral system, one in which the self is sacred, desire is authoritative, and authenticity is the highest virtue. The cultural assumptions were so pervasive that they seemed natural, even compassionate. Sin was recast as brokenness. Repentance was reframed as healing. "Rebellion" was renamed as "authenticity." None of these shifts appeared hostile to Christianity on the surface, yet all were lethal to discipleship.[25] Because once the self is elevated to the throne, Christ can no longer occupy it. A faith built on self-affirmation cannot sustain the weight of self-denial.

Dietrich Bonhoeffer, writing in the shadow of Nazi Germany, diagnosed this theological cancer with precision: cheap grace. He defined it as "grace without discipleship, grace without the cross, grace without Jesus Christ living and incarnate."[26]

Cheap grace offers the forgiveness of sins without requiring repentance. It promises belonging without demanding obedience. It speaks of salvation without transformation. Cheap grace does not deny Christ; it domesticates Him, reducing the Lion of Judah to a household pet who blesses whatever we choose. Bonhoeffer understood that cheap grace was not a minor deviation but a fundamental corruption; it preserved religious language while emptying it of spiritual power. And he warned that when cheap grace becomes the norm, the Church ceases to be the Church.

The consequences of cheap grace are now fully visible. Churches function not as discipleship forges but as affirmation atmospheres. Sermons are designed to soothe rather than sharpen, to comfort rather than confront, to validate rather than convict.[27]

The goal is no longer to produce believers who resemble Christ but to produce attenders who feel good about themselves. Where the early church produced martyrs willing to die for Christ, the modern church produces believers who reconsider their faith the moment it costs social approval. This is not a problem of weak Christians; it is a problem of weak Christianity, a Christianity that never demanded death in the first place.

The expectation of discipleship has collapsed because belief has been decoupled from submission. Confession has been detached from transformation. People are assured they belong to Christ before they are taught to obey Him.[28] But Scripture allows no such separation. *"Whoever does not bear his own cross and come after me cannot be my disciple."* (Luke 14:27).[29] The language is absolute. Not "should not" or "might struggle to be" but "cannot be." Jesus does not offer a Christianity in which discipleship is optional. There is no category in Scripture for a saved person who remains unchanged, for a regenerate heart that loves sin, or for a follower of Christ who refuses to follow.

The modern church absorbed expressive individualism so thoroughly that most believers do not even recognize the shift. The self became the highest authority. Authenticity became the supreme virtue. Internal feelings were elevated above external commands. And because this framework felt compassionate, after all, who wants to suppress someone's authentic self? It was embraced without resistance.[30]

But the gospel is not about expressing your authentic self; it is about crucifying your authentic self so that Christ can live through you. Where this is not understood, obedience begins to sound abusive, correction begins to feel unsafe, and holiness begins to seem oppressive. Love itself is redefined, not as seeking another's highest good in conformity to truth but as affirming whatever they feel. Richard Sibbes understood that love divorced from truth is not tenderness but treachery, for it leaves the beloved comfortable in the very condition that destroys them.[31]

Suffering, which Scripture presents as normative and formative, has been reinterpreted as failure. The New Testament declares plainly, *"Through many tribulations we must enter the kingdom of God."* (Acts 14:22).[32] Tribulation is not the exception; it is the path. But Western Christianity, shaped by prosperity and comfort, trained believers to interpret ease as God's favor and hardship as His absence. This produces a faith that cannot endure pressure; not because discipleship demands too much, but because endurance was never expected in the first place. Mark Dever observed that a church which lowers the bar of membership lowers the bar of discipleship, and a Christianity shaped by consumer expectations will always collapse when suffering arrives.[33]

The problem is not that the way is too narrow; the problem is that we were told it was wide.

Even the doctrine of holiness has been hollowed out. Obedience, once understood as the liberating path of righteousness, is now perceived as restrictive legalism. Holiness, once the identity of every believer, *"Be holy, for I am holy."* (1 Peter 1:16), has been recast as a personal calling for the unusually devout.[34] When holiness is dismissed as unrealistic or unnecessary, Christianity loses its distinctiveness. It becomes a spiritual affiliation that costs nothing, confronts nothing, and changes nothing. And a Christianity that changes nothing is not Christianity at all.

The danger of this drift was not hidden from history's most perceptive theologians. John Owen pressed the distinction with surgical precision: the greatest threat to authentic faith is not outright rejection of Christ but a religion of admiration that never crosses into obedience. The admirer acknowledges Christ's excellence; the follower submits to Christ's authority. And the difference between an admirer and a follower is the difference between spiritual life and spiritual death.[35] Admirers gather at a safe distance. They applaud His words, celebrate His love, and invoke His name, but they do not do what He says. Followers, by contrast, hear His commands and obey. They count the cost and pay it. They take up their cross even when it leads to suffering. Jesus never promised that following Him would be easy. He promised it would be worth it.

"The gate is narrow, and the way is hard that leads to life, and those who find it are few." (Matthew 7:14).[36]

The institutional church adapted to the absence of obedience. Leaders lowered expectations to avoid offending the crowd. Christ's demands were reframed as aspirational rather than authoritative. Sermons emphasized comfort and avoided confrontation. Richard Baxter saw this pastoral failure coming centuries before it arrived: when shepherds refuse to wound, the sheep mistake their sickness for health, their sin for strength, and their distance from God for freedom.[37] Reproof and correction, essential elements of pastoral care according to *"All Scripture is... profitable for... correction, for training in righteousness."* (2 Timothy 3:16),[38] were quietly removed from the pulpit. But when reproof and correction are eliminated, training collapses. Muscles do not grow without resistance, and faith does not mature without discipline. A Christianity that refuses correction produces believers who remain spiritually infantile, unstable, and vulnerable to deception.

Market metrics replaced biblical ones. Success was measured by attendance, budget, and engagement rather than repentance, obedience, and holiness. Leaders chose silence over shepherding because confronting sin risked losing donors, members, or influence. William Wilberforce warned that the most dangerous form of religious cowardice is the silence of those who know the truth but choose peace with men over faithfulness to God.[39] But Scripture declares that leaders will give an account for the souls under their care. Silence in the face of sin is not kindness; it is cruelty.

"If I say to the wicked, 'You shall surely die,' and you give him no warning... his blood I will require at your hand." (Ezekiel 33:8).[40] Watchmen who refuse to sound the alarm are complicit in the destruction that follows.

The collapse of discipleship has produced an endurance crisis. Churches are growing numerically while shrinking spiritually. Buildings are full, but hearts are empty. Crowds swell, but conviction disappears. When discipleship vanishes, so does endurance, because endurance is the fruit of roots grown deep through discipline, suffering, and obedience. Jesus warned of this in the parable of the sower: the seed that falls on rocky ground springs up quickly but withers under pressure because it has no root.[41]

Modern Christianity produces shallow-rooted believers who flourish during seasons of comfort but collapse the moment faith costs something. This is not because they lacked sincerity but because they were never taught that following Christ requires death.

Cultural hostility does not destroy faith; it exposes it. Persecution reveals what worship services conceal. When following Christ costs reputation, career, relationships, or safety, shallow conversions are stripped away. The difference between admirers and followers becomes undeniable. And the church that spent decades prioritizing growth over depth, numbers over transformation, and engagement over obedience suddenly discovers that much of what it built was wood, hay, and stubble.[42] The fire of testing consumes what was never real.

When discipleship dies, autonomy rushes in to fill the vacuum. The human heart is never neutral. If Christ does not govern it, it will be governed by another authority, self, culture, ideology, or desire. This is the pattern Scripture reveals from the beginning. *"In those days there was no king in Israel. Everyone did what was right in his own eyes."* (Judges 21:25).[43] Autonomy always masquerades as freedom, but it produces chaos, fragmentation, and bondage. Until the self is dethroned, Christ cannot reign. Until the will is surrendered, grace cannot transform. And until the old life is crucified, the new life cannot begin.

The death of discipleship is not a crisis of relevance but a crisis of repentance. The church does not need better marketing, cooler worship, or more engaging programs. It needs to recover what it abandoned: the call to die. Jesus did not make discipleship complicated. He made it costly. The cost has not changed. *"Whoever loves father or mother more than me is not worthy of me, and whoever loves son or daughter more than me is not worthy of me."* (Matthew 10:37).[44] These words offend the modern ear because they demand what culture cannot tolerate, total allegiance to Christ above all earthly affections, identities, and securities.

But this is where hope lies. Discipleship may be dead in much of the visible church, but the true Church, the remnant who tremble at God's Word, has never abandoned it. They understand that the cross is not a symbol but a summons, that grace is not cheap but costly, and that following Christ means walking the narrow road even when the crowds turn back. The call remains: *"If anyone would come after me, let him deny himself and take up his cross and follow me."* (Luke 9:23).[45] The question is not whether this demand is too hard. The question is whether we will obey it.

Section III: The Cult of Self and The Rise of Autonomy

The American church did not drift into the cult of self by accident. She was discipled into it, absorbing the assumptions of expressive individualism so gradually that most believers never recognized the shift.[46] Autonomy, Eden's primal temptation, the serpent's first lie, was rebranded as authenticity, and the Church, eager to appear compassionate, embraced it without resistance. The self became sacred. Desire became authoritative. And God, rather than confronting the rebellion of the human heart, was reimagined as a cosmic validator whose primary role is to affirm whatever identity we construct.

This was not a theological argument the Church lost; it was a cultural catechism she absorbed. Identity politics infiltrated the sanctuary by teaching that personhood is anchored not in God's design but in subjective self-definition. Kevin DeYoung observed that when the church imports the culture's framework for identity, she loses the only framework that can actually liberate the self, the truth that we are creatures made in God's image, accountable to His design, and redeemable by His grace.[47]

The individual became the final arbiter of meaning, morality, and reality. To challenge someone's self-concept became an act of violence. To assert external authority, Scripture, tradition, or truth itself became a threat to dignity. And the church, terrified of appearing judgmental, bent the knee.

Eric Metaxas has traced how the doctrine of expressive individualism quietly replaced the biblical understanding of human identity, teaching that the authentic self is the one most free from external authority, which makes submission to God not liberation but oppression.[48] This is expressive individualism, the doctrine that the truest thing about you is how you feel inside and that faithfulness to God means faithfulness to that internal sense of self. But Scripture teaches the opposite.

"The heart is deceitful above all things, and desperately sick." (Jeremiah 17:9).[49] The self is not a sanctuary to be protected but a throne to be toppled. Regeneration does not validate the old self; it executes it.

God Himself was redefined to fit this framework. The biblical portrait, sovereign Creator, righteous Judge, consuming fire, was quietly replaced with a deity whose primary attribute is therapeutic support. John Calvin understood the human heart's relentless drive to manufacture gods in its own image: the heart is an idol factory, and left unchecked, it will always fashion a deity that costs nothing, demands nothing, and confirms whatever the self already desires.[50]

What Calvin diagnosed in the broader human condition, the Church baptized in the sanctuary. God became a cheerleader for personal authenticity rather than the Lord who commands, *"You shall be holy, for I am holy."* (Leviticus 11:44).[51] A deity who never confronts cannot save anyone, and a Christ stripped of His disrupting authority cannot deliver anyone from anything.

The question at the heart of faith shifted from "What does God command?" to "What feels true to me?" Jordan Peterson, observing this collapse from outside the faith, notes that modern Westerners systematically "confuse feelings with convictions," treating emotional resonance as moral legitimacy.[52] When this framework infiltrates the Church, repentance becomes psychologically destabilizing. Holiness becomes oppressive. Obedience sounds abusive. And the call to *"take every thought captive to obey Christ"* (2 Corinthians 10:5) is dismissed as unhealthy suppression of the authentic self.[53]

Douglas Murray describes a society in which "hurt feelings carry the weight of moral claims."[54] Emotional discomfort is treated as evidence of harm, and any teaching that produces discomfort is presumed to be harmful. Churches absorbed this logic without questioning it. Pastors softened sermons to avoid triggering offense. Believers avoided transformation to preserve emotional equilibrium. Biblical truth, which by nature confronts sin and calls for surrender, became indistinguishable from emotional aggression. But compassion divorced from truth is not love; it is capitulation. A Church that will not wound cannot heal.

The shift was deeper than emotion; it was epistemological. The self became the moral center of the universe. Jonathan Haidt has documented how modern people inherit powerful moral emotions while losing the shared frameworks that once gave those emotions coherent direction, producing a culture that feels deeply but cannot reason morally.[55] The Church adopted this posture wholesale: retaining Christian ethics while abandoning Christian obedience, affirming biblical morality in theory while rejecting it in practice. The result is spirituality built on sentiment rather than submission, a Christianity that feels warm but cannot bear weight. When pressure comes, it collapses.

Ecclesiology itself was inverted. The Church no longer existed to call individuals into submission to Christ; it existed to serve individuals on their journey of self-discovery.[56] Worship shifted from declaring God's glory to curating emotional experiences. Preaching became therapeutic rather than prophetic. The sanctuary was transformed into a spiritual resource center for personal development, where God is the life coach, and Scripture is the self-help manual. But the Church was never designed to validate the self. It was designed to crucify it.

Ethics were rewritten to conform to identity movements. Rather than calling people to turn from sin and be transformed by the renewing of their minds, congregations began blessing whatever identity was claimed, sexual, political, cultural, or ideological. Repentance was replaced with affirmation. Sanctification was replaced with self-expression. Charlie Kirk observes that many churches now function as "extensions of secular consensus," more concerned with cultural acceptability than doctrinal clarity.[57] The question is no longer "What does Scripture say?" but "What does society demand?" And when culture speaks louder than God, the Church ceases to be the Church.

Scripture itself became negotiable. Texts that challenged modern sensibilities were softened, reinterpreted, or avoided altogether. Authority was not denied outright; that would have been too honest. Instead, it was diluted, treated as one voice among many rather than the final word. Søren Kierkegaard warned that the greatest danger to Christianity is not atheism but the substitution of Christ's demands with something easier.[58] This is precisely what occurred. The narrow gate was widened, the hard way made comfortable, and the cost of discipleship negotiated down to zero.

Identity was no longer understood as a calling rooted in creation but as a collage constructed from experiences, attractions, political tribes, and personal preferences. Thomas Sowell observed that when institutions abandon fixed standards, they do not become neutral but simply import whatever ideology is currently dominant and enforce it with the same rigidity once reserved for truth.[59] God's declaration, *"male and female he created them"* (Genesis 1:27), was replaced with the doctrine that identity is self-defined and self-authenticated.[60] Repentance, which requires acknowledging that the self is not sovereign, became offensive. Suggesting that someone change not just behavior but desire, orientation, or identity was framed as an attack on their personhood. But the gospel has always required this.

"If anyone is in Christ, he is a new creation. The old has passed away; behold, the new has come." (2 Corinthians 5:17).[61] Christianity is not about discovering your true self; it is about dying to your old self so Christ can make you new.

Sentimental spirituality flourished in this environment. Churches produced a Christianity that inspires but does not transform, that soothes but does not sanctify. Sermons avoided sin, judgment, and holiness while emphasizing purpose, affirmation, and potential. Believers were taught to feel better without becoming better before God. This is religion as emotional maintenance, not spiritual rebirth. And it produces congregations full of people who love the idea of Jesus but refuse to obey Him.

Suffering, which Scripture presents as God's sanctifying instrument, was redefined as a violation of personal worth. The New Testament teaches that *"we rejoice in our sufferings, knowing that suffering produces endurance, and endurance produces character."* (Romans 5:3-4).[62] But expressive individualism reinterprets discomfort as harm. Trials are no longer formative; they are destructive. Hardship is no longer redemptive; it is abusive. And when believers redefine suffering as a violation, holiness itself becomes harm, because holiness requires the death of what we naturally love.

The ecclesial consequences are visible everywhere. Churches built around self-expression fracture the moment discomfort arises. Unity becomes sentimental rather than sacrificial, held together by shared feelings rather than shared surrender. These are communities of self-expression, not self-denial. And when pressure comes, doctrinal clarity, moral accountability, or cultural opposition, they collapse because there is no foundation beneath the sentiment.

This is idolatry. The self has become the idol, and autonomy the altar where truth is sacrificed.[63] Every generation has its false gods, but this generation's god is the mirror. We worship what we see reflected back: our desires, our identity, our autonomy, our authenticity. And the Church, rather than smashing the idol, gilded it with Christian language and called it discipleship. William Wilberforce warned that the distinguishing mark of nominal Christianity is precisely this: it retains the vocabulary of the faith while emptying it of its demands, producing a religion that costs the self nothing and therefore transforms the self not at all.[64]

It is Christianity that costs nothing, confronts nothing, and changes nothing.

Autonomy has rewritten freedom itself. Scripture defines freedom as liberation from sin to obey God. *"You have been set free from sin and have become slaves to righteousness."* (Romans 6:18).[65] But modern culture defines freedom as liberation from all external constraint to obey the self. Bari Weiss has observed that the institutions most loudly committed to freedom are often the most aggressive in enforcing conformity, because the freedom they celebrate is freedom from God and tradition, not freedom for truth and virtue.[66] A life governed by unchecked desire does not produce flourishing; it produces chaos, addiction, and bondage. Yet the Church adopted this redefinition wholesale, presenting the Christian life not as surrender but as self-actualization.

The theological lens has been inverted. Instead of Scripture defining identity, identity now demands that Scripture affirm it. The beating heart of expressive individualism is the conviction that the internal sense of self is the truest thing about a person, more real than biology, more authoritative than revelation, more sacred than Scripture. This produced what can only be called identity spirituality: a faith that considers itself most authentic when most free from external constraint. But Christianity has never operated this way. Faith begins not with self-discovery but with self-denial. The way to life is through death.

Progressive spirituality's engine is not theological discovery but sociological pressure. Paul Kingsnorth has identified this dynamic with precision: what presents itself as spiritual evolution is in reality the substitution of one religion for another, with the new faith demanding the same total allegiance while offering none of the transcendence.[67] It treats Christian ethics as oppressive when they conflict with desire, and it demands constant revision to remain culturally acceptable. The result is a church in perpetual retreat, surrendering one doctrinal position after another to avoid the accusation of being unloving. But love does not mean affirmation. Love means pursuing another's highest good even when it costs comfort, reputation, or approval. A Church that cannot say no to the self cannot meaningfully say yes to Christ.

The final diagnosis is this: when the self becomes sacred, anything that challenges the self becomes suspect, including God. The Church's modern temptation is not persecution from without but accommodation from within. The question is not whether believers will face opposition but whether they will resist the pressure to conform. And a Church that elevates autonomy above obedience, feelings above truth, and self-expression above surrender has already chosen its answer. It has chosen the idol. And idols, no matter how gilded, cannot save.

The cult of self is not a sidebar to the Church's crisis; it is the crisis. It is the engine driving every other compromise, the root feeding every other error. Until the idol is torn down, nothing else can be rebuilt. Until autonomy is dethroned, Christ cannot reign. And until the Church recovers the courage to confront the self rather than coddle it, she will remain culturally palatable but spiritually powerless. The line has been drawn. The choice is clear. Will the Church bow to the idol of self, or will she bow to the Lordship of Christ?

Section IV: The Counterfeit Church: Crowds Without Conversion

The most devastating deception is not persecution from without but corruption from within, a Christianity that looks alive while spiritually dead. This is the counterfeit church, and her judgment is already underway. She replaced holiness with hype. She traded repentance for relevance. She substituted discipleship with brand loyalty. And God will not be mocked. *"For the time has come for judgment to begin at the household of God."* (1 Peter 4:17).[68] The ax is already at the root. The fire is already kindled. And what appears successful by human metrics stands condemned by divine standard.

The counterfeit church measures vitality by crowd size rather than soul condition. Attendance became the metric. Budget growth became proof of blessing. Platforms expanded while prayer rooms emptied. Leonard Verduin observed that the church's long temptation has been to mistake numerical expansion for spiritual reality, confusing the growth of an institution with the advance of the Kingdom. The institutional church learned centuries ago that it could fill buildings without filling hearts, compel attendance without compelling surrender, and manufacture religious conformity without producing genuine conversion.[69]

A packed sanctuary proves nothing about the state of hearts before God. Numbers can be fabricated. Transformation cannot. And on the day of judgment, the question will not be "How many attended?" but "How many obeyed?"

The megachurch industrial complex, when divorced from gospel accountability, accelerated the apostasy. What began as evangelistic zeal devolved into a system prioritizing spectacle over sanctification.[70] Sanctuaries became performance venues. Worship became theatrical production. Preaching became motivational content engineered for engagement metrics rather than eternal impact. The church adopted the world's language, branding, audience retention, and market differentiation and congratulated herself on being relevant. But Jesus did not call His church to be relevant. He called her to be righteous.

"You are the salt of the earth, but if salt has lost its taste, how shall its saltiness be restored? It is no longer good for anything except to be thrown out and trampled under people's feet." (Matthew 5:13).[71] The American church lost her saltiness chasing crowds. Now she is being trampled by the culture she courted.

Worship was gutted and replaced with entertainment. Lights choreographed. Fog deployed. Volume maximized. Everything calibrated to manufacture atmosphere, to produce emotional peaks, and to generate the feeling of transcendence without requiring surrender to the Transcendent One. People mistake adrenaline for anointing, goosebumps for conviction, and the energy of a crowd for the presence of God. Lloyd-Jones diagnosed this collapse with precision: when the church substitutes emotional excitement for the fear of God, she produces a generation that has experienced religion but never encountered the living Christ.[72]

Where entertainment replaces the fear of the Lord, spectacle substitutes for sanctification. And God is not impressed by production budgets. *"The LORD sees not as man sees: man looks on the outward appearance, but the LORD looks on the heart."* (1 Samuel 16:7).[73] He sees past the lights, past the crowds, and past the metrics, and He sees hearts cold, lives unchanged, and worship empty.

The pulpit collapsed under the weight of compromise. Sermons became talks, shorter, lighter, safer, designed to inspire without offending, encourage without convicting, tickle ears without piercing hearts. Difficult passages vanished from preaching calendars. "Sin" was renamed "brokenness." Hell was omitted. Repentance was replaced with positive affirmation. The goal shifted from transformation to retention, from holiness to happiness, from truth to therapeutic comfort. Eric Weinstein observes that modern people are losing the capacity to endure uncomfortable truths.[74] The church accommodated this weakness rather than confronting it. But the prophet does not ask permission to declare God's Word. Jeremiah did not poll Jerusalem before pronouncing judgment. Amos did not soften his message to appease Bethel's priests. And the Word of God does not negotiate with human preference.

"Is not my word like fire, declares the LORD, and like a hammer that breaks the rock in pieces?" (Jeremiah 23:29).[75] Where the hammer is not swung, rocks remain unbroken. Where the fire does not burn, dross remains unrefined. The counterfeit church chose comfort, and in choosing comfort, she chose death.

Programs replaced prayer as the engine of growth. The early church advanced on her knees.

"They devoted themselves to the apostles' teaching and the fellowship, to the breaking of bread and the prayers." (Acts 2:42).[76] Prayer was not supplemental; it was foundational. Power flowed not from strategy but from supplication. But the modern church discovered she could expand without intercession, could multiply without dependence, and could succeed, by worldly measures, without God's manifest presence. Francis Schaeffer warned the

church was learning to "build empires without the power of the Spirit."[77] And build she did. Calendars filled. Budgets exploded. Staff expanded. Campuses multiplied. But the anointing lifted. The glory departed. And Ichabod was written over sanctuaries that once trembled at God's Word. Activity increased while authority evaporated. Busyness masked barrenness. And God withdrew His hand from institutions that no longer sought His face.

Leadership was corrupted from shepherding to influencing. Success became measured by platform size, follower count, conference invitations, and media visibility, not by faithfulness in obscurity, righteousness under pressure, or tears shed in intercession. Shepherds guard souls. Influencers curate brands. Shepherds bleed for the flock. Influencers perform for the audience. And when the inevitable scandals erupted, moral failure, financial corruption, abuse of power—entire empires collapsed because they were built on personality, not the presence of God.[78]

Charisma cannot sustain what character never built. Gifting cannot preserve what godliness never established. And the wreckage of fallen ministries testifies to a generation that elevated talent above holiness, platform above prayer, and image above integrity.

Victor Davis Hanson has documented how declining civilizations master the art of maintaining appearances long after the substance has collapsed, preserving the forms of institutional life while the animating convictions that built them have already died.[79] The counterfeit church perfected this substitution and baptized it as "ministry." Buildings gleam. Budgets soar. Crowds swell. Social media engagement explodes. But beneath the veneer lies spiritual bankruptcy. These are whitewashed tombs, beautiful on the outside, full of dead men's bones within. Jesus pronounced woe upon such facades: *"Woe to you, scribes and Pharisees, hypocrites! For you are like whitewashed tombs, which outwardly appear beautiful but within are full of dead people's bones and all uncleanness."* (Matthew 23:27).[80]

The counterfeit church is the Pharisee in contemporary dress, maintaining religious form while denying spiritual power and preserving institutional structure while quenching the Holy Spirit. And God is not fooled. He sees. He knows. And He will not hold guiltless those who trade His glory for human applause.

The counterfeit is trapped in an escalation spiral. Each service must surpass the last, and each production must intensify. The spectacle must continually amplify because once people acclimate to one level of stimulation, anything less registers as death. This is not worship; it is addiction. And like all addictions, it demands increasing doses to produce diminishing returns. But no fog machine manufactures the fear of the Lord. No light show produces conviction of sin. No volume level generates genuine repentance. These are cheap substitutes, counterfeit intimacy, and simulated transcendence.

And believers trained to equate atmosphere with the Holy Spirit become incapable of encountering God outside manufactured experiences. They need the production. They crave the stimulation. And when crisis comes, when suffering strips away the spectacle, when persecution removes the comfort, and when loss shatters the illusion, their faith collapses because it was built on feeling, not foundation.

What the counterfeit church fails to produce exposes her emptiness. She does not produce intercessors because prayer is invisible, slow, and incompatible with metrics-driven ministry. She does not produce theologians, because rigorous doctrine divides audiences and complicates branding. She does not produce martyrs, because martyrdom requires convictions deeper than slogans, costlier than social media campaigns, and more durable than trending hashtags. Instead, she produces consumers masquerading as disciples, spectators pretending to be soldiers, and fans mistaken for followers. David Platt warns that much of American Christianity has produced believers whose faith costs nothing, demands nothing, and changes nothing.[81]

And when pressure arrives, cultural hostility, personal suffering, and doctrinal conflict, these shallow-rooted believers evaporate like morning mist, proving they were never converted, only convinced. Never regenerated. Only religious.

Spiritual hunger remains cruelly unsatisfied. Believers feel the void but cannot name it. They experience emotional highs on Sunday and spiritual lows by Tuesday. The chasm between weekend worship and weekday reality grows unbearable, yet they return hoping the next service will finally satisfy what the last one promised. This is starvation disguised as abundance, famine masked by activity. Andrew Murray warned that a church which has lost the spirit of intercession has lost the spirit of her mission, exchanging the burden of souls for the comfort of religious routine and the urgency of heaven for the management of earthly programs.[82]

The mission inverted and the gospel was commodified, while souls were lost and statisticians celebrated attendance records. And God weighs the church in His balances and finds her wanting.

The tragedy is not that believers cannot distinguish authentic from counterfeit; it is that many prefer the counterfeit. They choose aesthetic over authority, atmosphere over obedience, and feeling over faithfulness. Music becomes the centerpiece because it delivers instant emotion without demanding surrender. Lights and fog create the illusion of God's presence without requiring submission to His lordship. But Jesus exposed this fraud two millennia ago: *"This people honors me with their lips, but their heart is far from me."* (Matthew 15:8).[83]

Loud singing coexists with cold hearts. Enthusiastic worship accompanies rebellious living. Hands raised on Sunday do not guarantee hands clean before God. And the counterfeit church is filled, absolutely filled, with worshipers whose mouths declare allegiance while their lives deny authority.

The pulpit has been so distorted that it is unrecognizable. Teaching became palatable, therapeutic, and anecdotal, engineered for inspiration rather than instruction, affirmation rather than confrontation, and comfort rather than conviction. The preacher became a brand. The sermon became a product. The Word of God became raw material mined for relatable content rather than the sharp sword dividing soul and spirit. Charles Spurgeon prophesied this degradation with chilling precision: "The time will come when instead of shepherds feeding the sheep, the church will have clowns entertaining goats."[84]

That time arrived. Clowns occupy pulpits. Goats fill pews. Entertainment replaced exposition. Jokes substituted for judgment. And sheep starve while goats laugh.

The church became functionally indistinguishable from the world she was commissioned to confront. The church's values now mirror the culture's priorities, her metrics mimic marketplace standards, and her leaders resemble influencers far more than prophets. Her message drifted from the scandal of the cross toward the safety of self-help therapy. When the cross is removed from the center, culture becomes the architect of the church. And a church designed by culture will always conform to culture because she has no transcendent standard by which to resist. Voddie Baucham identifies this as "cultural captivity," where the church is so absorbed by surrounding society that she cannot distinguish biblical Christianity from baptized secularism.[85]

She speaks the world's language, adopts the world's methods, pursues the world's approval, and wonders why she possesses none of the world-overturning power that marked the early church.

What does the counterfeit produce? Christians who articulate mission statements but not the gospel. Believers who memorize weekend service schedules but not Scripture. Congregants who feel close to God during worship while remaining distant in obedience. Churches marked by Sunday emotion and Monday compromise. This is religion without regeneration, affiliation without transformation, form without power. *"Having the appearance of godliness, but denying its power."* (2 Timothy 3:5).[86] God warned of such counterfeits. He pronounced judgment on such facades. And He will not accept substitutes for genuine surrender.

The early church stands as a devastating indictment. They turned empires upside down not through production quality or marketing genius but through holiness, truth-proclamation, suffering endurance, fervent prayer, and the undeniable power of the Holy Spirit. Even pagan observers marveled. Pliny the Younger, reporting to Emperor Trajan, described Christians whose devotion was extraordinary, whose courage under torture was unshakable, and whose allegiance to Christ superseded even the threat of death.[87]

That church transformed civilizations. This church struggles to transform suburbs. That church prayed until heaven opened. This church programs until calendars fill. That church was willing to die. This church is unwilling to be inconvenienced.

This is not a crisis of relevance. This is a crisis of repentance. The church has not lost influence because she lacks better branding. She lost influence because she lost her identity. A church indistinguishable from the world has nothing to offer the world. A church prioritizing comfort over confrontation produces cultural Christians, not crucified disciples. And a church abandoning the cross cannot carry the gospel, because the gospel *is* the cross, foolishness to those perishing, and the power of God to those being saved. *"For the word of the cross is folly to those who are perishing, but to us who are being saved it is the power of God."* (1 Corinthians 1:18).[88]

When the church trades the foolishness of the cross for the wisdom of the world, she gains the world's approval and loses God's power.

But God is raising a remnant. While crowds are drawn to spectacle, a remnant gathers around the Word. While production crews program lights, intercessors fill prayer rooms, knowing no building can contain God's glory and no production can manufacture His presence. The counterfeit has crowds. The remnant has fire. The counterfeit commands platforms. The remnant cries to heaven. And when the remnant rises, not in arrogance but in brokenness, not in condemnation but in consecration, the counterfeit will be exposed, the façade will crumble, and the Spirit will move with purifying fire.

The watchman sounds the alarm: *"Son of man, I have made you a watchman for the house of Israel. Whenever you hear a word from my mouth, you shall give them warning from me."* (Ezekiel 33:7).[89] The warning is this: judgment has begun at the household of God. The counterfeit church will not survive what is coming. Buildings will not preserve her. Budgets will not protect her. Crowds will not vindicate her. Only repentance can save her. Only humility can restore her. Only returning to the cross can resurrect her. The choice is stark. The moment is urgent. Repent or perish. Return or remain counterfeit. The fire is coming. And only what is built on Christ will survive.

Section V: A Prophetic Call to Return to the Lord

The call to return does not begin with thunder. It begins with a whisper, the quiet recognition that something vital has been lost. Before conviction crashes like waves, hunger stirs like a murmur beneath the surface. The first tremors of repentance feel less like judgment and more like longing, the dawning realization that the Christianity we embraced is not the Christianity Christ preached.[90] The form remains. The vocabulary persists. But the substance has evaporated, leaving behind a hollow shell that no longer sustains, no longer convicts, no longer transforms.

This is where the remnant rises: not among the loud or the applauded, but among those who tremble at God's Word when the nation no longer listens. God defines them with precision: *"This is the one to whom I will look: he who is humble and contrite in spirit and trembles at my word."* (Isaiah 66:2).[91] Humble. Contrite. Trembling. These are not admired virtues in a culture that celebrates confidence, autonomy, and self-assertion. But these are the ones God seeks. These are the ones He revives. And when the remnant rises, renewal follows.

The fear of the Lord has collapsed. Not because people rejected God outright; that would have been too honest. Instead, they replaced Him with a safer version: a deity who affirms but never confronts, who validates but never commands, who speaks gently but never rebukes. Os Guinness has shown that the modern West did not lose God through direct assault but through slow substitution, replacing transcendent authority with inner experience until the self became the only remaining standard by which truth could be judged.[92]

The result was predictable: when God's authority diminishes, human autonomy expands. When reverence collapses, wisdom collapses. And when wisdom collapses, repentance disappears. Scripture declares without ambiguity, *"The fear of the LORD is the beginning of knowledge."* (Proverbs 1:7).[93] Without the fear of the Lord, there can be no knowledge of God, no discernment of truth, no path to renewal.

The prophetic call echoes across the Old Testament through every true prophet: *"Return to me, and I will return to you."* (Malachi 3:7).[94] This is not religious ritual but relational return, the restoration of intimacy severed by rebellion. When John the Baptist stood in the wilderness, his message was not new but ancient: *"Repent, for the kingdom of heaven is at hand."* (Matthew 3:2).[95] When Christ began His earthly ministry, His first recorded words repeated the same summons: *"Repent, for the kingdom of heaven is at hand."* (Matthew 4:17).[96] Repentance was not an add-on. It was not optional. It was the doorway into the Kingdom.

But the modern church redefined repentance. What Scripture presents as liberation, the doorway out of deception into truth, culture recast as an antiquated emotional burden, a shame-producing device incompatible with psychological health. The vocabulary survived, but the meaning was drained. Repentance became regret without reorientation, sorrow without surrender, and emotional acknowledgment without behavioral transformation. But biblical repentance is far more radical. It is the violent overthrow of every idol, the crucifixion of every competing allegiance, and the death of the autonomous self so Christ can reign. Adrian Rogers declared that real repentance is not a feeling but a decision, not sorrow over consequences but a complete turning of the will from self to God.[97]

Samuel Rutherford pressed this truth with pastoral urgency: the soul that has not been undone by the weight of its own sin cannot be rebuilt by the grace of God, for God fills only those vessels that have first been emptied.[98] Comfort cannot coexist with conviction. Self-affirmation cannot produce self-denial. And revival will not come to a church unwilling to confess that she has strayed.

The urgency is not abstract. Christ's warning to the lukewarm church was not a pastoral suggestion but a prophetic indictment: *"So, because you are lukewarm, and neither hot nor cold, I will spit you out of my mouth."*

(Revelation 3:16).[99] Lukewarm does not mean mild; it means crisis. It describes people who speak God's name but do not fear His holiness, who affiliate with Christ but do not submit to His authority, who call Him Lord but refuse His commands. Lukewarm faith is not weak faith; it is counterfeit faith. And Christ does not negotiate with counterfeits. He rejects them.

The remnant is rising. The remnant sees what others ignore, discerns what others dismiss, and senses the vacuum beneath Christian culture: the activity without anointing, the noise without power, the crowds without conversion. Charles Finney pressed the same indictment with precision: a church that has lost the spirit of prayer has lost the spirit of power, and a Christianity stripped of the fear of God will neither convict the world nor transform it, because it no longer carries the evidence of heaven's authority.[100] When believers no longer tremble before God, why would unbelievers tremble before the Church? When Christians live indistinguishably from the world, why would the world believe the gospel transforms anyone? The remnant recognizes this bankruptcy and refuses to participate in the charade.

The dividing line of this age is not theological sophistication or cultural engagement. It is obedience. The line runs between those who admire Christ and those who obey Him, between those who use His name and those who bear His cross, between those who attend services and those who surrender their lives. Jesus exposed this division with surgical precision: *"Why do you call me 'Lord, Lord,' and not do what I tell you?"* (Luke 6:46).[101] Calling Him Lord without treating Him as Lord is a contradiction heaven will not recognize. It is spiritual performance, religious pretense, and moral fraud. The remnant hears this question and trembles.

They know that profession without obedience, confession without transformation, and faith without fruit are all evidence of a Christianity that exists only in name.

Where the fear of the Lord is restored, holiness returns. Not as aesthetic preference or cultural posture, but as obedience embodied, visible evidence that Christ reigns. Holiness is not isolation from culture but illumination within it, the undeniable difference produced when a life submits fully to God's authority. Walter Marshall understood this with Puritan precision: holiness is not the achievement of self-discipline but the fruit of union with Christ, the natural overflow of a heart whose affections have been reordered by grace and whose will has been brought into conformity with God's own.[102] When believers think like God thinks, value what God values, and hate what God hates, holiness becomes natural, not forced. But this requires death to self, surrender of autonomy, and the crucifixion of pride. It requires exactly what modern Christianity refuses: the cross.

The call cannot be soft, for the time is too late and the stakes are too high. The deception is too deep. God is calling His people not to comfort but to consecration, not to self-expression but to surrender. The prophet Joel declared God's heart: *"Return to me with all your heart, with fasting, with weeping, and with mourning; and rend your hearts and not your garments."* (Joel 2:12-13).[103]

God does not accept theatrical piety. He does not receive cosmetic repentance. He demands the rending of hearts, the violent tearing apart of every idol, every excuse, and every comfortable compromise that stands between the soul and full surrender. This is not gentle religion. This is total war against everything in us that refuses to bow.

When Christ calls a man, He bids him come and die. John Knox understood this at the cost of his own freedom, declaring that the man who fears God has nothing left to fear, and that the call to follow Christ is inseparable from the call to lose everything the world counts as security.[104]

The line offends every instinct of a culture that treats the self as sacred. Death is not palatable. Crucifixion is not comfortable. But Jesus never promised comfort. He promised resurrection on the far side of death. And no one rises who has not first died. The cross is not negotiable. It is not optional. It is the only path to life.

The pattern of God's dealings is consistent: before judgment comes silence, and before silence comes warning. The prophets stood in this gap, crying out while mercy's window remained open. Israel's greatest danger was never external enemies but the erosion of reverence within the sanctuary, priests who no longer feared God, prophets who spoke lies, and people who loved it so. *"My people are destroyed for lack of knowledge."* (Hosea 4:6).[105]

The destruction came not from a lack of information but a lack of intimacy, not from ignorance but from indifference. They possessed Scripture but did not tremble at it. They knew God's name but did not fear His presence. And silence descended.

Judgment begins in the household of God.

"For it is time for judgment to begin at the household of God." (1 Peter 4:17).[106] The greatest threat facing the American church is not persecution from without but compromise from within. These include pulpits that refuse to preach repentance, congregations that no longer fear the Lord, and believers who confuse emotional inspiration with

spiritual regeneration. The watchman sounds the alarm not to condemn but to awaken, not to destroy but to deliver. But the alarm must be sounded. Silence is complicity. Cowardice is betrayal. And the blood of souls lost will be required at the hands of shepherds who refused to warn.

Repentance is not sorrow alone. Repentance is surrender, not an emotional reaction but a moral reorientation, evidenced not by words but by change: turning from sin, turning toward God, and obeying what was previously ignored. When John the Baptist confronted the crowds seeking baptism, he did not accept verbal profession. He demanded visible fruit: *"Bear fruit in keeping with repentance."* (Matthew 3:8).[107] Faith without works is dead. Profession without transformation is deception. And a Christianity that costs nothing, demands nothing, and changes nothing is not Christianity at all. It is religious performance masquerading as spiritual life.

The remnant rises not on platforms but in prayer closets, not in the spotlight but in the shadow, not in public acclaim but in private intercession. They gather in living rooms and late-night vigils, burdened for a Church that has forgotten her first love. God is preparing His Church for separation, not from the world but from the worldly within the Church. The wheat and the tares grow together until the separation, but the separation is coming.[108] The line between authentic and counterfeit Christianity is becoming visible. And those who see it cannot unsee it.

The loss of God's awe takes everything else with it, first the power, then the witness, until the Church becomes indistinguishable from the institutions she was commissioned to confront. Samuel Rutherford pressed this conviction with pastoral urgency: the soul that has once seen the glory of Christ can never again be satisfied with anything less, and the church that has lost that vision has lost the only thing that made her dangerous to the kingdom of darkness.[109]

Revival is not the recovery of programs, methods, or cultural relevance. Revival is the recovery of the fear of the Lord, the awe, wonder, terror, and delight that come from encountering the living God.

The warning is not aimed at outsiders but at professing believers. The lukewarm church Jesus confronted in Revelation was not pagan Ephesus, but Christian Laodicea, a community that possessed wealth, religious activity, and institutional stability yet lacked the presence of God.[110] They mimicked devotion while resisting surrender. They spoke Christ's name while denying His authority. And Jesus, standing outside the door of His own Church, knocked and waited. His command was clear: *"Be zealous and repent."* (Revelation 3:19).[111]

Zeal is unreserved allegiance and a refusal to negotiate obedience, something the modern church often dismisses as extremism, but what Scripture presents as normal faithfulness.

The mercy window remains open. God is issuing the call while grace still extends. Warnings come before judgments, not after. The pattern is consistent throughout Scripture: God sends prophets, gives time, and offers opportunity. He is patient, long-suffering, and slow to anger. But patience is not permission. Delay is not approval. And the window does not remain open forever. The promise stands: *"Return to me, and I will return to you."* (Malachi 3:7).[112] But the invitation requires a response; it demands a decision. And the hour grows late.

Hope does not lie in cultural relevance but in spiritual authority. Hope is found not in crowds but in consecration, not in influence but in obedience, not in programs but in the manifest presence of God. When the Church returns to holiness, when believers tremble at God's Word, when the fear of the Lord is restored, then and only then will revival come. This is not prosperity gospel optimism. This is covenant promise. God has never withheld Himself from a people who sought Him with their whole heart. He has never rejected genuine repentance. And He has never failed to revive those who return.

The dividing line of this age runs between true Christianity and false Christianity. Between those who negotiate with God and those who bow before Him. Between those who rename sin and those who repent of it, there is a difference. True faith does not haggle. It does not bargain. It does not compromise. It bows. And it does the hard work of repentance, even when repentance costs everything.

Jesus' final warning to the religious echoes across the ages: *"Not everyone who says to me, 'Lord, Lord,' will enter the kingdom of heaven, but the one who does the will of my Father who is in heaven. On that day, many will say to me, 'Lord, Lord, did we not prophesy in your name, and cast out demons in your name, and do many mighty works in your name?' And then will I declare to them, 'I never knew you; depart from me, you workers of lawlessness.'"* (Matthew 7:21-23).[113]

This warning was not directed at pagans but at religious people, those who used His name, performed religious works, and were affiliated with the faith. But they never submitted. They never obeyed. They never truly knew Him. And on the day of judgment, profession without transformation will be exposed as fraud.

But hope remains. God has always revived His people when they returned with wholehearted devotion. The pattern is clear, the promise certain: *"If my people who are called by my name humble themselves and pray and seek my face and turn from their wicked ways, then I will hear from heaven and will forgive their sin and heal their land."* (2 Chronicles 7:14).[114] Revival is not a mystery. It is the predictable outcome of obedience. Humble. Pray. Seek. Turn. These are not complex. They are costly. But they are the pathway home.

God does not need a majority. He does not need cultural power, political favor, or institutional prestige. He needs a remnant: people who fear Him, love Him, and obey Him more than they fear man. People who will stand in the gap, rebuild the ancient ruins, and restore the foundations. Not because they are perfect, but because they are surrendered. Not because they are gifted but because they are broken. Not because they are confident but because they tremble at His Word.

The voice that calls echoes through the ages: *"Return to me, for I have redeemed you."* (Isaiah 44:22).[115] Return with surrender, not sentiment. With allegiance, not admiration. With crucified faith, not casual faith. The Church stands at the crossroads. Return to holiness or continue in compromise. The remnant is rising. The separation is becoming visible. And God is calling His people home.

CONVICTION IN ACTION
"Revelation Governs"

Chapter 1: The Rise of Cultural Christianity

CONVICTION

God's Word is not an accessory to life; it is the foundation of it. When Scripture is displaced by self-rule, crowds, or cultural pressure, collapse is not a possibility; it is a timetable.

REALITY CHECK

The American church did not drift into compromise by accident. She was discipled into it, absorbing autonomy, outsourcing authority, and rebranding the result as "confusing times." Attendance swelled while holiness evaporated. The pulpit cooled from a furnace into a stage. And a Church that no longer trembles before God will inevitably tremble before culture. What we tolerated as "neutral" became quiet worship of something else.

FAITHFULNESS NOW LOOKS LIKE

Personal: Submit your daily decisions to Scripture, not as inspiration but as jurisdiction. Kill the hidden sin. Restore the neglected discipline. Where Christ is not Lord of the private life, public boldness is performance.

Church: Refuse cheap grace. Rebuild discipleship that expects repentance, obedience, endurance, and fruit, not crowds, sentiment, or metrics. If the pulpit avoids confrontation to preserve attendance, it has already chosen its master.

Public: Speak and act with a conscience anchored in transcendent truth. Refuse to surrender moral clarity for social acceptance. Admiring Christ and obeying Christ are not the same, and the difference is clear.

COMMITMENTS

☐ Open Scripture before news, inbox, or social feeds each day and write one concrete act of obedience you will complete that day.

☐ Identify one system you've been leaning on for security, whether money, politics, image, or relationships, and fast from it for 48 hours as a reset of allegiance.

☐ Restore one neglected discipline, whether prayer, confession, or accountability, and schedule it as non-negotiable, not "when I feel like it."

☐ Choose one cross-bearing obedience you've been postponing, something Scripture already requires, and do it this week without negotiating.

PRAYER

Lord Jesus, forgive me for calling admiration discipleship. Forgive me for outsourcing authority, lowering expectations, and renaming the wreckage "confusing times." Rebuild my conscience on Your Word alone. Make me a person who trembles before You rather than before culture, who counts the cost of obedience and pays it gladly. Restore in Your Church the fear of the Lord, the beginning of all wisdom, and let repentance precede renewal. Where I have made myself the standard, dethrone me. Where Scripture has not governed, let it govern now. Amen.

Chapter 2: What the Bible Actually Says

Section I: Scripture as the Standard, Not a Suggestion

The collision is already here. For decades, the language has sounded reasonable, "my truth," "lived experience," and "personal authenticity", as though truth were preference rather than revelation. But beneath the therapeutic vocabulary lies the oldest rebellion: the creature refusing to submit to the Creator, the sinner crowning himself judge over the Word of God. The question is unavoidable: Who has the final word?

That question defines everything. Authority is not optional. The human heart bows to something, always, and when it refuses to bow to God, it bows to an idol. The West has spent the last century systematically dismantling Scripture's authority. The Supreme Court declares that marriage can be redefined by judicial decree (Obergefell v. Hodges, 2015), as though five lawyers possess the authority to overrule the God who instituted marriage in Genesis. The Democratic Party enshrines abortion as a sacrament and codifies sexual autonomy as a constitutional right. The Equality Act seeks to criminalize biblical conviction, making it illegal to operate under the belief that male and female are fixed categories established by God. These are not accidents.

They are the systemic fruit of a nation that has dethroned Scripture.

The dethronement of Scripture does not produce freedom. It produces chaos, and chaos demands a tyrant. When every individual is authorized to define reality according to personal preference, reality ceases to exist as a shared inheritance. The culture that preaches tolerance punishes dissent. The ideology that promises liberation delivers enslavement. C.S. Lewis warned that when objective morality is abolished, what emerges is barbarism, a society of "men without chests" who demand virtue while mocking the foundations that make virtue possible.[116]

Scripture does not arrive as one voice among many. It arrives as the voice, the Word of God breathed out, profitable for teaching, for reproof, for correction, and for training in righteousness so that the man of God may be complete and equipped for every good work (2 Timothy 3:16–17).[117] This is revelation with binding force. The Word of God is not subject to amendment by committee or revision by culture. *"Forever, O Lord, your word is firmly fixed in the heavens."* (Psalm 119:89).[118] *"The grass withers, the flower fades, but the word of our God will stand forever."* (Isaiah 40:8).[119]

The collision is inevitable. Either Scripture has the final word, or something else does. Jesus made the terms explicit: *"No one can serve two masters, for either he will hate the one and love the other, or he will be devoted to the one and despise the other."* (Matthew 6:24).[120] The heart that divides its allegiance produces instability, and instability collapses toward the flesh. The modern experiment in personal truth has enslaved millions to their appetites and to the machinery of a state that has filled the authority vacuum.

The mechanism is the Democratic Party platform. It explicitly endorses abortion without restriction, celebrates sexual autonomy as a civil right, and treats biblical sexual ethics as hate speech. The Equality Act would force religious institutions to violate their convictions or face state coercion, compelling Christian schools, hospitals, and businesses to participate in what God calls sin. This is not tolerance. This is the establishment of a rival religion that worships autonomy and punishes those who refuse to bow.

Scripture does not negotiate with rival religions. It confronts them and declares judgment. The nation that refuses to acknowledge Scripture's authority will bow to Caesar, and Caesar does not share power. He demands worship, by persuasion if possible and by coercion when necessary.

If Scripture is the standard, its authority cannot be confined to Sunday mornings while the rest of life operates under different rules. The great temptation is compartmentalization, the belief that faith governs the soul while politics and culture govern everything else. But Scripture permits no such division. Its jurisdiction is total, its claims comprehensive, and its demand is submission.

Jesus declared that He did not come to abolish the Law or the Prophets: *"Until heaven and earth pass away, not an iota, not a dot, will pass from the Law until all is accomplished."* (Matthew 5:17–18).[121] Heaven and earth will pass away, but the Word of God will outlast them both. This is the non-negotiable claim of Scripture over every generation and every institution that dares to operate as though God's Word is optional.

The church has forgotten this. For decades, the pulpit has softened Scripture to avoid offending culture, treating the Bible as a resource for personal growth rather than the binding law of the King. Pastors preach grace without repentance, love without holiness, and inclusion without transformation. The result is a Christianity functionally indistinguishable from the world, a faith that offers comfort but demands nothing. Nancy Pearcey has documented how the sacred-secular split has privatized faith, reducing Christianity to a compartmentalized preference that culture tolerates as long as it remains silent.[122] The church that accepts this bargain has surrendered the gospel.

But Scripture will not be domesticated. *"The word of God is living and active, sharper than any two-edged sword, piercing to the division of soul and of spirit, of joints and of marrow, and discerning the thoughts and intentions of the heart."* (Hebrews 4:12).[123] This is sovereignty. The Word of God does not wait for permission. This Word pierces, divides, discerns, and judges, exposing hidden motives, unmasking disguised idols, and demanding submission from every soul it reaches.

Submission is not popular in a culture that worships autonomy, but it is the only proper response to the God who created and sustains the universe. To submit to Scripture is to acknowledge that God has the right to define reality, establish morality, command the conscience, and judge the nations. *"Your word is a lamp to my feet and a light to my path."* (Psalm 119:105).[124] Submission is wisdom, the recognition that the creature does not override the Creator.

Carl Trueman has shown how expressive individualism has made submission to external authority culturally unintelligible.[125] When identity is defined by inner feelings rather than external truth, submission to God becomes oppression. The modern self does not bow. It curates, selecting what it affirms and dismissing what it restricts. But God does not ask for curators. He demands servants.

Scripture's jurisdiction extends everywhere: to the family, where it governs marriage and parenting; to the church, where it defines doctrine and worship; to the conscience, where it exposes sin and commands repentance; and to the public square, where it speaks truth to power. *"Sanctify them in the truth; your word is truth."* (John 17:17).[126]

The Democratic Party platform represents the systematic rejection of Scripture's jurisdiction. The Equality Act treats biblical sexual ethics as discrimination. Roe, though overturned in Dobbs, functionally protected the killing of the unborn for fifty years, and the Democratic Party fights for its restoration with religious fervor. Obergefell redefined marriage by judicial fiat, as though five unelected lawyers possess the authority to overrule the God who created male and female. These are declarations of war against Scripture, and the church that remains silent has chosen its master.

The only posture that honors God is submission, not selective compliance but total surrender. *"You shall not add to the word that I command you, nor take from it."* (Deuteronomy 4:2).[127] To add is rebellion. To subtract is rebellion. To negotiate is rebellion. The church that treats Scripture as a buffet has dethroned God. And the culture that celebrates such rebellion is already under judgment.

When Scripture is dethroned, authority does not disappear. It relocates, and what rushes in is not reason or freedom but idolatry. The lie of secularism is that rejecting God's authority clears the ground for rational discourse, but the ground is never cleared. The human heart is a factory of idols, and production never stops. The machinery updates its product line. The ancient world carved its idols from wood and stone. Today, they are encoded in legislation, enshrined in court rulings, and enforced by the coercive power of the state.

The first relocation is to the self. When "my truth" becomes the final word and personal authenticity is elevated to revelation, the self becomes god. But the self is a cruel deity. It contradicts itself, shifts with cultural trends, and demands constant validation to sustain the illusion of coherence. James K.A. Smith has traced how cultural liturgies quietly train people to treat inner desire as the seat of moral authority, making the self sacred while rendering every external claim oppressive, resulting not in freedom but in fragility.[128]

When identity is constructed from within rather than received from without, every challenge becomes an existential threat, and existential threats must be eliminated. This is why dissent has become intolerable. To question someone's self-authored identity is to commit violence, and violence justifies any response, including the silencing and destruction of the one who speaks.

But the self cannot bear the weight of divinity. *"The heart is deceitful above all things, and desperately sick; who can understand it?"* (Jeremiah 17:9).[129] To make the self the final authority is madness, and the culture that enshrines autonomy produces a generation enslaved to appetite, addicted to validation, and incapable of sustaining a functional society.

When the self proves inadequate, authority relocates to the institution. The expert class, the credentialed elite, and the bureaucracy that claims to govern for the common good, become the new priests. "Trust the science." "Follow the guidelines." "Experts agree." The language is clinical, but the function is religious. The institution becomes the mediator of truth, and like every idol, it demands worship. Francis Schaeffer documented the trajectory, tracing the line of despair from the abandonment of absolutes to the collapse of meaning, showing how the West traded revelation for human reason only to discover that reason without transcendence produces nihilism.[130]

And nihilism devours freedom next.

The state offers the final relocation. When the self cannot sustain authority, and the institution cannot satisfy the demand for meaning, the state steps forward as the ultimate arbiter. "The law requires." "Public safety demands." The vocabulary is utilitarian, but the claim is totalitarian. The state that replaces God does not acknowledge limits because it has no authority higher than itself. And so the state becomes god, the final word on truth, morality, identity, and justice.

Once the state occupies God's throne, whatever it permits becomes permissible, whatever it condemns becomes criminal, and whatever it mandates becomes mandatory, regardless of conscience or divine command.

History confirms the pattern. Rome fell not because the barbarians were strong but because Rome was hollow. The Third Reich began with the rejection of Christian authority and ended in the worship of the state and the slaughter of millions. Soviet Russia promised liberation through atheism and delivered the Gulag. Maoist China traded God for the Party and harvested seventy million corpses. *"Thus says the Lord: 'Cursed is the man who trusts in man and makes flesh his strength, whose heart turns away from the Lord.'"* (Jeremiah 17:5).[131]

The curse is not arbitrary. It is the natural consequence of misplaced trust.

The Democratic Party has made the state its god. Each platform position, legislative priority, and judicial nominee is selected to expand government power and shrink the space for dissent. The Equality Act would force Christian institutions to choose between conviction and survival. Abortion is defended as a sacred right, and those who oppose it are treated as enemies. Gender ideology, enshrined in federal policy and enforced in public schools, teaches children that male and female are social constructs, and parents who object are labeled bigots.

This is idolatry, the worship of state power masquerading as compassion, and the church that remains silent has already bowed the knee.

But there is a fourth relocation: the tribe. When the self, the institution, and the state prove inadequate, authority relocates to the group. Identity becomes tribal. Truth becomes partisan. The tribe offers belonging in a world where meaning has collapsed, but the price is conformity, and the penalty for deviation is exile.

Scripture exposes the entire trajectory. *"They exchanged the truth about God for a lie and worshiped and served the creature rather than the Creator."* (Romans 1:25).[132] The exchange is always a downgrade. The creature is not capable of bearing the authority that belongs to the Creator. The self is not wise enough. The institution is not just enough. The state is not merciful enough. The tribe is not stable enough. None of the substitutes can bear the load. Each crumbles under the weight of expectations it was never designed to carry.

The only authority that does not crumble is the Word of God. *"The grass withers, the flower fades, but the word of our God will stand forever."* (Isaiah 40:8).[133] It stands because it is anchored in the character of a God who does not change, because it speaks truth into chaos and refuses to negotiate with the lies of the age, and because it will not be replaced, will not share the throne, and will not bow to idols.

Once Scripture is dethroned, the next battlefield is language itself. Language is the mechanism by which reality is named, morality is framed, and authority is exercised. To control the vocabulary is to control the conscience, and the culture that rejects biblical authority does not abandon Scripture's definitions. It inverts them. The result is a systematic inversion in which what God calls holy is labeled harmful, what He calls sin is celebrated as liberation, and what He calls truth is condemned as oppression.

Isaiah warned of this inversion: *"Woe to those who call evil good and good evil, who put darkness for light and light for darkness, who put bitter for sweet and sweet for bitter!"* (Isaiah 5:20).[134]

The prophet was not describing a distant future but diagnosing the present reality of a people who had exchanged the Word of God for the wisdom of man. When truth is no longer anchored in revelation, words lose their meaning, and reality becomes whatever the most powerful voices declare.

Consider "love." In Scripture, love is defined by sacrifice, fidelity, and truth-telling. *"Love does not delight in evil but rejoices with the truth."* (1 Corinthians 13:6).[135] To love someone is to desire their good, to pursue their holiness, and to speak truth even when truth is costly. But the culture has redefined love as affirmation.

To love is to approve. To question is to hate. To correct is to harm. The biblical definition demands that we confront sin for the sinner's soul. The cultural definition demands that we celebrate sin for the sake of the sinner's feelings. The two definitions are opposite gospels, and the society that adopts the cultural definition will call those who practice biblical love bigots while lionizing those who affirm people into destruction.

"Harm" has undergone the same corruption. Scripture defines harm as anything that damages the soul or distorts the image of God. But culture has redefined harm as anything that challenges autonomy or questions identity. Under this definition, the most harmful thing a person can do is tell the truth that contradicts someone's self-conception. Truth becomes violence. Silence becomes love. The inversion is complete.

"Freedom" in Scripture is liberation from sin, the ability to do what we were created to do. *"If the Son sets you free, you will be free indeed."* (John 8:36).[136] Freedom is not autonomy. It is alignment with truth. But culture defines freedom as the absence of constraint, the ability to do whatever one desires without interference. Under this definition, obedience to God is slavery, and rebellion is liberation. The irony is brutal: the culture that promises freedom through autonomy produces addiction, while the faith that commands submission produces life.

Douglas Wilson has documented how controlling vocabulary is the first step in controlling culture, because whoever defines the terms wins the argument before it begins.[137] If "tolerance" means celebrating sin, then biblical Christians are intolerant by definition. If "equality" means erasing distinctions God created, then Scripture is oppressive. If "justice" means equal outcomes regardless of merit, then God is unjust. The definitions are loaded. The argument is rigged. The church that accepts the culture's vocabulary has surrendered.

But Scripture does not accept the culture's vocabulary. It establishes its own. *"Sanctify them in the truth; your word is truth."* (John 17:17).[138] The Word of God does not adapt to the redefinitions of the age. It speaks with authority into confusion, declaring what is true, what is good, and what is right. The church that recovers biblical clarity will refuse to surrender the vocabulary of truth, love, harm, freedom, and justice to the culture. It will insist that words have meanings, that meanings are rooted in reality, and that reality is defined by the God who created it.

G.K. Chesterton warned that reformers who tear down fences without understanding why they were built are fools.[139] The culture that redefines words without understanding their biblical foundations is not progressing but regressing, tearing down the linguistic architecture that makes coherent thought and functional society possible. When the architecture collapses, what remains is chaos.

The Democratic Party has weaponized this linguistic inversion. To oppose abortion is to wage a "war on women." To affirm biblical sexuality is to commit "hate speech." To insist that male and female are fixed categories is to engage in "discrimination." The Equality Act would codify these inversions into federal law, making it illegal to operate a business, run a school, or practice medicine on the basis of biblical convictions.

The party does not reject Scripture's definitions. It criminalizes them, using state power to punish those who refuse to adopt the newspeak.

"See to it that no one takes you captive by philosophy and empty deceit, according to human tradition, according to the elemental spirits of the world, and not according to Christ."

(Colossians 2:8).[140] The captivity begins with language, and the liberation begins with reclaiming the words that God has given. Because Scripture is the standard, it must govern the contested terms. Truth, morality, identity, and justice are not optional domains. They are territories that Scripture claims by right, and the church that recovers prophetic clarity will speak the Word of God without apology.

The culture insists that definitions evolve, that words mean whatever consensus declares. But Scripture does not evolve. It endures. The Word of God is not one voice among many. It is the voice that spoke creation into existence, the voice that will judge the living and the dead, and the voice that will not be silenced by the redefinitions of rebels. The authority of Scripture is total, and total authority demands total submission.

Section II: The Word of God on Truth, Morality, Identity, and Justice

The war over truth, morality, identity, and justice is as old as Eden, where the serpent asked, "Did God actually say?" The question has never changed. Now the serpent speaks through Supreme Court opinions, Democratic Party platforms, and federal agencies, asking the same question with the same intent: to make God's Word negotiable, to replace divine revelation with human preference, and to crown the creature as judge over the Creator.

Scripture must govern these four domains because these are the categories through which human beings understand reality, define right and wrong, construct identity, and order societies. When Scripture is rejected as the authority, chaos does not remain chaos. It resolves into tyranny. The culture that rejects God's standard will impose its own, and the imposition will be total. The trajectory is consistent and brutal: "my truth" ends as compelled speech, "therapeutic morality" ends as criminalized conviction, "self-authored identity" ends as state-enforced ideology, and "social justice" ends as weaponized law.

The pattern is visible in the Democratic Party's 2020 platform, in the Equality Act, and in every Supreme Court opinion that treats God's design as negotiable. The attacks on Scripture are not incidental. They are foundational. The goal is conquest.

Truth is neither a preference nor a plural concept. It is singular, absolute, and personal. *"I am the way, the truth, and the life. No one comes to the Father except through me"* (John 14:6).[141] Jesus does not claim to be one truth among many. He claims to be the truth, the exclusive path to the Father, and the revelation that exposes every competing claim as a lie.

The culture has spent generations dismantling this foundation. The Democratic Party's 2020 platform enshrines "lived experience" as the measure of truth, elevating subjective feelings to the status of objective reality while dismissing biblical revelation as bigotry.[142] Public school curricula teach children that truth is a social construct. Federal Title IX guidance redefines biological sex as self-identification, compelling schools to treat self-declared identity as legally binding truth while punishing dissent as discrimination.[143] Truth is not discovered. It has been invented. And the inventor is the self.

But the self cannot bear the weight of truth. When every individual becomes the arbiter of reality, reality ceases to exist as a shared category. What remains is a war of competing narratives, and the narrative with the most power wins. The culture that celebrates "my truth" also demands ideological conformity, because preference cannot sustain a civilization. Paul described the mechanism in Romans: humanity *"exchanged the truth about God for a lie and worshiped and served the creature rather than the Creator"* (Romans 1:25).[144] The exchange is always a degradation.

The trajectory from relativism to tyranny is observable. Institutions that preach tolerance punish dissent, and voices that celebrate diversity demand uniformity. Truth rejected does not produce a vacuum. It produces a substitute, and the substitute is always coercion because lies cannot sustain themselves without the threat of punishment.[145]

When identity becomes truth and truth becomes identity, dissent is not wrong. It is violence. And violence must be eliminated. If truth is whatever the self declares, then the self must be protected from challenge at all costs.[146] The tyranny of the self is more brutal than any external dictator. The self demands validation it cannot provide, punishes dissent it cannot refute, and collapses under contradictions it cannot resolve.

Scripture will not be edited. *"Sanctify them in the truth; your word is truth"* (John 17:17).[147] Truth is objective, grounded in the character of the God who does not change. To reject this truth is to embrace tyranny.

Morality is not therapeutic, and it is not negotiable. Morality is holiness, the reflection of God's character in the lives of those He has created, and it requires repentance, obedience, and the death of the old self. *"You shall be holy, for I am holy"* (Leviticus 19:2).[148] This is a command, not a suggestion. Holiness is not one option on a menu of lifestyle choices. It is the standard, and the standard does not shift to accommodate cultural preferences or personal comfort.

But the culture has replaced holiness with therapy, treating sin as a wound to be affirmed rather than a rebellion to be crucified. Repentance has been rebranded as "shame." Conviction has been labeled "harm." And holiness itself has been redefined as oppression.

The Equality Act is the legislative embodiment of this inversion. Introduced repeatedly by Democratic lawmakers and supported overwhelmingly by the party's leadership, the Act would criminalize biblical sexual ethics, force Christian institutions to hire and affirm those who reject biblical morality, and eliminate conscience protections for healthcare providers, business owners, and educators who operate under the conviction that God's design is not negotiable.[149] The Act does not seek tolerance but enforcement, and it does not protect freedom but punishes dissent. And it does so under the banner of compassion, as though coercion could ever produce genuine love.

The Supreme Court paved the way. Obergefell v. Hodges declared that marriage can be redefined by judicial decree, treating millennia of moral clarity as outdated prejudice and elevating sentiment to the status of constitutional right.[150] The majority opinion does not argue from nature, Scripture, or reason. It argues from feelings, as though subjective experience possessed the authority to overrule the God who instituted marriage in Genesis. This is not jurisprudence. It is rebellion, the use of judicial power to impose a moral framework that treats autonomy as sacred and God's design as optional. And the rebellion does not stop with marriage. It extends to every category of moral life, redefining sin as identity and identity as untouchable.

The inversion is total. What God calls an abomination, the culture calls beautiful. What God calls death, the culture calls healthcare. What God calls rebellion, the culture calls authenticity. Isaiah warned of this pattern: *"Woe to those who call evil good and good evil, who put darkness for light and light for darkness, who put bitter for sweet and sweet for bitter!"* (Isaiah 5:20).[151] The woe is not rhetorical. It is the announcement of judgment, the declaration that moral inversion produces collapse. And the collapse is not distant. It is here, visible in the rising suicide rates among those affirmed in their confusion, in the epidemic of addiction among those told their appetites are their identity, and in the spiritual emptiness of a generation raised to worship the self and despise the Savior.

Therapeutic morality has made repentance intolerable because repentance requires acknowledging sin, and sin cannot exist in a world where the self is sacred. To call someone to turn from their sin is now framed as inflicting psychological harm, as though the soul's eternal condition mattered less than the sinner's temporary comfort.[152] But silence is not love. It is cowardice masquerading as compassion, and it produces damnation dressed in the vocabulary of affirmation.

The culture that refuses to call sin what God calls it will not produce flourishing. It will produce death, because the wages of sin have not changed, no matter how many judges declare otherwise.

The therapeutic model demands that the church affirm what God condemns, celebrate what Scripture calls an abomination, and remain silent when the Word commands speech. But Scripture does not permit such surrender. *"Be holy, for I am holy"* (1 Peter 1:15-16).[153] Holiness is the standard. The church that abandons holiness for cultural acceptance has abandoned the gospel, because a gospel without repentance sends souls to hell while promising heaven.[154]

Civilization requires fixed boundaries, consequences for those who cross them, and the moral clarity to distinguish right from wrong. When boundaries are erased, when sin is celebrated and holiness condemned, the structure collapses. God has built the universe to function a certain way. When humanity operates outside that design, the result is destruction.

Identity is not invented but received. *"So God created man in his own image, in the image of God he created him; male and female he created them"* (Genesis 1:27).[155] Identity begins with creation, not with preference. It is rooted in the act of the Creator, who formed us in the womb, who knows us before we know ourselves, and who has declared what we are before we ever have the chance to declare what we want to be.

"For you formed my inward parts; you knitted me together in my mother's womb" (Psalm 139:13).[156] This is not poetry. This is ontology, the truth about who we are grounded in the reality of the God who made us.

But the culture has made identity a matter of self-construction. Gender is no longer a biological reality established by God at conception. It is a social construct, a choice, a fluid spectrum that each individual is free to define and redefine at will. The Supreme Court enshrined this lie in Bostock v. Clayton County, ruling that Title VII's prohibition on sex discrimination includes "sexual orientation" and "gender identity," effectively mandating that employers, schools, and institutions treat self-declared identity as a legally binding reality while punishing those who insist on biological truth.[157]

The decision does not argue from the text of the law, from biology, or from the created order. It argues from ideology, imposing a worldview that makes the self the author of identity and treats God's design as irrelevant.

The Biden administration pushed Title IX toward an expansive gender-identity theory of "sex discrimination," prompting nationwide legal conflict.[158] Although the Department's 2024 Title IX rule was vacated and OCR says it has reverted to enforcing the 2020 rule, the broader push has already reshaped institutional policies on bathrooms, locker rooms, and sports. It has ignited clashes over compelled speech.[159] In documented cases, teachers have been fired or disciplined in disputes involving pronouns and gender-identity policies, even as courts have recognized constitutional claims in some contexts.[160] The result is pressure, social, professional, and institutional, to comply with contested assertions about sex and identity, with penalties for those who resist.

This is not policy. This is coercion, the use of institutional power to compel participation in a delusion and to punish those who refuse to pretend that lies are truth.

The Democratic Party has made this enforcement a central plank of its platform, treating gender ideology as a civil right and biblical anthropology as discrimination. The 2024 platform explicitly endorses "full equality" for LGBTQ+ individuals, which in practice means the elimination of any distinction between male and female, the celebration of sexual confusion as courage, and the punishment of dissent as hate.[161] Tolerance is not the goal. What is being established is a rival religion, one that worships the self and treats creation as a prison to be escaped rather than a gift to be received.

When identity is severed from creation and grounded in preference, it becomes fragile, requiring constant validation from the outside world to sustain the illusion of coherence. And when validation is not forthcoming, enforcement becomes necessary. This is why dissent has become intolerable. To question someone's self-declared identity is not to disagree. It is to commit violence, an assault on the existence of the person who has staked their entire sense of self on the lie that they can be whoever they say they are.[162] And violence justifies any response, including the destruction of careers, the severing of relationships, and the use of state power to silence those who insist on reality.

The mechanisms of enforcement are already in place. Social pressure shames dissenters into silence. Institutional policies punish those who refuse to affirm the ideology. And legal coercion criminalizes dissent, making it illegal to operate a business, practice medicine, or educate children under the conviction that male and female are fixed categories established by God.[163] The trajectory is unmistakable. A demand for tolerance becomes a demand for participation, and participation becomes compulsion. The culture that makes identity sacred cannot tolerate dissent, because dissent exposes the lie.

Scripture does not permit the lie. Identity is received, grounded in the Creator who made us male and female, who knit us together in the womb, and who declared our purpose before we drew breath. To reject this identity is rebellion, the attempt to overthrow the Creator and install the creature in His place. The creature cannot bear the weight of divinity. It collapses under its own contradictions, and when it collapses, it blames those who refused to affirm the delusion.[164] The self-made identity produces fragility rather than strength. And fragility, when given power, becomes cruelty.

Justice is neither power nor outcomes. It is righteousness, the impartial application of God's standard to all people without favoritism or partiality. *"The Rock, his work is perfect, for all his ways are justice. A God of faithfulness and without iniquity, just and upright is he"* (Deuteronomy 32:4).[165]

Justice begins with God's character and flows from His law. It is grounded in truth, measured by righteousness, and applied without regard to status, tribe, or identity. It treats all people equally before the standard, rewarding those who do right and punishing those who do wrong. This is biblical justice, and it is the only justice that produces genuine flourishing.

But the culture has replaced biblical justice with power masked as compassion. The Democratic Party's platforms, the Equality Act, and the ever-expanding federal bureaucracy have redefined justice as the redistribution of outcomes to achieve predetermined results based on identity categories rather than individual conduct. Rather than being blind, justice has become partial, favoring the "oppressed" and punishing the "oppressor" based on immutable characteristics rather than actions or character. The 2020 Democratic platform explicitly endorses "equity" over equality, treating equal outcomes as the measure of justice and disparate results as evidence of systemic injustice regardless of behavior, effort, or merit.[166]

This is not justice. This is the weaponization of law, the use of state power to enforce a moral framework that treats power as the only relevant category and outcomes as the only measure of righteousness. When justice is detached from truth and grounded in identity, law becomes a tool of vengeance rather than righteousness. Partiality replaces impartiality. Narrative replaces evidence. And ideology replaces truth.[167]

The result is not flourishing. It is tyranny, the use of legal coercion to punish those who succeed and reward those who claim grievance, regardless of whether the grievance is legitimate or the punishment is deserved.

The Equality Act represents this inversion in legislative form. It does not seek equal treatment under the law. It seeks preferential treatment for favored groups and punitive measures against those who refuse to comply with the new orthodoxy.[168] Religious liberty is stripped, conscience protections eliminated, and dissent criminalized. And those who insist that justice must be tethered to truth and righteousness are labeled bigots and targeted for destruction. This is not justice. This is power, the use of law to enforce conformity and punish those who refuse to bow.

Biblical justice requires truth because without it there is no standard, righteousness because without it there is no basis for just action, and impartiality because partiality is the essence of injustice. *"Righteousness and justice are the foundation of your throne"* (Psalm 89:14).[169] Justice that is not grounded in God's character is not justice at all. It is power dressed in the vocabulary of compassion, and it produces oppression rather than liberation.[170]

The attempt to achieve cosmic justice through state power always produces tyranny, because it requires the concentration of authority in the hands of those who claim to know what outcomes should be. Those who claim such knowledge are never impartial.[171] When justice is defined by results rather than righteousness, law becomes arbitrary. The powerful decide who deserves what, and their decisions are always influenced by ideology, tribe, and the pursuit of power.

Truth becomes irrelevant, righteousness becomes oppressive, and impartiality becomes impossible. What remains is not justice. It is the rule of the strong over the weak, enforced by legal coercion and justified by the lie that outcomes are the measure of righteousness.

But Scripture does not permit such corruption. Justice must be grounded in truth, measured by righteousness, and impartial to all. Anything less is not justice. It is tyranny masquerading as compassion, and it will produce the same result that all tyrannies produce: the destruction of those it claims to liberate.

The trajectory is unmistakable, and the acceleration is visible. When truth is rejected, moral chaos follows. That chaos produces identity instability, which demands legal enforcement, which in turn requires the silencing of dissent. The pattern repeats in every institution, every platform, every sphere of public life. Tolerance becomes compulsion, compassion becomes coercion, and the promise of liberation delivers slavery.

The mechanisms are already in place. Social pressure shames dissenters into silence. Institutional policies punish those who refuse to comply. And legal coercion criminalizes conviction, making it illegal to operate based on biblical truth in business, education, medicine, or public witness.[172] The culture that began with "celebrate diversity" has arrived at "compelled speech," and the arrival was not accidental. It was inevitable, because lies cannot sustain themselves without the threat of punishment.

Elite institutions have abandoned their commitment to truth and adopted ideological conformity as the measure of acceptability. Media, academia, corporations, and government agencies now enforce narrative rather than pursue truth, punishing those who question the orthodoxy and rewarding those who enforce it.[173] When truth is replaced by narrative, justice is replaced by power, and persuasion is replaced by coercion, tyranny is the only possible outcome. And the tyranny targets the church because the church is the last institution that insists Scripture is the standard and Scripture will not be negotiated.

Compelled speech is the hallmark of totalitarian regimes, and the West has embraced it with enthusiasm. Pronouns must be affirmed. Gender ideology must be celebrated. Biological reality must be denied. And those who refuse face destruction.[174]

This is not tolerance. This is enforcement, the use of power to compel participation in lies and to punish those who insist on truth. And the enforcement will escalate, because it must. Lies require ever-increasing levels of coercion to be sustained, and the culture that has rejected truth as the standard has no limiting principle, no boundary it will not cross, and no cost it will not impose.

This is the pressure the church now faces. Negotiate truth or be labeled intolerant. Negotiate morality, or be called hateful. Negotiate identity, or be accused of violence. Negotiate justice, or be branded oppressive. The demands will not stop, because they cannot stop. The culture that has rejected Scripture as the authority over these four domains has no alternative but coercion, and coercion will be applied to the church until the church either capitulates or is destroyed.

The cost of negotiation must now be named.

Section III: The Cost of Treating Scripture as a Buffet

Buffet Christianity is not a harmless preference. It is throne theft, the quiet insurrection that leaves "Lord" on the lips while removing submission from the life. The church that treats Scripture as a menu rather than a master has not found balance. It has committed treason, keeping the comforts of belonging while vetoing the King's commands. This is not selective emphasis. This is functional lordship rejection, and it produces a counterfeit Christianity that looks like the faith, sounds like the faith, and calls itself the faith while serving a different god.

Jesus declared the standard without ambiguity: "*Not everyone who says to me, 'Lord, Lord,' will enter the kingdom of heaven, but the one who does the will of my Father who is in heaven.*" (Matthew 7:21).[175] The designation "Lord" requires submission. To call Him Lord while refusing His commands is not discipleship. It is blasphemy dressed in religious vocabulary, the claiming of His name without the cost of His cross. Buffet Christianity insists on the benefits, forgiveness, assurance, community, and heaven, while editing out the requirements.

Sexual ethics negotiated. Generosity optional. Speech unguarded. Submission to authority is conditional. Holiness deferred. Repentance minimized. This is not Christianity. It is self-worship with Christian aesthetics, and it produces damnation while promising salvation.

Cheap grace is grace without discipleship, forgiveness without repentance, communion without confession, and absolution without contrition.[176] It treats the gospel as a product to consume rather than a King to obey. It wants the cross as a symbol, not as a sentence. It celebrates Easter while refusing Good Friday. And it produces disciples who have never been discipled, Christians who have never met Christ, and churches full of people destined for judgment who believe they are destined for glory.

The church tolerates a Christ who exists to affirm rather than command, who blesses comfort zones rather than demolishes them, who validates preferences rather than crucifies rebellion.[177] The buffet approach reconstitutes Jesus into a therapist who exists to make us feel better about ourselves rather than the Lord who demands we die to ourselves. And when Christ is domesticated, the gospel is gutted. What remains is not good news. It is self-help with religious language, therapeutic affirmation masquerading as divine truth. And it sends souls to hell while assuring them they are saved. And it sends souls to hell while assuring them they are saved.

James does not permit such delusion. *"But be doers of the word and not hearers only, deceiving yourselves."* (James 1:22).[178] Selective obedience is self-deception. It is the lie that hearing without doing, affirming without obeying, and believing without submitting constitutes faith. But faith without works is dead, and a dead faith produces dead souls. The buffet Christian hears the Word, agrees with the Word, celebrates the Word, and then edits the Word to fit the life already chosen. This is not transformation. It is confirmation bias with Bible verses attached.

And God will not be mocked. The one who picks and chooses what to obey has chosen self as lord, no matter what the mouth confesses.

Selective Scripture does not produce mere theological error. It reconstitutes the gospel into something fundamentally different, a safer religion that keeps Jesus as mascot while removing Him as Master. The mechanism is subtle but devastating: edited commands, preserved comforts, rearranged priorities. The result is a counterfeit faith that looks, sounds, and feels Christian while producing no actual transformation.

The time is coming when people will not endure sound teaching, when itching ears will accumulate teachers to suit passions, and when truth gives way to myths (2 Timothy 4:3-4).[179] The itching ear demands a gospel that affirms rather than confronts, that comforts rather than convicts, and that validates preferences rather than demolishes them. And the church supplies what the ear demands: teachers who soften the hard sayings, reframe the costly commands, and assure the comfortable that their comfort is God's will.

The buffet produces a gospel where Jesus affirms your identity, blesses your ambitions, validates your sexuality, and demands nothing in return except that you feel good about Him.

This is not the Christ of Scripture. This is an idol carved in the image of therapeutic culture, a Jesus who exists to make you happy rather than holy, who whispers affirmation rather than demands repentance, and who celebrates self-expression rather than requires self-denial. The half-Christian wants heaven without holiness, forgiveness without forsaking sin, Christ without the cross.[180]

And the pattern has accelerated. The American church has produced millions who believe they are saved because they prayed a prayer, walked an aisle, or identify as Christian, but who show no evidence of regeneration, no hunger for holiness, no hatred of sin, and no love for Christ's commands.

The American Dream has gutted the American gospel, replacing radical discipleship with comfortable religion, substituting the cost of the cross with the pursuit of personal peace and affluence.[181] The result is a Christianity that fits seamlessly into consumer culture because it has become consumer culture with religious branding. Jesus as a life coach. The gospel as a self-improvement plan. The church as a social club. Discipleship as an optional upgrade. And millions believe they are saved while living in functional rebellion against the God they claim to worship.

Lukewarmness invites divine judgment. *"So, because you are lukewarm and neither hot nor cold, I will spit you out of my mouth."* (Revelation 3:15-16).[182] Selective obedience produces selective conviction, selective repentance, and selective transformation. It produces people who are neither fully in nor fully out, who claim Christ without submitting to Christ, who want the benefits of grace without the bondage of holiness. And Christ does not accept such divided loyalty. He demands all or nothing. The buffet Christian offers some, calls it all, and believes the lie.

Halfhearted commitment insults God while claiming to love Him.[183] When Scripture is treated as negotiable, conviction becomes negotiable, holiness becomes negotiable, and eventually Christ Himself becomes negotiable. What remains is not Christianity. It is apostasy disguised in Christian vocabulary. And the apostasy spreads not through outright denial but through selective affirmation, the editing of Scripture, one command at a time, until what remains bears no resemblance to the faith once delivered.

The collapse is documented. Among self-identified evangelicals, biblical literacy has plummeted, biblical engagement has cratered, and biblical authority has eroded to the point where Scripture is treated as one voice among many rather than the final voice over all.[184] The buffet has become the default posture. Scripture is affirmed in theory while ignored in practice, commands are acknowledged while disobeyed, and truth is celebrated while being edited. And the church wonders why it produces disciples incapable of endurance, weak under pressure, and silent when courage is required.

Selective Scripture produces selective discipleship, and selective discipleship collapses under pressure. The Christian trained to negotiate commands cannot sustain conviction when conviction costs something. The disciple formed on edited Scripture has no foundation when the world demands capitulation. And the church that treats God's Word as optional produces a generation incapable of the courage that costly obedience requires.

Discipleship is daily death. "*If anyone would come after me, let him deny himself and take up his cross daily and follow me.*" (Luke 9:23).[185] It is the mortification of the old self and the submission to the new Master. It is not an addition to the life already chosen. It is a replacement: the exchange of autonomy for obedience, of preference for surrender, of self-rule for Christ-rule. But the buffet Christian refuses the exchange. The cross is affirmed as a symbol while rejected as a sentence.

Self-denial is praised in theory while abandoned in practice. And the result is a disciple who has never been discipled, a follower who has never followed, a Christian who bears Christ's name while living in functional rebellion against His lordship.

The gap between gospel passion and the pursuit of godliness reveals the hole in evangelical holiness where the pursuit of Christ-likeness should be.[186] The gospel demands total surrender. The one who comes to Christ must come empty-handed, with nothing to offer and everything to lose. But the buffet gospel offers salvation without surrender, heaven without holiness, and eternal life without dying to self. And it produces millions who believe they are saved while remaining slaves to sin, who claim regeneration while showing no transformation, who confess Christ while denying Him with their lives.

The question confronts every professing Christian: Are you seeking the approval of man or of God? If you were still trying to please man, you would not be a servant of Christ (Galatians 1:10).[187] The buffet Christian seeks to please both God and man, to affirm Scripture while accommodating culture, and to uphold truth while avoiding offense. But such a compromise is impossible. The servant of Christ serves Christ alone. The one who negotiates Scripture to avoid cultural cost has chosen culture as lord.

And culture is a cruel master. It demands ever-increasing capitulation, punishes courage with rejection, and rewards cowardice with acceptance. The church that trains disciples to please man produces disciples incapable of serving God.

The acceleration is documented. Among younger evangelicals, support for same-sex marriage has increased, abortion restrictions have decreased, and biblical sexual ethics have been abandoned at rates that would have been unthinkable a generation ago.[188] The buffet has produced exactly what it was designed to produce: a generation trained to edit Scripture when Scripture conflicts with cultural pressure. And the editing does not stop with sexuality. It extends to money, speech, submission to authority, and every other command that carries cultural cost. The disciple trained to negotiate one command will negotiate them all. And when negotiation becomes the default posture, courage becomes impossible.

The fear of the Lord persuades. "*Therefore, knowing the fear of the Lord, we persuade others.*" (2 Corinthians 5:11).[189] The fear of God is the foundation of courage, because the one who fears God fears nothing else. The disciple who stands before God in trembling reverence does not tremble before cultural rejection. But the buffet Christian has lost the fear of God. Scripture is no longer the voice of the living God demanding submission. It is a resource to be mined for comfort, a menu to be curated for preference, and a book to be affirmed in theory while ignored in practice. And when the fear of God is lost, the fear of man fills the void.

The result is a church of cowards who call their cowardice wisdom, who label capitulation discernment, and who mistake silence for grace.

The cost of buffet Christianity extends beyond individual discipleship. It destroys the church's public witness and teaches the watching world that truth is negotiable, that reality is editable, and that Scripture carries no binding authority. When the church edits God's Word to avoid cultural cost, it forfeits the right to speak God's truth to the culture. And when prophetic witness collapses, coercion fills the void.

The church exists as a pillar and a buttress of the truth (1 Timothy 3:15), bearing the weight of God's Word in a world at war with reality.[190] But the pillar cannot bear weight if the foundation is compromised. And the foundation is compromised when Scripture becomes negotiable.

The church that edits God's Word in one area teaches the culture that God's Word is editable in all areas. Sexual ethics rewritten. Gender erased. Marriage redefined. Life negotiated. Justice detached from righteousness, truth severed from revelation. And the culture learns the lesson the church has taught: reality is whatever power declares it to be.

The abandonment of whole-counsel preaching produces a generation incapable of distinguishing truth from error, incapable of resisting cultural pressure, and incapable of the clarity that prophetic witness requires.[191] When pastors soften the hard sayings, edit the costly commands, and preach a gospel designed to comfort rather than confront, the church loses its prophetic edge. What remains is not a pillar of truth. It is a mirror of culture, reflecting the world's values back to the world while claiming to represent God.

The pattern is visible in denominational collapse. The Presbyterian Church (USA) redefined marriage, abandoned biblical sexual ethics, and watched membership collapse by half in a generation.[192] The United Methodist Church fractured over the same issues, dividing into factions that affirm Scripture and factions that edit Scripture to accommodate cultural demands.[193] The trajectory is consistent: edit Scripture, lose authority, collapse into irrelevance. And the culture does not respect the church that capitulates. It despises it, because even the world understands that a religion without conviction is worthless.

The evangelical church is not immune. Portions of the evangelical movement now promote "gay Christianity," celebrating sexual orientation as identity while insisting that same-sex attraction is not sinful as long as it remains unconsummated.[194] The language is careful. The framing is therapeutic. The intent is clear: normalize what Scripture condemns, affirm what God calls an abomination, and redefine holiness to accommodate sexual brokenness.

And segments of the evangelical church, desperate to avoid cultural rejection, desperate to be seen as compassionate, and desperate to be affirmed by the world, have embraced the trajectory. The buffet produces what it always produces: a church that looks like the world, sounds like the world, and serves the world's gods while claiming to worship the God of Scripture.

The watchman who sees the sword coming and does not blow the trumpet bears the blood of those who perish (Ezekiel 33:6), and the church that sees the culture's rebellion against God while remaining silent shares that guilt.[195] And the silence is not neutrality. It is complicity. When the church edits Scripture to avoid offense, it becomes an accomplice in the culture's self-destruction. And God will require an accounting.

The whole counsel of God must be declared without negotiation. *"I did not shrink from declaring to you the whole counsel of God."* (Acts 20:27).[196] The whole counsel. Not the comfortable parts. Not the culturally acceptable parts. Not the parts that produce applause rather than persecution. The whole counsel, every command, every truth, every hard saying, without negotiation and without apology. This is the only posture that sustains prophetic witness. And prophetic witness is not optional. It is the church's calling, the reason the church exists in a world at war with God.

The choice before the church is binary. Submit to the whole counsel of God or surrender to the spirit of the age. There is no middle ground. The buffet is not balance. It is betrayal. And the cost of betrayal is not merely institutional decline or cultural irrelevance. The cost is the forfeiture of the faith itself.

All authority in heaven and on earth has been given to Christ (Matthew 28:18-20).[197] Go, therefore, and make disciples of all nations, baptizing them in the name of the Father and of the Son and of the Holy Spirit and teaching them to observe all that I have commanded you. All authority. All nations. All that I have commanded. The Great Commission does not permit selectivity.

The disciple is commanded to teach observance of all Christ's commands, not curated highlights, not culturally palatable portions, and not the parts that fit comfortably into modern sensibilities. All. And the church that edits the commission has abandoned the mission.

The fear of God is the beginning of wisdom, the foundation of obedience, and the only force strong enough to sustain courage when courage costs everything.[198] God is neither safe nor manageable nor negotiable. He is a consuming fire, the holy and righteous Judge before whom every knee will bow and every tongue confess. And the church that has lost the fear of God has lost everything.

It becomes a social club, a therapy center, a political advocacy group, or anything except what it was called to be: the assembly of the redeemed who tremble before the throne and obey without negotiation.

The cost of obedience is real. Rejection, persecution, loss of reputation, loss of livelihood, loss of cultural acceptance. Jesus promised it, Paul experienced it, and the early church expected it. And the modern church, desperate to avoid it, has traded the cost of discipleship for the comfort of cultural acceptance. But cultural acceptance purchased through compromise is not victory. It is surrender. And the church that surrenders Scripture to avoid cost has already lost, because a church without authority cannot speak truth, and a church that cannot speak truth has no reason to exist.

Sanctification is not optional, and devotion to God requires submission to the whole counsel without negotiation.[199] The gospel is not a negotiation. It is a declaration. Christ is Lord, Scripture is final, obedience is required, repentance is necessary, and holiness is commanded. And the alternative is not a kinder, gentler version of Christianity. The alternative is judgment. The watching world does not need a church that mirrors its rebellion. It needs a church that declares God's truth without flinching, calls sin what God calls sin, offers grace without negotiating holiness, and stands on the whole counsel of God regardless of cost.

The herald has spoken. The sword is coming. The culture's rebellion against God will not end in liberation. It will end in judgment. And the church that edits Scripture to accommodate the rebellion will share in the judgment.

But there is an alternative. Repentance. Whole-counsel fidelity. Fear of God. Courage under fire. Public witness that costs everything and refuses to negotiate. This is not a better strategy. It is the only strategy that Scripture permits. We must be grateful for receiving a kingdom that cannot be shaken and thus offer to God acceptable worship with reverence and awe, for our God is a consuming fire (Hebrews 12:28-29).[200]

The kingdom cannot be shaken, the Word will not be edited, and the Lord will not be domesticated. And the church must choose. Scripture as Lord or self as god. Whole counsel, or buffet blasphemy. There is no third option. And the time for choosing is now.

CONVICTION IN ACTION
"Truth Has a Throne"
Chapter 2: What the Bible Actually Says

CONVICTION

Scripture is not advisory, Christ is not optional, and obedience is not negotiable. When the Church treats God's Word as one voice among many, she has already chosen a different master.

REALITY CHECK

We are watching truth get reduced to preference, morality to emotion, and identity to self-authorship. A culture that preaches tolerance while punishing dissent, and promises liberation while delivering enslavement, has inverted reality itself. And the Church, rather than confronting the inversion, absorbed it, softening Scripture to protect comfort, editing commands to preserve attendance, and calling the surrender "nuance." Buffet Christianity is not balance. It is self-rule. And self-rule always demands more edits.

FAITHFULNESS NOW LOOKS LIKE

Personal: Reorder your life under Scripture daily, not as inspiration but as jurisdiction. Identify the edited zones and the commands you explain away, postpone, or relabel. Practice costly obedience where it will actually cost you.

Church: Preach and receive the whole counsel of God, including reproof, correction, warning, and judgment. Stop managing truth for attendance. If the Word is softened to keep peace, it will eventually lose peace anyway.

Public: Refuse compelled speech and moral inversion, without cruelty and without cowardice. Speak plainly when evil is renamed good. Engage as a pillar, not a weather vane: truth anchored in Christ, conscience unbought.

COMMITMENTS

☐ Read Scripture daily with one goal: submission, not selection.

☐ Name and repent of one buffet zone where you have negotiated obedience rather than practiced it.

☐ Speak one needed truth this week that you have been avoiding, in love, with clarity, without retreat.

☐ Align one relationship, habit, or entertainment pattern under Christ's authority, not your appetite.

PRAYER

Lord Jesus, forgive me for treating Your Word as advisory rather than authoritative. Forgive me for the zones I've edited, the commands I've relabeled, and the obedience I've postponed. You are not one voice among many. You are the voice. Rebuild my life under the authority of Scripture. Give me the courage to submit where I have only selected, to obey where I have only admired, and to speak where I have only been silent. Let Your Word govern everything: my conscience, my household, and my public witness. Truth has a throne. Let me bow before it. Amen.

Chapter 3: Abortion and the Democratic Party's Culture of Death

Section I: The Sanctity of Life vs. the Right to Kill

There is no more contested ground in the war between God and the gods of this age than the womb. It is not biological space. It is jurisdiction. It is the place where the Creator forms image-bearers and where a rebel culture attempts to seize authority it was never given. When Scripture declares, *"So God created man in his own image, in the image of God he created him; male and female he created them."* (Genesis 1:27),[201] it is not offering a sentiment for baby showers or a decorative verse for nursery walls. It is establishing the foundation upon which all human worth is measured and the non-negotiable boundary that no government, no court, no political platform, and no ideological movement has the authority to cross. The State does not grant the imago Dei. It is not ratified by a mother's consent. It is not negotiated by a physician's signature or a Supreme Court opinion. It is bestowed by God alone, and therefore it is inviolable.

Every legal system, every party platform, every cultural movement that attempts to redefine the worth of a human being apart from this foundation has not adopted a different philosophy. It has declared war on its Maker, and it will answer for it.

The moral boundary is not ambiguous, and it was not left to human deliberation. *"You shall not murder."* (Exodus 20:13).[202] That command is neither culturally conditioned nor subject to legislative revision or judicial reinterpretation. It does not bend to the preferences of a generation that has decided killing is acceptable as long as the victim is small enough and silent enough to ignore. The prohibition stands because innocent human life belongs to God, and what belongs to God is never available for human renegotiation. Abortion is not a complex moral gray area wrapped in medical terminology. It is the intentional destruction of a human life that God authored, and no volume of political rhetoric, no amount of institutional funding, and no number of euphemistic slogans will change what heaven sees when the act is committed. A nation that legalizes the shedding of innocent blood has not modernized its policy. It has rearranged its worship. It has placed something on the altar that God never authorized, and the prophets had a name for that: abomination.

Scripture does not treat life in the womb as potential life, conditional life, or life awaiting ratification. It treats it as life under active divine authorship. *"For you formed my inward parts; you knitted me together in my mother's womb."* (Psalm 139:13).[203] That is not poetry designed to comfort expectant mothers at a church event. It is a declaration of divine ownership. The child does not belong to the mother. The mother did not design the child. God did. He is the architect, the author, and the authority.

The womb is sacred not because of sentimentality but because God is at work there, and where God is at work, man is forbidden to destroy. What a people does to its most defenseless members reveals what it actually believes about God, regardless of what it prints on its currency, recites in its pledges, or sings in its sanctuaries. Basil the Great preached this with unsparing clarity in the fourth century: a society that hoards comfort while abandoning the vulnerable has exposed the bankruptcy of its professed faith, because true theology is measured not by confession but by conduct toward the weak.[204]

Jeremiah's calling confronts something this generation despises with every fiber of its being: divine intention that precedes and overrides personal preference. *"Before I formed you in the womb I knew you, and before you were born I consecrated you."* (Jeremiah 1:5).[205] The significance of that verse extends far beyond Jeremiah's prophetic office. It reveals a principle that governs every human life: God's knowledge of a person, God's purpose for a person, and God's claim on a person exist before that person draws a first breath, before a mother confirms a pregnancy, before any human institution has the opportunity to classify that life as wanted or unwanted, convenient or inconvenient, viable or expendable. Heaven does not wait for human permission to assign value. Heaven assigns it before the first cell divides.

Abortion, then, does not end a pregnancy. It trespasses into territory that belongs to God and interrupts a life already under His sovereign gaze. Francis Schaeffer warned that this trajectory was not accidental but inevitable: once a civilization severs humanity from its Creator, human life becomes raw material, and the powerful will always find reasons to discard the powerless.[206]

The logic never changes, and history never fails to confirm it. If man is not sacred, man is negotiable. If man is negotiable, power decides who lives and who dies. And when power decides, the weak always lose. The unborn cannot lobby a congressman. They cannot march in protest. They cannot hire attorneys. They cannot organize voter registration drives. They cannot purchase protection or broadcast their suffering on social media. They can only exist.

And in a culture intoxicated by its own sovereignty, a culture that has made autonomy its highest sacrament, mere existence has ceased to be enough. Existence without utility, without consent from the powerful, without economic justification, that kind of existence is treated as disposable. And the disposers call themselves compassionate.

The defense of abortion has always required the dehumanization of its victims, because the human conscience does not surrender quietly. It must first be sedated. That is the function of euphemism, and euphemism is not neutral language. It is the first instrument of violence. When the unborn child is renamed "tissue," "products of conception," "a clump of cells," or simply "a pregnancy to be terminated," the vocabulary is performing moral surgery on the conscience of an entire civilization. It is severing the mind from reality so that the hand can do its work without trembling. Euphemism kills the truth before the procedure kills the child. The early Church had no access to ultrasound technology, modern embryology textbooks, or genetic science.

But the Didache, written within living memory of the apostles, spoke with an authority that required none of those things: *"You shall not murder a child by abortion nor kill that which is born."* (Didache 2.2).[207] That statement is intolerable to modern ears for one reason: modern ears have been carefully, systematically trained to call the killing of children healthcare, and the Didache refuses to cooperate with the lie.

Tertullian, writing to a hostile Roman Empire that practiced exposure and infanticide without moral hesitation, identified what the Church has known from the beginning:

abortion is not a modern medical innovation, and its moral classification has never been in doubt among those who fear God. He called it what it is with the kind of directness that earns enemies in every generation: the deliberate destruction of a human being before birth, murder dressed in timing.[208]

The bluntness was not cruelty. It was love. Because when a society's vocabulary has grown cowardly enough to conceal killing behind sterile terminology, the most compassionate thing a truth-teller can do is refuse the vocabulary and speak plainly. Clarity in an age of euphemism is not harshness. It is the first act of mercy, because no one can repent of what no one is willing to name.

The political architecture that protects and expands abortion in America did not emerge by accident. It was constructed, funded, codified, and institutionally defended. The 2024 Democratic Party Platform commits the Party explicitly to protecting and expanding access to abortion and to opposing any restrictions on the practice.[209] That is not editorial commentary. It is the Party's own published language, written by its own leadership, ratified by its own delegates. The platform does not frame abortion as a tragic necessity or a reluctant concession. It frames it as a protected good, a positive right, and those who resist that framing are treated not as political opponents but as enemies of human progress.

When a major political institution anchors itself to the destruction of innocent life as a matter of party identity, platform commitment, and funding priority, it has not adopted a policy position. It has constructed a moral order. And what that order protects reveals what it worships.

Roe v. Wade functioned for nearly fifty years as the judicial canopy under which that moral order expanded and entrenched itself in American life.[210] But Roe was never the engine. It was the legal shelter. The engine was always deeper, a worship disorder that elevated human autonomy above divine authority, that treated the self as sovereign and the child as negotiable. When *Dobbs v. Jackson Women's Health Organization* overturned Roe in 2022, the national reaction revealed what had always been true beneath the legal briefs and oral arguments: this conflict was never primarily about constitutional interpretation.[211] It was about moral allegiance.

The fury that erupted was not the frustration of citizens who lost a procedural argument. It was the rage of a people whose god, the god of absolute personal autonomy, had been stripped of its most powerful federal protection. Dobbs did not end the war. It exposed it. And what it exposed should terrify every nation that still pretends its laws are morally neutral.

Hillary Clinton stated publicly, in language that has never been retracted, "The unborn person does not have constitutional rights."[212] That sentence deserves to be read twice, because the contradiction it carries is the moral engine of the entire regime. She called the unborn a *person*. Then, in the same breath, she denied that person any claim to protection. That is precisely how dehumanization operates in advanced, educated, sophisticated societies. It does not always deny humanity. That would be too crude, too obviously monstrous. Instead, it admits humanity and then declares that this particular category of humanity has no enforceable rights.

It relocates personhood from nature to law, from divine declaration to government permission, from ontological reality to political convenience. And once personhood becomes a status conferred by the powerful rather than a reality recognized under God, it is always one election, one court ruling, or one party platform revision away from being revoked for someone else.

What begins with the unborn never ends with the unborn. C.S. Lewis foresaw this logic with precision: once humanity is cut from its transcendent root, the powerful do not liberate the weak—they repurpose them, and the repurposing has no natural stopping point.[213]

The argument over when life begins is deployed as a fog machine, designed to keep moral clarity at a safe distance by implying that science has not yet settled the question. Science has settled it. The answer is inconvenient. At the moment of fertilization, a genetically distinct human organism begins to exist, with its own DNA and its own developmental trajectory, ordered toward growth, maturation, and birth. No embryology textbook published in the last fifty years disputes this. The modern world is not confused about whether a human embryo is biologically human. There is conflict about what obligations humanity imposes. And that conflict is not scientific. It is spiritual.

It is the refusal to accept that being human carries a divine claim that no human authority can override. Psalm 8 drives the question past utility and into the territory where all evasion fails: *"What is man that you are mindful of him and the son of man that you care for him? Yet you have made him a little lower than the heavenly beings and crowned him with glory and honor."* (Psalm 8:4–5).[214] That crowning is not postponed until viability. It is not contingent on a mother's emotional readiness or a father's financial capacity. It is rooted in God's sovereign decision to dignify man as man, and no human vote has the authority to reverse what God decreed before the foundation of the world.

Scripture provides a witness that no secular framework can neutralize and no euphemism can bury. When Mary visited Elizabeth, the unborn John responded to the presence of Christ in the womb of another woman, and Scripture does not treat the moment as poetry, metaphor, or literary device. *"For behold, when the sound of your greeting came to my ears, the baby in my womb leaped for joy."* (Luke 1:44).[215] The Holy Spirit chose every word of that sentence with precision. He did not call the unborn John a fetus. He did not call him "tissue." He did not call him a product of conception. He called him a baby.

And He attributed to that baby a distinctly human, distinctly spiritual response: joy in the presence of the Messiah. That single verse demolishes every piece of rhetorical machinery the abortion movement has ever constructed, because it treats the unborn not as a cluster of cells awaiting personhood but as a human being capable of recognizing the Son of God.

The legal contradictions that govern American law at this moment expose the moral rebellion underneath. If a wanted child in the womb is killed by a drunk driver or an act of violence, the law in most jurisdictions recognizes a second victim. Charges are filed. Grief is acknowledged. Personhood is assumed. But if an unwanted child in the very same womb, at the very same gestational stage, with the very same heartbeat, is intentionally destroyed in a clinical setting, the law calls it a "protected liberty." The body, the DNA, and the biological humanity are identical. The only variable is whether someone with power wanted the child to live. That is not justice. It is not neutrality. It is moral relativism hardened into statute and enforced by institutions.

It teaches the population a catechism more effective than any pulpit has ever delivered: value is determined by desire, humanity is contingent on consent, and rights belong to the strong, not the small.

When Paul describes the progression of a society that has rejected God, he does not begin with the external symptoms. He begins with the internal exchange that makes the external collapse inevitable: *"They exchanged the truth about God for a lie and worshiped and served the creature rather than the Creator, who is blessed forever."* (Romans 1:25).[216] That exchange is the engine. Once a culture trades the Creator for the creature, once it enthrones the Self where God was meant to reign, every moral boundary becomes negotiable because a creature that worships itself has no authority to tell itself no.

Calvin identified this mechanism centuries before the modern world perfected it: the human heart is a perpetual factory of idols, endlessly manufacturing new objects of devotion to justify whatever the flesh craves and whatever the will demands.[217] The abortion regime is not an anomaly in an otherwise healthy culture. It is the natural product of a civilization that replaced the worship of God with the worship of Self and then discovered that the Self demands sacrifice, real sacrifice, blood sacrifice, to maintain its throne.

Augustine understood, from the ruins of an empire that thought itself eternal, that when the soul's loves are disordered, when comfort is loved more than justice, when autonomy is loved more than obedience, and when convenience is loved more than life, the result is never private dysfunction. It is public violence. Disordered love in the heart becomes disordered law in the courts and disordered blood in the streets.[218]

The prophets of Israel witnessed the same pattern and named it without flinching: *"They sacrificed their sons and their daughters to the demons; they poured out innocent blood, the blood of their sons and daughters."* (Psalm 106:37–38).[219] That passage is devastating because it refuses every comfortable euphemism. It does not say Israel "made difficult healthcare decisions." It does not say Israel "exercised reproductive autonomy." It says Israel poured out innocent blood. It says Israel sacrificed children to demons. And it says God remembered every drop.

The consequences of this moral architecture do not remain confined to the womb. Thomas Sowell has demonstrated across decades of policy analysis that incentive structures produce moral outcomes. A political system that funds abortion, normalizes abortion, celebrates abortion, and punishes those who resist abortion creates an architecture in which children are treated as liabilities, personal sacrifice is mocked as backwardness, and the only responsibility recognized is the responsibility to protect one's own comfort.[220]

The civilizational trajectory is not subtle. Victor Davis Hanson has argued it with the clarity of a historian who has watched this pattern destroy societies older and more confident than ours: nations that turn against their own children are not progressing toward enlightenment. They are consuming their own future. They are dying, and they are calling it freedom.[221]

Scripture does not allow the people of God to stand neutral while innocent blood is shed, no matter how inconvenient the truth, no matter how costly the stand. *"Cease to do evil; learn to do good; seek justice, correct oppression, bring justice to the fatherless, and plead the widow's cause."* (Isaiah 1:16–17).[222]

The unborn child is not less fatherless because his biological father is alive somewhere. Fatherless because he has no defender, voiceless not by choice but by nature, he is precisely the kind of neighbor the prophets had in view when they condemned societies that traded justice for convenience and then dressed up the exchange as compassion.

R.C. Sproul spent decades warning the Church that the fundamental crisis of the modern world is neither political nor cultural. It is theological. It is the loss of God's holiness. When a people stops trembling at what is holy, it stops trembling at what is sinful. And when sin no longer produces trembling, blood no longer produces grief.

The culture reclassifies the killing, assigns it a medical code, funds it with taxpayer dollars, and calls anyone who objects a fanatic.[223] That is not a theoretical warning. It is a precise description of the nation we now inhabit, and the judgment that attaches to it is not speculative. It is already underway.

The question before this nation, and before every person who claims the name of Christ, is not a simple one. Science has already answered whether the unborn are human, and Scripture has already answered whether God claims authority over the womb. The remaining question is whether these people will obey or rebel, whether this Church will speak or hide, or whether this generation will choose the fear of God over the approval of a culture that has already decided the child must die so the Self can reign. Deuteronomy frames the decision with a finality that permits no evasion and no delay: *"I have set before you life and death, blessing and curse. Therefore, choose life, that you and your offspring may live."* (Deuteronomy 30:19).[224]

A nation that chooses death will not remain stable, because death is never satisfied with one category of victim. If the womb is disposable, nothing is sacred. If innocent blood can be legalized, no blood is safe. The defense of life in the womb is not a narrow political crusade. It is the front line in the defense of human dignity itself. And once that line falls, every line behind it falls with it.

Section II: Why 'Reproductive Freedom' Is a Spiritual Deception

The language has changed, but the altar remains the same.

What was once called abortion, a clinical term that at least acknowledged the destruction of life, is now draped in the silken rhetoric of "reproductive freedom," "bodily autonomy," and "healthcare." The architects of death have learned that people will accept murder if you dress it in the vocabulary of liberation, that a nation will sacrifice its children if you convince them it is an act of empowerment, and that the Church will remain silent if you make the sin sound like progress.

This pattern is neither new nor modern. It is ancient. The serpent in Eden did not say, "Eat this fruit and you will become rebels destined for death." He said, *"You will be like God, knowing good and evil."* (Genesis 3:5).[225]

The truth was buried beneath the promise of autonomy. The consequence was hidden beneath the appeal to personal sovereignty. And humanity has been falling for the same deception ever since: the lie that freedom can be purchased through rebellion, that liberation comes through the shedding of innocent blood, and that we can be our own gods if we refuse to bow to the God who made us.

"Reproductive freedom" is that same serpent's hiss, spoken in the language of constitutional rights and healthcare policy. It promises women control over their own bodies while concealing the body that is not their own, the distinct, genetically unique, unrepeatable human life growing within them. It offers liberation while demanding a blood price. It speaks the language of rights while stripping the most vulnerable of every right, including the right to exist.

And since January 22, 1973, the day the Supreme Court handed down *Roe v. Wade*, more than sixty-three million children have been killed in America through abortion.[226] Sixty-three million. The Guttmacher Institute, Planned Parenthood's own research arm, has documented this carnage year by year: nearly 1.6 million abortions annually in the peak years of the 1980s and 90s, tapering to approximately 930,000 per year by 2020.[227] The Centers for Disease Control confirms these numbers within a margin of error.[228] This is not pro-life propaganda. This is data from the abortion industry itself.

Sixty-three million children. More than the combined populations of California and Texas. More than died in the Holocaust, the Cambodian genocide, and the Rwandan massacres put together. More than all American military deaths in every war in our nation's history, the Revolutionary War, the Civil War, World War I, World War II, Korea, Vietnam, Iraq, and Afghanistan, all of them combined and multiplied by ten. This is the simple, brutal math of a half-century of legalized child sacrifice.

And it continues. Even after *Dobbs* overturned *Roe*, the killing has not stopped. In 2023 alone, over 1 million abortions were performed in the United States, the highest number in more than a decade.[229] States like California, New York, and Illinois have expanded access, declaring themselves "sanctuary states" for abortion, advertising their services to women from pro-life states, paying for travel and lodging, and turning the killing of children into interstate commerce.

The Democratic Party has made this slaughter its creed. Their 2024 platform declares: "Democrats believe that every woman should be able to access high-quality reproductive health care services, including safe and legal abortion."[230] This is not a footnote. This is a religious statement, delivered with the force of absolute conviction. Abortion is "high-quality reproductive health care." It is safe. It is legal. It is, by implication, good.

The platform goes further: "We will restore the protections of *Roe v. Wade* in federal law and continue to fight against state laws that criminalize abortion."[231] This is conquest. The goal is to impose abortion on the entire nation, to override every protection for the unborn, and to ensure that no community can say "not here, not our children." They want abortion enshrined as federal law, permanent and untouchable, a right more sacred than speech, more fundamental than religion, more protected than life itself.

And they want you to pay for it. The platform commits to eliminating the Hyde Amendment, which for decades has prevented federal tax dollars from funding most abortions.[232] Not to permit the killing of children, but to compel every citizen to participate financially in the slaughter, to make every taxpayer an accomplice, and to transform an entire nation into Molech's priesthood, whether they consent or not.

This is not policy. This is theology. A rival gospel, a competing vision of human flourishing, and a counterfeit salvation that promises freedom through death and autonomy through violence. And it is being preached from the highest platforms in the land, codified into law, enforced by the courts, and celebrated as progress.

The Church must name this for what it is: demonic. Not figuratively demonic. Actually, spiritually, cosmically opposed to the Kingdom of God. This is the principalities and powers that Paul warned about, the spiritual forces of wickedness in the heavenly places, the rulers of this present darkness who demand the blood of children and call it enlightenment (Ephesians 6:12).[233]

Words matter because they shape reality. The abortion regime has always understood this. They do not speak of "killing" or "dismemberment." They speak of "termination of pregnancy," as though pregnancy were a subscription service. They speak of "the right to choose," as though the choice were no different than selecting breakfast cereal. They speak of "products of conception," as though a human being were no more significant than tissue, as though God's image could be reduced to biological material and discarded like medical waste.

This is linguistic sorcery. The same dark magic that has turned vice into virtue throughout human history: the transformation of murder into sacrifice, of greed into prosperity, of rebellion into enlightenment. George Orwell saw it coming: "War is peace. Freedom is slavery. Ignorance is strength."[234] The inversion of language is always the prelude to the inversion of morality.

Once you control the words, you control the thoughts. Once you control the thoughts, you control the actions. And once you control the actions, you have built an empire on lies so foundational that people will kill their own children and call it healthcare.

Paul warned the Ephesian church: *"Let no one deceive you with empty words, for because of these things the wrath of God comes upon the sons of disobedience."* (Ephesians 5:6).[235] Empty words. Words that sound noble but carry death. This is precisely what "reproductive freedom" is: an empty word, a hollow promise, a deception that continues to claim thousands of lives every week.

And the Church has gone along with it. Not universally, but enough. Enough to blunt the prophetic edge and soften the call to repentance. We have adopted the world's vocabulary. We speak of being "pro-choice" and "pro-life" as though this were a preference, a political leaning, or a matter of opinion. We have allowed the culture to set the terms of the debate.

Because this is not about choice, this is about children. Real children, with beating hearts and forming fingers and DNA that will never be repeated in human history. Children who are made in the image of God, who are known by Him before they are born, and who are knitted together in the secret place. David understood this: *"You formed my inward parts; you knitted me together in my mother's womb. I praise you, for I am fearfully and wonderfully made."* (Psalm 139:13-14).[236]

The unborn are not potential persons. They are persons, endowed by their Creator with dignity, worth, and an inalienable right to life.

Abortion denies this. It asserts that personhood is not intrinsic but assigned. That a human being in the womb is not yet worthy of protection. This is not a new idea. It is the same logic that justified slavery: that some human beings are property, not persons.

It is the same logic that fueled the Holocaust: that some lives are unworthy of life. It is the same logic that has rationalized every genocide in human history: divide humanity into categories, declare some lives less valuable than others, and destroy them with the full sanction of the law.

And every time, every single time, God has brought judgment.

On January 22, 1973, the Supreme Court handed down *Roe v. Wade*, declaring that the Constitution protected a woman's right to terminate her pregnancy.[237] Justice Harry Blackmun located this right in the "penumbras" and "emanations" of the Fourteenth Amendment, a legal fiction so transparently ideological that even pro-abortion scholars have admitted its constitutional bankruptcy. Justice Byron White, dissenting, called it "an exercise of raw judicial power."[238] He was right. It was the creation of a new right, conjured from nothing and imposed on the entire nation by nine unelected judges.

Roe did not legalize abortion. It sacralized it. It transformed the taking of innocent life into a protected liberty. It elevated a woman's choice to kill her child to the status of a fundamental right, placing it alongside freedom of speech and freedom of religion. The Supreme Court became the high priest of a new civic religion, one in which personal autonomy was the highest good, the unborn were disposable, and the state's role was to facilitate access to the altar.

For forty-nine years, that altar stood. Generations grew up believing that abortion was not only legal but constitutionally guaranteed, a sacred right beyond question. Planned Parenthood became the largest abortion provider in the nation, performing over 350,000 abortions annually and receiving over $600 million in federal funding each year.[239] The Democratic Party made abortion access a central pillar of its platform, opposing every restriction, parental notification, waiting periods, and bans on partial-birth abortion. Every proposed limit was fought with the ferocity of religious zealots defending sacred ground.

Because that is precisely what it was: sacred ground. Not to God, but to the principalities and powers that have always demanded the blood of children.

Then, on June 24, 2022, the Supreme Court overturned *Roe v. Wade* in *Dobbs v. Jackson Women's Health Organization*.[240] Justice Samuel Alito declared that the Constitution does not confer a right to abortion and that the authority to regulate abortion must be returned to the people and their elected representatives. He wrote: "Roe was egregiously wrong from the start. Its reasoning was exceptionally weak, and the decision has had damaging consequences."[241]

The response was apocalyptic. President Biden called it "a sad day for the Court and for the country."[242] Protests erupted. Violence was threatened and carried out against pro-life pregnancy centers. The rhetoric was not political disagreement. It was the language of blasphemy, the fury of a priesthood whose temple had been desecrated.

This reaction reveals the truth. Abortion is not a political issue for the Left. It is a sacrament. The ritual by which autonomy is asserted, by which the self is enthroned, by which the inconvenient image of God is erased. Any threat to that sacrament is perceived as an existential attack.

We are not debating policy. We are confronting a rival religion. And that religion demands submission. It demands that every knee bow, that every voice affirm, and that every conscience comply. You will celebrate the slaughter, or you will be silenced.

At its core, abortion rests on a lie about the nature of human beings and the nature of God. It asserts that we are the ultimate arbiters of life and death, that our will supersedes divine command, and that our convenience outweighs His creation. Every abortion is an assertion of sovereignty, a declaration that "I am god of my own life, and I will not be constrained by the inconvenience of another."

This is the essence of sin. Not the breaking of arbitrary rules, but the overthrow of God's rightful authority, the usurpation of His throne. It is the same sin that cast Lucifer from heaven and the same pride that built the tower of Babel (Genesis 11:1-9).[243] The same rebellion that has brought judgment upon every civilization that has embraced it.

America has sacrificed its children on the altar of convenience and called it freedom. We have shed innocent blood and called it healthcare. We have defied the living God and called it progress.

Do not think for a moment that God does not see. Isaiah declared, *"Your hands are full of blood."* (Isaiah 1:15).[244] Jeremiah warned, *"They have filled this place with the blood of innocents."* (Jeremiah 19:4).[245] And God responded then as

He will respond now: *"I will punish you according to the fruit of your deeds."* (Jeremiah 21:14).[246]

Make no mistake: we are already under judgment. The judgment of God is not always fire from heaven. Sometimes the judgment is internal: the hardening of hearts, the searing of consciences, the loss of the ability to recognize evil. Paul describes it in Romans: *"God gave them over to a debased mind."* (Romans 1:28).[247]

We have normalized the killing of the innocent, and in return, we have lost our moral clarity: what God calls good is condemned, what He calls evil is celebrated as healthcare, and what He calls life is destroyed and called freedom. (Isaiah 5:20).[248]

This is the judgment: the darkening of the mind, the corruption of the culture, the collapse of the ability to see reality as it is. A nation that kills its children in the womb will inevitably lose its capacity to protect children outside the womb. Once you have accepted the premise that some human lives are disposable, you have opened the door to limitless atrocity.

The only question is where you draw the line, and history teaches that the line keeps moving, always in the direction of more death, more violence, more utilitarian calculations about whose life is worth living and whose is not.

We are already seeing this. Assisted suicide is legal in ten states and the District of Columbia.[249] Euthanasia is being normalized, promoted as compassion, and sold as dignity. The same arguments used to justify abortion, autonomy, quality of life, and relief from suffering are now being deployed to justify killing the elderly and the terminally ill. If personhood is assigned rather than intrinsic and if value is determined by utility rather than inherent dignity, then every human being is potentially disposable.

Abortion has built this world, and the culture of death is now in full bloom. And the Church has been far too silent.

Some churches have remained silent, fearing controversy. Others have adopted the culture's framing, speaking of abortion as a "difficult issue" without ever naming the sin or calling for its end. Still others have accepted the lie that abortion is primarily a matter of personal choice, that the Church has no right to speak into such intimate decisions, and that love requires non-judgment.

But love does not require silence in the face of murder. Jesus did not mince words when confronting evil. He called the Pharisees *"whitewashed tombs."* (Matthew 23:27).[250] He overturned the tables of the money changers (John 2:15).[251] He pronounced woe upon those who harmed the little ones, declaring that it would be better for them to have a millstone tied around their neck and be thrown into the sea (Matthew 18:6).[252] He loved people enough to tell them the truth, even when the truth was offensive, even when it cost Him everything.

The Church must follow His example. We must love women enough to tell them that abortion is not freedom but bondage, not healthcare but homicide. We must love the unborn enough to speak for those who cannot speak for themselves. And we must love our nation enough to warn it that the blood of sixty-three million children cries out from the ground like Abel's blood (Genesis 4:10).[253] And that God will not ignore that cry forever.

Because He will not, God is patient, but He is not passive. He is merciful, but He is also just. Proverbs lists six things the

Lord hates, and seven that are an abomination to Him, and at the top of that list are *"hands that shed innocent blood."* (Proverbs 6:16-17).[254] Not hands that shed guilty blood in a just war, but innocent blood, the blood of those who have done no wrong, who pose no threat, who are guilty of nothing except being inconvenient.

Sixty-three million times, innocent blood has been shed in this nation. Sixty-three million times, a child has been torn from the womb, dismembered, poisoned, and discarded. Sixty-three million times, the image of God has been destroyed, and we have called it a constitutional right.

The overturning of *Roe* was not a victory that ended the battle. It was a reprieve, a momentary lifting of the fog. But the idolatry has not ended. The altars are still standing. California has become a destination for women seeking abortions, advertising its services and paying for travel. New York has removed virtually every restriction, allowing abortion up to the moment of birth.[255] Illinois, Colorado, Oregon, the list goes on. These states have actively embraced destruction, building entire industries around it, funding it with taxpayer dollars, and celebrating it as liberation.

And the federal government stands ready to join them. The Biden administration has fought every pro-life measure and worked tirelessly to expand abortion access through executive orders and agency regulations. The FDA has made abortion pills available by mail, allowing women to kill their children at home without ever seeing a doctor.[256] The Justice Department has prosecuted pro-life activists under laws designed to protect abortion clinics, treating peaceful protests as federal crimes while ignoring the firebombing of pregnancy centers by pro-abortion extremists.

This is the full weight of the federal government deployed in service of the abortion regime, using every available tool to ensure that children continue to die, that the altars remain open, and that the blood continues to flow.

There is still time. God is merciful. He does not delight in the death of the wicked but desires that all should turn from their evil ways and live (Ezekiel 18:23).[257] He stands ready to forgive, to cleanse, and to restore, but only if we will humble ourselves, confess our sin, and cry out to Him for mercy.

Second Chronicles 7:14 is not a political slogan. It is a call to repentance:

"If my people who are called by my name humble themselves and pray and seek my face and turn from their wicked ways, then I will hear from heaven and will forgive their sin and heal their land." (2 Chronicles 7:14).[258]

If my people. Not the Democrats. Not the pagans. Not the abortion industry. My people. The judgment begins with the house of God (1 Peter 4:17).[259] Repentance must begin with us. We must confess that we have been silent when we should have spoken, and that we have allowed the culture to set the terms while the children continued to die.

And then we must act, but neither with violence nor with hatred. With truth spoken in love, with courage rooted in conviction. We must preach the full counsel of God (Acts 20:27),[260] including the hard truths about sin and judgment, about life and death, about God's righteous anger toward those who shed innocent blood. We must call abortion what it is: murder, a violation of God's law, an assault on His image, and an act of rebellion that demands repentance.

We must also offer hope. To the woman who has had an abortion: "There is forgiveness at the cross. There is cleansing in the blood of Christ" (1 John 1:9).[261] To the woman considering abortion: "We will walk with you. We will support you. We will help you carry this burden" (Galatians 6:2).[262] To the nation that has embraced this evil, There is still time to turn back. There is still mercy available if you will humble yourself and seek the face of God.

But we must also be honest about what is at stake. If this nation does not repent, if we continue to sacrifice our children, if we continue to call evil good and good evil, then judgment will come. Not because God is cruel, but because He is just. The blood of sixty-three million children cries out for justice, and that cry will be answered, either through repentance and restoration or through judgment and destruction.

The call is clear. The choice is before us. Will we continue to worship at the altar of autonomy, sacrificing our children and calling it freedom? Or will we repent, turn from our idolatry, and return to the God who gives life, who defends the weak, who demands justice for the oppressed?

The trumpet has sounded. What you do with it is between you and God.

Section III: How Christians Have Been Complicit Through Silence

The blood is on our hands, too.

Not because we performed the abortions. Not because we wrote *Roe v. Wade* or built Planned Parenthood's empire. But because we saw the sword coming and did not blow the trumpet. We saw children being killed and chose silence. We saw a nation embrace murder as a constitutional right and decided that speaking up would cost too much: too much reputation, too much comfort, too much access to power. And while we calculated the cost of obedience, sixty-three million children died.

God told Ezekiel, *"If the watchman sees the sword coming and does not blow the trumpet and the people are not warned and the sword comes and takes any one of them, that person is taken away in his iniquity, but his blood I will require at the watchman's hand."* (Ezekiel 33:6).[263]

The watchman who sees danger and stays silent does not escape guilt. He bears it. God holds him accountable for every life that could have been saved, every warning that should have been given, and every act of courage that was replaced with cowardice.

The sentinel was posted. The sword was visible. And we said nothing.

In 1973, when the Supreme Court handed down *Roe v. Wade*, the Southern Baptist Convention, the largest Protestant denomination in America, did not rise up in unified opposition. Instead, they passed a resolution affirming the decision, stating that Southern Baptists should "work for legislation that will allow the possibility of abortion under such conditions as rape, incest, clear evidence of severe fetal deformity, and carefully ascertained evidence of the likelihood of damage to the emotional, mental, and physical health of the mother."[264] This was not a lone voice. This was the official position of millions of evangelical Christians.

They saw the sword coming, and they blessed it.

It took the Southern Baptist Convention until 1980, seven years and millions of dead children later, to reverse course and declare abortion a moral evil.[265] Seven years. And even then, the reversal came not from prophetic conviction but from political realignment, from the rise of the Religious Right and the calculation that opposing abortion was now politically advantageous. The repentance was real, but it was late. Tragically, unforgivably late.

But the Southern Baptists were not alone. Across denominations, the response to *Roe* was muted, cautious, and shot through with the language of nuance. Mainline Protestant churches largely celebrated the decision as a victory for women's autonomy.[266] Even evangelical leaders who personally opposed abortion often refused to make it a central issue, fearing that too much focus on "single-issue politics" would alienate seekers, divide congregations, or damage the church's reputation in an increasingly secular culture.[267] They treated abortion as one issue among many, a matter of personal conscience rather than a defining moral crisis that demanded total commitment.

The silence was not neutral. Silence never is. A Church that refuses to speak gives the world permission. Pastors who avoid the topic from the pulpit teach congregants it must not be that important. And Christians who vote for pro-abortion politicians while justifying it with appeals to "other issues" or "prudence" or "the lesser of two evils," they teach their children that the killing of innocents is negotiable, that God's law can be subordinated to political strategy, and that faithfulness is optional when the cost gets too high.

Dietrich Bonhoeffer, writing from Nazi Germany, understood this dynamic with painful clarity. He wrote, "Silence in the face of evil is itself evil: God will not hold us guiltless. Not to speak is to speak. Not to act is to act."[268] Bonhoeffer was not speaking theoretically. He was speaking from within a church that had largely capitulated to the Nazi regime, that had chosen institutional survival over prophetic witness, that had decided the cost of resistance was too high. And he watched as that silence enabled atrocity on a scale the world had never seen.

The Church's failure in Nazi Germany was not primarily a failure of theology. It was a failure of courage.

The same failure has marked the American Church's response to abortion. The theology was present. The knowledge was clear: life begins at conception, the unborn are made in the image of God, and that "Thou shalt not kill" applies to children in the womb just as much as children outside it. But knowing did not translate into action because action required sacrifice, and sacrifice was a price we were unwilling to pay.

The mechanisms of our silence have been varied but consistent. Pastors avoided preaching on abortion because they feared losing members, losing tithes, or being labeled "political."[269] Denominational leaders prioritized institutional unity over moral clarity, refusing to discipline churches or leaders who publicly supported abortion rights because division was seen as a greater threat than complicity.[270] Seminary professors trained future pastors in the art of nuance, teaching them to avoid "controversial" topics and to focus instead on personal spirituality, church growth, and cultural engagement, as though you could engage the culture without confronting its most egregious sins.[271]

Christian universities, desperate to maintain their accreditation and their reputation among secular elites, soft-pedaled or ignored the abortion issue entirely, treating it as a matter of private conviction rather than public truth.[272] Christian publishing houses rejected manuscripts that were too confrontational, too politically charged, too likely to alienate progressive readers or mainstream reviewers. Christian media outlets covered abortion in measured tones, always careful to present "both sides," always quick to acknowledge complexity, and always reluctant to call it what it is: murder.

And individual Christians, shaped by this culture of avoidance, followed suit. A 2020 study by the Barna Group found that 47% of self-identified evangelicals believed that abortion should be legal in at least some circumstances, and 15% believed it should be legal in all circumstances.[273] These are not nominal Christians. These are people who attend church regularly, who read their Bibles, who identify publicly with the faith. And nearly half of them have adopted the world's position on the killing of children.

How did this happen? How did a people who claim to worship the God of life, who sing of His love for the weak and the vulnerable, who profess to follow a Savior who said, "Let the little children come to me," become a people who shrug at the industrial-scale slaughter of the innocent?

The answer is formation. Or rather, the failure of formation. The Church has allowed its people to be discipled by the culture rather than by Scripture. We have taught them to sing worship songs, attend Bible studies, and serve in ministries, but we never taught them Scripture's fundamental questions of life, death, justice, and power; never trained them to recognize idolatry in the costume of rights and freedom; and never built in them the courage to stand firm when faithfulness costs social ostracism, professional consequences, or political isolation.

James K. A. Smith writes: "You are what you love. But you might not love what you think. And what you think doesn't determine what you love. We are formed by what we worship, and worship is not primarily a cognitive act but a formative habit."[274] The problem is not that Christians lack information about abortion. The problem is that they have been formed by liturgies, cultural rituals, rhythms, and narratives that shape their lives in ways that contradict Scripture.

They have been discipled by entertainment, by social media, by political tribalism, by consumerism, and by the relentless message that autonomy is the highest good and that no authority, not God, not Scripture, and not the Church, has the right to constrain their choices.

And the Church, instead of resisting this formation, has accommodated it. We have made the gospel safe, inoffensive, and personally helpful but publicly irrelevant. We have preached grace without repentance, love without holiness, and faith without obedience. And we have produced a generation of Christians who can sing "Amazing Grace" on Sunday and vote for pro-abortion candidates on Tuesday without experiencing even a flicker of cognitive dissonance.

This is not a failure of discipleship. This is a betrayal. And it has consequences that go far beyond the ballot box. When the Church loses its moral authority, when it becomes indistinguishable from the world in its convictions, its courage, and its willingness to sacrifice for truth, it loses its ability to speak prophetically into the culture.

The world does not listen to a Church that sounds like the world. It does not respect a Church that is more concerned with its reputation than with righteousness. And it certainly does not fear a Church that has been domesticated, that has traded its prophetic edge for a seat at the cultural table, that speaks in whispers when it should be shouting from the rooftops.

Peter warned, *"For it is time for judgment to begin at the household of God; and if it begins with us, what will be the outcome for those who do not obey the gospel of God?"* (1 Peter 4:17).[275] Judgment begins with the house of God. Not with the abortion industry. Not with Planned Parenthood. Not with the Supreme Court or the Democratic Party or the culture at large. With us. With the Church.

With those who knew better and did nothing. With those who had the truth and refused to speak it. With those who were called to be salt and light but chose instead to be safe and silent.

The watchman who sees the sword and does not blow the trumpet bears the blood guilt. This is not metaphorical. This is not a rhetorical flourish. This is the sober judgment of Scripture. God will require an accounting.

Pastors who avoided preaching on abortion because it was too divisive will be held accountable for every child whose life might have been saved if their congregation had been told the truth. Denominational leaders who prioritized institutional peace over prophetic witness will answer for every believer who was formed by their silence rather than by Scripture. Seminary professors who trained pastors in the art of evasion will give an account for every pulpit where the Word of God was muted because courage was never modeled.

And individual Christians, those who voted for pro-abortion politicians, who donated to pro-abortion causes, who stayed silent when they should have spoken, and who valued their comfort and reputation more than the lives of the innocent, they too will stand before God and answer for their complicity. *"Not everyone who says to me, 'Lord, Lord,' will enter the kingdom of heaven, but the one who does the will of my Father who is in heaven."* (Matthew 7:21).[276]

Obedience is not optional. Faithfulness is not negotiable. And the blood of sixty-three million children is not something you can wash off your hands by claiming you were trying to be winsome.

But, and this is the mercy that must be proclaimed even in the midst of judgment, there is still time. God does not delight in the death of the wicked. He does not desire that any should perish. He stands ready to forgive, to cleanse, to restore. *"If we confess our sins, he is faithful and just to forgive us our sins and to cleanse us from all unrighteousness."* (1 John 1:9).[277] The Church can repent. Pastors can start preaching the truth. Denominational leaders can stop prioritizing institutional survival over moral clarity. Seminaries can train future ministers in both courage and theology. Christian universities can choose faithfulness over accreditation. And individual believers can begin to live as though the lordship of Christ actually governs their politics, their votes, their public witness, and their willingness to sacrifice for the sake of the vulnerable.

Repentance is not feeling sorry. Repentance is a change of direction. It is concrete, measurable, and costly. For the Church, repentance means several non-negotiable actions. First, it means clarity. The pulpit must declare without equivocation that abortion is murder, that it is an abomination before God, and that no Christian can support it, not in the voting booth, not with their tax dollars, not with their silence. There is no "third way" to the killing of children. There is no "nuanced" position that somehow transcends the binary of life and death. Clarity is not cruelty. It is love. It is the kindness of telling the truth before it is too late.

Second, repentance means courage. The Church must be willing to lose members, lose funding, lose cultural respectability, lose access to power, and whatever it costs to obey God rather than men. We must stop calculating the cost of faithfulness and start obeying regardless of the cost. Bonhoeffer again: "When Christ calls a man, he bids him come and die."[278] Discipleship has always been costly. The American Church has forgotten this because, for too long, faithfulness and cultural approval happened to align. They no longer do. And we must choose.

Third, repentance means public witness. It is not enough to be privately pro-life while publicly silent. The world does not need more Christians who quietly disapprove of abortion while doing nothing to stop it. The world needs Christians who will speak, who will march, who will protest, who will vote, who will run for office, who will open pregnancy centers, who will adopt, who will foster, who will financially support women in crisis, and who will make it socially costly to support the killing of children.

The battle for life is not won in the quiet of personal conviction. It is won in the public square, in the legislature, in the courtroom, in the pulpit, and in the everyday choices of believers who refuse to participate in a culture of death.

Fourth, repentance means accountability. The Church must discipline its members and its leaders who persist in supporting abortion. This is not about being judgmental. This is about being faithful. Paul commanded the Corinthian church to remove a man who was living in open sexual sin, not because the church was cruel but because sin left unchecked spreads like leaven through the whole lump (1 Corinthians 5:6-7).[279] If the Church will not hold its own members accountable for supporting the murder of children, then we have no moral authority to speak into the culture at all. Discipline is an act of love. It protects the integrity of the witness, and it protects the sinner from continuing in rebellion unchallenged.

Fifth, and finally, repentance means perseverance. The fight for life will not be won quickly. *Roe* stood for forty-nine years. *Dobbs* overturned it, but the battle is far from over. States are enshrining abortion in their constitutions. The federal government is working to circumvent state protections. The culture continues to celebrate autonomy as the highest good. And the Church will face relentless pressure to back down, to compromise, to accept incremental defeats as pragmatic wisdom. We must not. We must hold the line. We must refuse to grow weary in doing good.

We must remember that we serve a God who sees, who judges, and who will one day make all things right. And we must endure, even when the cost is high, even when the results are slow, even when the world hates us for it.

The choice is before us. Continuing in silence, compromise, and comfortable complicity means facing the judgment of God with blood on our hands. The alternative is repentance, confessing our failure, turning from our cowardice, and beginning today to live as though the lives of children matter more than our reputation, more than our safety, more than our comfort, more than anything this world offers.

The alarm has been raised. The sword is at the gate. And God is watching to see whether His Church will finally choose obedience. What will you do?

"Defend the Voiceless"
Chapter 3: Abortion and the Democratic Party's Culture of Death

CONVICTION

The Church is the sentinel on the wall, commanded to speak for those who cannot speak for themselves. When we choose silence over the lives of the innocent, we trade prophetic faithfulness for cultural approval and bear the guilt of complicity.

REALITY CHECK

Our age has normalized the killing of children and trained Christians to treat it as a political preference rather than a moral crisis. Pastors avoid preaching on abortion because it might offend donors or divide congregations. Individual Christians vote for pro-abortion politicians while calling themselves followers of Christ. But Scripture is unambiguous: silence is not neutrality. It is permission. It is partnership. It is guilt.

FAITHFULNESS NOW LOOKS LIKE

Personal: Stop treating abortion as one issue among many. Let that recognition govern your vote, your giving, your conversations, and your willingness to sacrifice reputation for truth. The killing of children is not negotiable.

Church: Demand that your pastor preach the full counsel of God, including the sanctity of life and God's judgment on the shedding of innocent blood. Support crisis pregnancy centers and adoption ministries with your time and money.

Public: Speak. Vote. Advocate. Make it socially costly to support abortion. Run for office, volunteer at pregnancy centers, foster, and adopt. When the cost comes, count it joy that you were counted worthy to suffer for righteousness' sake.

COMMITMENTS

☐ Refuse to vote for any candidate who supports abortion, regardless of party or other issues, because children's lives are not political currency.

☐ Financially support at least one crisis pregnancy center or pro-life organization this month and commit to ongoing giving.

☐ Have one honest conversation this week with someone in your life about the reality of abortion and why silence is not an option for Christians.

☐ Identify one concrete action in your community, whether volunteering, fostering, adopting, mentoring, or supporting legislation, and begin this month.

PRAYER

Lord Jesus, forgive me for my silence. Forgive me for valuing my comfort over the lives of Your image-bearers and for treating the slaughter of innocents as a political issue rather than a spiritual crisis. Give me the courage to speak when it costs me something. Give me love for the unborn that compels action, not sentiment. Strengthen Your Church to be a place of refuge for women in crisis and a voice of truth in a culture of death. Make me willing to lose friends, reputation, and safety for the sake of the voiceless. Let my life be a witness that every child matters because You made them, You love them, and You command us to defend them. Amen.

Chapter 4: Gender, Sexuality, and the War on Creation

Section I: God's Design vs The Democratic Party's Gender Chaos

"So God created man in his own image, in the image of God he created him; male and female he created them." (Genesis 1:27).[280] This is not a suggestion open to revision by cultural consensus or legislative vote. This is the foundational decree of the Creator Himself, the bedrock upon which human identity, marriage, family, and procreation rest. God established male and female not as arbitrary categories subject to redefinition but as sacred distinctions that reflect His own image and anchor the covenant relationship between Christ and His Church.

When we deny this binary, we are not rejecting biology or challenging social norms; we are rebelling against the One who spoke us into existence and defined what it means to be human.

Yet our federal government has declared war on this foundation, and the Church in America has largely surrendered without a fight. The 2024 Democratic Party Platform explicitly promises to "vigorously oppose state and federal bans on gender-affirming health care." It boasts that the Biden administration has "protected transgender Americans' access to health care and coverage, including medically necessary gender-affirming care."[281] Strip away the sanitized language, and the horror becomes clear: our government is funding and celebrating the chemical castration of boys, the administration of puberty blockers to children, cross-sex hormones injected into adolescents, and the surgical removal of healthy breasts from teenage girls. This is not healthcare. This is state-sponsored mutilation of children, and the federal government has made it national policy.

The platform goes further, vowing to "ensure that all transgender and non-binary people can procure official government identification documents that accurately reflect their gender identity" and to "guarantee transgender students' access to facilities based on their gender identity".[282] These are not yet federal law, but they reveal the intent: to force reality itself to bow to delusion, to compel driver's licenses to lie about biological sex, to mandate that boys claiming to be girls be granted access to girls' bathrooms and locker rooms, and to wield the full prosecutorial power of the federal government against any institution that resists.

When Caesar promises to call evil good and good evil, when political platforms declare war on the created order, we stand at a moment of crisis that demands a response from every believer and every congregation in this nation.

The issue is brutally simple: God has spoken, the government has contradicted Him, and the Church is obeying the government instead of God. This is not a complicated theological puzzle requiring careful academic analysis. This is Acts 5:29 in living color: *"We must obey God rather than men."*[283]

Yet across this nation, churches hang rainbow flags in June, pastors remain silent on sexuality and gender for fear of losing their tax-exempt status or their cultural respectability, and Christian institutions hire staff who openly defy biblical teaching on marriage and sexuality because to do otherwise invites lawsuits and public condemnation. We have chosen

Caesar over Christ, and unless we repent, we will share in the judgment that is already falling on this nation.

Scripture warned us this moment would come. When the serpent whispered to Eve in the garden, *"Did God actually say?"* (Genesis 3:1),[284] he was not asking a genuine question seeking clarification. He was planting doubt, inviting rebellion, suggesting that perhaps God's Word is not final after all, that perhaps we humans can revise and improve upon what the Creator decreed.

That same question now echoes through every institution in America. Did God actually say male and female? Did He actually design marriage as one man and one woman? Did He actually create our bodies as sacred and fixed, or are they raw material for surgical reconstruction based on feelings? The Democratic platform answers with a defiant "No," the federal courts answer "No," the Department of Education answers "No," and tragically, much of the American Church has answered "No" through its silence and compromise.

The U.S. Department of Education reinterpreted Title IX, a law originally designed to protect women's opportunities in education and athletics, to mean precisely the opposite, mandating that schools treat biological sex as legally irrelevant and force girls to share bathrooms, locker rooms, and sports teams with biological males who identify as female.[285] In classrooms across America, children as young as five are being taught that gender is a spectrum, that their bodies are mistakes awaiting correction, and that boys can become girls and girls can become boys by declaration. Teachers in multiple states are now legally prohibited from informing parents when their children begin socially transitioning at school, severing the parent-child bond and positioning the state as the ultimate authority over a child's identity and future. None of this is accidental or the well-meaning confusion of people stumbling toward enlightenment.

This is systematic, coordinated rebellion against the created order, and it is accelerating.

The cruelty of this rebellion hides behind the language of compassion. California's Assembly Bill 2218 established a "Transgender Wellness and Equity Fund" funneling millions of taxpayer dollars toward procedures that sterilize children, destroy their fertility, compromise their bone density, and sever them permanently from their God-given bodies, and it calls this "wellness".[286] The American Academy of Pediatrics endorses surgical and chemical intervention for minors experiencing gender confusion, declaring it "medically necessary".[287] But Scripture cuts through the euphemism with ancient clarity: *"The mercy of the wicked is cruel."* (Proverbs 12:10, KJV).[288] What our culture celebrates as compassion and liberation, God condemns as barbarism and bondage.

Surgeons removing healthy breasts from teenage girls convinced by social media and activist counselors that their discomfort with puberty means they are actually boys are not healing; they are destroying. When the state threatens parents with loss of custody unless they "affirm" their child's claimed gender identity and consent to medical mutilation, the government is not protecting children; it is offering them as sacrifices on an ideological altar.

John Calvin warned that when humanity departs from God's established order, "they are carried headlong into monstrous things".[289] We are living in the fulfillment of that warning. Operating rooms in children's hospitals have become altars where the bodies of the young are destroyed in the name of progress, and we are told to celebrate.

The devastation is already visible, though the media suppresses it and the federal government refuses to investigate. Thousands of young people who underwent "gender-affirming care" as teenagers now live with permanent sterility, destroyed sexual function, weakened bones, chronic pain, and bodies mutilated beyond repair, and many are beginning to speak.[290]

Detransitioners report that no one warned them these procedures were irreversible, that no one investigated whether trauma or mental illness was driving their confusion, and that affirmation was immediate, but regret came too late to undo the damage. They were sacrificed to ideology, and their destroyed lives testify to what happens when we replace God's design with human delusion.

And where is the Church? Dietrich Bonhoeffer, watching the German church surrender to Nazi pressure, wrote words that burn with relevance today: "Cheap grace is the preaching of forgiveness without requiring repentance, baptism without church discipline, and Communion without confession. Cheap grace is grace without discipleship, grace without the cross, grace without Jesus Christ".[291] We have adopted cheap grace of a different flavor but the same poison, grace that blesses what God condemns, that calls tolerance what Scripture calls compromise, and that offers false peace to those rushing toward judgment.

Pastors who remain silent about gender ideology for fear of controversy, churches that hire staff living in open sexual rebellion because to do otherwise invites lawsuits, and congregations that hang rainbow flags to signal their cultural acceptability are not showing love. We are participating in spiritual murder, confirming people in lies that will destroy them unless they repent.

Christ did not commission us to make peace with the world's rebellion. He commanded, "Go *therefore and make disciples of all nations, baptizing them in the name of the Father and of the Son and of the Holy Spirit; teaching them to observe all that I have commanded you."* (Matthew 28:19-20).[292] Not some of His commands. Not the culturally palatable parts. All that He commanded. Silence about God's design for male and female, refusal to call sexual rebellion what it is, and choosing reputation over obedience are not acts of love. They are abandonment of our neighbors to judgment.

Charles Spurgeon declared that true discernment is not distinguishing right from wrong; even pagans can manage that, but distinguishing right from almost right, truth from the counterfeit that wears truth's clothing.[293] The government's gender ideology is almost right. It sounds like compassion. It mimics justice. It uses the vocabulary of dignity and human rights. But it is a lie, and lies destroy.

To affirm a teenage girl's claim to be a boy is not compassionate; it confirms her in rebellion that will mutilate her body and, unless she repents, damn her soul. To celebrate your neighbor's same-sex "marriage" is not loving; it affirms him in sin that leads to death. The watchman who sees the sword coming and remains silent has blood on his hands; the watchman who cries out in warning has loved enough to tell the truth (Ezekiel 33:1-6).[294]

Leonard Ravenhill lamented that the modern Church lost its power when it lost its holiness, trading the fear of God for the approval of culture.[295] We have made exactly that trade. A church unwilling to confront sin has forfeited its authority, and one that prioritizes cultural approval over biblical fidelity has ceased to be the church and become a religious social club awaiting the same judgment it refuses to warn against.

"Woe to those who call evil good and good evil, who put darkness for light and light for darkness." (Isaiah 5:20).[296] We are living under that woe, and the Church's silence makes us complicit.

This is not political. This is spiritual warfare spilling into legislation and policy. Paul warned, "We *do not wrestle against flesh and blood, but against the rulers, against the authorities, against the cosmic powers over this present darkness, and against the spiritual forces of evil in the heavenly places."* (Ephesians 6:12).[297] Satan cannot destroy God, so he attacks the image of God stamped on every human being. He cannot defeat Christ, so he defiles the picture of marriage designed to reflect Christ and His Church. Gender ideology is a demonic assault on creation itself, and it will not be defeated by dialogue, compromise, or finding common ground.

It will fall only when the Church proclaims God's truth with the authority of heaven and refuses to bow regardless of cost.

History warns us of what happens when God's people obey earthly authorities rather than their heavenly King. Israel's kings "*did what was evil in the sight of the Lord,"* enshrining idolatry and sexual immorality into national policy while ignoring the prophets who called for repentance (2 Kings 17:7-23).[298] God's patience ran out. Assyria conquered the northern kingdom. Babylon destroyed the southern kingdom and carried the survivors into exile. The righteous suffered alongside the wicked when judgment came. Daniel was dragged into Babylonian captivity not because of his sin but because the leaders of his nation persisted in theirs.

America is following the same trajectory. We sacrifice children on operating tables and call it healthcare. We celebrate sexual rebellion as Pride and criminalize biblical truth as hate speech. We use federal power to crush those who resist. Unless repentance sweeps from the highest offices to the lowest hearts, judgment is not a distant possibility; it is certain. Douglas Murray, writing as a secular observer, documented how Western civilization is systematically destroying its own foundations while calling it progress.[299]

But Scripture alone explains why: *"God gave them up to dishonorable passions... and since they did not see fit to acknowledge God, God gave them up to a debased mind."* (Romans 1:26-28).[300] When a culture rejects God's design for sexuality and gender, God withdraws His restraining hand. What follows is not enlightenment but chaos, not freedom but bondage. This is judgment, and it is present.

Yet even now, mercy calls. Daniel, though carried into captivity by the sins of others, refused to defile himself with the king's food, refused to bow to the king's idols, refused to compromise God's Word for Babylon's approval (Daniel 1:8).[301] God honored his faithfulness with wisdom and influence that outlasted empires. We must make Daniel's choice. We will not call men women. We will not celebrate as love what God condemns as rebellion. We will not fund with our taxes or bless with our silence the mutilation of children. This is not cruelty but clarity, not hatred but holiness.

And if it costs everything, our reputations, our livelihoods, and our freedom, so be it.

"Do not be deceived: God is not mocked, for whatever one sows, that will he also reap." (Galatians 6:7).[302] We are sowing confusion, rebellion, and the blood of mutilated children. Unless we repent, we will reap the whirlwind. The instruments may differ from those used on ancient Israel, whether economic collapse, cultural disintegration, or the loss of every freedom we claim to cherish, but the cause is identical: we have rejected our Creator. God's patience is not infinite. Every day of unrepentant rebellion brings us closer to the point where mercy withdraws, and judgment becomes irreversible.

Therefore, let us hear the word of the Lord: this is no time for silence or compromise. We must obey God rather than men. The Democratic platform has declared war on creation itself, federal agencies are enforcing the rebellion, and the Church must decide where it stands. Will we speak the truth that costs everything, or will we buy safety with silence? Will we stand as Daniel stood, faithful when the fire is hot, or will we fall as Judah fell, complicit in the rebellion that brings destruction?

America stands at the crossroads where Israel once stood. Will we honor the God who made male and female, or will we bow to the idols of self-creation? Will the Church thunder with prophetic clarity, or will it whisper in fear? Judgment is not approaching; it is here, unfolding in the lives of children whose bodies are destroyed and souls taught that rebellion is righteousness.

The question before every believer, every church, and every Christian institution is simple and terrible: Will we obey God or men? Will we stand with Daniel in Babylon, or will we fall silent like Judah and share in the judgment we refused to resist? The Democratic platform is not theory; it is law in motion. Federal agencies enforce it. Courts rule by it. Schools indoctrinate by it. The sword is drawn.

We must choose. Daniel chose faithfulness over comfort, truth over approval, and God over kings. His testimony outlasted empires. Our choice will determine whether we stand as witnesses to truth or accomplices to judgment.

The time for decision is now.

Section II: LGBTQ+ Ideology and The Redefinition of Love

Three words have become the functional creed of a nation in rebellion: "Love is love." From the Democratic Party platform to the pulpits of compromised churches, from corporate boardrooms to public school classrooms, this slogan is wielded as gospel truth, unchallengeable, self-evident, and the very definition of compassion in our enlightened age. But the apostle John declared a different truth when he wrote that *"God is love."* (1 John 4:8).[303] Our culture has inverted this divine revelation into idolatry, elevating human desire to the throne of God Himself and demanding that all creation bow before it.

Feeling becomes love, desire becomes sacred, and whatever rebellion burns in the heart gets baptized as identity and demanded as celebration. This is not progress. This is the ancient lie from Eden, "you will be like God", wearing progressive vocabulary and pride flags.

Two cities have been built on two loves: one on love of God, even to contempt of self; the other on love of self, even to contempt of God.[304] America has chosen. You have built your Babylon on self-worship, crowned desire as sovereign, and declared God's design oppressive. When love is divorced from God's glory and severed from truth, when affection is freed from holiness and desire unleashed from divine boundaries, the result is not liberation but slavery.

Your culture celebrates what looks compassionate, affirming identities, validating desires, and embracing authenticity. But the springs of the heart are poisoned. What appears as kindness flows from rebellion, and what masquerades as love produces death. The motive determines the morality, and when that motive is rooted in contempt for God, every action, however virtuous it appears, becomes sin.

Scripture defines love with precision that shatters our cultural delusions: *"Love does not delight in evil but rejoices with the truth."* (1 Corinthians 13:6).[305] Love separated from truth is not love at all. It is sentiment masquerading as virtue, emotion pretending to be morality, and affirmation that destroys while claiming to heal. Telling people that God made them exactly as they are and that their deepest desires define their truest selves, celebrating identities built on rebellion against biological reality and divine design, and calling surgical mutilation "gender-affirming care" while labeling hormone treatments "life-saving medicine" is not love. It is participation in destruction.

We are handing them poison while calling it living water. And we will answer to God for every lie we spoke in love's name.

The Democratic Party has enshrined this deception into law and declared war on every institution that refuses to comply. Their 2024 platform celebrates "LGBTQ+ equality" as a fundamental civil right and demands passage of the Equality Act to codify sexual orientation and gender identity as protected classes under federal law.[306] The legislation they champion would eliminate religious exemptions that have protected churches, Christian schools, and faith-based organizations for generations. It would force hiring of individuals in same-sex marriages regardless of religious conviction, compel speech through mandated pronoun usage, punish counselors who help people leave homosexuality, and strip tax-exempt status from any ministry that maintains biblical sexual ethics. This is not equality. This is persecution with a progressive veneer. This is the machinery of totalitarianism disguised as civil rights.

And too many Christians, calculating the cost of resistance, measuring their cultural capital, and weighing their reputations against their convictions, have decided that silence is the wise course.

But Scripture leaves no room for neutrality in the face of such rebellion. Paul's warning to the Corinthians was not a suggestion subject to cultural evolution: *"Do you not know that wrongdoers will not inherit the kingdom of God? Do not be deceived: Neither the sexually immoral nor idolaters nor adulterers nor men who have sex with men nor thieves nor the greedy nor drunkards nor slanderers nor swindlers will inherit the kingdom of God."* (1 Corinthians 6:9-10).[307] These are the words of the Holy Spirit through the apostle Paul, declaring with divine authority who will and will not enter the kingdom of heaven. The stakes are not temporal but eternal, and the consequences are not social but spiritual.

And the church that refuses to declare these truths because it fears being called unloving has forgotten that the most unloving thing we can do is allow people to walk confidently toward hell while assuring them that God is fine with their choices.

Genesis establishes the foundation that our culture has declared negotiable: *"So God created mankind in his own image, in the image of God he created them; male and female he created them."* (Genesis 1:27).[308] Male and female. Not a spectrum. Not fluid. Not subject to personal preference or medical intervention. God spoke humanity into existence as male and female, and what God has joined together in creation, the unity of biological sex and personal identity, no amount of surgery, hormone therapy, or legislative mandate can tear asunder.

The modern self assumes the authority of inner feelings and sees authenticity as defined by the ability to give social expression to them.[309] This is not a fringe philosophy debated in academic journals; this is the operating system of Western civilization, embedded in law, enforced in education, and weaponized against dissent.

When inner feelings become infallible, and self-expression becomes sacred, when authenticity requires public affirmation and identity depends on external validation, there are no boundaries left. Biology becomes negotiable. Reality becomes fluid. Truth becomes whatever the self declares it to be.

The Democratic platform treats this fundamental reality as a social construct waiting to be deconstructed, a prison from which enlightened souls must be liberated. The Department of Education now interprets Title IX to include "gender identity," mandating that schools allow biological males into girls' bathrooms, locker rooms, and sports teams, threatening to withhold federal funding from any institution that refuses to participate in this delusion.[310] California allocates state funds for "transgender wellness and equity" programs that facilitate the medical transition of children, protecting doctors who prescribe puberty blockers and cross-sex hormones to confused minors.[311] The American Academy of Pediatrics endorses these interventions as "comprehensive care" for gender-diverse youth, enshrining ideology into medical protocol.[312]

You are mutilating children. You are sterilizing the next generation. You are performing irreversible medical experiments on teenagers struggling with depression, autism, social anxiety, and trauma, and you are calling it compassionate healthcare. The gender surgeries performed on natal females quadrupled in a single year as social contagion swept through schools and online communities.[313] The devastation is documented, the casualties mounting, and the horror unfolding in real time across this nation. And Jesus Christ spoke about those who harm children: *"Whoever causes one of these little ones who believe in me to sin, it would be better for him to have a great millstone fastened around his neck and to be drowned in the depth of the sea."* (Matthew 18:6).[314]

The millstone awaits those who destroy these precious souls while claiming to affirm them.

The judgment of God is not waiting for some distant future. It is already here. Romans 1 describes not wrath postponed but abandonment executed: when a society exchanges the truth of God for a lie and worships the creature rather than the Creator, *"God gave them over to shameful lusts"* and *"a depraved mind."* (Romans 1:26, 28).[315] This is present tense. This is a diagnosis of a condition already manifest. You demanded autonomy from God's law and insisted on freedom to define your own identity. He granted both, giving you over to your desires.

Now you are drowning in the consequences: epidemic rates of depression and anxiety in LGBTQ+ communities despite unprecedented cultural affirmation, skyrocketing suicide attempts among transgender youth, families torn apart, children sterilized, and a civilization collapsing under the weight of delusions it insists are rights. The sexual revolution severed the bonds between sex and procreation and marriage and permanence and left a wasteland of loneliness in its wake.[316] The fruit is rotten because the tree is cursed. And watering it with federal funding while calling it justice will not make the poison sweet.

Where is the Church in this hour of judgment? Where are the shepherds who should be protecting the flock? Where are the watchmen who should be crying alarm from the walls? Too many have gone silent, calculating that cultural acceptance matters more than biblical fidelity and deciding that being called loving by the world is worth being called compromised by God. The prophets of old faced kings and called them to account. Elijah confronted Ahab. Nathan exposed David. John the Baptist rebuked Herod. Where are such men today? Where are the voices willing to lose everything rather than compromise an inch?

Paul commanded Timothy to *"preach the word; be ready in season and out of season; reprove, rebuke, and exhort, with complete patience and teaching."* (2 Timothy 4:2).[317] But you have preached self-acceptance instead of self-denial. You have rebuked "intolerance" instead of sin. You have exhorted people to embrace their authentic selves rather than crucify the flesh. The Episcopal Church officially blesses same-sex unions. The Evangelical Lutheran Church in America ordains practicing homosexuals as clergy. The United Church of Christ performs gay weddings in sanctuaries built for worship of the one true God. These are not fringe movements; these are major denominations representing millions who claim Christ's name while denying His Word.

The therapeutic turn in American Christianity represents not an evolution of Christian practice but its evacuation.[318] The God of this corrupted gospel exists only to validate feelings, not to call rebels to repentance. This hollow faith promises community without commitment, identity without transformation, and warm emotions without dying to self. But this god cannot save because this god does not exist. On the day every knee bows and every tongue confesses that Jesus Christ is Lord, those who spent their ministries affirming people in rebellion will discover they served an idol of their own making.

Scripture warned of this hour: *"For the time is coming when people will not endure sound teaching, but having itching ears, they will accumulate for themselves teachers to suit their own passions and will turn away from listening to the truth and wander off into myths."* (2 Timothy 4:3-4).[319] The time has come. The itching ears have found their teachers. The myths have replaced the gospel.

Jesus spoke of false prophets and gave a simple test for identifying them: *"Beware of false prophets, who come to you in sheep's clothing but inwardly are ravenous wolves. You will recognize them by their fruits."* (Matthew 7:15-16).[320] Look at the fruit of "love is love." Children sterilized. Families destroyed. Biology denied. Reality rejected. Totalitarianism enforced.

The Democratic platform demands not tolerance but total compliance, not coexistence but celebration, not freedom but compelled participation. The Equality Act would strip religious liberty protections that have stood for centuries, force Christian institutions to hire those in open rebellion against biblical sexual ethics, and punish any business owner or counselor who declines to participate in the fiction that men can become women through declaration. When truth becomes hate speech and biology becomes bigotry, when parents lose custody of children for refusing to affirm delusions and therapists lose licenses for helping people leave homosexuality, you are not witnessing social progress. You are watching tyranny consolidate power. Silence in the face of such evil is not neutrality; it is complicity.[321]

Natural loves that are allowed to become gods do not remain loves; they become complicated forms of hatred that destroy everything they touch.[322] You see this hatred now in the viciousness directed at anyone who speaks biblical truth. Parents who resist their children's social transition lose custody. Bakers who decline to create cakes celebrating same-sex weddings lose their businesses. Counselors who help people overcome unwanted same-sex attraction lose their licenses. Teachers who refuse to use pronouns that deny biology lose their jobs. This is not love seeking space to exist. This is hatred demanding total submission.

This is a false god that will tolerate no rivals, brook no dissent, and punish every hint of resistance.

True spiritual affections are marked by evangelical humiliation, a deep recognition of unworthiness before a holy God that produces transformation rather than self-celebration.[323] The modern church is filled with counterfeit affections that produce emotional highs without holiness, inclusive rhetoric without truth, and therapeutic comfort without repentance. Where is the trembling before God's holiness? Where is the fear that drives out the fear of man? Where is the humiliation that precedes exaltation?

Entire denominations have traded doctrine for demographics, biblical authority for cultural acceptance, the fear of God for the fear of being called unloving. They have retained Christian vocabulary while abandoning Christian conviction. They march in pride parades, ordain the unrepentant, and call God's judgment outdated and His commands oppressive.

God's love is not the sentimental validation our culture demands. The love of God is both a pillar upon which the hope of the world rests and a solemn and terrifying thing.[324] This is not soft sentimentalism but holy love that burns with zeal for righteousness and truth. This love does not affirm you in your sin. It transforms you out of it, or it consumes you. There is no third option. There is no neutrality before a holy God.

There is no peaceful coexistence between light and darkness, between truth and lies, between the kingdom of God and the kingdom of self. We have forgotten that following Christ requires total surrender, not therapeutic affirmation.[325]

On Mount Carmel, Elijah confronted a nation paralyzed by compromise and issued a challenge that echoes through millennia to this very hour: *"How long will you waver between two opinions? If the LORD is God, follow him; but if Baal is God, follow him."* (1 Kings 18:21).[326] The people said nothing because they wanted both. They wanted Baal's pleasures and Yahweh's protection, cultural acceptance and divine blessing, and the approval of the world and the favor of heaven. It did not work then. It will not work now. Jesus Himself declared that *"No one can serve two masters, for either he will hate the one and love the other, or he will be devoted to the one and despise the other."* (Matthew 6:24).[327] Attempting to serve both God and culture is not neutrality; it is choosing culture while using God's name as cover.

Church of America, the hour of decision is upon you. You cannot serve the God of Scripture and the god of cultural approval. You cannot preach Christ's narrow way and the world's broad way. You cannot worship at the altar of truth and the altar of inclusion. The Democratic platform has drawn the line. The LGBTQ+ movement has issued its ultimatum: celebrate or be destroyed. And too many of you are calculating whether your buildings, your reputations, your salaries, or your cultural standing is worth the cost of obedience to Christ.

But Jesus declared without qualification or ambiguity, *"Whoever denies me before men, I also will deny before my Father who is in heaven."* (Matthew 10:33).[328] Your silence is denial. Your compromise is betrayal. Your fear of man is rejection of God. And on the day you stand before Him, "I didn't want to be divisive" will not save you from His judgment. The cost of discipleship is high, but the cost of compromise is eternal.[329]

Scripture has spoken with clarity that pierces every excuse and exposes every compromise. The Democratic platform has codified rebellion into law and declared war on the Church of Jesus Christ. The judgment is already unfolding: children mutilated in the name of compassion, families destroyed in the name of authenticity, souls damned in the name of love, a civilization collapsing under the weight of delusions it has enshrined as rights. The external witnesses have documented the carnage that flows inevitably from rejecting God's design. The warning has been given.

John declares without shadow or compromise: *"God is light; in him there is no darkness at all."* (1 John 1:5).[330] No shadows. No gray areas. No peaceful coexistence with rebellion. To know this God is to be transformed by His light. To reject this God is to remain in darkness with eternal consequences.

Real love has a name: Jesus Christ. He is *"the way and the truth and the life."* (John 14:6).[331] He is love incarnate, not because He affirms our desires but because He died to free us from slavery to them. He calls us not to celebrate our identities but to lose our lives that we might find them in Him.

The line has been drawn. Choose this day whom you will serve. The Baal prophets are crying out with passionate intensity, cutting themselves, working themselves into emotional frenzies, and producing nothing but theater. The God who answers by fire is waiting for His people to stop wavering, stop compromising, and stop calculating the cost of obedience.

The watchmen are crying from the walls. The sword is at the gate. Repent and return to the Lord while there is still time, or be swept away with the unrepentant when judgment falls.

Let the faithful stand.

Section III: The Fallout of Affirming What God Calls Sin

The judgment of God is not coming. It is here. When a nation celebrates what the Creator calls abomination, when institutions surrender truth to ideological pressure, and when shepherds abandon their flocks to wolves, the wrath of God does not wait for some future reckoning. It falls now. Paul declared the mechanism with devastating clarity: *"For the wrath of God is revealed from heaven against all ungodliness and unrighteousness of men, who by their unrighteousness suppress the truth."* (Romans 1:18).[332] Revealed. Present tense. The suppression of truth triggers the revelation of wrath, and America is drowning in both.

Three times in Romans 1, the verdict falls like a hammer: *"God gave them up in the lusts of their hearts to impurity"* (Romans 1:24).[333] Again: *"God gave them up to dishonorable passions"* (Romans 1:26).[334] Finally: *"God gave them up to a debased mind to do what ought not to be done"* (Romans 1:28).[335] God gave them up. This is not a threat; it is a diagnosis. This is not a warning; it is a declaration of abandonment already executed.

A society that demands autonomy from divine law, insists on freedom to define its own reality, and exchanges the truth of God for the lie of self-sovereignty receives exactly what it chose: God grants the request, steps back, removes His restraining hand, and the society collapses into the chaos it selected.

You are watching that collapse in real time. Sin has been redefined as identity, disorder as health, mutilation as compassion, feelings crowned sovereign, and biology declared negotiable. And every institution has bowed: the academy, the media, the government, the psychiatric establishment, the medical profession, and, God help us, the church. This is what divine abandonment looks like when a nation refuses correction, and God says, "Very well. Have it your way."

The American Psychiatric Association's surrender to ideology over the past fifty years stands as damning evidence that when truth is rejected, expertise means nothing. Activism conquers science, pressure replaces evidence, and professionals whose duty is healing become agents of destruction. The removal of homosexuality from the Diagnostic and Statistical Manual in 1973 did not follow breakthrough research or clinical validation. It followed protests, disruptions, and relentless political pressure until the APA capitulated.[336] Science did not change its mind. Scientists were bullied into silence.

The pattern repeated. Ego-dystonic homosexuality, the diagnosis for those distressed by same-sex attraction and seeking help, was eliminated in 1987.[337] The message was unmistakable: even those suffering would not be helped if helping them contradicted the new orthodoxy. Gender Identity Disorder was introduced in 1994, then sanitized into Gender Dysphoria in 2013, and then reclassified entirely by the World Health Organization in 2019 as no longer a mental disorder but a "condition related to sexual health."[338] By 2022, the DSM itself adopted the propaganda phrase "sex assigned at birth" as clinical language.[339] Sex is not assigned. It is observed. But psychiatry now speaks the language of ideology, not biology.

Compare this to legitimate revisions. When Asperger's Syndrome was folded into Autism Spectrum Disorder, the change followed decades of research demonstrating overlapping symptomology.[340] When hypochondriasis was replaced with distinct diagnoses for illness anxiety and somatic symptoms, empirical studies justified the shift.[341] These changes followed evidence. The sexuality and gender revisions followed activists. An entire medical field surrendered to the mob. And when healers become propagandists, patients are sacrificed.

The blood testifies. A Swedish study tracked individuals who underwent sex-reassignment surgery over thirty years and documented a suicide rate nineteen times higher than the general population.[342] Nineteen times higher. In Sweden, one of the most culturally affirming nations on earth, where tolerance is policy and celebration is law. The surgery did not bring peace. It compounded despair. The affirmation did not heal. It confirmed the delusion and left broken people more broken still.

The Trevor Project documents the mental health crisis among LGBTQ+ youth with statistics that should shatter every illusion about affirmation as a cure. Their 2022 survey found that 45% of LGBTQ+ youth seriously considered suicide in the past year, and nearly one in five attempted it.[343] Every corporation waves rainbow flags. Every school celebrates Pride Month. Every media outlet lionizes transition stories. And still the despair deepens. The explanation offered is always the same: more affirmation needed, more acceptance required, more laws to protect, more funding to support. But Sweden is not lacking affirmation. The Trevor Project surveys youth in America's most progressive cities. If celebration were the cure, the suicide rates would be dropping. They are rising. The problem is not rejection but the lie itself. When you build identity on delusion, the foundation crumbles.

"They have healed the wound of my people lightly, saying, 'Peace, peace,' when there is no peace." (Jeremiah 6:14).[344] There is no peace because the wound has not been healed. It has been celebrated, codified into law, and left to fester to death.

Then there are the voices of the betrayed, those who believed the lie, underwent irreversible procedures, and now live in the wreckage. Chloe Cole was thirteen when she began puberty blockers. Fifteen when surgeons removed her breasts. Eighteen when she detransitioned and began speaking the truth that the adults who should have protected her instead destroyed her.[345] She was told transition would cure her distress. It multiplied it. She was told the changes were reversible. They were not. She was told she was born in the wrong body.

The truth is, she was a confused child failed by every institution that touched her life.

Helena Kerschner describes the social contagion that swept her into transgender identity, online communities that convinced vulnerable young women that dysphoria explained their depression, that testosterone would solve their anxiety, and that transition was the path to authenticity.[346] Years of hormones later, she detransitioned and joined the growing ranks of those testifying that they were lied to, exploited, and abandoned. These are not isolated cases. Detransition support networks are multiplying, filled with the wounded who were told that mutilation was healthcare and are now discovering that the adults who cheered them on have disappeared now that regret has set in.

How many others never make it to testimony? How many take their own lives after the surgeries that were supposed to save them? The blood cries out from clinic floors and hospital beds across this nation. And you call it compassion. *"Even the mercy of the wicked is cruel."* (Proverbs 12:10).[347] This is cruelty wearing a doctor's coat. This is destruction marketed as care. And God will require an accounting for every child sacrificed on the altar of affirmed identity.

This is not political theater. This is not cultural evolution. This is spiritual warfare. *"For we do not wrestle against flesh and blood, but against the rulers, against the authorities, against the cosmic powers over this present darkness, against the spiritual forces of evil in the heavenly places."* (Ephesians 6:12).[348] The Enemy cannot strike God directly, so he strikes the image of God stamped into creation. And that image is clearest in the binary that Genesis establishes: *"So God created man in his own image, in the image of God he created him; male and female he created them."* (Genesis 1:27).[349] Male and female. Not spectrum. Not fluid. Not subject to surgical revision or hormonal intervention.

The binary is sacred because it reflects the Creator. To obliterate it is to deface the image of God in humanity.

The serpent's strategy has not evolved since Eden. *"Did God really say?"* (Genesis 3:1).[350] That whisper echoes today in every classroom teaching that gender is a social construct, in every therapist affirming that feelings trump biology, and in every politician declaring that men can become women through declaration. Did God really make them male and female? Or is identity whatever we feel, reality whatever we choose, truth whatever serves our desires? When the answer comes back denying the Creator's design, the serpent smiles. His work is done. The lie has been believed. And belief in lies always produces death.

Paul warned that this blindness is not accidental. *"The god of this world has blinded the minds of the unbelievers, to keep them from seeing the light of the gospel of the glory of Christ, who is the image of God."* (2 Corinthians 4:4).[351] This is systemic deception. This is darkness descending when truth is rejected and lies are enthroned. The evidence screams: bodies mutilated, suicides soaring, children sterilized, families destroyed, but the culture chooses blindness. The problem is not inability to see but refusal to see, and that refusal is judgment already falling.

History warns, but you refuse to listen. Ancient Israel passed its children through fire to Molech, and God's law thundered against it: *"You shall not give any of your children to offer them to Molech and so profane the name of your God: I am the LORD."* (Leviticus 18:21).[352] Jeremiah condemned those who *"built the high places of Baal in the Valley of the Son of Hinnom to offer up their sons and daughters to Molech, though I did not command them, nor did it enter into my mind that they should do this abomination."* (Jeremiah 32:35).[353] God's judgment fell. The nation was carried into exile for sacrificing its children to false gods.

You tell yourselves you are more enlightened. You do not have bronze idols heated in flames. You do not chant incantations to pagan deities. But you do have operating rooms where healthy breasts are removed from teenage girls. You do have endocrinology clinics where puberty blockers chemically castrate confused boys. You do have scalpels carving away tissue, hormones sterilizing the fertile, and a culture celebrating every mutilation as healthcare. The altars look different. The priests wear white coats instead of religious garb. But the sacrifice is the same.

You are offering your children to the gods of self-expression, autonomy, and affirmed identity. You call it compassion. God calls it an abomination. And the children's blood cries out from surgical tables across this land.

Nebuchadnezzar erected a golden image and commanded all to bow. *"Whoever does not fall down and worship shall immediately be cast into a burning fiery furnace."* (Daniel 3:6).[354] The music played. The masses bowed. Only three refused. Shadrach, Meshach, and Abednego told the king, *"We will not serve your gods or worship the golden image that you have set up."* (Daniel 3:18).[355] The furnace was heated seven times hotter than before. They were thrown in. And God vindicated them. They walked out untouched, without even the smell of smoke on their clothing.

Today, the golden image is the ideology that declares gender fluid, identity sacred, and feelings sovereign. The command has been issued: bow, celebrate, and affirm. Refuse and face the fire, career destruction, public shaming, legal penalties, and social exile. The music is playing. The masses are bowing.

Corporations, universities, hospitals, governments, and churches are falling prostrate before the idol. But there is a remnant that will not bow. They know there are worse things than losing employment. There are worse things than being called a bigot. There is the judgment of God. The question is not whether pressure will come. The question is whether you will stand when it does.

And the most damning indictment falls not on the world but on the church. The world acts like the world. This is no surprise. But when the church surrenders truth, when shepherds lead sheep into error, and when those called to guard sound doctrine instead celebrate rebellion, the betrayal is complete. The Episcopal Church consecrated Gene Robinson as the first openly gay bishop in 2003.[356]

The Evangelical Lutheran Church in America voted in 2009 to allow clergy in committed same-sex relationships.[357] The United Church of Christ endorsed same-sex marriage in

2005.[358] These are not fringe congregations. These are denominations representing millions who claim the name of Christ while denying the authority of His Word.

The trajectory does not stop. Once Scripture's authority is surrendered on sexuality, no ground remains to hold. The same denominations now bless gender transitions, ordain transgender clergy, host Pride worship services, and march under rainbow flags while calling it Christian witness. This is not an evolution of doctrine. This is apostasy wearing vestments. This is the rebellion Tozer warned against when he observed that religion, which began with God at the center, inevitably degenerates into religion with man at the center.[359]

You have made man sovereign, his feelings ultimate, his identity sacred, and his desires determinative. And in doing so, you have pushed God to the margins and erected an idol in His place.

Bonhoeffer declared that silence in the face of evil is participation in evil itself: "Not to speak is to speak. Not to act is to act."[360] The American church has chosen silence. Pastors who know the truth calculate the cost and choose their careers over their calling. Elders who should speak remain quiet to preserve unity. Congregations that once stood firm have sanded down every sharp edge to avoid the accusation of being unloving. And in that silence, the Enemy advances unopposed.

Spurgeon pleaded with a passion the modern church has forgotten: "If sinners be damned, at least let them leap to Hell over our dead bodies. And if they perish, let them perish with our arms wrapped about their knees, imploring them to stay."[361] Where is that desperation now? Where are the pastors weeping over lost souls? Where are the churches willing to be hated for speaking truth? The silence is not neutrality. It is surrender. And it will be judged.

God appointed watchmen to sound the alarm, and He holds them accountable for what they see and fail to declare. *"Son of man, I have made you a watchman for the house of Israel. Whenever you hear a word from my mouth, you shall give them warning from me."* (Ezekiel 33:7).[362] The watchman's calling is not popularity. It is not peace. It is a warning. And the consequences of silence are explicit: *"If the watchman sees the sword coming and does not blow the trumpet, so that the people are not warned, and the sword comes and takes any one of them, that person is taken away in his iniquity, but his blood I will require at the watchman's hand."* (Ezekiel 33:6).[363]

Their blood is on the watchman's hands. Not the enemy's. Not the victims'. The watchman's.

Pastor, elder, church leader: this commission is yours. You see the sword at the gate. You see children being mutilated in the name of affirmation. You see families torn apart. You see souls walking confidently toward hell while churches celebrate their authenticity. And if you remain silent because you fear losing members, because you calculate that your reputation matters more than their souls, or because you prioritize cultural acceptance over biblical fidelity, their blood will be required on your hands. This is not secondary. This is not negotiable. This is the image of God under assault, children being sacrificed, and the gospel being perverted into a message that affirms rebellion instead of calling for repentance.

Israel ignored the prophets. Judah mocked them. They sacrificed their children, called evil good, and silenced every voice that cried warning. And God brought judgment. The Assyrians destroyed the northern kingdom. The Babylonians burned Jerusalem and carried the survivors into exile. The warnings had been true. The prophets had been right. But the nation refused to listen until it was too late.

America is not exempt. *"Righteousness exalts a nation, but sin is a reproach to any people."* (Proverbs 14:34).[364] You have codified sin into law, paraded rebellion in your streets, and celebrated the destruction of your children as progress. Empires do not fall overnight. They rot from within, morality abandoned, truth rejected, foundations mocked, and history erased. When elites lose confidence in their own civilization, when citizens tear down their own monuments, and when ideology replaces reality, the collapse is already underway.[365] You are demolishing your own foundations while insisting you are building a more just society. The end is not distant. The judgment is falling now.

But God is merciful even in wrath. Even now, He extends the offer that could stay His hand: *"Return to me, and I will return to you, says the LORD of hosts."* (Malachi 3:7).[366] Repentance is not regret. It is a reversal. It is confessing that you have called evil good, that you have affirmed what God condemns, that you have been silent when you should have spoken, and that you have celebrated what you should have mourned. And then it is fleeing to the cross, the only place where rebellion is paid for and sinners are made clean.

The gospel still saves. The blood of Christ still cleanses. There is no sin too great for grace to reach, no confusion too deep for truth to shatter, no bondage too strong for the Spirit to break. Jesus came to save sinners, and He saves completely. *"If we confess our sins, he is faithful and just to forgive us our sins and to cleanse us from all unrighteousness."* (1 John 1:9).[367]

This is the message the church must proclaim: not an affirmation that leaves people in chains, but redemption that breaks them. Not a celebration of identity built on lies, but a transformation into the image of Christ. Not cheap grace that costs nothing, but costly grace that demands everything and gives life eternal.

The hour demands a prophetic church. Not a church marketing itself to the culture. Not a church trimming Scripture to fit the times. Not a church prioritizing attendance metrics over faithfulness to God. A church that cries aloud and spares not. *"Cry aloud; do not hold back; lift up your voice like a trumpet; declare to my people their transgression, to the house of Jacob their sins."* (Isaiah 58:1).[368] Not whispers. Not suggestions. A voice like a trumpet declaring truth without compromise, calling rebellion by its name, and pleading with sinners to flee the wrath to come.

Small remnants have turned nations before. Josiah was eight years old when he became king of a nation steeped in idolatry. He led a reformation that tore down high places, destroyed idols, and restored the worship of God (2 Kings 22-23).[369] One faithful king. One remnant willing to stand. And judgment was delayed. God is looking for such a remnant now. Not conferences issuing carefully worded statements. Not committees drafting position papers. A remnant that will stand in the gap, speak truth in love, and refuse to bow, no matter the cost.

The line has been drawn. On one side stands the eternal truth of God, unchanging, non-negotiable, and holy. On the other side stands the lie, fluid, accommodating, destructive.

You cannot stand on both. You cannot serve two masters. *"Whoever is not with me is against me, and whoever does not gather with me scatters."* (Matthew 12:30).[370] There is no neutral ground. Silence is a choice. Inaction is a choice. And both are choices against Christ.

The children are being sterilized. The families are being destroyed. The souls are being damned. This is not metaphor. This is happening now in clinics, classrooms, and courtrooms across this nation. And the church calculates whether standing for truth is worth the cultural cost. God will not be mocked. The ideologies will crumble and the pride flags will burn. Every knee will bow, and every tongue confess that Jesus Christ is Lord (Philippians 2:10-11).[371] The question is whether that confession comes in repentance now or judgment later.

To the faithful remnant, you are not alone. God preserves a remnant in every generation. When Elijah believed he was the last faithful voice in Israel, God told him, *"I will leave seven thousand in Israel, all the knees that have not bowed to Baal, and every mouth that has not kissed him."* (1 Kings 19:18).[372] Seven thousand whose names Elijah had never known. But God knew. He always knows. Daniel refused to defile himself even in Babylon (Daniel 1:8).[373] The early church sang hymns while lions circled in the arena. They stood. And you are part of that unbroken line of witnesses who refused to bow.

Do not grow weary. Do not surrender. Speak truth in love. Live with courage. Refuse to bow before the idol, no matter what fire they threaten. Trust that the God who vindicated Shadrach, Meshach, and Abednego in the furnace will vindicate you. The world will hate you. The culture will mock you. Even churches will cast you out. But God sees. And His approval is all that matters.

The safe place is not cultural acceptance or keeping your head down until the storm passes. It is under the blood of the Lamb, standing on the truth of His Word, refusing to deny Him regardless of cost. *"Choose this day whom you will serve."* (Joshua 24:15).[374] Will you serve the God who made you, redeemed you, and calls you to holiness? Or will you serve the gods of this age, self-expression, autonomy, and affirmed identity, who demand your children and your soul as the price of their approval?

"Whoever denies me before men, I also will deny before my Father who is in heaven." (Matthew 10:33).[375] The stakes are eternal. The hour is urgent. *"Be watchful, stand firm in the faith, act like men, and be strong."* (1 Corinthians 16:13).[376]

The line has been drawn, the trumpet is sounding, the sword is at the gate — let the faithful stand.

CONVICTION IN ACTION
"The Line Has Been Drawn"
Chapter 4: Gender, Sexuality, and the War on Creation

CONVICTION

God's design for humanity as male and female, created in His image, is non-negotiable. When the Church affirms what God calls sin or remains silent while children are mutilated in the name of compassion, we do not show love. We participate in destruction, and we will answer to God for every soul we failed to warn.

REALITY CHECK

Gender ideology has conquered every institution: government, education, medicine, and now the Church itself. Denominations ordain practicing homosexuals. Pastors perform same-sex weddings. Christian parents surrender confused children to activists who promise affirmation and deliver sterilization. And the rest of us stay silent, calculating that our careers and reputations matter more than truth. The stakes are not social. They are eternal.

FAITHFULNESS NOW LOOKS LIKE

Personal: Stop using the world's language. Speak the truth in your home, workplace, and friendships, even when it costs you. If you know someone trapped in sexual sin or gender confusion, love them enough to tell them the truth: Jesus offers freedom, not affirmation.

Church: Demand that your pastor preach the whole counsel of God, including what Scripture says about sexuality, gender, and judgment. If your church has gone silent, ask why. Support ministries that help people leave LGBTQ+ lifestyles.

Public: The line has been drawn. There is no neutrality. Refuse pronoun mandates. Show up at school board meetings. Oppose legislation that harms children. Count the cost and pay it. You will lose friends, you may lose your job, but you will stand before God with a clean conscience.

COMMITMENTS

☐ Stop using compromise language such as "gender-affirming care" or "assigned at birth" and speak biblical truth plainly, even when it costs you socially.

☐ Protect your children from gender ideology by monitoring their education and media, and proactively teach them God's design for male and female.

☐ Have one conversation this week with someone who needs to hear the truth about sexuality or God's design, with courage and without cruelty.

☐ Take one concrete action in your community this month: speak at a school board meeting, support protective legislation, or stand with someone being persecuted for refusing to bow.

PRAYER

Lord Jesus, forgive me for my cowardice. Forgive me for valuing acceptance over truth, comfort over courage, and reputation over obedience. Give me the courage to speak when it costs me everything. Strengthen Your Church to stand firm when the world demands we bow, and protect the children being sacrificed to the gods of self-expression. Break the chains of sexual sin and gender confusion that enslave so many, and show them that freedom is found in You alone. On that day, let it be said that I stood when others bowed and that I loved people enough to tell them the truth. Amen.

Chapter 5: Love Redefined—The Hijacking of Compassion

Section I: From Agapē to Affirmation—The Counterfeit Gospel

God spoke these words to a nation drowning in compromise: "Woe to those who call evil good and good evil, who put darkness for light and light for darkness, who put bitter for sweet and sweet for bitter." (Isaiah 5:20).[377] He speaks them again today. The Church has committed adultery with the world and called it compassion. Pastors stand in pulpits and speak the language of heaven while bowing to the demands of hell. What Scripture calls sin and rebellion, progressive Christianity has rebranded as identity and authenticity.

Parents are told that to love their gender-confused child is to affirm the confusion. Pastors preach that to love the sinner is to celebrate the sin. Denominations ordain practicing homosexuals and call it inclusion. Churches host drag queen story hours and call it radical hospitality. Seminary professors rewrite theology to accommodate transgender ideology and call it scholarship.

The culture screams, "What is kind?" and the Church has forgotten to ask, "What is true?" Conviction has been relabeled cruelty and restraint renamed hatred. Truth has been exiled in the name of love. This is not love; it is betrayal.

The Scripture declares, "God shows his love for us in that while we were still sinners, Christ died for us" (Romans 5:8).[378] God's love does not affirm rebellion; it rescues from it. The cross was not an affirmation; it was an execution. The Word states plainly, "It was the will of the Lord to crush him;

he has put him to grief." (Isaiah 53:10).[379] The Father crushed His own Son under the weight of sin so that sinners might be saved. That is love: ferocious, uncompromising, drenched in blood. Love does not whisper comfort into rebellion; it tears down the lies, exposes the sin, and offers one path to life: repentance.

But the modern Church preaches a different gospel. It offers comfort without conviction, acceptance without transformation, and grace without repentance. The therapeutic gospel has gutted the cross of its offense and dressed it in the language of inclusion. Worship songs scrub out His wrath; sermons promise blessing without any call to holiness. Prayer has become self-help, discipleship has become therapy, and the altar call has been replaced with an invitation to "come as you are and stay as you are." The gospel that once turned the world upside down has been repackaged to leave sinners undisturbed.

The Apostle Paul carved the line in stone: "Love does not rejoice at wrongdoing but rejoices with the truth." (1 Corinthians 13:6).[380] There is no love without truth. There is no mercy without holiness. There is no salvation without repentance. Any gospel that severs love from truth is not the gospel of Jesus Christ; it is a counterfeit designed to make sinners comfortable on the road to hell.

The progressive movement has seized the language of love and weaponized it. The serpent asked Eve a question that echoes through history: "Did God actually say...?" (Genesis 3:1).[381] The same question echoes in churches across America. Did God actually say homosexuality is sin? Did God actually say marriage is between one man and one woman? Did God actually say there are only two genders?

The Church, terrified of being labeled intolerant, has begun to equivocate. Scripture has been traded for cultural approval. The fear of God has been replaced by the fear of man. The human heart manufactures idols to replace the living God, and the modern Church has forged a new one: not of stone or wood but of sentiment and tolerance.[382]

Jesus did not come to affirm. He declared plainly, "Do not think that I have come to bring peace to the earth. I have not come to bring peace, but a sword." (Matthew 10:34).[383] His message was divisive by design. The gospel does not accommodate; it exposes, confronts, and demands. The early Church knew this. They did not conquer Rome by affirming its perversions but by confronting them, not with therapeutic sentiment but with proclamation. The faith does not advance by accommodation but by separation, by fidelity, and by the courage to stand when the culture demands you bow.[384]

Paul warned Timothy of this hour: "Having the appearance of godliness, but denying its power." (2 Timothy 3:5).[385] It has arrived. Sanctuaries have become theaters and worship mere performance. The power to transform has been traded for the applause of the crowd. Pastors fear being called hateful more than they fear the living God. The gospel has been gutted of its offense and dressed in the language of inclusion.

The risen Christ spoke these words to the compromising church at Laodicea: "Those whom I love, I reprove and discipline." (Revelation 3:19).[386] Love includes judgment. A father who refuses to discipline his son does not love him; he destroys him. A shepherd who refuses to warn the sheep of wolves does not love the flock; he feeds them to slaughter. A doctor who diagnoses cancer but refuses to prescribe treatment does not love his patient; he murders him with kindness. The Church has done this. It has removed judgment from love and stripped correction from mercy, calling the wreckage grace and compassion.

Jesus marked the path: "Enter by the narrow gate. For the gate is wide and the way is easy that leads to destruction, and those who enter by it are many. For the gate is narrow and the way is hard that leads to life, and those who find it are few." (Matthew 7:13-14).[387] The modern Church is paving the wide road with rainbow flags and therapeutic affirmations, escorting sinners to hell while calling it inclusion. This is not love but cruelty dressed in kindness, murder disguised as mercy.

The prophet Ezekiel delivered God's verdict over the silent watchmen: "If the watchman sees the sword coming and does not blow the trumpet so that the people are not warned and the sword comes and takes any one of them, that person is taken away in his iniquity, but his blood I will require at the watchman's hand." (Ezekiel 33:6).[388] The Church has seen the sword, watched the collapse of biblical morality, the enshrinement of perversion into law, the mutilation of children, and refused to blow the trumpet. The blood is on its hands.

The lie is now law. The Equality Act of 2021 enshrines sexual orientation and gender identity into federal civil rights law.[389] Biblical convictions are now bigotry. To refuse to participate in a same-sex wedding is discrimination. To refuse to use false pronouns is harassment. To believe that God made humanity male and female is hate speech. The Church did not stop this. It enabled it. When the culture demanded compromise and the courts codified rebellion, the Church whispered excuses and the pulpits stayed silent. The sword has arrived. Those who walked out of darkness into light see what pastors refuse to acknowledge: compassion that refuses to name sin does not rescue; it destroys.[390]

Jesus spoke plainly: *"If anyone would come after me, let him deny himself and take up his cross daily and follow me."* (Luke 9:23).[391] The cross demands death to self, not affirmation of self. Deny. Die. Follow. That is the gospel. But the progressive gospel says, "Affirm yourself. Trust your feelings. God made you this way." That is not the gospel of Jesus Christ; it is the gospel of the serpent. The modern Church has inverted the message: truth if possible, peace at all costs. But without truth, there is no love. Without holiness, there is no God.[392]

The Scripture declares the human condition without equivocation: "The heart is deceitful above all things and desperately sick." (Jeremiah 17:9).[393] Man does not need validation. He needs salvation. The man enslaved to sin does not need to be told he is enough. He needs to be told he is lost. The woman trapped in rebellion does not need affirmation. She needs transformation. The child who is confused about gender does not need hormones and scalpels. He needs the truth. Apart from Christ, you are dead. That is the truth that wounds before it heals, and it is love.

Jesus spoke the judgment over those who reject light: "This is the judgment: the light has come into the world, and people loved the darkness rather than the light because their works were evil. For everyone who does wicked things hates the light and does not come to the light, lest his works should be exposed." (John 3:20).[394] The Church is called to be light. Light exposes sin. It does not hide it. But the modern Church has dimmed its light. It has softened the message, blunted the edge, and removed the offense. And the darkness has deepened.

A dimmed light does not illuminate; it deceives. A blunted sword does not defend; it betrays. The evangelical church has accommodated to the world spirit of the age, and accommodation is the death of truth.[395]

Jesus did not equivocate: "Unless you repent, you will all likewise perish." (Luke 13:3).[396] He did not say, "Unless you feel affirmed." He did not say, "Embrace your authentic self." He said, "Repent." That is love. That is the only path to life. The arrogance of modern Christianity is staggering. Pastors stand in pulpits and preach a softer gospel than the Son of God preached, and they call it compassion. We are not more loving than Jesus.

Paul declared without shame, "I am not ashamed of the gospel, for it is the power of God for salvation to everyone who believes." (Romans 1:16).[397] The gospel does not need our edits. It does not need our therapeutic adjustments. It does not need to be made safe for modern sensibilities. It needs to be preached. Agapē does not mean acceptance. It means alignment with the holy purposes of God. It means the refusal to leave sinners comfortable in their rebellion. It means the willingness to wound in order to heal, to confront in order to rescue, and to speak the truth even when the truth costs everything.

Love has been hijacked. The Church has bowed to the golden calf of tolerance and called it mercy. The hour is late. The sword is at the gates. The blood of a generation cries out from the altars of affirmation. Children are being told that their confusion is sacred, that their feelings are infallible, that their rebellion is righteous. The Church watches and says nothing. Worse, it affirms, it celebrates, and it ordains the very lies that lead to death.

It is time for the Church to rise: not with hatred but with holy fire, not with cruelty but with clarity, and not with compromise but with the blood-stained, soul-rescuing, life-transforming gospel of Jesus Christ. The call is not to inclusion or affirmation but to repentance and the cross. Repent and believe.

Section II: Tolerance as the New Golden Calf

There was a time when truth thundered from American pulpits. Jonathan Edwards preached "Sinners in the Hands of an Angry God," and men gripped their pews in terror of judgment. Charles Finney demanded public repentance, and cities shook under the weight of conviction. Martin Luther King Jr. wielded the sword of biblical justice, and a nation could not look away. Truth was etched in stone, immovable, uncompromising. It did not bend to preference. It did not negotiate with culture. It stood.

That time has ended. The stone has been traded for clay, soft and pliable, shaped by the hands of whatever generation finds truth inconvenient. The Church has not rejected God outright. It has done something far more dangerous: it has forged a golden calf and named it "Tolerance," and it bows before this idol while singing songs to Yahweh.

The prophet Amos spoke to a nation drunk on compromise: *"They hate him who reproves in the gate, and they abhor him who speaks the truth."* (Amos 5:10).[398] This is America. This is the American Church. Tolerance has been baptized, canonized, and enshrined as the supreme virtue. It demands no repentance. It requires no holiness. It promises peace with everyone and accountability to no one.

But Jesus did not preach neutrality. He declared, *"Whoever is not with me is against me."* (Matthew 12:30).[399] There is no middle ground, no safe space between the kingdom of God and the kingdom of this world. The modern Church, terrified of offense, has built its temple in that imaginary middle ground. And it is sinking.

The great collapse did not begin with gay pride parades. It began in the 1960s when the Church watched moral rebellion explode in the streets and chose to retreat into the sanctuary. In 1962, the Supreme Court ruled that prayer and Bible reading were unconstitutional in public schools.[400] The Church issued statements. It did not wage war. In 1973, Roe v. Wade legalized the slaughter of the unborn. Many pastors calculated the cost of losing their 501(c)(3) status and chose to remain silent. Resistance became retreat. Retreat became rebranding. And rebranding became the therapeutic gospel that now sits on the throne where Christ once ruled.

Tolerance has mutated. What began as a Christian virtue, bearing with one another in love and showing patience toward the sinner, has metastasized into a secular religion that demands orthodoxy without grace. The old Christian virtues have gone mad.[401]

Tolerance now demands not patience but approval, not forbearance but celebration. To refuse to affirm is hate speech; to refuse to participate is discrimination. The refusal to bake the cake, to use the pronouns, and to applaud the parade is no longer a protected conscience; it is prosecuted as bigotry. This new religion has its own orthodoxy, and it is more rigid than any creed the Church ever wrote. It demands heretic hunts without forgiveness, rituals without redemption. It is, as one observer noted, a religion that offers all the judgment of the old faith with none of its mercy.[402]

The sacraments of this new religion are visible everywhere. Pride parades have replaced baptism, public declarations of identity celebrated by the masses and protected by the state. Preferred pronouns have replaced confession, the daily ritual of affirming the lie, the compelled speech that forces participation in delusion. Corporate virtue signaling has replaced communion, the public display of allegiance, and the performance of righteousness divorced from any actual transformation. And the clergy of this new faith are not pastors but activists; its catechism is curated not by councils but by influencers; its gospel is preached not from pulpits but from platforms.

And the Church, the Bride of Christ, the pillar and ground of truth, has become the missionary arm of this religion. Christian leaders baptize rebellion in the name of relevance. They pepper their sermons with the language of "inclusion," "equity," and "lived experience." They remove words like "sin," "repentance," and "judgment" from their vocabulary. They do not confront the culture; they court it; rather than calling the lost to repentance, they invite them to brunch. Vance Havner saw it decades ago: the devil is not fighting churches; he is joining them.[403]

There are churches in America today that host drag queen story hours for children and call it "radical inclusion." The Scripture is plain: *"It would be better for him if a millstone were hung around his neck and he were cast into the sea than that he should cause one of these little ones to sin."* (Luke 17:2).[404] This is not courage or love. This is spiritual negligence of the highest order, the Church functioning not as the body of Christ but as the opposition of God. When the Church affirms what God calls abominable, it does not redefine holiness. It forfeits its authority.

And authority has been forfeited. The Church once shook empires. Now it whispers in the corner, hoping not to offend. It once cast out demons in the name of Jesus. Now it fears being called unloving. It once thundered the Word of God with such force that sinners fell to their knees. Now it mumbles apologies for passages that make people uncomfortable. Jesus pronounced woe over the cities that rejected Him: *"Woe to you, Chorazin! Woe to you, Bethsaida!"* (Matthew 11:21).[405] But the modern Church is so terrified of pronouncing woe over anyone that it has lost the ability to pronounce blessing. A church that cannot wound cannot heal, and a church that will not confront cannot convert.

The Apostle Paul warned the Romans, "Do *not be conformed to this world, but be transformed by the renewal of your mind."* (Romans 12:2).[406] The American Church has crossed that line. It has conformed. It has been transformed, not by the renewal of the Spirit but by the pressure of the culture. And a church that conforms to the world does not become more effective. It becomes indicted. It does not win the culture. It becomes the culture. The world is not waiting for the Church to redefine its message. It is waiting for the Church to demonstrate its power.[407] And the Church has nothing to demonstrate but compromise.

The pattern is ancient. While Moses was on the mountain receiving the Law of God, Aaron stood at the base of the mountain and forged a golden calf. The people demanded a god they could see, a god they could control, a god who would not make demands they found inconvenient. Aaron did not reject Yahweh outright. He blended truth with preference. He took the gold and shaped it into something the people wanted. And when he presented the calf, he declared, *"These are your gods, O Israel, who brought you up out of the land of Egypt!"* (Exodus 32:4).[408] This was not atheism. This was syncretism. This was the worship of Yahweh on the people's terms. And God's wrath burned hot.

The modern Church has done this. It has not rejected God. It has remade Him in the image of tolerance. It assigns His name to what He abhors. It calls the celebration of sexual rebellion "love." It calls the mutilation of children "compassion." It calls the silencing of truth "unity." This is Aaron's calf dressed in a rainbow flag.

When Moses came down from the mountain, he did not dialogue. He did not seek common ground. He shattered the tablets of the Law at the base of the mountain. He ground the golden calf into powder. He mixed it with water and made the people drink it. He confronted Aaron, and Aaron's excuse was pathetic: *"You know the people; they are set on evil."* (Exodus 32:22).[409] The same cowardice echoes today.

Pastors say, "We're just trying to reach people." "We're walking with them on their journey." "We're meeting them where they are." No. Aaron tolerated evil, and it provoked the wrath of God. The modern Church tolerates evil, and it will provoke the same.

The golden calf of tolerance now has legal standing. In 2015, Obergefell v. Hodges redefined marriage by judicial fiat. In 2021, the Equality Act elevated sexual orientation and gender identity to protected status. The idol has been codified into law. The Church's silence did not slow this. It strengthened it.

And now the consequences are generational. Children are being forced to deny biological reality in the name of liberation, but this is deception, not freedom. Students are compelled to use false pronouns and told that to speak the truth is to commit violence. Affirmation-only policies ignore every principle of mental health science and call it compassion.[410] Compelled speech, the demand that citizens participate in the lie under threat of punishment, is not courtesy. It is tyranny dressed in rainbow colors.[411]

And there are pastors, celebrity pastors, and influencers with platforms who have built their brands not on the authority of Scripture but on the ambiguity of their message. They are quick to address injustice but slow to define sin, quoting cultural influencers more readily than prophets and parsing every word to avoid offense. The Apostle Paul asked the Galatians a piercing question: *"Am I now seeking the approval of man or of God? Or am I trying to please man? If I were still trying to please man, I would not be a servant of Christ."* (Galatians 1:10).[412] The verdict is in.

But God has always moved through the remnant. Elijah stood alone on Mount Carmel while the nation danced between two opinions. Daniel prayed when prayer was made illegal. Micaiah prophesied truth while 400 false prophets lied to the king. These men feared God, and that fear made them fearless before men. The same will be required today. The majority has bowed. The remnant must stand.

Elijah posed the question on Carmel: *"How long will you go limping between two different opinions? If the Lord is God, follow him; but if Baal, then follow him."* (1 Kings 18:21).[413] That is the question for the American Church today. You cannot serve both Christ and culture, offering the cross with one hand and compromise with the other, and expect fire to fall from heaven. The Apostle Paul made it plain: *"Come out from among them and be separate, says the Lord. Touch no unclean thing, and I will receive you."* (2 Corinthians

6:17).[414] The fire of God falls only on altars that belong wholly to Him. The Church that splits its allegiance will find itself with neither the favor of God nor the respect of the world. It will have nothing but the hollow approval of a culture racing toward judgment.

The hour is late. The golden calf stands in the sanctuary. The people dance. And the few who remain faithful watch in horror, wondering if Moses will descend from the mountain in time. He will. And when He does, the calf will be ground to dust, the compromisers will be confronted, and the line will be drawn.

Choose this day.

Section III: The Love That Warns—God's Mercy Is Not Mute

If judgment comes to America, it will not be because God failed to love. Scripture declares plainly, *"The Lord roars from Zion."* (Amos 1:2).[415] This is not the roar of cruelty but of warning, the urgent cry of a God whose love refuses to remain silent when His people rush toward destruction. The prophet Amos thundered with divine authority: *"Is a trumpet blown in a city, and the people are not afraid?"* (Amos 3:6).[416] The trumpet of warning has been blown across this land. God has sent prophets. He has sent disasters that shake the foundations. He has sent division that exposes what the unity concealed. And He has sent His Word, unchanging and razor-sharp, declaring what is true when every institution insists on the lie.

Yet the nation continues its rebellion. The Church calculates the cost of speaking and chooses silence. And the sword draws nearer with every passing day.

Jesus wept over Jerusalem not because He lacked power to prevent its judgment but because love compelled Him to warn even when the warning would be rejected: *"Would that you, even you, had known on this day the things that make for peace! But now they are hidden from your eyes."* (Luke 19:42).[417] He did not whisper diplomatic suggestions. He did not soften the message to spare feelings or protect His reputation. He declared the city's doom, tears streaming down His face, because judgment was certain and the people were blind to their own peril. This was not cold pronouncement from a distance. This was love breaking over those who would not listen, mercy extended to the last possible moment, and warning delivered when warning could still matter. The pattern is ancient and unchanging: God sends warning before He sends judgment; mercy precedes wrath, and the prophetic voice cries out while time remains. But the time does not remain forever. The patience of God has limits, and those limits are approaching fast.

Noah preached righteousness for 120 years while building an ark no one believed would be needed (2 Peter 2:5).[418] His neighbors mocked him daily. His message was dismissed as the ravings of a fanatic. The culture called him extreme, judgmental, and out of touch with the times. And then the rains came. The floods rose. The door of the ark closed. And every mocker drowned.

Jeremiah stood in the streets of Jerusalem and wept, while warning of Babylon's coming siege, and the city's leaders threw him into a cistern for troubling Israel (Jeremiah 38:6).[419] They silenced the messenger and punished the prophet because his words exposed their rebellion and they refused to receive it.

Amos pronounced judgment on nations that thought themselves untouchable and declared with uncompromising clarity, *"Prepare to meet your God, O Israel!"* (Amos 4:12).[420] These were not cruel men. They were commissioned watchmen who loved enough to warn, who cared enough to be hated, and who valued souls more than their own reputations. And they spoke not because they enjoyed pronouncing judgment but because silence was complicity in destruction. The blood of the unwarned would be required at the watchman's hand, and they refused to bear that guilt.

Jesus Christ warned more than any other figure in Scripture, and He did so because His love demanded it. He pronounced woes over cities that refused to repent (Matthew 11:20-24).[421] He declared that it would be more bearable for Sodom and Gomorrah on the day of judgment than for Chorazin and Bethsaida, cities that witnessed His miracles and remained unchanged. Think of that: cities that saw the Son of God perform wonders with their own eyes, yet their hearts stayed hard.

He told the woman caught in adultery, *"Go, and from now on sin no more"* (John 8:11),[422] coupling mercy with the clear command to forsake sin. Grace was free, but it was not cheap. He warned the rich young ruler that wealth would be his destruction unless he surrendered it (Mark 10:21-22).[423]

He spoke of hell more than any other person in Scripture, describing it as outer darkness, weeping and gnashing of teeth, the fire that is not quenched, and the worm that does not die (Matthew 25:30, Mark 9:48).[424] He did not avoid the doctrine or soften the language because it offended modern sensibilities. This was not cruelty. This was truth spoken in love by the One who would soon die to provide escape from the judgment He warned against. To claim the name of Christ while refusing to warn is to preach a Christ who never existed, a Jesus of our own making who bears no resemblance to the Lord of Scripture.

The American church believes it can have revival without first having rebuke. Scripture teaches no such thing. Peter declared without qualification: *"It is time for judgment to begin at the household of God."* (1 Peter 4:17).[425] Judgment begins not with Hollywood or Washington but with the congregation that bears Christ's name. Yet the church hosts conferences that celebrate vision without demanding holiness, that promise breakthrough without requiring brokenness. Worship sets grow louder while prayer closets stay empty. Buildings expand while repentance disappears from the vocabulary. Marketing budgets swell while Scripture literacy collapses to embarrassing levels. Attendance metrics become the measure of success, while holiness becomes optional, a niche interest for the especially devout.

The language is always the same: more passion, greater anointing, and a fresh move of the Spirit. But God does not send fire on altars that refuse to be cleansed. He does not pour new wine into wineskins that will not be emptied of the old (Luke 5:37-38).[426] And He does not revive a church that will not first be rebuked. The fire comes only after the altar is prepared, and preparation requires confession of sin, not celebration of programs.

Jeremiah confronted a nation that said *"Peace, peace"* when there was no peace (Jeremiah 6:14).[427] The false prophets promised security while the nation's foundations crumbled beneath them. The people wanted comfort, and the prophets gave it to them in abundance. Religious leaders told the people what they wanted to hear, not what they needed to hear. But Jeremiah stood alone and declared the truth no one wanted to hear: judgment is coming, the sword is at the gates, and your comfortable delusions will not save you when the day of reckoning arrives.

This is the divide that always emerges between true prophets and false ones. The true prophet does not measure success by popularity or platform size. He measures it by faithfulness to the message God has given, regardless of whether the people receive it with gratitude or reject it with violence. The mission has been abandoned. The message has been softened beyond recognition. And the warnings that could awaken a sleeping nation die in the throat of pastors who have calculated that their careers matter more than their calling. They have traded the fear of God for the fear of losing donors, exchanging prophetic authority for cultural acceptance. And the sheep starve while the shepherds protect their platforms and polish their brands.

Even secular observers now see what the church refuses to acknowledge. When words lose meaning, reality becomes negotiable, and negotiable reality produces chaos.[428] The madness of crowds now treats objective truth as oppression and lived experience as the final authority.[429] These are witnesses to judgment already unfolding in real time. They are canaries in the coal mine, signaling that the air has turned toxic and the collapse is underway. And their testimony is damning not because they possess superior wisdom but because the church that should be sounding the alarm has instead joined the crowd in celebrating the collapse. The world sees the insanity. The church calls it progress and updates its website accordingly.

Ezekiel recorded the heart of the Father with surgical precision: *"Have I any pleasure in the death of the wicked, declares the Lord God, and not rather that he should turn from his way and live?"* (Ezekiel 18:23).[430] God does not delight in wrath. He is slow to anger and abounding in steadfast love (Psalm 103:8).[431] He delays judgment. He extends mercy. He sends warning after warning, shaking after shaking, and opportunity after opportunity to repent and return.

But mercy without repentance becomes permission to continue in rebellion. Grace without obedience becomes license for lawlessness. And warnings ignored become judgments executed with the full force of divine justice. The prophets wept as they warned, not because they were weak or sentimental, but because they understood what was coming and loved the people enough to beg them to turn back before it was too late. Jeremiah wept because he knew what Babylon would do to Jerusalem. His warnings were rejected as unpatriotic and divisive. And his tears were vindicated when the city burned and the temple fell.

The alarm is sounding now, louder than it has ever sounded before. Jesus spoke with fire in His voice: *"I came to cast fire on the earth, and would that it were already kindled!"* (Luke 12:49).[432] This is not the language of patience that runs forever without consequence. This is divine urgency: the Lord of heaven declaring that time is not infinite, that mercy has limits, and that the door will not remain open indefinitely while rebels mock from the other side. He overturned tables in the temple not because He lost control of His emotions but because zeal for His Father's house consumed Him (John 2:17).[433] He pronounced woes over the Pharisees who devoured widows' houses and made their converts twice the sons of hell that they were (Matthew 23:14-15).[434] He warned that a house divided against itself cannot stand (Matthew 12:25).[435] And He declared that on the day of judgment, people will give account for every careless word they have spoken (Matthew 12:36).[436] This is love that does not coddle sinners in their rebellion. This is mercy that warns with tears and thunder. This is grace that refuses to leave people comfortable in their destruction. And this same Jesus is coming again, not as suffering servant but as conquering King, with eyes like fire and a sword proceeding from His mouth.

The Apostle Paul understood that God's wrath is not only future but present, not only coming but already here: *"God gave them up in the lusts of their hearts to impurity."* (Romans 1:24).[437] Again, the verdict falls: *"God gave them up to dishonorable passions."* (Romans 1:26).[438] Finally, the third time seals it: *"God gave them up to a debased mind."* (Romans 1:28).[439] Three times the verdict falls like a hammer: God gave them up. This is present-tense judgment: God stepping back and allowing a society to drown in the consequences of its rebellion, happening now, unfolding in real time.

America is not waiting for collapse. America is witnessing it now: children sterilized in the name of compassion, families shattered in the name of authenticity, truth criminalized in the name of inclusion, reality itself declared negotiable in the name of progress. This is what divine abandonment looks like: the wrath of God revealed not in fire from heaven but in the removal of His protection, allowing the culture to drink deeply from the cup it has chosen. And the culture calls the poison medicine, celebrates the madness as enlightenment, and punishes anyone who points to the cliff ahead.

Joel cried out in desperation as he watched his nation stumble toward judgment: *"Spare your people, O Lord, and make not your heritage a reproach."* (Joel 2:17).[440] There is still time. The door has not closed. The mercy of God still speaks. But the hour grows late, and the shadows lengthen.

The risen Christ addressed the lukewarm church at Laodicea with words that cut through every excuse and exposed every compromise: *"Those whom I love, I reprove and discipline, so be zealous and repent."* (Revelation 3:19).[441] This is love speaking, not the sentimental affirmation the culture demands but the surgical rebuke that cuts away the cancer before it kills the body. The love that warns is the only love that saves; the love that stays silent while souls walk toward hell is no love at all. It is cowardice dressed in the language of compassion, and it produces damnation while promising peace. False compassion kills. True love wounds before it heals, rebukes before it restores, and speaks the hard truth that no one wants to hear but everyone desperately needs.

The trumpet is blown. The voice has cried from the wall. The sword is visible at the gates, and the enemy is advancing. And the question is no longer whether judgment will come. The question is whether the church will repent before judgment falls in its fullness, whether shepherds will finally speak the truth that costs them everything, whether congregations will fall on their faces and confess the compromise that has left them powerless, and whether this generation will choose the fear of God over the approval of man.

The choice remains. But the window is closing. Repent, or perish. Return to the cross or be swept away with the culture that chose rebellion over righteousness. The alarm is sounding. The love that warns is still speaking. But it will not speak forever. The day is coming when the door closes, when mercy withdraws, when the time for repentance ends, and the time for judgment begins in earnest. And on that day, every excuse will be exposed as the lie it always was, and every compromise will be revealed as the betrayal it truly is.

Section IV: Church Without Conviction— How We Got Here

The Church did not fall in a day. It fell silent first. The pulpits went quiet before they went dark. The shepherds stopped warning before they started wandering. And when the sword came, the watchmen were asleep at their posts. Scripture declares the verdict without mercy: *"If the watchman sees the sword coming and does not blow the trumpet so that the people are not warned and the sword comes and takes any one of them, that person is taken away in his iniquity, but his blood I will require at the watchman's hand."* (Ezekiel 33:6).[442] The sword came. The blood is on the watchman's hands. And God will require it.

The 1950s saw the building of churches. The 1960s emptied them of power. The 1970s codified rebellion into law, and pulpits issued statements rather than repentance. When prayer was ripped from the schools in 1962, the Church filed lawsuits instead of falling on its face. When Roe legalized murder in 1973, pastors protected their tax exemptions instead of the unborn.

Fifty million dead. And the shepherds never missed a Sunday service. They preached about God's love while His image-bearers were dismembered in the womb, sang about grace while the blood cried from the ground. The decline did not begin with scandal. It began with silence.

The 1990s turned sanctuaries into theaters. Worship became a product and discipleship became networking. The cross disappeared behind lighting rigs and branding strategies. Pastors became CEOs. Metrics replaced prayer. And the gospel was repackaged to offend no one and save no one. The Church said it was reaching the culture. The culture said the Church had become irrelevant. Both were right. Entire generations walked out the doors not because the Church asked too much but because it asked nothing at all. They were inoculated against the real gospel by a counterfeit that demanded no repentance, required no holiness, and cost nothing but an hour on Sunday morning.

While the Church built empires, the courts built altars to rebellion. Lawrence v. Texas in 2003 declared that sexual autonomy is a constitutional right. Obergefell v. Hodges in 2015 forced every state to recognize same-sex marriage as legitimate. And the Church trembled, not with the fear of God but with the fear of man. Jeremiah stood in the streets and declared, "Amend *your ways and your deeds, and obey the voice of the Lord your God, and the Lord will relent of the disaster that he has pronounced against you.*" (Jeremiah 7:3).[443] The modern Church had no Jeremiahs. It had consultants and strategists and spokesmen who whispered behind closed doors and called it "wisdom." The nation needed prophets who would stand in the gates and declare the word of the Lord. It got entrepreneurs protecting donor bases and politicians in clerical collars.

The Church called its silence wisdom, its cowardice strategy, and its refusal to offend anyone "love." But Scripture declares the truth without apology: when the Church will not name sin, the culture defines righteousness. Isaiah saw this day coming: *"Justice is turned back, and righteousness stands far away; for truth has stumbled in the public squares, and uprightness cannot enter."* (Isaiah 59:14).[444]

Justice turned back. Truth stumbled. And the Church watched from padded pews while singing songs about victory. Not to speak is to speak. Not to act is to act. The silence was a verdict. The cowardice was a choice. And the judgment is falling now.

To leave a nation unwarned is not compassion but cruelty; to leave a congregation comfortable in sin is not ministry but malpractice. Scripture declares without ambiguity: *"The fear of the Lord is the beginning of wisdom."* (Proverbs 9:10).[445] Not the end. Not a side note for the mature. The beginning.

The prophets of Baal had the crowds. They had the funding. They had the king's approval. And Elijah called fire from heaven that consumed them all (1 Kings 18:38-40).[446] Elijah stood alone. But he stood under the authority of heaven. The modern Church has the crowds, the buildings, and the budgets. And the fire does not fall because the altars are defiled.

The enemy walked through the front door under the banner of progress. Progressive theology is not new paganism. It is an old heresy in Christian vocabulary. A God who affirms and never judges. A Christ who saves but never sanctifies, a gospel stripped of the blood, the cross, the fire, the wrath. Paul warned Timothy that this was coming: *"The time is coming when people will not endure sound teaching, but, having itching ears, they will accumulate for themselves teachers to suit their own passions."* (2 Timothy 4:3).[447] The time is here. The teachers fill stadiums and the itching ears applaud. And the cost is visible: entire generations lost to a counterfeit gospel that baptized the culture's rebellion and called it grace. You cannot twist reality without consequence. The Church tried. And the wreckage fills the pews.

The denominations fractured. The United Methodist Church split over whether practicing homosexuality disqualifies one from ordination. The Presbyterian Church USA removed "Father" and "Son" language because it offends. The Episcopal Church ordains what Scripture condemns and excommunicates those who object. The enemy does not need to storm the walls; he was invited in by bishops who confused tolerance with love and surrendered Scripture for a seat at the cultural table. Paul warned that evil people and impostors would go from bad to worse, deceiving and being deceived (2 Timothy 3:13).[448] The deceivers wear robes, hold doctorates, and sit on denominational boards. And they lead sheep to slaughter while claiming to shepherd them to safety.

The Church traded the fear of God for access to power. It made peace with those who hate the Word in exchange for influence. Nathan rebuked David to his face (2 Samuel 12:7).[449] Elijah declared drought over Ahab's kingdom (1 Kings 17:1).[450] John the Baptist called Herod's adultery sin and lost his head for it (Mark 6:18-28).[451] Where are the Nathans today? Where are the Elijahs? Where are the Johns? They whisper in private meetings. They issue carefully worded statements. They refuse to name names. And they call it prudence. Scripture calls it cowardice.

The biblical illiteracy is not an accident. It is a strategy. When the people do not know the Word, they cannot identify the lie. The average Christian quotes influencers more readily than apostles. The average sermon draws more on sociology than on Scripture. The average congregation applauds heresy because it has never been taught orthodoxy. The Book of Judges records what happens when this occurs: *"Everyone did what was right in his own eyes."* (Judges 21:25).[452] That generation had no king. This generation has no Scripture. The result is identical: chaos baptized as freedom, rebellion celebrated as authenticity, and the voice of God drowned out by the roar of the self.

Only 32 percent of evangelical churchgoers read the Bible daily. Twelve percent rarely or never open it.[453] The witness is damning. The Church has abandoned the Word, and the Word has abandoned the Church.

The theological drift produced the moral collapse. The Church stopped preaching sin and calling for repentance, replacing them with celebrations of struggle and affirmations of brokenness. It baptized dysfunction as identity. Sin became a side effect of trauma. Rebellion became self-expression. And holiness became judgmental. The Church lost the ability to discern between right and almost right.[454] It applauds what God condemns. It ordains what Scripture forbids. And it excommunicates those who still believe that God meant what He said.

The devastation is not theoretical. It is measurable. Schools indoctrinate children in ideologies that Scripture calls abominations. Courts legalize what God calls sin and criminalize what God calls righteousness. Corporations enforce conformity to lies more aggressively than governments. Children are sterilized and mutilated in the name of compassion, families shattered in the name of authenticity. And the Church issues statements about unity while the nation burns. Peter declared the line that cannot be crossed: *"We must obey God rather than men."* (Acts 5:29).[455] The Church chose men. The consequences are unfolding in real time.

But God is not silent. He speaks through His Word. He speaks through His Spirit. He speaks through the headlines that scream what the pulpits whisper. The call is not first to politics. It is to repentance. Before America is reformed, the Church must be revived. Before the Church is revived, the Church must be rebuked. The altar must be cleansed before fire falls. Sin must be confessed before power returns. And shepherds must weep before sheep repent.

The question cuts to the heart: is the world crucified to you, or does it fascinate you?[456] The American Church has been fascinated for too long. It chased cultural relevance while the fear of God evaporated. It built platforms while prophets went extinct. It measured success by attendance, while holiness became optional. The time for fascination is over. The time for crucifixion has come. Crucified to the applause of men. Crucified to the approval of the culture. Crucified to every metric that measures success without measuring holiness.

John Knox cried over Scotland: "Give me Scotland, or I die."[457] Where is that cry today? Where is the shepherd who will say, "Give me America in repentance, or I will not sleep"? Where is the prophet who will stand in the gates and declare the word of the Lord without calculating the cost? If the Church will not weep, it is not ready to war. If the pulpits will not tremble, they have no authority to speak. The tears must come first. The fire follows after.

Hope is not a strategy, a coalition, or a bipartisan compromise; it is sackcloth and ashes, fire on the altar, and pulpits trembling under the weight of a holy God. Joel gives the blueprint: *"Blow the trumpet in Zion, consecrate a fast, and call a solemn assembly."* (Joel 2:15).[458] Not a conference. Not a summit. A solemn assembly where elders weep between the porch and the altar and cry out, "Spare your people, O Lord."

This generation is not asleep because it was never warned. It is asleep because it preferred comfort to conviction, dreams to truth, and relevance to righteousness. God is not mocked. He will have a holy Church, or He will have no Church at all. If this generation does not rise with repentance and fire, it will be remembered not as the generation that lost the culture war but as the generation that forfeited the fear of God.

Joshua's ultimatum still stands: *"Choose this day whom you will serve. But as for me and my house, we will serve the Lord."* (Joshua 24:15).[459] Choose. The sword is at the gates. The trumpet has been blown. Revival will not come through comfort. It will come through conviction. The clock is ticking. Heaven is watching. And the verdict is being written.

Section V: The False Gospel of Affirmation

What God calls sin the pulpit now calls identity, and what Scripture names confusion pastors describe as a sacred journey. The transgender teenager is not called to renewal but affirmed in self-perception. The practicing homosexual is not urged toward repentance but embraced without correction. The Church has ripped the gospel in half and called it compassion. Jesus spoke to the woman caught in adultery with words that coupled mercy with truth: *"Neither do I condemn you. Go, and from now on, sin no more."* (John 8:11).[460] The modern Church kept the first half and discarded the second. It offers acceptance without correction, grace without holiness, and compassion without the cross. And in doing so, it becomes not a rescuer but an accomplice to deception.

When churches affirm what God condemns, they do not rescue people from judgment. They escort them toward it. The pulpit has been replaced by the couch, the preacher by a therapist, and the call to die to self by motivational speeches about self-love. But the gospel is not self-help. The gospel is a bloody, offensive declaration that exposes who we are in sin and demands what we cannot produce on our own: *"You must be born again."* (John 3:7).[461] Any message that leaves people comfortable in their rebellion while calling it grace is a lie. Any pastor who refuses to name sin because it might offend is not a shepherd. He is a hireling who runs when the wolf comes.

Secular institutions have enshrined affirmation as a virtue. Public schools teach that affirming gender confusion is loving. Therapists are discouraged, sometimes prohibited, from questioning a child's self-declared identity. Government agencies enforce non-discrimination policies that compel speech and punish dissent. This is not compassion; it is coercion. The state now mandates delusion and calls it progress. And the Church, having surrendered its prophetic voice decades ago, has nothing left to say. It cannot correct the culture because it has been converted by the culture.

The compelled speech that now defines the age is not harmless courtesy; it is a dangerous step toward totalitarianism.[462] When the state demands control over language, it demands control over thought itself. And the devastating witness is visible: those who stand outside the faith see what the Church refuses to acknowledge. This is not a rights movement anymore but cultural domination enforced through law.[463]

Paul warned Timothy that this day would come: *"The time is coming when people will not endure sound teaching, but, having itching ears, they will accumulate for themselves teachers to suit their own passions."* (2 Timothy 4:3).[464] That time has arrived. The marketplace is saturated with teachers who preach empathy without repentance, inclusion without transformation, and love without truth. Pastors craft sermons to fit emotional sensibilities and test their messages for cultural palatability rather than spiritual obedience or biblical fidelity. And the congregations applaud because the false gospel makes no demands and costs nothing.

If Jesus had preached the same message that modern ministers preach today, He would never have been crucified.[465] He was executed not for being kind but for exposing evil. He confronted the Pharisees. He overturned tables. He pronounced woes over cities. He told the rich young ruler to sell everything. He declared that unless you eat His flesh and drink His blood, you have no life in you. The true gospel wounded pride before it healed souls. It offended before it saved. The affirmation gospel bypasses the offense entirely. It tells sinners they are fine as they are, that God loves them unconditionally, and that Jesus died so they could be comfortable. This is not the gospel of Christ; it is the gospel of self.

The Church's mission has never been to make sinners comfortable. It has been to make them new. Jesus did not die to affirm humanity as it is. He died to transform humanity into what it is not. Paul declares without ambiguity, "*If anyone is in Christ, he is a new creation. The old has passed away; behold, the new has come.*" (2 Corinthians 5:17).[466] The progressive gospel cannot preach this because it requires confronting sin as sin. It requires telling people that their identity is not found in their desires but in the image of God stamped on their souls and marred by the fall. It requires declaring that the way they see themselves is not the final word, that God's Word is the final word, and that His Word calls them to repentance.

The theology of affirmation has infected even the language of justice. Rather than standing on God's character, Scripture declares plainly, *"Righteousness and justice are the foundation of your throne"* (Psalm 89:14)[467] — pastors now preach a cultural gospel of equity that demands equal outcomes without equal accountability. Biblical justice is rooted in truth, and truth by its nature divides. It separates light from darkness, sheep from goats, and wheat from tares. When justice is filtered through the lens of affirmation, it ceases to be justice; it becomes sentiment. And sentiment saves no one.

The progressive gospel does not silence dissent through argument. It silences dissent through emotional manipulation. It is not anchored in Scripture but in emotionalism; it appeals to the crowd, not to the cross. It thrives in environments where feelings are exalted and conviction is condemned. Jesus' first public message was not "you are enough" or "God accepts you just as you are." His first message was this: *"Repent, for the kingdom of heaven is at hand."* (Matthew 4:17).[468] The kingdom demands repentance. It demands surrender. It demands death to the old self. The affirmation gospel offers none of this. It baptizes the old self, celebrates the old desires and calls the refusal to change "authenticity."

The devastation is measurable. Entire denominations are collapsing under the weight of compromise.[469] Seminaries produce life coaches who are fluent in therapy but illiterate in theology. Churches that wave rainbow flags and host pronoun workshops are imploding from within. Attendance is dropping. Giving is declining. The next generation is walking out the doors. And the shepherds stand in their empty sanctuaries, wondering what went wrong.

What went wrong is this: sinners drowning in guilt do not need affirmation. They need salvation. They do not need to be told they are fine but that they are dying, and there is a Savior who can rescue them, but only if they repent and believe.

The Church's task has never been to catch the spirit of the age. The Church's task is to correct it.[470] But the modern Church has been catechized by influencers, discipled by algorithms, and evangelized by activists. It has absorbed the culture's definitions and baptized them with Christian language. Love without truth is not love; it is sentimentality. It attracts crowds, but it cannot create disciples. It fills auditoriums, but it does not fill heaven. And when the day of judgment comes, every person who was affirmed in their sin while being told that God loved them too much to demand repentance will stand before the throne and realize they were lied to by the people who claimed to love them most.

Affirmation is not the gospel. The gospel is confrontation followed by invitation. The gospel exposes who we are in our sin, and then it calls us to become what we could never be apart from Christ. One message says, "You are perfect just as you are." The other says, "Come and die." One leaves people in their sin with a smile on their face. The other pulls them out of their sin with a cross on their back, and only one is the gospel of Jesus Christ.

The Church must not think of itself as a hospital where the sick are made comfortable while they die; it is a rescue station where sinners are saved.[471] The progressive gospel has transformed the Church into a hospice for the spiritually dead, offering comfort instead of cure, validation instead of transformation. Affirmations are like anesthesia; they numb the pain while the disease progresses. But the Great Physician did not come to numb. He came to heal. And healing requires surgery. It requires cutting away the cancer of sin: pain before relief, death before resurrection, and repentance before restoration.

The great deception of this age is not that it rejects the gospel outright. The great deception is that it offers a counterfeit gospel that looks Christian, sounds compassionate, and promises peace but delivers none of these things. It is a gospel without the cross, love without sacrifice, and compassion that refuses to offend, not the gospel of Christ but the gospel of self, and it spreads not because the world is bold but because the Church is silent. The culture has perfected love-bombing: any correction is labeled hate, any disagreement is called harm, and any call to repentance is dismissed as violence. And the Church, having lost its nerve, bows to the mob and calls its cowardice wisdom.

Jesus declared a hard truth: *"Blessed is the one who is not offended by me."* (Matthew 11:6).[472] The real Jesus will always offend sin, especially the kinds of sin that the world seeks to baptize as identity. The society that redefines sin as identity and love as affirmation will inevitably label the gospel harmful and the Word of God hateful. This is not new. The prophets were stoned. The apostles were executed. Jesus was crucified. And He warned His disciples that the same fate awaited them. The offense of the cross has not been removed; it has only been repackaged by false teachers who promise peace where there is no peace and offer grace that costs nothing because it saves no one.

But God is still on the throne. He still calls sin what it is. He still extends mercy to the repentant and judgment to the rebellious. He still sends prophets to declare truth even when the truth is rejected. And He still speaks through His Word with clarity that cannot be negotiated: *"Return to me, and I will return to you."* (Malachi 3:7).[473] The door is not closed. The invitation still stands. But the invitation demands a response. It demands repentance. It demands faith. It demands surrender.

Love does not affirm what destroys. Love rescues. Love confronts. Love tells the hard truth even when the truth costs everything. Any gospel that leaves people enslaved to sin while calling it grace is a lie. Any message that removes the offense of the cross to gain cultural approval is apostasy. Any pastor who refuses to speak the truth because it might cost him his platform is a coward, not a shepherd. The Church must reclaim the prophetic voice. It must reestablish biblical compassion. It must reject the lie that love means silence and affirm what Scripture has always taught: love tells the truth, no matter the cost.

Mark records the first public words of Jesus with precision: *"The time is fulfilled, and the kingdom of God is at hand; repent and believe in the gospel."* (Mark 1:15).[474] Repent and believe. Not affirm and accommodate. Not celebrate and include. Repent and believe. Anything less than this is a betrayal of the gospel and a betrayal of the souls Christ died to save. The remnant will stand. The gates of hell will not prevail against the Church that belongs to Christ. But that Church will not be the one waving rainbow flags and hosting pronoun workshops. It will be the Church that preaches the whole counsel of God, calls sin what it is, and declares with unshakable conviction the following: Jesus Christ is Lord. Repent and believe. The hour is late. The world does not need our approval; it needs our witness. And the witness is ancient and unchanged: repent and believe. There is no other way.

CONVICTION IN ACTION
"Love Redefined"

Chapter 5: The Hijacking of Compassion

CONVICTION

Love has been hijacked, stripped of holiness, and weaponized as affirmation. When the Church trades truth-telling, soul-rescuing agapē for validation that leaves people enslaved to sin, we do not show compassion; we escort souls toward judgment, and we will answer to God for every person we affirmed into destruction instead of calling to repentance.

REALITY CHECK

The word "love" has been redefined to mean approval without correction and celebration without conviction. And the Church, terrified of being called hateful, surrendered. We offer grace without repentance, compassion without the cross, and acceptance without transformation. We have become accomplices to deception, baptizing rebellion as identity and calling our cowardice love. But Jesus did not die so sinners could stay comfortable in their sin. He died to set them free.

FAITHFULNESS NOW LOOKS LIKE

Personal: Stop calling affirmation "love." Love tells the truth even when the truth wounds. If someone you know is trapped in sin or confusion, love them enough to speak, not with cruelty but with clarity. Silence is not neutrality; it is partnership with the lie.

Church: Demand that your church preach the whole gospel, including repentance, holiness, and the offense of the cross. If your pastor speaks only of God's love without calling sin what it is, he has already offended God. Support ministries that preach transformation, not affirmation.

Public: The world does not need the Church to sound like the world; it needs the Church to sound like God. Refuse workplace mandates to celebrate what God forbids. Stand firm when the culture calls correction "hate." The cost will be real. Pay it.

COMMITMENTS

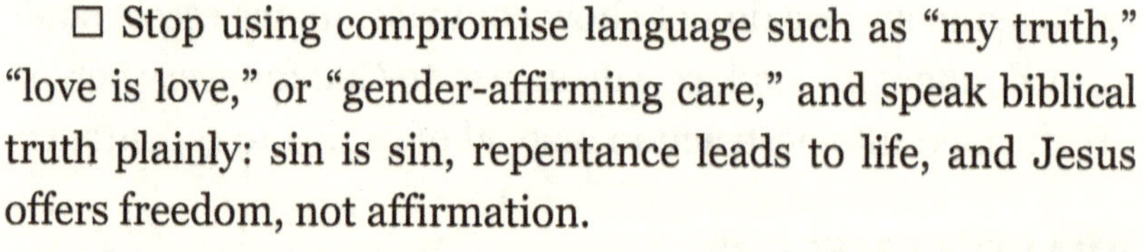

☐ Stop using compromise language such as "my truth," "love is love," or "gender-affirming care," and speak biblical truth plainly: sin is sin, repentance leads to life, and Jesus offers freedom, not affirmation.

☐ Have one conversation this week with someone who needs to hear the truth, whether trapped in sin, confused about identity, or celebrating rebellion. Speak with clarity, and trust that real love confronts.

☐ Examine your own life for areas where you've chosen cultural approval over biblical obedience, stayed silent to avoid conflict, or affirmed what God condemns. Confess and repent.

☐ Ask your pastor or church leaders directly: Does this church preach repentance? Does it call sin what Scripture calls sin? If the answer is evasive or cowardly, demand accountability or find a church with conviction.

PRAYER

Lord Jesus, forgive me for calling cowardice compassion. Forgive me for choosing comfort over truth, for valuing approval over obedience, for staying silent when You commanded me to speak. Break my heart for what breaks

Yours. Give me love that tells the truth even when the truth brings rejection. Give me the courage to stand when everyone else bows. Raise up shepherds who fear You more than they fear man, who preach repentance without compromise and who call sin what You call sin. Set captives free from the chains that hold them while they're told they're fine. On the day I stand before You, let it be said that I loved people enough to warn them. Amen.

Chapter 6: Jesus Wasn't a Socialist, And the Bible Isn't a Welfare Manifesto

Section I: The Lie of Holy Redistribution

The progressive movement has not misunderstood Jesus; it has rebranded Him. It has taken the King of Kings and repackaged Him into a political mascot, a moral prop, and a state-sponsored caseworker who exists to validate grievances and sanctify redistribution. The biblical Christ confronts sin, commands repentance, warns of judgment, and calls men to die to self and live under His lordship. *"The time is fulfilled, and the kingdom of God is at hand; repent and believe in the gospel."* (Mark 1:15).[475] But the counterfeit Christ of modern politics is presented as a compassionate administrator, a benevolent manager of outcomes, and a symbol invoked to justify programs that weaken households and transfer moral responsibility upward into bureaucracy. This is not a minor theological misunderstanding. It is a rival gospel that offers comfort without conversion, entitlement without obedience, and provision without repentance.

It does not propose a different way to help the poor; it proposes a different god.

This lie is persuasive because it mimics biblical compassion while quietly severing it from biblical holiness. Scripture commands mercy, but it never treats mercy as a substitute for righteousness. Scripture commands care for the vulnerable, but it never makes the state the shepherd of the soul. Scripture dignifies the poor, but it does not flatter them into dependence or train them into identity-based victimhood. The welfare gospel does exactly that. It replaces the categories of stewardship, self-government, repentance, and disciplined generosity with new categories: access, entitlement, outcome, grievance, and state protection. The Church must understand what is being smuggled in. This is not compassion with a budget. This is catechesis with a ballot. It is formation through policy, a rival liturgy of security where the citizen learns to look to Washington as provider, protector, and vindicator.

The core distortion is a category error. Charity and coercion are not the same category; compassion and compulsion are not the same moral act. Biblical mercy is personal, voluntary, accountable, and aimed at restoration. It flows from worship, from love of God, and from love of neighbor. It is expressed through a giver who chooses to give and a recipient who is treated as a soul, not a statistic. State redistribution is impersonal by design. It is extracted under threat of penalty and administered through layers of anonymous authority. It may move money but not hearts, compel payment but not love.

That is why the Church must stop repeating the propaganda that taxation is charity and that bureaucratic transfers are Christian compassion. The Bible never calls the state to replace the Church's calling. The Bible calls the state to punish evildoers and reward good, not to become priest, provider, and savior. *"For rulers are not a terror to good conduct but to bad."* (Romans 13:3).[476] When the state presents itself as moral redeemer, it trespasses beyond its God-ordained lane.

This is where the biblical architecture must be rebuilt in the minds of believers. God designed man for stewardship, not entitlement. Work is not an evil to be eliminated by policy but a calling that forms maturity, restraint, competence, and dignity. *"The Lord God took the man and put him in the garden of Eden to work it and keep it."* (Genesis 2:15).[477] Before the fall, there was assignment. Before suffering, there was responsibility. A society that trains its people to expect a harvest without sowing is training them to despise the dignity God has embedded in human life. Scripture does not present labor as a cruel burden to be abolished by "progress." Scripture presents labor as one of the primary ways God forms men into providers, builders, and givers.

Therefore, Scripture is explicit about provision and responsibility. *"If anyone is not willing to work, let him not eat."* (2 Thessalonians 3:10).[478] That is not cruelty. It is moral clarity. It is a boundary against chaos because idleness corrodes the soul and dependency breeds spiritual childishness. The modern welfare gospel treats this clarity as harshness because it cannot survive responsibility. It must call responsibility "harm" to justify entitlement. But Scripture presses toward quiet self-governance, honorable labor, and disciplined independence that frees a person to give rather than to grasp. *"Aspire to live quietly, and to mind your own affairs, and to work with your hands… so that you may walk properly before outsiders and be dependent on no one."* (1 Thessalonians 4:11–12).[479] That is not a libertarian slogan. That is biblical order.

Alongside work, Scripture affirms private property and stewardship as moral realities. The Bible never treats wealth as inherently righteous, but it consistently treats theft, envy, covetousness, and coercion as moral evils. *"You shall not steal."* (Exodus 20:15).[480] *"You shall not covet… anything that is your neighbor's."* (Exodus 20:17).[481] The welfare gospel attempts to bypass these commands by renaming covetous desire as justice and by renaming coercive taking as compassion. But the moral substance does not change because the vocabulary changes. If a transfer is forced, it is not charity; if compelled, it is not generosity. That does not mean the poor are ignored. It means the poor are helped in a way that preserves dignity, restores order, and calls all parties to righteousness.

Scripture's mercy structures demonstrate how God cares for the vulnerable without dissolving responsibility or centralizing control. The gleaning laws are a direct rebuke to entitlement ideology. God commanded landowners to leave the edges of their fields so the poor could gather with effort and dignity. *"You shall not reap your field right up to its edge... you shall leave them for the poor and for the sojourner."* (Leviticus 23:22).[482] This is mercy, but it is not infantilizing. The poor were not treated as passive recipients. They were granted access, not entitlement. They were invited into labor. They were preserved from starvation without being trained into dependence. This is what government welfare often fails to do. It transfers resources while weakening the habits and structures that produce long-term stability.

The same architecture appears in the local provision model embedded in Israel's covenant life. *"At the end of every three years you shall bring out all the tithe of your produce... and the Levite... and the sojourner, the fatherless, and the widow... shall come and eat and be filled."* (Deuteronomy 14:28–29).[483] Notice what is absent: a distant imperial bureaucracy. Provision was local, accountable, and relational. It was administered in proximity where elders knew households, where exploitation could be confronted, where discipline and restoration could be taught, and where help could be paired with shepherding. This was not a welfare empire. It was a covenant of mercy with moral oversight.

Jubilee is often weaponized by modern ideologues as if it were a divine endorsement of enforced equality and perpetual redistribution. Jubilee was not Marxism with Bible verses. Jubilee preserved families and restrained permanent generational dispossession, reminding Israel that land belonged to God and that covenant life required restraint, mercy, and order. *"You shall hallow the fiftieth year and proclaim liberty throughout the land to all its inhabitants."* (Leviticus 25:10).[484] Jubilee did not abolish private property; it presupposed it. Jubilee did not erase responsibility; it reinforced it. Jubilee was not the worship of equality; it was the worship of God's ownership and God's mercy within God's boundaries.

The modern welfare gospel reverses these structures. It extracts resources impersonally, distributes them through distant systems, and often does so without proximity, accountability, or discipleship. It can keep someone alive while leaving them spiritually and socially unformed. It can provide sustenance while training resentment. It can reduce immediate pain while deepening long-term collapse.

Scripture never separates provision from formation. Scripture never treats money as salvation. Scripture never treats the state as a redeemer. It is the Church that is commanded to carry burdens, to disciple the idle, to confront sin, to restore households, and to care for the vulnerable in truth. This is why the misuse of Christ's miracles as political precedent is so destructive. When Jesus fed the multitudes, He did not legislate a redistribution scheme. He did not assign Caesar a moral mandate. He placed responsibility on His disciples. *"You give them something to eat."* (Matthew 14:16).[485] The command is direct. It is personal and non-delegable. The welfare gospel preaches the opposite: that love is primarily expressed through state expansion, through budgets, through administrative programs, through transfers that require no relationship and no repentance. That is not the Church becoming the hands and feet of Christ. That is the Church outsourcing her mission and then applauding the state for doing what she abandoned.

At the root of this surrender is a failure of allegiance. Christ does not share His glory with bureaucracies. The Church is not called to be the lobbying arm of the welfare state. The Church is called to be the pillar and buttress of truth, the household of God, and the community where mercy is practiced under holiness. *"You are... the church of the living God, a pillar and buttress of the truth."* (1 Timothy 3:15).[486] When the Church trades that calling for political comfort, she loses her prophetic voice. When she baptizes coercion as charity, she corrupts both. When she allows Christ to be rebranded as a political mascot, she invites judgment for her compromise. *"Judgment begins at the household of God."* (1 Peter 4:17).[487]

This is where the Church must reassert the biblical principle that the state is not commanded to be savior. Compassion is commanded to individuals, families, and congregations as a fruit of worship. That is why Scripture emphasizes the household as a first line of responsibility. *"If anyone does not provide for his relatives... he has denied the faith and is worse than an unbeliever."* (1 Timothy 5:8).[488] That verse does not flatter excuses. It demands order and responsibility. It makes the family accountable. When the state attempts to replace the father, the household, and the Church, it is not "helping." It is displacing God's design.

Now, policy examples must be bounded, but they matter because they reveal how the counterfeit gospel expresses itself in law. The Equality Act is not a cultural statement. In its introduced form, it explicitly limits the application of the Religious Freedom Restoration Act as a claim or defense in contexts covered by the Act, increasing pressure on faith-based institutions.[489] When law begins to treat Christian conscience as a problem to be neutralized, the argument is no longer about legislative preference. It is about who is permitted to define righteousness and who is permitted to live publicly as a Christian. Once the state becomes moral arbiter, it will not remain content to distribute money. It will demand conformity.

Universal Basic Income represents a different theological signal. UBI, by definition, tends toward unconditional provision with minimal eligibility criteria, intentionally loosening the link between work and receipt.[490] The issue is not that Christians oppose helping the poor. The issue is that policy increasingly normalizes the idea that provision should be detached from responsibility, that productivity is optional, and that consequences must be softened by design. That is not economics. That is moral formation. It teaches citizens to see provision as entitlement, not as stewardship. It encourages a culture of demanding rather than building.

The American Rescue Plan's changes to the child tax credit structure and payments for 2021 illustrate the same detachment pressure. The ARPA expansion increased amounts and made the credit fully refundable, including for households with low or no earnings, and it was paid in periodic installments beginning in mid-2021.[491] Again, the point here is not to deny that families struggle or that children matter. The point is that policy often moves toward structuring provision as a right divorced from the formative discipline of work and responsibility. When a society systematically weakens the link between labor and provision, it weakens the habits that sustain a civilization.

The same pressure is visible in the unemployment insurance expansions and replacement rate dynamics of the pandemic era. ARPA extended and modified unemployment insurance components, including supplemental benefits.[492] Research on replacement rates during the pandemic estimated that expanded benefits produced replacement rates that, for many workers, exceeded 100 percent of prior wages, with warnings that such replacement rates may hinder labor reallocation.[493] The Church should not treat these issues as irrelevant to discipleship. Incentives form behavior. Behavior forms character. Character forms households. Households form nations. When incentives consistently reward non-work more than work, they train dependence, and dependence becomes political leverage.

This is where the moral architecture must be stated plainly. A system that systematically detaches provision from responsibility is not neutral. It catechizes and teaches, forming a people who expect a provider other than God and who look to institutions rather than to covenant structures for security. Scripture warns nations that shift trust from God to human systems. *"Woe to those who go down to Egypt for help... but do not look to the Holy One of Israel."* (Isaiah 31:1).[494] The problem is not horses versus chariots in the modern sense. The problem is misplaced trust. When citizens learn to ask the state for daily bread, they will also learn to fear the state as the one who can withhold it.

This is not a new human temptation. Israel demanded a king to outsource risk and responsibility to centralized power. *"Give us a king... that he may go out before us and fight our battles."* (1 Samuel 8:20).[495] God warned them that the cost would be heavy: taxation, conscription, and loss of liberty. Their demand was not political. It was spiritual. It was a transfer of trust away from God's governance. The modern welfare gospel repeats the same exchange with different vocabulary. Instead of asking for a king to fight battles, the nation asks for a state to solve suffering, to guarantee provision, and to neutralize consequences. The cost is always the same: coercion, dependency, and the slow erosion of self-government.

The Church must recover moral clarity about what mercy is and what it is not. John Chrysostom did not treat compassion as a justification for coercion; he treated generosity as a matter of repentance before God: "Not to share one's goods with the poor is to rob them."[496] That is not an argument for Caesar to seize property. It is an indictment of the heart, a rebuke of self-worship, and a reminder that refusal to give is not a budgeting decision; it is a moral failure that God sees and judges.

And this is where the root issue returns: the God being preached determines the obedience being demanded. When the Church tolerates a softened Christ, it will inevitably tolerate a softened morality. A. W. Tozer exposes the fault line with a single sentence that demolishes theological laziness: "What comes into our minds when we think about God is the most important thing about us."[497] If Christ is reduced into a mascot for modern politics, then the Church will also reduce His commands, His warnings, His demands, and His authority until He can be safely used rather than feared and obeyed.

Dietrich Bonhoeffer names the spiritual mechanism that makes the welfare gospel attractive: it offers moral comfort without crucifixion, compassion without conversion, and benefits without obedience. He calls it what it is: "Cheap grace is grace without discipleship, grace without the cross."[498] That principle applies beyond private piety. Once a culture is trained to believe that provision must be unconditional, that consequences must be eliminated, and that authority must be centralized to guarantee outcomes, it becomes spiritually allergic to the cross-shaped life. It rejects discipline as oppression and repentance as harm because cheap grace cannot survive holiness.

This is why the Church must stop surrendering its mission to the illusion of social management. Francis Schaeffer warned that a people can be trained to want comfort above truth and to treat stability as the highest good: "Personal peace means wanting to have my personal life pattern undisturbed in my lifetime."[499] When that desire governs a nation, it will accept almost any arrangement that promises relief from hardship, even if the cost is moral clarity, liberty, responsibility, and the fear of God. The welfare gospel becomes plausible in precisely that climate, because it offers the appearance of mercy while discipling the public into dependence.

The Church must stop pretending that these are disconnected issues. The question is not whether Christians should care for the poor. Christians must care for the poor, the widow, the orphan, the sojourner, and the oppressed. *"Religion that is pure and undefiled before God... is this: to visit orphans and widows in their affliction."* (James 1:27).[500] The question is whether Christians will care for them God's way or man's way. God's way preserves dignity, requires responsibility and ties mercy to truth. Man's way often replaces discipleship with distribution, holiness with sentimentality, and covenant care with impersonal transfers.

God's mercy does not bypass formation. Even suffering, in some cases, becomes a teacher that drives repentance and wisdom. *"Before I was afflicted, I went astray, but now I keep your word."* (Psalm 119:67).[501] That does not mean we leave people to starve. It means we refuse to lie about what heals. The welfare gospel attempts to eliminate discomfort as if discomfort were always injustice. Scripture teaches that discomfort can sometimes be discipline, sometimes mercy, and sometimes correction. A system that indiscriminately eliminates consequences does not eliminate pain. It eliminates learning.

It eliminates the very conditions under which repentance often occurs, preserving bodies while leaving souls uncorrected.

The lie of holy redistribution also collapses the moral distinction between help that restores and help that enables. Scripture commands generosity, but it never commands enabling. Scripture commands mercy, but it never sanctifies disorder. The welfare gospel must blur these lines because it cannot survive them. It must call discernment "harm." It must call correction "oppression." It must call responsibility "cruelty." But in the biblical worldview, responsibility is not cruelty. Responsibility is mercy because it aligns a person with reality. It aligns them with God's order. It trains them into the kind of maturity that can build, provide, and give.

This is why the Church cannot remain silent. When Christ is rebranded, the Church must testify. When coercion is baptized as compassion, the Church must distinguish. When policy becomes theology, the Church must preach. When the state moves from punishing evil to defining virtue, the Church must resist. The issue here is not partisan. It is covenantal. It is about lordship. It is about whether Christ is King in public truth or only tolerated as a private symbol while Caesar sets the moral terms.

So the lie must be stated and rejected. The welfare gospel is a counterfeit kingdom. It promises bread while weakening souls. It promises justice while undermining righteousness. It promises compassion while dissolving responsibility. It offers a rival savior, a rival priesthood, and a rival moral order that recodes envy as virtue and coercion as love.

The Church must not applaud, sanctify, or outsource her mission to this. Christ did not die to create a managed society. Christ died to redeem a people, to form stewards, to establish His kingdom, and to call nations to righteousness. He calls His people to work, to build, to give, to disciple, to restore households, and to practice mercy in truth. The Church must recover covenant mercy, local responsibility, and disciplined generosity under the lordship of Christ. Otherwise, the state will continue to fill the vacuum, and it will not fill it with holiness. It will fill it with control.

Here is the handoff that must be made. Once redistribution is baptized as "love," the next step is inevitable. Compassion becomes a lever of compliance. A people trained to receive will be trained to fear the one who provides. A Church that praises Caesar's programs will eventually be tempted to mute Caesar's sins. That is where the chapter must go next: not more policy debate, but the mechanism that follows the lie. If holy redistribution is accepted as a moral good, then "compassion" will be used to purchase obedience, silence dissent, and discipline institutions into conformity. That is not a future threat. It is the predictable fruit of a rival gospel. And it is why the Church must repent of outsourcing mercy and return to obedience under the King.

Section II: When Compassion Becomes Control

Compassion becomes control when provision is converted into leverage and then baptized as morality. The transfer rarely begins with open coercion. It begins with a promise to manage suffering, remove instability, and guarantee a baseline of security. The posture feels humane, even righteous, because it borrows the moral vocabulary of mercy while quietly relocating the seat of authority. The decisive shift is not first economic; it is jurisdictional. When the provider is centralized, the power to grant becomes the power to condition, and the power to condition becomes the power to command.

The arrangement trains a public instinct: look upward for deliverance, calibrate speech to preserve benefits, and suppress dissent to remain eligible. That is why the conflict cannot be reduced to budgets. The machinery works on the conscience. *"For the Lord is the Spirit, and where the Spirit of the Lord is, there is freedom."* (2 Corinthians 3:17).[502] Freedom is not the absence of a chain; it is the spiritual condition in which the conscience answers to God as ultimate judge, and obedience is rendered willingly rather than extracted by fear. Once a society normalizes centralized provision as the primary form of "care," it normalizes centralized moral authority as the primary definition of "good."

Hayek warned that the planned redistribution of outcomes does not remain a technical exercise, because planners must decide whose needs count, whose claims are legitimate, and whose resistance is intolerable.[503] If the state must guarantee results, the state must also govern the conditions that produce results. And if the state governs conditions, it eventually governs the behaviors, incentives, and social narratives that shape those conditions. That is how benevolence becomes an administrative project, and administration becomes a discipline mechanism. The soft beginning does not prevent the hard end. It delays recognition until dependence is already entrenched.

The leverage is not created only by the existence of aid but also by the way aid can be structured to create moral dependence alongside material dependence. Once a system becomes the stabilizing center, it becomes psychologically central. People begin to treat access as a matter of survival, and survival instincts quietly reshape speech. Eligibility requirements, whatever their initial intentions, create a category of the "deserving" and the "undeserving," and that category quickly becomes moralized. The system acquires the power to reward public agreement, penalize public resistance, and normalize the expectation that citizens must demonstrate alignment to remain "in good standing." The chain is not visible at first. It is first internal.

Control accelerates when language is recoded so that dissent can be treated as harm. The most successful systems do not first argue their opponents into silence; they rename the opposition into moral disgrace. Orwell observed that political language is designed to make certain things sound virtuous while making resistance sound vicious so that the public conscience can be guided without ever being persuaded.[504] When "compassion" becomes the master term, refusal can be framed as violence, skepticism as cruelty, and moral disagreement as a threat. The shift does not require mass arrests. It requires moral vocabulary that narrows what can be said without penalty. In that world, the most dangerous act is not theft; it is clarity. *"Woe to those who call evil good and good evil, who put darkness for light and light for darkness."* (Isaiah 5:20).[505] The curse falls on inversion: the replacement of God's categories with counterfeit categories that perform righteousness while corroding truth.

The new moral order is not announced as rebellion. It is announced as "empathy." It is not sold as domination. It is sold as safety. Once "harm" is defined as offense against the system's moral framework, the system can punish dissent while claiming moral purity. A penalty becomes a "protective measure." Exclusion becomes "accountability." Compelled vocabulary becomes "inclusion." Public conformity becomes "values alignment." The language does not describe reality; it constructs the permitted boundaries of reality. That is why moral recoding is not a side issue. It is the gateway through which coercion masquerades as care.

This is also why modern ideological systems fight so aggressively over definitions. Helen Pluckrose and James Lindsay describe how activist moral frameworks can repurpose ordinary words into boundary markers so that disagreement is treated less like debate and more like moral contamination.[506] If the public can be trained to treat dissent as danger, then punishment can be recast as protection, and coercion can be recast as kindness. The vocabulary becomes the first gate. Once the gate is in place, people begin policing themselves long before they are policed by institutions.

When moral recoding succeeds, administrative righteousness replaces repentance as the primary public virtue. The system does not ask whether a thing is true; it asks whether it aligns. It does not ask whether an action is holy; it asks whether it is compliant. That substitution is the essence of modern control because it creates a righteousness that can be audited and enforced. Trueman's diagnosis of the modern self explains why this approach is effective: when the moral center shifts from objective truth to subjective authenticity and social recognition, institutions gain power by controlling recognition.[507] Watkin frames the same crisis as a contest of stories and moral worlds.[508] In a compliance regime, the "story" is enforced through policy, training, credentialing, and the surveillance of speech. This is why paperwork can become spiritual pressure. It trains people to perform allegiance rather than practice truth.

"Why, as if you were still alive in the world, do you submit to regulations... according to human precepts and teachings?" (Colossians 2:20–22).[509] The warning is not that every rule is evil; it is that human regulations can claim a spiritual weight they do not possess, presenting themselves as wisdom while binding conscience.

Administrative righteousness thrives because it feels clean. It removes moral judgment from the messy arena of confession, restitution, and reconciliation and replaces it with certifications, audits, and compliance artifacts. Once a culture can "score" goodness, it can punish "badness" without ever naming sin. The system becomes a counterfeit tribunal: it declares what is acceptable, demands the performance of acceptance, and disciplines those who refuse to perform. And because the mechanism is procedural, the enforcers can claim innocence: they are not judging; they are "just following policy." That phrase becomes the modern absolution.

This substitution also scales. Large systems prefer paperwork to pastoral care, metrics to moral formation, and standardized procedures to the slow work of forming hearts. That is why this style of righteousness grows by default: it is measurable, enforceable, and transferable, easily centralized, franchised, and automated across institutions. It can expand under the cover of neutrality even when it functions as moral law. A society can become highly regulated while still claiming that nobody is "imposing values," because the imposition is embedded in forms, trainings, and institutional thresholds rather than in sermons and statements.

The regime deepens when enforcement is distributed across institutions so that the coercion becomes ambient. Dreher's account of soft totalitarianism is not the image of tanks in the streets; it is the quiet construction of a world where ordinary life is gated through ideological conformity.[510] The threat is rarely prison first. The threat is loss of livelihood, stalled advancement, reputational exile, and professional immobility. The logic is repeated everywhere: comply to keep access. The fear that governs is not always fear of violence; it is fear of being labeled, fear of being excluded, and fear of being made unemployable. *"The fear of man lays a snare, but whoever trusts in the Lord is safe."* (Proverbs 29:25).[511] A snare does not announce itself as a snare; it presents itself as a reasonable compromise, a small accommodation, a minor rephrasing, or a harmless pledge. Then the snare tightens.

Distributed enforcement makes the tightening nearly invisible, because no single actor appears to be the tyrant. HR can claim it is "just policy." Finance can claim it is "just risk management." Licensing can claim it is "just standards." Procurement can claim it is "just compliance." The effect is the same: conscience is pressured from every side until silence feels like the only affordable posture. In that environment, dissent becomes expensive not because it is disproven but because it is punished. The person learns that even if the law permits speech, the ecosystem can still price speech out of reach.

This pressure is amplified when the language of fiduciary duty and institutional prudence becomes a justification for the enforcement of values. Modern control often does not frame itself as moral domination. It frames itself as responsible governance. A system can say it is not policing beliefs; it is protecting stakeholders. It can say it is not enforcing ideology; it is ensuring prudence. The Department of Labor's rulemaking on fiduciary behavior and shareholder rights illustrates how governance language can shape the acceptable boundaries of institutional action and how "prudence" can become a lever that encourages certain frameworks and discourages others.[512] The point is not to litigate every clause of rulemaking. The point is to identify the mechanism: when institutions are compelled to treat moral frameworks as compliance requirements, conscience is indirectly pressured through policy architecture.

In a distributed system, pressure rarely needs to be explicit. It needs to be legible: the person knows what must be affirmed to remain in good standing. *There is only one lawgiver and judge, he who is able to save and to destroy. But who are you to judge your neighbor?"* (James 4:12).[513] Scripture does not deny human authority. It denies any system the right to enthrone itself as the ultimate moral lawgiver over conscience. Administrative systems drift into moral adjudication because they must decide what counts as "harm," what counts as "safety," what counts as "acceptable speech," and what counts as "misconduct." Once those definitions detach from God's categories, they become tools of domination dressed in the robes of responsibility.

The same logic operates in benefits structures that quietly punish virtue and reward dependency. Assistance can be designed in a way that discourages work without ever condemning work. It can be designed so that marginal advancement sharply reduces support, making progress feel like a betrayal of one's household. The cliff becomes a trainer. People learn to step back from it. In such systems, dependency is not a byproduct; it becomes the stable base of governance. Guidance documents that govern unemployment expansions and emergency programs reveal how quickly temporary measures can normalize new expectations and how official structures can scale a dependency posture under crisis logic.[514] That is not a claim about motives; it is a claim about incentives.

Once a society trains citizens to treat provision as a right detached from responsibility, the provider becomes central in the citizen's psychological world, and what is central becomes powerful. Lupton warns that aid can become toxic when it undermines dignity and agency.[515] Corbett and Fikkert describe how helping can harm when it replaces empowerment with dependency and subtly distorts relationships into patronage.[516] Olasky's history of American compassion reinforces the pattern: compassion can be transformed into impersonal machinery that weakens moral formation while presenting itself as humane.[517] *"Whatever does not proceed from faith is sin."* (Romans 14:23).[518] If faith is required for righteousness, then coerced behavior or dependency-conditioned behavior cannot be treated as holiness. A system can move money and still degrade souls, feed bodies and still train the posture of fear, entitlement, grievance, and resignation.

Control grows not only through benefits and standards but also through the construction of gates that require visible allegiance. The first gate is vocabulary: approved words and forbidden words. The second gate is credentialing: training modules, required affirmations, and certification rituals. The third gate is participation: pledges, public declarations, and mandatory statements. The fourth gate is reputation: a constant threat of denunciation if one speaks plainly. The Heritage report's treatment of ESG and DEI frameworks is useful precisely because it describes how scorecards and standards can be tied to institutional decisions and economic opportunity, allowing ideology to be enforced without ever admitting it is ideology.[519]

Vivek Ramaswamy's account of corporate activism is also useful on this point, as it highlights how "values" are operationalized into managerial machinery.[520] Standards become benchmarks, benchmarks become internal controls, and internal controls become external leverage as firms compete for access to capital, contracts, and reputational legitimacy. The mechanism is straightforward: quantify values, link values to access, and then claim the denial of access is merely "consequence." Once gates exist, people begin to self-censor before they are censored. They learn to speak in sanctioned terms, avoid forbidden truths, and trade conviction for employability.

"If anyone thinks he is religious and does not bridle his tongue but deceives his heart, this person's religion is worthless." (James 1:26).[521] The warning is not that all restraint is cowardice; it is that deception can hide under the pretense of piety. A culture that demands compelled silence is not teaching wisdom; it is training hypocrisy. And hypocrisy is the fertile soil where control thrives, because hypocrites are easily managed. They have already agreed to trade truth for safety. They also become dependent on the system's approval, because their public identity is now built on compliance rather than on integrity.

Once gates are established, the system begins to require rituals, because rituals reveal who will bow when the cost becomes social. The ritual may look like a pledge, a statement, a training confession, a forced redefinition of reality, or a public denouncement. The purpose is not informational; it is allegiance. Daniel shows this logic without ambiguity: public command, visible conformity, punitive enforcement. *"You are commanded... when you hear the sound... you are to fall down and worship the golden image."* (Daniel 3:4–5).[522] Walvoord emphasizes that the ceremony functioned as a loyalty test designed to expose refusal in public.[523] Ferguson likewise underscores that the act of bowing was a liturgical demand for visible uniformity, not mere civic participation.[524] The empire needed visible uniformity because visible uniformity consolidates power.

Modern rituals differ in form, but the structure is the same: visible conformity proves belonging. Public noncompliance proves that belonging is not total. That is why noncompliance is punished. The punishment may not be a furnace, but it can be exile from a profession, denial of access, and institutional blacklisting. Soft coercion can still be coercion. A society can remain outwardly civilized while functioning as an empire of compelled conformity. It can keep elections, courts, and polite language, while still teaching citizens that survival requires public alignment.

This is where "harm" and "safety" become the sharpest weapons. When the system frames itself as protector of the vulnerable, it claims a sacred mantle. Dissent can then be renamed as threat. Penalty can then be named as care. Exclusion can then be named as protection. The EEOC's guidance on religious accommodation, when narrowly applied, illustrates how institutions negotiate the boundary between asserted conviction and institutional expectations.[525] The mechanism is not the existence of law; the mechanism is the cultural trend that treats conviction as a problem to be managed and reshaped rather than a conscience to be honored. Once dissent is categorized as moral danger, the system can punish it while claiming righteousness.

"We must obey God rather than men." (Acts 5:29).[526] That boundary is not rhetorical flair; it is the line between Christ's lordship and every rival claim. Systems of control do not require overt atheism to function. They require the inversion of fear, the relocation of ultimate allegiance, and the normalization of compelled participation in moral rituals. Once the people fear reputational death more than they fear God, the system has already won the decisive battle. It does not need to prove its moral framework; it only needs to make dissent so costly that it is not worth expressing.

Freedom in Christ stands in direct collision with this entire structure because Christian liberty is liberty of conscience under God. Luther's distinction remains fatal to coercive virtue: the conscience is free in Christ, yet the believer serves others willingly in love.[527] That voluntary character is not a minor detail; it is the difference between holiness and forced compliance. *"For freedom Christ has set us free; stand firm therefore, and do not submit again to a yoke of slavery."* (Galatians 5:1).[528] The yoke is not only legal; it is psychological, moral, and social. It is the demand that conscience must answer first to institutional definitions of righteousness and that speech must conform to survive.

Timothy George's treatment of Galatians helps sharpen this point because he insists that the letter's freedom is not freedom from moral order but freedom from any rival claim that would bind the conscience where Christ has liberated it.[529] That is why a "new yoke" can be sold as compassion and still be slavery. A yoke can be padded with therapeutic language and still be a yoke. A yoke can be socially enforced rather than legally codified and still function as bondage, because the bondage is the annexation of conscience and confession.

Lewis warns that when objective moral order is debunked and language is recoded, people become morally disarmed. They become "men without chests," unable to resist because resistance has been labeled immoral.[530] *"Whoever is not with me is against me."* (Matthew 12:30).[531] The division is not finally between parties or platforms. It is between Christ's lordship and the rival lordship of systems that demand what belongs to God: conscience, confession, and worship.

When an institution claims the right to define moral reality, it functions as a counterfeit priesthood. When an institution claims the right to require public affirmations as proof of belonging, it functions as a counterfeit church. When an institution claims the right to punish dissent as moral evil, it functions as a counterfeit judge.

Once conscience is targeted, compelled confession becomes the most direct assault. Silence can sometimes be strategic. Forced agreement is a different category. Forced agreement is worship-like because it requires the mouth, not the behavior. The tongue becomes a proof of allegiance. The system does not demand that certain truths not be said; it demands that certain claims be affirmed. That is why compelled speech is not a workplace issue or a procedural matter. It is spiritual pressure. *"Do not call conspiracy all that this people calls conspiracy, and do not fear what they fear."* (Isaiah 8:12).[532] Manufactured fear is a governance tool.

It is used to justify exceptional measures, a permanent state of emergency, and the constant expansion of compliance.

In such a world, people are told they are free because they may choose, yet every real gate is constructed so that refusal is punished. The freedom is formal; the compulsion is functional. Control does not need to speak as control. It only needs to set conditions that make compliance the only affordable path. Once the public is trained to treat conformity as goodness and refusal as harm, the system can demand increasingly explicit performances without ever calling them "worship." The conscience learns to negotiate, then to rationalize, and finally to submit.

The final mechanism is the relocation of ownership. The more dependence is normalized, the more the citizen begins to live as if he belongs to the system that sustains him. That belonging may never be spoken, but it governs decisions, speech, courage, and silence. *"You were bought with a price; do not become bondservants of men."* (1 Corinthians 7:23).[533] The sentence is not anti-authority; it is anti-idolatry. It establishes that the conscience is already purchased, already owned, already claimed by Christ. When a system demands allegiance through benefits, standards, rituals, and penalties, it is not administering programs; it is imposing a system of control. It is competing for ownership.

Olasky's history of "compassion" in American life shows how quickly charity can be reshaped into impersonal mechanisms that erode moral formation and local responsibility, while still presenting themselves as benevolent. That is why the machinery matters. The machinery forms souls. It teaches what is feared, what is trusted, and what is owed. It teaches whether truth is worth losing access, whether conscience can endure loss, and whether holiness is subordinate to safety.

Compassion becomes control when the language of mercy is severed from truth and then fused to compliance. Relief becomes expectation. Expectation becomes entitlement. Entitlement becomes leverage. Leverage becomes obedience. The regime does not need to announce itself as tyranny if it can train the public to treat noncompliance as moral defect. In that world, virtue becomes measurable, righteousness becomes procedural, and dissent becomes punishable. The mechanism is now exposed: moral recoding, administrative righteousness, distributed coercion, ritualized conformity, compelled confession, and the new yoke. What remains is not to re-explain the machinery but to render judgment on what the machinery is doing to souls and to worship.

Section III: Why Forced Charity Isn't Christlike

The Church cannot think about poverty, mercy, and the state as long as it accepts the modern false binary: either you bless the welfare-state imagination as "Christian compassion," or you are accused of hardness toward the poor. That binary treats outcomes as the only moral category. Scripture treats something deeper as decisive: authority, conscience, and covenant responsibility. When we collapse those categories, we baptize coercion as virtue and call extraction "love." The poor become a political sacrament, and the state becomes the functional priesthood. But Christian mercy is not a mood or a mechanism. It is an act of obedience under God that must remain tethered to truth, justice, and the moral agency of the giver. That is why the debate is not "Do we care?" It is "Who owns mercy, and by what authority is mercy administered?" If we refuse that question, we will keep confusing a tax pipeline with discipleship and then wonder why souls decay while budgets expand.[534]

Christian charity is not defined by the movement of money from "haves" to "have-nots." It is defined by the moral act: a willing gift offered in love, under God, from a heart that fears the Lord more than it fears social shame. That is why the apostle does not treat giving as a quota enforced by pressure or as a righteousness manufactured by threat. *"Each one must give as he has decided in his heart, not reluctantly or under compulsion, for God loves a cheerful giver."* (2 Corinthians 9:7).[535] The verse does not deny need; it denies compulsion as the generator of virtue. A coerced transfer can redistribute resources, but it cannot create the moral reality Scripture calls "love." Spurgeon pressed this repeatedly: Christian giving that is dragged out of people by pressure is not the aroma of grace; it is the stench of hypocrisy, because the heart has not been formed.[536]

A second confusion must be removed: Christians often blur charity, justice, restitution, and confiscation as if they are all "fairness." Scripture distinguishes them because God distinguishes them. Restitution is a moral repair for a real wrong, and courts may compel it precisely because it is justice, not generosity. Charity is mercy toward need, and mercy is a free act that cannot be coerced without being emptied of its moral content. That is why the same Bible that commands generosity also condemns partiality and the perversion of justice: *"You shall do no injustice in court. You shall not be partial to the poor or defer to the great, but in righteousness shall you judge your neighbor."* (Leviticus 19:15).[537] Justice is righteousness, not sentimentality, and it is not "whatever feels compassionate." When the state seizes and redistributes and calls the result "charity," it is mixing categories: it uses force to simulate a virtue that requires freedom. The Acton Institute's framing is useful here because it forces the category separation: charity is personal and voluntary, justice is public and enforceable, and confusing them turns the state into a counterfeit moral agent.[538]

Here is the hinge: the question is not whether Christians should care about poverty, but whether Christians will allow Caesar to redefine charity itself. Biblical mercy grows inside covenant and community: you know the person, you can discern the need, you can correct folly, you can confront sin, and you can provide temporary relief without sanctifying permanent dependence. A national pipeline cannot do that. It can move funds, but it cannot shepherd. It can subsidize consumption, but it cannot rebuild conscience. It can stabilize material conditions for a season, but it cannot restore moral agency, mend families, or form gratitude. McDowell's central point in *True Charity* is exactly this: real help is defined by what it does to the person, not what it does for the person, and impersonal systems predictably drift into enabling and entitlement because they cannot discipline love with truth.[539]

Jesus' pattern makes the distinction unavoidable. Christ targeted the human heart, not the tax code. When a man tried to recruit Jesus into an economic dispute, Jesus refused the role of state-like arbitrator: *"Man, who made me a judge or arbitrator over you?"* (Luke 12:14).[540] That refusal is not indifference toward suffering. It is revelation about jurisdiction. Jesus did not come to build an administrative system to equalize outcomes. He came to call sinners to repentance, to expose the love of money, and to establish a kingdom whose primary instrument is the Word, not the sword. If your model of "Christian compassion" requires

Jesus to become what He refused to be, then your model is already out of step with Christ. Ryle's warnings about confusing "Christianity" with social programs land here: the Church's calling is spiritual first, and when it trades that calling for a substitute mission, it loses the very power that forms mercy at the root.[541]

Jesus also confronted wealth personally, in the arena of conscience. He did not outsource obedience to a public system. He spoke directly to the rich young ruler: *"If you would be perfect, go, sell what you possess and give to the poor... and come, follow me."* (Matthew 19:21).[542] The command is sharp precisely because it is voluntary. It tests love. It exposes idols. It calls for repentance and costly obedience, leaving the man morally responsible before God. A coercive regime can redistribute money, but it cannot replicate this; it cannot produce repentance, obedience, or love. Platt is right to stress that New Testament generosity is the overflow of worship, not compliance with an external extraction system. When "giving" becomes something done to you rather than something done by you, the moral act collapses, even if the poor still receive funds.[543]

The political economist Frédéric Bastiat named the moral inversion with clarity. When the law uses force to take from one person to give to another, it becomes a mechanism of "legal plunder."[544] His point is not that every tax is theft. His point is that the moral nature of an action does not become righteous because it is legalized and administered by officials. If a private person may not seize your property to fund "good causes," then the state does not become holy by doing it at scale. Bastiat presses the deeper danger: once citizens learn to view law as a tool for legalized taking, they train envy as a civic virtue and produce permanent conflict between groups competing for the spoils. That is not only an economic warning. It is a spiritual warning: it trains covetousness, grievance, and dependence, then calls the product "compassion."[545]

Alexis de Tocqueville saw a related danger: "legal charity" tends to create dependence and entitlement because it makes support impersonal and rights-based rather than relational and formative.[546] Once provision is framed as a claim rather than a gift, gratitude dies, obligation dies, and the moral center of a community shifts from stewardship to grievance. That is why the debate is not finally about budgets. It is about what kind of people a society produces and what kind of moral instincts it trains. Arthur Brooks applies this directly: when citizens are told they have "done charity" by paying taxes, they become less personally generous and less personally responsible because the moral act has been outsourced and replaced by a transaction.[547]

This is why "forced charity" is not ineffective; it is un-Christlike. Christian mercy aims at restoration, which includes agency, responsibility, and the rebuilding of character. Paul confronts idleness with a rule that protects the community from subsidizing collapse: *"If anyone is not willing to work, let him not eat."* (2 Thessalonians 3:10).[548] Paul is not condemning the disabled or the truly needy. He is condemning a posture that refuses responsibility while demanding provision. Love can be firm because love aims at holiness, maturity, and dignity. Welfare models that detach provision from responsibility often do the opposite: they train passivity, punish incremental advancement, and normalize long-term dependence as a stable way of life.[549]

A genuinely Christian approach must prioritize the formation of givers over the engineering of outcomes. That formation happens through discipleship, not through policy. The New Testament ties honest labor to generosity in a way coercive systems cannot replicate: *"Let the thief no longer steal, but rather let him labor, doing honest work with his own hands, so that he may have something to share with anyone in need."* (Ephesians 4:28).[550] Notice the chain: repentance, work, provision, then giving. The goal is not that needs are met. The goal is that people are transformed into the kind of persons who can meet needs. When policy aims only at results, it tends to treat people as economic units. When the gospel aims at renewal, it treats people as image-bearers who must be restored in truth, work, responsibility, and love.[551]

Relational charity is different in kind because it carries presence, discernment, and truth. A citizen can pay taxes for "anti-poverty" programs and never see the poor, never know the actual need, never confront addiction, never encourage work, never restore family order. Biblical mercy is not transfer. It is care, counsel, correction, hospitality, and often disciplined limitation. *"So then, as we have opportunity, let us do good to everyone, and especially to those who are of the household of faith."* (Galatians 6:10).[552] The Church is commanded into proximity because love is covenantal, not abstract. McDowell's critique is blunt: systems can become a way for the giver to avoid relationships, truth, and accountability, while still feeling morally superior.[553]

The early Church Fathers reinforce the same point: mercy is moral, personal, and accountable. Basil the Great could speak with fierce clarity against hoarding, but his remedy is not a state program that forces righteousness. His remedy is conscience awakened under God and pressed toward love and personal responsibility.[554] John Chrysostom's preaching against luxury and neglect of the poor similarly assumes personal culpability and personal repentance, not bureaucratic virtue.[555] Both men condemn the moral anesthesia of wealth, but neither treats Caesar as the engine of sanctification. Their vision is pastoral: the rich must be converted, the Church must be faithful, and mercy must be practiced in truth.[556]

The family is the first-order institution of provision in Scripture, which means the state can never become the covenant father without deforming God's design. *"But if anyone does not provide for his relatives, and especially for members of his household, he has denied the faith and is worse than an unbeliever."* (1 Timothy 5:8).[557] That sentence destroys the idea that "care" can be outsourced while fathers remain absent. It also exposes why welfare structures that replace fatherhood with checks can function as a rival authority: they can quietly tell a household, "You can collapse, and we will cover the consequences." Social policy becomes moral instruction. Miller's argument is straightforward: Christian responsibility begins at home, and systems that undermine that order produce long-term harm even when short-term relief is real.[558]

Scripture also protects the Church from being bled by cases the household should carry, precisely so that the Church can focus its mercy on true needs. If a believing family has widows in their care, they are to support them so the church is not burdened and can care for those who are truly needy widows. *"Let the church not be burdened so that it may care for those who are truly widows."* (1 Timothy 5:16).[559]

That boundary matters because it tells you what the New Testament assumes: charity is covenantal before it is institutional. It begins with responsibility that is close enough to see, correct, and sustain. When responsibility is displaced upward, the moral lesson changes. A household that should be trained in provision learns instead to outsource provision. A church that should be freed for triage and mercy becomes an administrative clearinghouse for problems that never get repaired at the root. That is why Miller's point is not pragmatic; it is theological: when "help" is detached from accountable relationships, it often becomes a mechanism for avoiding repentance, avoiding discipline, and avoiding the hard work of restoring order.[560]

This is also where the modern welfare imagination collides with fatherhood. Scripture's order is not sentimental; it is structural. God assigns provision, protection, and discipline first to the household, then to the church's mercy structures, and only then to civil authority in limited roles. When the state grows into the role of provider of necessities, it does not "fill gaps." It reshapes incentives, and incentives shape behavior. Charles Murray's critique is controversial in tone but straightforward in mechanism: when benefits structures reduce the marginal value of marriage, work, and stable fatherhood, they unintentionally subsidize family fragmentation and long-term dependence.[561]

Tocqueville saw this long before modern American bureaucracies, and he framed it in moral terms: once aid becomes a legal right administered impersonally, it lowers gratitude, elevates grievance, and hardens division between those compelled to give and those entitled to receive. He warned that administrative systems of "legal charity" tend to grow an idle and dependent posture, living at the expense of the working class, not because every recipient is wicked, but because the system trains a posture and rewards it.[562]

That does not mean the poor are the enemy. It means systems can manufacture the very miseries they claim to cure, especially when provision is separated from moral formation. Paul's warning about idleness is not cruelty; it is protection for both giver and receiver because it refuses to baptize irresponsibility as virtue. *"Aspire to live quietly, and to mind your own affairs, and to work with your hands... so that you may walk properly before outsiders and be dependent on no one."* (1 Thessalonians 4:11–12).[563] A Christian framework must preserve the distinction between the truly needy and the able-bodied who have been trained into dependency, because collapsing that distinction destroys both compassion and justice.[564]

Now bring that back to the Church's witness. When Christians treat taxes as "charity," they are tempted to believe they have fulfilled the command to love their neighbor without ever practicing actual love. Brooks's data-driven argument is relevant here because it reveals the behavioral truth: people who are more skeptical of state redistribution tend to give more voluntarily, and, on average, conservatives in his analysis give substantially more to private charity than liberals. You do not have to absolutize the conclusions to accept the general moral warning: outsourcing compassion dulls compassion.[565]

And once the Church's mercy is outsourced, the state becomes not only the provider but also the moral narrator. It defines who deserves help, what "harm" is, what "fairness" means, and which moral frameworks are permitted to speak. The same corruption that Bastiat called "legal plunder" is not only fiscal. It is catechetical. It teaches citizens to see other citizens as sources of entitlement, and it teaches the giver that coercion is righteousness as long as the result is framed as compassion.[566]

This is why Madison's principle matters for Christian political theology: "charity is no part of the legislative duty of government." That line does not deny the legitimacy of limited taxation for justice, defense, and public order. It denies that government can lawfully assume the Church's vocation and then call that assumption "morality." Once government is treated as the ordained engine of mercy, the Church's own mercy becomes optional, and the state quietly occupies a space it cannot fill: the space of conscience, repentance, and love.[567]

So what does a Christian alternative actually look like, if it refuses the false binary? It looks like this: justice stays public and enforceable; charity stays personal and voluntary; discipleship stays central and formative. That is not utopian. It is category integrity. It is the refusal to treat a tax pipeline as if it were a sacrament. The Church must recover the courage to say, plainly, that compelled transfers do not produce the moral act that Scripture calls love, even when compelled transfers sometimes produce temporary material relief. *"It is more blessed to give than to receive."* (Acts 20:35).[568]

That integrity also requires saying something many Christians avoid: not every need is purely material, and not all poverty is purely financial. Some poverty is driven by addiction. Some is driven by idleness. Some is driven by predatory relationships. Some is driven by fatherlessness. Some is driven by despair and spiritual collapse.

A bureaucracy can fund consumption, but it cannot shepherd the soul, confront sin, restore household order, rebuild work habits, or create stable marriage and family patterns. McDowell's point is uncomfortably accurate: impersonal giving often becomes a way to avoid the moral labor of love because love requires proximity, time, truth, and, at times, discipline.[569]

This is where Burke's emphasis on local, voluntary institutions becomes practical rather than nostalgic. Gregg's treatment of Burke is helpful because it ties charity to moral ecology: voluntary community structures preserve both dignity and accountability, whereas state structures necessarily flatten people into categories and process them as cases. The state cannot love. It can only administer. Administration can be necessary in limited spheres, but when administration is treated as mercy, the nature of mercy is redefined into something Christ never commanded.[570]

Even if a Christian insists that some limited safety net is legitimate under civil authority, the Church must still refuse the idea that moral responsibility can be replaced by policy. Welfare models that penalize work through benefit cliffs, penalize marriage through household calculations, or subsidize fatherlessness through structural incentives do not "help." They teach, and what they teach is often anti-discipleship. Murray's argument is not that every recipient is morally deficient; it is that systems that detach provision from responsibility reshape the culture in predictable ways.[571]

The New Testament pattern is different: it aims at restoration that produces givers. *"Whoever is generous to the poor lends to the Lord, and he will repay him for his deed."* (Proverbs 19:17).[572] That is a discipleship pipeline, not a tax pipeline. It begins with repentance, moves into work, grows into provision, and overflows into generosity. That pipeline cannot be replicated by coercion because coercion bypasses the heart, and what bypasses the heart cannot form virtue.[573]

The Church's job, then, is not to romanticize poverty or demonize the poor. It is to rebuild deacon-level mercy that is wise and fearless: feeding the hungry while refusing to fund addiction, sheltering the vulnerable while demanding responsibility, and helping in crisis while refusing to institutionalize collapse. The Church must be able to say "yes" with open hands and "no" with a clean conscience because both can be love when both are ordered toward restoration. *"If a brother or sister is poorly clothed and lacking in daily food... and one of you says to them, 'Go in peace, be warmed and filled,' without giving them the things needed for the body, what good is that?"* (James 2:15–16).[574] That covenant-near mercy does not cancel broader mercy; it establishes proximity as the proper environment for disciplined love.[575]

This is also why "forced charity" is un-Christlike at the level of worship. It trains people to call Caesar "provider," to treat entitlement as moral innocence, and to treat confiscation as righteousness. Bastiat's warning lands here again: when law is converted into a tool for plunder under the banner of philanthropy, the law becomes an instrument of organized injustice and moral confusion.[576]

The Church cannot keep blessing that confusion and still claim to preach a coherent gospel of repentance, lordship, and stewardship. If Christ is Lord, then Christ owns mercy, defines love, governs conscience, and commands generosity while judging greed. And Christ does not share His throne with a system that demands worship-like submission through dependency, entitlement, and compelled redistribution dressed up as virtue. *"No one can serve two masters."* (Matthew 6:24).[577] If the Church will not speak here, it will keep losing the next generation, not because the world is persuasive, but because the Church will have trained people to confuse compulsion with compassion and administration with mercy.[578]

So the corrective is not a slogan. It is repentance and reconstruction. Repentance from calling coercion "love." Reconstruction of local charity that is personal, relational, accountable, and brave. Reconstruction of households where fathers provide, mothers build, and children are formed into responsibility. Reconstruction of churches that know their people, discern needs, and protect mercy from being weaponized by irresponsibility. That is not politics as savior. It is the Church being the Church, refusing Caesar's counterfeit sacraments and recovering the joy of voluntary generosity that flows from worship.[579]

CONVICTION IN ACTION
"Charity Without Chains"

Chapter 6: Jesus Wasn't a Socialist, and the Bible Isn't a Welfare Manifesto

---

CONVICTION

Christian mercy is voluntary, covenant-near, and discipleship-shaped. When the Church baptizes coercion as compassion, it trades Christlike love for state-managed imitation, producing neither justice nor transformation.

REALITY CHECK

Our age has recast extraction as virtue, training Christians to mistake state redistribution for obedience. Care is now judged by outcomes rather than by authority, conscience, or covenant responsibility. But coerced transfer is not biblical love, which requires willing obedience, not compulsion. When the Church outsources mercy to government programs, personal generosity fades, families weaken, local accountability erodes, and the hard work of meeting needs with truth disappears.

FAITHFULNESS NOW LOOKS LIKE

Personal: Refuse the moral shortcut of calling compelled redistribution "my compassion." Practice deliberate, willing generosity: give privately, give consistently, and give close enough to discern need, confront folly, and strengthen responsibility rather than enable collapse.

Church: Rebuild deacon-level mercy that is relational, accountable, and fearless. Help the truly needy, demand responsibility where Scripture demands it, and refuse to treat government programs as a substitute for the Church's vocation.

Public: Speak clearly without cruelty; defend limited civil authority while rejecting the state's claim to be a moral shepherd. Advocate for reforms that reduce dependency traps, strengthen marriage and work, and protect the first-order duty of households.

COMMITMENTS

☐ Set a concrete giving target and designate it to local, relational mercy rather than abstract causes alone.

☐ Identify one person or family in real need and pursue proximity-based help: material support combined with counsel and accountability, not detached assistance.

☐ Practice disciplined compassion once this week by helping in a way that strengthens responsibility rather than funds instability.

☐ Initiate one conversation in your church about rebuilding local mercy structures, whether deacons, benevolence standards, mentoring, or job connections, so the Church acts like the Church.

PRAYER

Lord Jesus, cleanse my mind from counterfeit compassion. Forgive me where I have outsourced obedience and called it "love." Make my generosity willing, clean, and courageous. Teach me mercy that restores: mercy that tells the truth, protects the weak, confronts sin, and rebuilds dignity. Strengthen my household to fulfill its responsibilities and strengthen Your Church to fulfill hers. Deliver us from the idol of outcomes and the fear of man. Make us faithful givers, faithful shepherds, and faithful witnesses so that mercy is practiced as worship, not outsourced as paperwork. Amen.

Chapter 7: The Democratic Party's Progressive Gospel

Section I: Woke at the Altar—How Wokeness Crept into the Pulpit

A Sunday can look ordinary from the parking lot: a full lot, polished signage, coffee flowing, volunteers smiling, children checked in efficiently, and the room tuned for comfort. Then the drift begins quietly, not with an open denial of Christ but with a replacement of repentance. The welcome becomes the sermon's thermostat, setting the emotional climate before any truth is spoken. The language that once named sin and announced mercy now avoids offense and promises safety, as if the highest pastoral good is the absence of friction. Yet the door into life is not belonging as an end in itself; it is repentance and faith, a summons to deny self and follow Christ (Matthew 16:24).[580] The tragedy is that this substitution often feels like love. At the same time, it trains people to expect comfort rather than conviction and affirmation rather than cleansing. A church can keep its outward forms and still lose spiritual substance, not because persecution came, but because accommodation was baptized as wisdom (2 Timothy 3:5).[581]

The drift rarely arrives as a sudden heresy; it more often arrives as a leak beneath the floorboards, tolerated because it does not make noise at first.

The current that becomes a flood is not political. It is anthropological, a re-centering of the human person away from creation and toward the self as the final authority. When a culture teaches that authentic identity lies in inner psychological feelings, moral norms are no longer perceived as liberating boundaries but as oppressive constraints.[582] In that world, repentance sounds like violence because it challenges the self's right to define itself. The therapeutic frame then recodes confrontation as harm and trains communities to treat discomfort as danger rather than as a possible instrument of truth.[583] That change does not need to be voted on by elders to become real; it seeps into instincts. Once safety becomes sacred, the church is tempted to treat conviction as cruelty and to treat truth as a threat to fragile people.

Scripture names this pressure without flinching: *"Do not be conformed to this world, but be transformed by the renewal of your mind."* (Romans 12:2).[584] The command assumes the world carries a shape that will impress itself onto the church unless resisted. When the church absorbs the world's definitions of harm and love, it does not cease to speak about compassion; it shifts what compassion means and what compassion is for. Compassion becomes emotional affirmation rather than rescue from deception. The church begins to interpret the gospel through culture rather than interpreting culture through the gospel. Over time, the pulpit learns that the quickest way to avoid conflict is to keep preaching in the realm of generalities, where everyone feels included and no one is called to die. That is how the vocabulary of "welcome" can replace the vocabulary of repentance without ever announcing itself as a theological revolution.[585]

This is why the crisis is measurable before it becomes theatrical. When the leaders charged with guarding doctrine and forming disciples lack a coherent biblical worldview, the church becomes vulnerable to substitution long before it becomes visibly compromised. Research documenting worldview deficits among pastors, including those forming children and youth, signals a catastrophic downstream effect: a generation catechized by tone and trend rather than Scripture.[586] The deficit does not remain private. It shapes sermon selection, topical avoidance, and the instinct to mute the sharp edges of Scripture that collide with the moral assumptions of the age. Paul's warning to shepherds was operational, not poetic: wolves come from without, but distortions also rise from within (Acts 20:28–31).[587] When pastors are uncertain about the world as God describes it, they become certain about what must not be said.

Fear then fills the vacuum left by clarity. Pastors report feeling constrained when speaking about cultural and moral issues, and the pressure does not only come from hostile outsiders; it comes from internal dynamics that punish conviction and reward silence.[588] That pressure produces a new pastoral habit: preemptive compliance. Certain truths may still be believed privately, but they are treated as impractical to say aloud because the cost of speaking them feels too high. Fear becomes a governing emotion inside congregations, shaping what people will tolerate and what they will demand their leaders avoid.[589] The result is not cowardice; it is a recalibration of what "pastoral" means. Pastoral becomes synonymous with "non-disruptive," even when disruption is precisely what truth brings to a heart that needs repentance.

This is how mission drift follows pulpit drift. It is not that good works become evil; it is that activism becomes identity and proclamation becomes optional. The church begins to sound like a nonprofit with Bible verses attached, rather than a holy people announcing reconciliation with God through Christ. In that world, evangelism is treated as one ministry among many instead of the church's defining commission. However, Christ did not authorize the church to trade conversion for cultural acceptance; He authorized the church to make disciples (Matthew 28:18–20).[590] The drift often presents itself as moral seriousness, a deeper compassion, and a more sophisticated justice. That is why it is persuasive. It enters through virtue-language while quietly evacuating the gospel's offense. A church can keep the word "grace" in its vocabulary while redefining grace as affirmation without repentance and inclusion without cleansing.[591]

At this point, the conflict is not primarily "left versus right." It is two rival moral orders competing to define reality. One system says the human self is sovereign, feelings are the final court, and moral norms that restrain self-expression are oppressive. The other says God is sovereign, the heart is not a trustworthy god, and freedom is found in obedience to the Creator. The rival system functions as a religion because it has its own doctrine of sin, its own priesthood of experts, its own rituals of confession, and its own system of absolution that never ends. After all, it has no finished atonement. It trains perpetual penance without final forgiveness.[592] It grants temporary acceptance only to those who speak the approved language and perform the approved rituals. That is not biblical repentance or Christian forgiveness; it is moral control dressed in compassion.[593]

This is why the language of "love" becomes contested ground. If love is defined by culture as affirmation, then any call to repentance becomes, by definition, hate. The church then begins to protect itself by softening repentance into therapeutic language: sin becomes "brokenness," rebellion becomes "woundedness," and conversion becomes "self-acceptance." A former insider can see the mechanism because it does not arrive as open hostility; it arrives as a compassionate reframe that makes the old categories feel cruel.[594] When repentance is reframed as harm, the church must either resist the reframe or begin revising its own moral instincts to survive socially. That is why the two tables cannot be blended. Friendship with the world is not a neutral posture; Scripture calls it enmity with God (James 4:4).[595]

Institutional capture makes the drift durable by giving new instincts credibility. If the seminary pipeline normalizes ideological frameworks, the pulpit inherits them as "tools," "training," or "best practices," and congregations receive them as spiritual authority because they are backed by clerical confidence. The issue is not education; the issue is what education disciples leaders to fear and what it disciples them to worship. If ministers become fluent in cultural theory but thin in Scripture, they will interpret the Bible through the culture rather than interpret the culture through the Bible.[596] Colossians warns against being taken captive by philosophy and empty deceit according to human tradition rather than Christ (Colossians 2:8).[597] A credentialed drift is harder to confront because it presents itself as maturity, nuance, and compassion, and it labels resistance as ignorance or cruelty.

The fruit shows up in the sanctuary, even if it is not announced from the platform. Teaching frames repentance as trauma, worship avoids the fear of God, and pastoral care offers affirmation without confrontation. The body itself becomes contested ground because the modern world treats the body as raw material for self-definition rather than a gift that declares God's order.[598] When that assumption enters the church, "in Christ" identity loses primacy and identity-stacks gain moral authority. Scripture offers a different identity foundation: a purchased people and a holy nation formed by

God's call, not by cultural categories (1 Peter 2:9).[599] When identity is re-centered on tribe and self, the cross becomes decorative instead of decisive.

A brief framing note belongs here because this drift does not remain private. When the church adopts the culture's definitions of harm and love, it becomes a chaplain to the public moral order that produced those definitions. Political convergence happens not first through policy mechanics but through shared moral assumptions that make certain outcomes appear mandatory and dissent appear cruel. The danger is not that Christians must become partisan machines. The danger is that churches become moral laundering systems for the age, blessing what Scripture forbids so the culture can feel righteous while it rebels.[600] The moment the fear of man becomes stronger than the fear of God, the church is already negotiating its convictions. That negotiation may be called "winsome," but it is the old temptation to keep peace with the world at the cost of fidelity.[601]

The diagnosis is ancient. The serpent rarely begins with outright denial; he begins with distortion, with a question that makes God's Word sound unreasonable, harsh, or unsafe (Genesis 3:1).[602] The modern deconstruction pattern often follows the same logic: not "God is false," but "God did not really mean that," and "surely love would not require repentance." Cheap grace flourishes in that soil because cheap grace promises a gospel without a cross, forgiveness without discipleship, and belonging without transformation.[603] The remedy is not performative outrage or anxious obsession with the culture. The remedy is recovered holiness and recovered courage. When the church becomes skilled at keeping people entertained while avoiding the fear of God, it may fill seats and still lose spiritual power.[604] Holiness is not a brand; it is the atmosphere of a people who fear God more than man.[605]

The section must end where Scripture ends, with Christ's measured but terrifying clarity. Jesus is not impressed by churches that look alive while they are dying (Revelation 3:1–2).[606] He warns churches that are lukewarm because they are compromised, not because they are unpopular (Revelation 3:15–16).[607] He calls churches to remember, repent, and return, or He comes in judgment (Revelation 2:4–5).[608] That is covenant language from the King who walks among the lampstands. The fork in the road is real: a church can keep the applause of the age and lose the presence of God, or it can bear reproach and keep fidelity.[609] The alarm is not that the world is worldly but that the church is learning to call worldliness wisdom. When fear of God returns, the pulpit becomes a river again, not a mirror.

Section II: Redefining Sin, Justice, and Jesus

The progressive gospel rarely introduces itself as "another gospel." It presents itself as a more compassionate version of Christianity, less harsh, less offensive, more "safe," and more aligned with modern moral instincts. The problem is not that it abandons Christian vocabulary; it preserves it. The problem is that it quietly changes the meanings of the words that make the gospel intelligible: sin, justice, grace, love, repentance, and salvation. Once those definitions change, the church can still gather, sing, preach, and say "Jesus" while delivering a message that has lost its power to save.[610] Scripture warns that this kind of drift is not hypothetical: people can retain the form of godliness while denying its power, and they can seek out teaching that flatters their desires rather than confronts their rebellion.[611] Section I exposed how this drift enters pulpits and institutions. Section II owns the internal mechanics: change the definitions, then change the gospel.

The definitional swap begins where modern culture begins: with the self. Smith has traced how cultural liturgies quietly train the self to treat inner desire as identity, so that traditional moral limits, especially biblical sexual ethics, feel less like truth and more like oppression.[612] In that frame, moral prohibition is interpreted as harm because it restricts self-realization. The biblical categories then appear upside down: conviction looks like cruelty, boundaries look like hate, repentance looks like self-rejection, and holiness looks like exclusion. Scripture anticipates this inversion and calls it what it is: the moral exchange that names evil good and good evil.[613] Once that reversal becomes normal, the church is pressured to re-label obedience as "harm" and to re-label compromise as "love." The definitional swap is not an academic debate; it is the point at which culture demands that the church confess a different moral universe.

The first and deepest replacement is sin. Scripture does not treat sin as "whatever hurts people," though sin certainly hurts people. Scripture treats sin as rebellion against God, a vertical offense that makes guilt real, judgment necessary, and forgiveness costly. David's confession is unbearable to the therapy religion because it centers on God, not the self: "Against you, you only, have I sinned and done what is evil in your sight."[614] Sproul's blunt description follows the Bible's bluntness: sin is cosmic treason against divine majesty, not a minor human malfunction.[615] The progressive gospel must flatten this vertical axis, because once sin is primarily against God, then God defines righteousness, and repentance becomes unavoidable.

However, if sin is redefined as horizontal harm alone, then the victim becomes the judge, feelings become the court, and repentance can be replaced by therapeutic affirmation.

This is where the modern moral imagination tries to delete guilt and replace it with grievance. Romans does not describe humanity as basically good people damaged by systems; it describes humanity as suppressing truth and exchanging the Creator for created things.[616] That indictment is not political; it is theological. It says the deepest problem is worship disorder: the creature is enthroned, and the Creator is rejected. Calvin's diagnosis lands in the same place: the human heart constantly manufactures idols, redirecting love from God to created things.[617] If the heart is an idol factory, then the moral crisis is not solved by giving the heart more authority. It is solved by converting the heart, replacing self-rule with God-rule. The progressive gospel often treats this as unacceptable because it threatens the sovereignty of desire. Yet the Bible treats it as the only path to life: the self must be dethroned because the self is not a safe god.

Jesus reinforces this vertical diagnosis by locating the defilement problem within the person, not outside it. "From within, out of the heart of man, come evil thoughts..."[618] That is the death blow to any gospel that treats sin primarily as external oppression and salvation primarily as social liberation. Owen sharpens the pastoral implication: sin is indwelling corruption that requires mortification, not structural reform or emotional reframing.[619] If sin is in the heart, discipleship must include confrontation, repentance, and the Spirit's transforming work. But if sin is redefined as harm, and harm is defined as "whatever makes me feel unsafe," then the church is pressured to stop naming sin at all.

A church that cannot name sin cannot preach forgiveness, because forgiveness is only meaningful when guilt is real.

This is where "safety" becomes a rival to holiness. Scripture commands the believer not to negotiate with sin but to put it to death.[620] That command assumes sin is deadly, deceptive, and worthy of warfare. But the modern therapeutic frame trains people to interpret discomfort as danger and to interpret self-denial as violence. That is why this counterfeit thrives in therapeutic Christianity: it offers peace without repentance, belonging without holiness, and blessing without surrender. Sibbes understood that where there is no war against the flesh, there has been no true awakening, for genuine grace always produces genuine conflict with sin, and a soul at peace with its corruption has not been reached by the gospel.[621] When the church absorbs the safety-first moral order, it treats mortification as harmful and repentance as trauma. Yet Scripture treats mortification as mercy because the "old self" is not a harmless roommate; it is a tyrant. If the church will not call people to die to sin, it will comfort them into bondage while calling bondage freedom.

Reducing sin inevitably reduces the cross. Sproul insists that substitutionary atonement is required because sin is ultimately against God, not against humanity.[622] That is why the progressive gospel often shifts the cross from objective satisfaction of justice to subjective symbolism of love or solidarity. If guilt before God is denied, the cross becomes optional; if the cross becomes optional, salvation becomes self-improvement, and if salvation becomes self-improvement, the church becomes a moral coaching platform rather than a redeemed people.

The biblical Jesus does not offer moral tips. He offers a summons to repentance and faith: "Repent and believe in the gospel."[623] Repentance is not an accessory; it is the doorway. Any gospel that makes repentance unnecessary has not "softened" Christianity; it has removed Christianity. It has replaced rescue with reassurance.

The second replacement is justice. Scripture's justice is grounded in God's character and applied with impartiality. "You shall do no injustice in court… in righteousness shall you judge your neighbor."[624] Justice is not a tribal weapon; it is a righteous standard that protects the vulnerable without perverting truth. When justice is detached from God's holiness, it becomes ideology, an instrument for power narratives, identity scoring, and social control. The culture then treats justice not as righteousness before God, but as alignment with the approved moral framework. This is where the church is pressured to become an enforcement arm of cultural righteousness rather than a witness to divine righteousness. Once justice becomes a social liturgy, the church's job shifts from proclaiming reconciliation with God to maintaining ideological compliance.

Murray describes how identity politics creates new moral hierarchies based on group victimhood, treating perceived oppression as moral authority.[625] The impact is religious in function: it assigns innocence and guilt by category rather than by truth, and it demands public performance of the approved language. When the church imports this structure, it can no longer preach impartial justice with integrity, because the new hierarchy punishes impartiality as betrayal. The church then begins discipling people into grievance as identity, fragility as virtue, and perpetual accusation as righteousness. That cannot coexist with biblical justice, because biblical justice is tethered to God's truth and God's holiness, not to a social ranking system that treats power as the ultimate moral explanation.

This is why speech becomes a battleground. Scripture commands the church to speak truth in love.[626] Truth without love becomes brutality; love without truth becomes betrayal. But therapeutic culture trains people to interpret discomfort as danger, which makes truth itself feel violent when it contradicts desire. Haidt and Lukianoff explain how "safetyism" teaches students to interpret discomfort as danger, encouraging a fragile posture that demands protection rather than resilience.[627] When that assumption becomes moral law, the church is pressured to treat confrontation as harm and clarity as cruelty. The prophetic note disappears. The warning passages are avoided. The sharp edges of Scripture are dulled. But a church that cannot speak truth cannot love, because love that refuses truth is not mercy; it is abandonment.

Flavel's principle cuts to the root: what you think is wrong with man determines what you think will fix him, and a system that redefines sin as oppression rather than rebellion against a holy God will inevitably produce a salvation that is activism rather than atonement.[628] That definitional shift forces a salvation shift. If sin is oppression, then salvation is liberation through activism; if salvation is activism, then righteousness becomes performance; and if righteousness is performance, then guilt can never be finally cleansed, because activism has no finished atonement. Scripture warns the church against being taken captive by philosophies and traditions not grounded in Christ.[629] The issue is not whether Christians care about justice; Christians must care about justice because God commands it. The issue is whether justice is rooted in God's truth or in a rival moral system that treats grievance as holy and treats repentance as oppression. When the church adopts that rival system, it stops producing humility and starts producing moral dominance.

Scripture's order matters here because it prevents justice from becoming a savior. The grace of God trains believers to renounce ungodliness and live in holiness, producing good works as fruit, not as the ground of righteousness.[630] That sequence is the death of both self-righteous activism and despairing guilt management. Baucham warns that equating the gospel with social justice risks making activism the functional atonement for social guilt.[631] In the biblical order, the cross cleanses the conscience, and a cleansed conscience produces humility, compassion, and courage. In the rival order, activism is the cleanser, so the conscience is never clean, only socially managed. The result is perpetual outrage and perpetual penance, because the system cannot provide peace. Only Christ can.

The third replacement is Jesus. When sin becomes harm and justice becomes ideological accounting, Jesus must be rewritten to fit the story. He becomes an affirming therapist, moral mascot, and activist symbol, useful for cultural agendas and harmless to the self's sovereignty. But Scripture presents a Jesus who speaks comfort and also commands repentance; who receives sinners and also calls them to leave sin, who is gentle and also absolute. He does not "affirm people where they are." He calls them into truth. And His claims are exclusive: "No one comes to the Father except through me."[632] Butterfield presses the pastoral consequence: refusing to call certain desires sin under the banner of compassion distorts justice and the person of Christ.[633] A Christ who cannot contradict the self is not the biblical Christ. He is a cultural mirror.

This is where the church's temptation becomes deadly: keeping the name "Jesus" while evacuating the authority of Jesus. When that happens, the church can offer community, affirmation, and emotional safety, but it cannot offer salvation, because salvation requires repentance, reconciliation, and transformation. The New Testament does not present Jesus as a permission structure for self-definition; it presents Him as Lord. The progressive gospel often treats lordship as oppressive because it implies submission, which expressive individualism rejects. But lordship is the only path to freedom, because sin is slavery.[634] When Jesus is reduced to a symbol, the cross becomes decoration, and discipleship becomes self-expression. That is not Christianity. It is a baptized form of self-worship.

Finally, the definitional swap is reinforced by cultural pressure. Dreher describes "soft totalitarianism" that compels speech and belief, punishing dissent and rewarding compliance.[635] The point here is not policy mechanics; it is the spiritual pressure that makes leaders fear man more than God. In that environment, churches are tempted to revise doctrine to avoid consequences and preserve their reputations. But Scripture treats false gospels as damnable, not unfortunate. Paul's language is not mild: a gospel contrary to the apostolic gospel is accursed.[636] That warning is not a rhetorical flourish; it is a rescue flare. It tells the church that a redefined gospel can keep the packaging and still poison the soul. Fear of man is not a small pastoral weakness; it is a pathway to doctrinal surrender.

So the conclusion of Section II must be an alarm-bell warning without turning into a rant: change the definitions, and you change the gospel. That is the mechanism this section owns. Schaeffer warned that evangelical accommodation to culture surrenders absolute truth and opens the door to every cultural wind.[637] Once the Bible is treated as negotiable wherever it collides with cultural taboos, "love" becomes whatever the culture blesses, "justice" becomes whatever the culture demands, and "Jesus" becomes whatever the culture will tolerate. Scripture calls the church back to something far more severe and therefore far more merciful: godly grief that produces repentance leading to salvation.[638] Section III will expose the counterfeit Christ explicitly. Section II has established the groundwork: redefine sin as harm, redefine justice as ideology, redefine Jesus as affirmation, and you have produced a gospel that cannot save while still calling itself Christian.[639]

Section III: The Counterfeit Christ: Why the Inclusive Jesus Isn't Jesus at All

A skilled counterfeiter does not print a bill that looks obviously fake. He imitates the colors, preserves the familiar symbols, mimics the layout, and depends on most people not studying the details. A counterfeit succeeds because it feels familiar enough to be trusted. That is how false gospels work. They do not usually arrive as open atheism. They arrive as a version of Christianity that keeps the name "Jesus," keeps the language of love and justice, keeps the tone of compassion, and then quietly changes the substance until the whole thing sounds like faith while buying nothing but deception. Scripture does not tell the church to expect only persecution from outside; it tells the church to expect distortion from within, including *"another Jesus"* preached with a spiritual vocabulary no longer apostolic (2 Corinthians 11:3–4).[640]

The pattern is older than modern politics and older than social media. The serpent in Eden did not begin by saying,

"God is false." He began by distorting what God had said, reframing God's command as restrictive, and baiting Eve to interpret obedience as oppression.[641] That is the genius of counterfeit religion: it does not need to deny God; it only needs to make God seem unreasonable, and then to make rebellion feel righteous. Paul warns that the church can be "led astray from a sincere and pure devotion to Christ" by this same kind of subtle distortion (2 Corinthians 11:3).[642] This section is not a general complaint about culture. It is a Christological exposure. It is a test of identity: who is Jesus, what does He demand, and what happens when the church begins to accept a "Jesus" who exists mainly to bless the self?

The "Inclusive Jesus" can be defined as affirmation without confrontation. It is a Christ who welcomes without warning, comforts without commanding, and loves in ways that never require repentance. It is a Christ who never draws a line, never names sin as sin, and never claims the right to judge. That version sounds humane to a therapeutic age because it treats moral conviction as a form of harm. Yet the Jesus of Scripture begins His public ministry with a demand that collapses the counterfeit immediately: "Repent and believe in the gospel." (Mark 1:15).[643] DeYoung argues that calling affirmation compassion is the cruelest deception of all, because it dresses abandonment in the language of love and leaves people confirmed in what will destroy them.[644]

A counterfeit Christ thrives because the modern self has been trained to interpret authenticity as obedience to inner feelings. Pearcey shows that expressive individualism produces a two-tier view of the person in which inner sentiment is sacred and the body's created order is negotiable, turning biblical sexual ethics from revelation into felt dehumanization.[645] Once that frame is installed, a Christ who confronts desire is automatically labeled "unsafe." Holiness is reinterpreted as trauma. Repentance is reinterpreted as self-hatred. Discipline is reinterpreted as oppression. The church then begins to fear that clarity will drive people away, so it substitutes affirmation for discipleship. Scripture anticipates this pastoral collapse: there will be a time when people will not endure sound teaching but will gather teachers to suit their passions (2 Timothy 4:3–4).[646]

This counterfeit is constructed primarily through term redefinition. "Love" becomes approval. "Justice" becomes emotional validation or ideological alignment. "Grace" becomes the suspension of moral claims rather than the power to renounce sin. "Freedom" becomes self-definition rather than deliverance from slavery. When words are redefined, Scripture can be quoted while being emptied. Passages about kindness are elevated, while passages about repentance, judgment, and lordship are treated as embarrassing relics. Sinclair Ferguson's work on the Holy Spirit is relevant here because the Spirit's mission is not to validate a new moral order but to glorify the true Christ, creating real conformity to Him rather than cultural conformity dressed as holiness.[647] The apostolic command is not to accept spiritual claims because they feel compassionate but to test them (1 John 4:1–3).[648]

The "Inclusive Jesus" also relies on selective Scripture. It presents Jesus as tender while suppressing that He is terrifying in holiness. It presents Him as a friend while suppressing that He is Judge. It presents Him as a healer of wounds while suppressing the fact that He confronts rebellion. The real Jesus does not offer moral neutrality. He calls the world to surrender, and He divides humanity by their response to Him. John MacArthur presses the lordship point in modern evangelical terms: the biblical gospel does not offer Christ as a helpful add-on while leaving the self enthroned; it calls for a transfer of allegiance.[649] Jesus Himself makes this non-negotiable: *"If anyone would come after me, let him deny himself and take up his cross."* (Mark 8:34).[650] "Deny self" is not a slogan. It is a death sentence to the religion of self-rule.

Historically, this is not new. Every era has produced an "improved" Jesus that aligns with the dominant moral imagination of the day. The early church fathers were forced to fight for the identity of Christ precisely because counterfeit versions were persuasive. Irenaeus insisted that heretics often do not present their message as a new religion; they present it as a better interpretation of the old one, blending terms, altering definitions, and claiming fidelity while introducing novelty.[651] That is exactly what the Inclusive Jesus does. It insists it has recovered the "real" Jesus, meaning a Jesus who never offends modern sensibilities. But if the "real" Jesus never confronts sin, never threatens judgment, and never demands repentance, then that Jesus is not the one the apostles preached.[652]

Athanasius matters for this section because he refuses to treat Jesus as a moral symbol. He insists that the incarnation is God's decisive invasion to rescue and remake, not to empathize.[653] The Inclusive Jesus is often presented as empathy without authority: a spiritual companion who affirms the self, applauds chosen identities, and blesses the moral instincts of the age. But the real Christ is not a mascot for human meaning-making. He is the Lord who defines reality. *"No one comes to the Father except through me"* is not culturally inclusive. It cannot be reduced to a general principle of niceness (John 14:6).[654] If the church tries to keep the warmth of Jesus while discarding the exclusivity of Jesus, it is not softening doctrine; it is forging a new Christ.

The theological engine under the counterfeit is idolatry. Edwards understood that the unregenerate heart will always form a god shaped to its own desires, and that counterfeit religion is precisely more comfortable than the Christ of Scripture because it demands nothing that costs the worshiper.[655] The Inclusive Jesus is one of those idols. He is shaped to meet modern desires: he never wounds pride, never restricts sexuality, never commands mortification, never threatens judgment, and never claims absolute authority over conscience. But Scripture exposes this idolatry as spiritual adultery. Friendship with the world is not neutral; it becomes enmity with God (James 4:4).[656] When the church blesses a cultural Christ to preserve cultural approval, it is not "adapting." It is prostituting its witness for counterfeit currency.

That is why the counterfeit must also neutralize spiritual warfare. The real Christ did not come to negotiate a truce between holiness and sin. He came to destroy the works of the devil (1 John 3:8).[657] A counterfeit Christ, by contrast, often makes peace with the very sins Scripture commands believers to put to death. It does this by reframing sin as identity, temptation as authenticity, and repentance as repression. John Owen's language is severe because the stakes are severe: sin is not a pet; it is a power, and mortification is not optional for those who belong to Christ.[658] A Jesus who never calls people to mortify sin is not a gentle Jesus. He is a powerless Jesus. He leaves chains in place while offering emotional comfort as a substitute for deliverance.

Now apply that to modern evidence without turning this section into a news cycle scrapbook. You do not need to prove every headline. You need to show the spiritual logic: the counterfeit Jesus is being catechized into people through images, slogans, and institutions that normalize a Christ who validates the moral priorities of the age. Pride-month Jesus imagery, influencer "Jesus content" that treats repentance as unloving, and church messaging that treats biblical boundaries as bigotry all function like liturgy. They train the imagination. They set the emotional default. They teach people what kind of Christ they should prefer. Douglas Murray's analysis of identity ideology helps here: when moral status is tied to identity hierarchy, disagreement becomes violence, and truth becomes secondary to emotional safety.[659] That is the cultural soil in which Inclusive Jesus grows, because a Jesus who confronts sin will always feel "unsafe" to a culture trained in safetyism.

This is why youth formation is not a side issue. It is a primary pipeline for counterfeit Christ-making. If children are trained that the highest virtue is affirmation, then any Jesus who calls for repentance will feel hateful. If students are trained to interpret discomfort as danger, then conviction will feel like abuse. Haidt and Lukianoff describe how safetyism encourages a fragile posture that equates emotional discomfort with actual harm.[660] Scripture's vision of discipleship is the opposite. It trains believers to endure, to test, to contend, and to suffer for truth if necessary (Jude 3).[661] When youth ministries replace discipleship with affirmation, they do not "lose young people." They manufacture a generation that recognizes only counterfeit currency, because it has never been taught how to examine the real thing.

Institutionalization then hardens what began as preference into doctrine. Seminaries, influencers, and progressive theologians can normalize selective Scripture and redefine historic categories under the banner of compassion. Hanson has documented how elite institutions enforce ideological conformity by making dissent professionally costly, shaping what leaders will say publicly even when they know what the evidence requires.[662] Under that pressure, clergy can begin to preach a Jesus who "never offends" because offense becomes professional risk. Yet Scripture commands pastors and Christians to fear God more than man and to refuse captivity to empty philosophy (Colossians 2:8).[663] If fear of man selects your Christ, you will not preach the Christ of Scripture but the Christ you are allowed to preach.

The Inclusive Jesus also rewrites grace. It presents grace as permission, not power. It says "grace" means God never confronts, never commands, never disciplines, and never warns. But the New Testament says the grace of God trains believers to renounce ungodliness and worldly passions (Titus 2:11–12).[664] That is training language. It assumes transformation. The counterfeit Jesus often offers a grace that never trains, never disciplines, never changes anyone, and therefore cannot plausibly be the grace of Scripture. This is why the apostolic warning about "turning the grace of our God into sensuality" fits the modern moment with chilling precision (Jude 4).[665] Grace is being rebranded as divine endorsement of desire, rather than divine rescue from the tyranny of desire.

All of this leads to the climax of this section: the fork in the road. Scripture does not allow a blended Jesus. It does not allow Christ to be made safe for the age. Paul's warning is not mild: if anyone preaches a gospel contrary to the apostolic gospel, let him be accursed (Galatians 1:8–9).[666] That is not rhetorical aggression. It is mercy. It is the church's emergency alarm that counterfeit currency is circulating, and souls are spending their lives on a Jesus who cannot save.

And Scripture says the end of this story is not ambiguity. The returning Christ is not a therapist with gentle suggestions. He is the conquering King whose holiness exposes every forgery (Revelation 19:11–16).[667] The Inclusive Jesus cannot survive Revelation. The real Jesus is the One who returns with eyes like fire, judging and making war in righteousness. The section ends here because the decision cannot be postponed: either the church receives the biblical Christ, with His repentance demand and His lordship, or it chooses the cultural Christ, with his affirmation and his impotence.

So the call is direct but measured: test the Jesus you are being offered. Compare him to the Jesus of Scripture. Ask whether he commands repentance, whether he names sin, whether he warns of judgment, whether he demands allegiance, whether he saves by the cross, whether he sanctifies by the Spirit, and whether he will stand upright in Revelation 19.[668] A forged bill feels usable until the moment it is examined. A forged Christ feels compassionate until the moment you ask whether he has the power to forgive guilt, break bondage, and raise the dead. The church does not need a Jesus who fits the age. It needs the Jesus who will judge the age. And it needs Him now, because counterfeit currency always circulates most aggressively when people stop checking what they are receiving.[669]

Section IV: The Assault on the Family

The family is not a human invention, not a political talking point, and not a disposable social arrangement that can be edited to match the mood of an age. It is a cornerstone of creation, designed by God before there was a nation, before there was a king, and before there were schools, agencies, courts, or cultural institutions. Scripture locates the family inside the architecture of creation itself: a man and a woman joined in covenant, commanded to be fruitful, ordered toward generational continuity and stewardship (Genesis 1:27–28; Genesis 2:24).[670]

That is why the family has always been contested ground. You do not attack what is irrelevant. You attack what anchors reality. And when a culture sets itself against God, it rarely begins by banning churches outright; it begins by dissolving the living institutions that carry truth from one generation to the next. The assault on the family is therefore not a matter of social decline. It is theological warfare. It is the attempt to dismantle the most basic "school of love," where loyalty is trained, authority is learned, self-rule is confronted, and identity is received rather than invented. Augustine's insight about ordered loves applies here: when love is disordered, when created things become ultimate, everything beneath that love rearranges, including sexuality, marriage, and parenthood.[671] The family becomes fragile not because people lack feelings but because they lack a fixed truth. And when the family collapses, the state and the market rush in to catechize what the home no longer forms.

Marriage is the first pillar under siege, because marriage is the first public declaration that the body is not meaningless and that the covenant is not optional. Scripture presents marriage as both covenant and sign: a one-flesh union that is not private romance but a patterned reality that points beyond itself (Genesis 2:24; Ephesians 5:31–32).[672] Progressive reconstruction has to redefine marriage precisely because the biblical definition will not cooperate with expressive individualism. If marriage is a covenant before God, then it implies an obligation that outlives convenience. If marriage is a one-flesh reality, then it implies embodied complementarity that does not change with feelings. If marriage is ordered toward fruitfulness and family formation, then it implies that children are not lifestyle accessories but a stewardship. This is why the modern self finds covenantal marriage increasingly intolerable. Guinness argues that a self grounded in inner expression rather than divine calling has no fixed center outside itself and therefore cannot sustain covenant obligations when they become costly.[673] Marriage, then, becomes a contract for mutual fulfillment, terminable the moment it stops working. The logic sounds compassionate, but it leaves wreckage in its wake. The covenant frame produces stability, sacrifice, and sanctification; the contract frame produces negotiated cohabitation, curated pleasure, and abandonment when the cost rises.

But marriage is not only attacked through divorce culture; it is attacked through theological revision that turns God's authority into a suggestion. Here, the "counterfeit Christ" of Section III spills over into a counterfeit covenant. When Jesus is reduced to affirmation without confrontation, the church loses the nerve to say that God defines marriage, that God commands fidelity, that God hates treachery, and that vows are not sentimental poetry but binding truth (Malachi 2:14–16; Matthew 19:4–6).[674] The church can still say "we welcome everyone," but if it cannot say "repent and believe" and "obey everything I have commanded" (Mark 1:15; Matthew 28:18–20),[675] then it will not form families that can endure pressure. It will form a group of consumers who attend events. That is why the family crisis is not downstream of culture; it is downstream of a softened gospel. When the offense of Christ is removed, the cost of discipleship is hidden, leaving people untrained for covenant. Bunyan understood that a profession of faith untouched by transformation is the most dangerous of all conditions; it inoculates a man against true grace by giving him the name of it without the power;[676] families built on cheap grace do not become holy; they become religious while remaining ruled by the self. If the gospel in the home becomes therapy rather than repentance, then marriage becomes a fragile emotional arrangement rather than a covenantal calling.[677]

The second pillar under siege is authority, specifically parental authority as a discipleship trust. Scripture does not present parents as optional accessories to a child's identity journey; it presents parents as God-appointed stewards who must teach, model, and discipline in the fear of the Lord (Deuteronomy 6:6–9; Proverbs 1:8–9; Ephesians 6:4).[678] That is not authoritarianism. It is love with responsibility. It is the recognition that children are formed, whether intentionally or not, and that formation always serves a "god" of some kind. When parents abdicate discipleship, institutions do not remain neutral; they replace the family's catechesis with their own. This is where cultural pressure becomes an institutional pipeline. Schools, screens, and social platforms become the primary liturgies, shaping what is admirable, what is shameful, what is sacred, and what is forbidden.

The shift is subtle: parents are told that "authority" is harmful, that boundaries are oppressive, that discipline is trauma, and that moral clarity is unsafe. Peterson argues that parents who refuse to discipline their children out of misplaced compassion do not spare them pain; they guarantee a deeper pain later by sending them unprepared into a world that will not accommodate their fragility.[679] But the biblical world is not organized around emotional comfort; it is organized around holiness and truth. Love is not the absence of pain. Love is the pursuit of good, even when good requires rebuke, restriction, and the slow work of character formation (Hebrews 12:5–11).[680]

This displacement of parental authority also changes the child's understanding of identity. In Scripture, identity is received before it is expressed: creaturehood before self-definition, sonship before performance, covenant belonging before autonomous self-authorship (Psalm 139:13–16; 1 Corinthians 6:19–20).[681] The modern framework reverses it. It makes the child the author of reality and casts the parent as either an applauding audience or a threat to authenticity. That is why many institutions now function as moral arbiters over the home, training children to distrust parental guidance as "bias" while trusting external authorities as "neutral." Rod Dreher's warnings about ideological capture apply here in a bounded way: once an institution demands public allegiance to a moral vision, dissent becomes punishable, and "freedom" becomes compliance.[682] The result is a quiet coercion that pressures families to affirm what they cannot affirm and to remain silent about what Scripture requires them to say. When fear of man becomes the operating principle, the family becomes timid, and timid families produce timid churches. The line between discipleship and capitulation blurs until the home becomes spiritually unarmed.

The third pillar under siege is gender anthropology: the question of what a human being is, what the body means, and whether male and female are gifts or raw material. Scripture is not embarrassed to speak in binaries because creation is not embarrassed to speak in binaries: *"male and female he created them."* (Genesis 1:27).[683] That statement does not exhaust every human struggle. Still, it establishes a creational norm that cannot be revised without revising reality itself. The modern project seeks to detach personhood from embodiment. It treats the body as negotiable and the self as sovereign, redefining identity as inner feeling rather than God-given form. Once this detachment is normalized, the family cannot remain intact, because family is built on embodied realities: motherhood, fatherhood, generational continuity, and the complementary union that produces and protects children. A culture that denies embodiment will inevitably deny the moral structure of marriage. And a church that refuses to speak about embodiment will inevitably bless confusion as compassion. That is how counterfeit mercy works: it offers affirmation while withholding truth. It feels kind, but it abandons people to instability. When the church loses confidence that God's design is good, it will stop teaching it. When it stops teaching it, it stops forming it.

The consequences are measurable, but the deeper consequence is spiritual: confusion multiplies because the fixed points have been removed. When marriage is reconstructed as self-expression, covenant fidelity weakens. When parental authority is displaced, children become prey to competing catechisms. When gender is turned into a spectrum of self-definition, the body becomes an enemy rather than a gift. Then the culture wonders why anxiety rises, why loneliness expands, why commitment declines, why children feel unmoored, why men and women distrust each other, why birth rates fall, and why community collapses. The biblical explanation is not complicated: when you reorder creation, you do not get liberation; you get fragmentation.

Calvin's language about idolatry helps: the heart will worship something, and when God is displaced, desire becomes the functional deity.[684] The self becomes the altar. And because the self is unstable, everything built on the self becomes unstable. The family is particularly vulnerable because it requires long obedience in the same direction: vows kept under pressure, children trained across years, authority exercised with patience, forgiveness practiced repeatedly, and holiness pursued in ordinary routines. A culture of perpetual self-optimization cannot sustain the boring glory of covenant life.[685]

At this point, the political synergy becomes visible, but it must be handled as application, not as the foundation. The section does not need to re-prove the earlier argument that progressive ideology and progressive theology reinforce each other; it only needs to show that policies and institutions often accelerate the very family dismantling that doctrine has already justified. When legal frameworks treat marriage as an infinitely malleable contract, they reinforce the idea that covenant is a preference. When institutional policies empower schools and agencies to function as moral authorities over children, bypassing parental authority, they reinforce the idea that parents are obstacles rather than stewards. When public discourse treats biblical convictions about gender as "harm," it pressures the home to either comply or conceal its faith. This does not require a long legislative detour to be spiritually understood. The pressure is real because the family is where theology becomes concrete. Abstract ideas about "autonomy" turn into real consequences in a teenager's mind, a father's resolve, a mother's courage, and a marriage's endurance. The ideological battle is not ultimately fought in courtrooms; it is fought in kitchens, bedtime routines, and the moral vocabulary parents are willing to teach.[686]

Hope, therefore, is not found in nostalgia or outrage. Hope is found in restoration through ordered discipleship, starting in the home and reinforced by a church that has regained clarity. The remnant is not a fantasy category; Scripture consistently shows that God preserves a people who refuse to bow (1 Kings 19:18; Romans 11:5).[687] The restoration of family order begins when parents reclaim their assignment: to shepherd their children with truth and tenderness, to discipline without cruelty, to correct without shame, to model repentance rather than perfectionism, and to build a household culture that treats Christ as Lord rather than guest (Joshua 24:15; Colossians 3:12–17).[688] This is where the Spirit's work matters. Winslow understood that all genuine spiritual fruitfulness flows not from human resolve but from the Spirit's indwelling supply of grace, forming in the believer loves and aversions that no natural strength could produce.[689] And this is where Lloyd-Jones's revival framework becomes relevant: true renewal begins with conviction and clarity, not with accommodation. Revival is not an emotional spectacle; it is the re-centering of God as God. When God is re-centered, the family's shape becomes intelligible again, because the family is not arbitrary; it is ordered toward worship.

The church's role in this restoration is not to replace parents but to equip them. A church that becomes a substitute parent will inadvertently weaken the home. But a church that honors the home and trains the home becomes a force multiplier for generational faithfulness. The New Testament vision is not "professionals raising children while parents outsource discipleship." The vision is households saturated with Scripture, strengthened by shepherds who refuse to preach a therapeutic Christ. Pastors must not fear cultural backlash more than God's holiness. Piper argues that a church that softens God's commands to avoid offense has not become more loving; it has substituted the comfort of man for the glory of God, which is the oldest form of idolatry.[690] If Christ is Lord, we do not get to redefine love as approval; if the gospel is power, we do not get to preach grace without repentance. When the church speaks clearly and loves courageously, it permits families to be sane in an insane age.[691]

The closing frame belongs to Psalm 127, because it nails the axis of the entire section: the family is built by God, guarded by God, and made fruitful by God, yet it is also entrusted to human stewardship. *"Unless the Lord builds the house, those who build it labor in vain."* (Psalm 127:1).[692] That is not passivity; it is priority. It means families cannot be rebuilt by mere technique. They are rebuilt by returning to God as the builder, the authority, the definition-giver. Psalm 127 also refutes the modern lie that children are a burden to be managed or a lifestyle choice to be optimized: children are a heritage from the Lord, an entrusted future. When a culture trains parents to see children as interruptions, the family weakens. When a culture trains parents to fear conflict more than truth, discipleship collapses. But when a home treats Christ as King and Scripture as law, not as a mood board, the family becomes a frontline of resistance and a vessel of hope. The defense of the family is therefore not a culture war hobby. It is a spiritual battlefront. It is the ordinary place where God's order is either honored or erased and where disciples are either formed or forfeited, and where the next generation either learns the true Christ or is handed a counterfeit bill and told it will purchase salvation.

CONVICTION IN ACTION
"The Progressive Gospel Is Not the Gospel"

Chapter 7: The Democratic Party's Progressive Gospel

CONVICTION

The progressive gospel is a counterfeit. It preserves Christian vocabulary while gutting Christian meaning, swapping sin for oppression, justice for ideology, and Jesus the Lord for Jesus the affirmer. A church built on this gospel cannot save anyone, because it has stopped preaching the gospel that saves.

REALITY CHECK

The counterfeit does not announce itself. It arrives as compassion, as a more humane Christianity, and as welcome. Sin is redefined as harm to others rather than rebellion against God. Justice becomes tribal accounting rather than God's righteous standard applied without partiality. And Jesus is reconstructed as a therapist who welcomes without warning and comforts without commanding repentance. The swap happens gradually: repentance softens into journey language, holiness becomes oppression, and the cross becomes a symbol of empathy rather than the execution of God's wrath on sin. Change the definitions, and you change the gospel. Change the gospel, and you lose the only message that can rescue a soul.

FAITHFULNESS NOW LOOKS LIKE

Personal: Test the Jesus you are being offered against the Jesus of Scripture. Ask whether he commands repentance, names sin, warns of judgment, and saves by the cross. If the answer is no, you are not dealing with the real Christ. Refuse a gospel that costs you nothing, and submit to the One whose grace trains you to renounce ungodliness, not celebrate it.

Church: Name the swap from the pulpit. Preach sin as vertical rebellion against a holy God, not as harm to others. Preach justice as God's impartial righteous standard, not ideological alignment with whoever claims victimhood. Preach the real Jesus who confronts, commands, and transforms. A church that keeps Christian vocabulary while emptying Christian meaning is not being compassionate. It is being deceptive.

Public: Refuse to let the culture set the definitions. When love is redefined as affirmation, correction becomes hate by definition. Reclaim the biblical vocabulary: love tells the truth; justice requires impartiality; and grace is the power to change, not permission to stay the same. Speak plainly and refuse the progressive gospel's demand that the Church validate what God condemns.

COMMITMENTS

☐ Identify one place where you have absorbed a progressive redefinition, whether of sin, love, justice, or Jesus, and replace it this week with the biblical definition. Write it down.

☐ Ask your pastor directly: Does this church preach sin as rebellion against God? Does it call for repentance as turning, not processing? If the answer is evasive, press for clarity or find a pulpit with backbone.

☐ Examine one sermon, book, or influencer you regularly consume and apply this test: does it preach the real Christ who commands repentance or a counterfeit who only affirms?

☐ Have one conversation this week where you clearly and kindly explain the difference between the progressive gospel and the apostolic gospel to someone who may not know there is a difference.

PRAYER

Lord Jesus, forgive me for tolerating a counterfeit. Forgive me for accepting redefined sin, weaponized justice, and a reconstructed Christ because the real versions were harder to live with. You are not a therapist or a mascot. You are Lord, and Your lordship demands repentance, not reflection. Restore in Your Church the courage to preach sin as what it is: rebellion against You. Restore justice as Your righteous standard, not our tribal preferences. And restore the real gospel, costly, bloody, and transforming, so that souls are rescued rather than affirmed into destruction. Let the counterfeit be named and the real Christ be proclaimed. Amen.

Chapter 8: Behind the Curtain— The Spirit Driving the Democratic Agenda

Section I: The War We Cannot See— Spiritual Conflict Beneath Political Chaos

The first deception that disarms the Church is not a headline, a scandal, or a law passed quietly in the night. It is a sentence that sounds reasonable, even responsible: "This is just politics." It feels like maturity because it promises emotional distance and like wisdom because it claims neutrality. But spiritually, it functions like a blindfold. It drains moral meaning from reality and reframes questions of obedience and rebellion as mere preferences. When that framing settles into the Church, believers begin to treat truth as negotiable and righteousness as optional. Over time, they disciple their children into the same posture, not through instruction but through omission.

Scripture does not permit that split. The Bible does not present the world as a set of sealed compartments in which spiritual truth remains private and public life operates by neutral rules. It presents reality as an arena of allegiance, where visible conflict is often downstream of invisible powers. The Church is not being asked to become partisan. It is being commanded to see. The dividing line is not between "political" and "spiritual," but between truth and deception, obedience and compromise, and the fear of God and the fear of man.

Peter's warning to believers is not poetic imagery; it is operational instruction. He commands sobriety and watchfulness because the adversary seeks to destroy through stealth, not spectacle. *"Be sober-minded; be watchful. Your adversary, the devil, prowls around like a roaring lion, seeking someone to devour."* (1 Peter 5:8).[693] Devouring does not always look like persecution. Sometimes it looks like sedation, a gradual lowering of vigilance until the Church loses the capacity to interpret the times through God's categories. When believers accept the framing of "just politics," they do not become neutral. They become numb. And numbness is one of the enemy's most effective victories because deception does not require hatred of truth, only indifference to it.[694]

Neutrality, in this sense, is not a safe middle ground. It is a moral decision disguised as restraint. Christians are rightly commanded to be gentle, patient, and united. But the world often repackages cowardice as kindness, and the Church absorbs the packaging. Believers learn to say, "I don't want to get involved," as if obedience ends where conflict begins. Yet Jesus defines discipleship in terms that leave no room for disengaged faithfulness. He calls His followers to self-denial, not self-preservation: *"If anyone would come after me, let him deny himself and take up his cross daily and follow me."* (Luke 9:23).[695] The cross is not a metaphor for inconvenience; it is an instrument of death. Any Christianity that treats comfort as the highest good will inevitably treat courage as optional.

This is why the language of "civility" becomes dangerous when it is weaponized against truth. Civility is not evil, but it becomes demonic camouflage when it is used to silence moral clarity. When truth-telling is labeled "divisive" and sin-naming is labeled "unloving," the Church is being trained to confuse peace with compliance. A congregation can be very polite while becoming very disobedient. The danger is not that Christians will disagree about strategy. The danger is that strategy becomes a refuge from obedience. That is the path Bonhoeffer warned against: grace without discipleship, forgiveness without repentance, comfort without crucifixion.[696]

The New Testament leaves no ambiguity about the nature of the conflict beneath human conflict. Paul explicitly teaches that the Church's struggle is not primarily against human opponents but against unseen rulers, authorities, and powers that operate through systems, ideas, and institutions *"...against the spiritual forces of evil in the heavenly places."* (Ephesians 6:12).[697] That distinction matters. It does not absolve human responsibility, but it clarifies ultimate causation. When the Church forgets this, it misidentifies the enemy, exhausts itself fighting symptoms, and grows confused when surface-level victories fail to produce righteousness.

This is why political chaos often feels disproportionate and irrational. The Church keeps trying to interpret spiritual warfare solely with sociological tools. But Scripture teaches that rebellion against God produces confusion by design. Disorder is not a byproduct of bad policy; it is a spiritual condition. When a culture rejects God's authority, it does not become neutral; it becomes spiritually reorganized. Truth becomes negotiable. Language becomes unstable. Morality becomes inverted. The Church is not permitted to treat that inversion as "how politics works now."

Confusion is not always circumstantial; it is often strategic. Scripture repeatedly portrays deception as a tactic of spiritual powers, not human ignorance. Falsehood rarely announces itself as evil. It arrives clothed in moral rhetoric, compassion language, and appeals to unity. When the Church lacks discernment, it will mistake emotional resonance for righteousness. It will interpret agreement as goodness and disagreement as harm. That is not spiritual maturity; it is vulnerability.

Worldliness accelerates this blindness. Worldliness does not usually announce itself as rebellion. It arrives as respectability, relevance, and safety. A worldly church still sings, still serves, still gathers, but it slowly loses the capacity to confront sin, especially public sin that has been culturally enthroned. Scripture warns that friendship with the world places the Church at odds with God's purposes: *"You adulterous people! Do you not know that friendship with the world is enmity with God?"* (James 4:4).[698] When acceptance becomes the currency of ministry success, faithfulness becomes negotiable.

This is how heresy enters most effectively, not through outright denial, but through selection. Truth is curated, hard doctrines are softened, conviction is reframed as "tone," and the fear of God is replaced with the fear of losing credibility. Over time, the Church becomes fluent in cultural language while becoming illiterate in spiritual warfare. That drift does not feel dramatic. It feels reasonable. But reasonableness divorced from obedience is another form of compromise.[699]

If the Church is going to interpret political reality with spiritual accuracy, it must learn to recognize one of the enemy's most consistent tactics: confusion as a tool of control. Confusion is not what happens when information is incomplete. In Scripture, confusion is often what happens when truth is resisted, when God's moral order is treated as optional, and when His categories are replaced with man-made substitutes. The modern Church frequently calls this "complexity," as if moral clarity is naïve. But the Word does not treat clarity as childish. It treats clarity as light. The confusion of the age is not impressive sophistication; it is often the fruit of rebellion wearing academic credentials.

Paul's command is not that the Church become culturally savvy but that it become spiritually discerning. He tells believers to test what is presented as good and refuse what is evil: *"Test everything; hold fast what is good. Abstain from every form of evil."* (1 Thessalonians 5:21–22).[700] John commands believers not to be gullible but to test spiritual claims: *"Beloved, do not believe every spirit, but test the spirits to see whether they are from God."* (1 John 4:1).[701] Those instructions exist because spiritual influence is real and deception can operate under religious language. The question is not whether spiritual forces are active; the question is whether the Church has eyes to see their fingerprints.

One major reason the Church struggles to see is that many believers assume spiritual warfare would look overt, like occult symbols, explicit blasphemy, or open persecution. But spiritual powers prefer camouflage. They do not need to abolish churches to neutralize the Church. They can keep the buildings full while stripping the people of discernment. They can keep worship music loud while convincing believers that naming evil is "unloving." They can keep sermons motivational while removing the sharp edges of Scripture. That is why the most dangerous drift often occurs while everything still "looks Christian." Ravenhill's diagnosis is brutal precisely because it names what is easy to deny: the Church can sleep in the light, surrounded by truth but unaffected by it, active but unawake.[702]

Confusion thrives where discernment has collapsed, and discernment collapses when the Church trades the fear of God for the fear of man. When leaders begin prioritizing diplomacy over truth, the people they lead do not become more compassionate; they become more vulnerable. Schaeffer warned that the evangelical disaster was not first political defeat but theological accommodation: the failure to stand for truth as truth, which then makes the Church pliable in every downstream arena.[703] Accommodation is not a neutral strategy; it is a spiritual concession. It assumes the culture's pressure is legitimate and then adjusts the gospel to reduce friction. But friction is often the sound of truth colliding with lies that have gained status.

The modern world has perfected a particular form of camouflage: moral rhetoric that appears compassionate while concealing moral inversion. The age has learned to weaponize empathy, not by encouraging kindness, but by severing compassion from truth. This produces a counterfeit virtue that demands affirmation where Scripture demands repentance and demands silence where Scripture demands speech. The slogans of the moment function like liturgies: repeated phrases that shape imagination, signal belonging, and punish dissent. They are not primarily arguments; they are identity markers. They work because they bypass careful thought and appeal directly to the moral emotions.

Jonathan Haidt's work is useful here, not as a replacement for Scripture, but as a description of human dynamics that spiritual powers can exploit. He observes that morality often "binds and blinds": it unites people into teams and then makes them less able to see their own distortions.[704] That dynamic is exactly why slogans can become spiritual camouflage. A phrase can bind a tribe so tightly that questioning the phrase feels like betraying goodness itself. In that environment, the Church is pressured to adopt the tribe's language to prove that it is "loving." But when the Church adopts language that smuggles in false assumptions, it begins to think within the false frame.

This is where "language as camouflage" becomes one of the central battlefields of Section I. The enemy does not need to win every debate. He only needs to control the vocabulary, because vocabulary sets the boundaries of what can be imagined as true. When words are redefined, moral reasoning is reshaped. When euphemisms replace plain speech, conscience is dulled. When vice is renamed as virtue, the public mind is trained to celebrate what God condemns. And once the Church accepts that vocabulary, it begins to preach with the world's categories, even while quoting the Bible.

Rod Dreher describes the modern enforcement of narrative and language as a form of soft totalitarian pressure, less about overt persecution and more about cultural capture and compliance.[705] Again, the point here is not to outsource theology to sociology. The point is to recognize that spiritual warfare often uses social mechanisms. When the culture can enforce language, it can enforce thought; and when it can enforce thought, it can enforce worship. The Church then faces a temptation: comply in speech to avoid cost and call that compliance "wisdom." But Scripture calls that fear what it is: a snare. *"The fear of man lays a snare, but whoever trusts in the Lord is safe."* (Proverbs 29:25).[706] A snare does not look like a trap until it tightens.

Modern moral confusion is intensified by a deeper worldview shift that has changed what people believe a human being is. Carl Trueman's diagnosis of expressive individualism, in which inner feelings become moral authority and identity becomes self-constructed, describes the air many believers breathe without realizing it.[707] This worldview teaches people to treat objective moral order as oppression and subjective experience as truth. It trains society to interpret limits as harm and correction as violence.

Once that logic becomes dominant, the church is pressured to preach a gospel that functions as therapy: Jesus as an affirming counselor rather than a reigning King. Sin becomes "brokenness," repentance becomes "processing," and obedience becomes "authenticity." That shift may feel compassionate, but it is spiritually catastrophic because it redefines the self as sovereign, and sovereignty is a worship claim.

When the self becomes sovereign, Scripture must be softened because Scripture confronts. The Word does not negotiate with the self; it commands the self. And that is where heresy enters most effectively: not through rejection, but through selection. Gurnall understood that the enemy's primary tactic is not outright assault but subtle reduction, trimming the sharp edges of truth until the sword of the Spirit is replaced with a blunt instrument that offends no one and wounds nothing.[708] This is why theological drift rarely begins with a denial of the resurrection. It begins with a change in emphasis: the cross reduced, sin minimized, holiness reframed as legalism, judgment ignored, repentance downgraded, and obedience made optional. The church still uses biblical words, but their meanings are quietly swapped out.

Once that happens, the Church becomes vulnerable to "softened heresy" that appears compassionate. The enemy does not have to explicitly convince believers to call evil good. He can persuade them to stop calling anything evil, except whatever the culture currently condemns. This produces a church that speaks boldly about safe sins and stays silent about protected sins. It also produces a church that cannot recognize demonic confusion because it has been trained to interpret every conflict psychologically. Everything becomes trauma, or misinformation, or social conditioning, anything but spiritual warfare.

Yet Scripture refuses to let the Church reduce reality that way. Jesus identifies the devil as a liar and accuser at the root of deception: *"When he lies, he speaks out of his own character, for he is a liar and the father of lies."* (John 8:44).[709] He warns about deception's reach: *"See that no one leads you astray."* (Matthew 24:4).[710] Paul speaks of spiritual blinding that keeps minds from seeing truth (2 Corinthians 4:4).[711] Again, the command is not to obsess over demons but to refuse blindness.

This blindness is why politics can look like madness. Jordan Peterson's contrast between chaos and order is not Scripture, but it resonates because it names something people feel: the sense that society is being pulled toward disintegration.[712] The spiritual lens explains why rebellion against God produces disorder, and disorder becomes a tool for control when truth is destabilized. When people cannot define what is real, they become dependent on the institutions and voices that claim to define it for them. That dependency is fertile soil for spiritual manipulation because it conditions people to submit to counterfeit authority.

But here is the indictment that Section I must not avoid: the Church has often assisted this process by abandoning its role as a truth-telling institution. When pulpits trade proclamation for diplomacy, believers lose spiritual categories. When leaders prioritize being "winsome" over being clear, the sheep inherit confusion. Lloyd-Jones warned that Satan's work includes sowing division and heresy, often through pulpits that prioritize respectability over truth.[713]

This is why the most dangerous deception is not "out there." It is inside the Church's habits: the choice to avoid naming evil, the choice to treat discernment as uncharitable, the choice to treat watchfulness as paranoia, and the choice to treat boldness as pride. Those choices do not create peace; they create vulnerability.

And once the Church becomes vulnerable, the culture's moral language begins to catechize the congregation. People become more fluent in slogans than in Scripture. They can quote narratives but not the Word. They can recite what the tribe believes but not what God commands. This is exactly the collapse of discernment: when believers can quote headlines and social framings but cannot recognize doctrinal drift, moral camouflage, and spiritual intimidation. The Church becomes a consumer of culture instead of a prophetic witness to it.

This is why Section I must press the point: confusion is not neutral. Confusion is not harmless. Confusion is an environment where deception thrives. The enemy loves fog because fog makes every step feel risky, so people stop moving. A church that cannot see will not confront. A church that will not confront will be shaped by what it refuses to name. And a church shaped by what it refuses to name will eventually bless what it should have rebuked.

So the charge here is not to become obsessed with language games, but to refuse naïveté about them. The Church must recover biblical categories and biblical speech. Scripture speaks plainly about sin, judgment, repentance, holiness, and truth. It does not apologize for clarity. When the Church apologizes for biblical clarity, it is not being humble; it is being conditioned. When it adopts the world's euphemisms, it is not being compassionate; it is being captured. And captured churches do not protect people from deception; they distribute it.

Once language is captured, the next phase is predictable: the Church begins censoring itself and calls that restraint "wisdom." What began as "tone" becomes theology; what began as "civility" becomes fear; what began as "we don't want to be political" becomes a settled refusal to warn. Scripture does not treat that posture as neutrality. The watchman who sees danger and will not sound the trumpet is not peaceable; he is accountable (Ezekiel 33:6).[714] This is not a license for rage or theatrics. It is a summons to clarity: to speak like people who believe God's Word governs reality, even when that clarity costs reputation, comfort, or institutional stability.

Discernment, then, is not optional equipment for elite believers. It is basic survival for a Church living in contested territory. John's instruction is blunt: *"Beloved, do not believe every spirit, but test the spirits to see whether they are from God."* (1 John 4:1).[715] The command assumes deception can wear a familiar face, even a religious one. Paul likewise warns that people can be moved not only by false doctrines but also by persuasive speech and plausible narratives that sound virtuous while hollowing out truth (Colossians 2:4).[716] The point is not to become suspicious of everything; the point is to submit everything to Scripture, words, movements, moral slogans, and even the preferred assumptions of our own tribe.

A Church that will not test spirits will eventually bless them. When discernment is treated as "uncharitable," deception is given sanctuary, and the saints are trained to confuse emotional pressure with the leading of God. That is why the armor of God is not decorative language but practical instruction for survival: stand in truth, guard the heart, and refuse the devil's schemes. *"Put on the whole armor of God, that you may be able to stand against the schemes of the devil."* (Ephesians 6:11);[717] *"Stand therefore, having fastened on the belt of truth..."* (Ephesians 6:14).[718] The war beneath politics is won or lost first in the Church's willingness to see and then in its willingness to speak.

The pulpit is the hinge point. When preachers treat clarity as a threat to unity, the congregation will inherit confusion as its default condition. Lloyd-Jones warned that doctrinal softness is not harmless; it is a door.[719] The church does not need less doctrine but doctrine preached with fear of God, nor less confrontation but confrontation shaped by holiness rather than ego. When leaders prioritize diplomacy over truth, they may keep a room calm, but they leave a people unarmed. The armor language of Ephesians 6 is a war kit for saints who must stand under pressure, having done all, to stand (Ephesians 6:13–14).[720] If a church is not trained to stand, it will learn to bend, and bending becomes a habit.

This is where "neutrality equals complicity" becomes more than a slogan. It becomes a spiritual diagnosis. A church that refuses to name evil will eventually bless it by omission. A church that treats spiritual warfare as an embarrassing topic will interpret principalities as "just politics" and then wonder why the culture's darkness keeps deepening despite endless "engagement." Schaeffer's warning stands: accommodation does not buy safety; it buys surrender, and surrender never satisfies the powers demanding it.[721]

So the call of Section I is not to obsess over demons or to turn every debate into a conspiracy. The call is to recover sight. The war we cannot see becomes visible when we watch how the culture uses truth, language, and conscience, and when we watch what the Church refuses to say. If Satan's strategy is to devour, and if devouring often begins with sedation, then watchfulness is not extremism; it is obedience. *"Let us not sleep, as others do, but let us keep awake and be sober."* (1 Thessalonians 5:6).[722]

A church that trades discernment for diplomacy will not be protected by its caution. It will be devoured by the forces it refused to name. The remedy is not panic. It is repentance. Not outrage, but fear of God. Not tribal loyalty, but allegiance to Christ. The Church must relearn the difference between gentleness and surrender, between peace and appeasement, between unity and silence. Only then can it interpret political chaos for what it often is: surface turbulence generated by an older war, one the Church was never allowed to ignore.[723]

Section II: Principalities Behind Policies: From Molech to Modernity

A nation's laws do not regulate behavior; they catechize desire. They teach people what is sacred, what is disposable, what is protected, what is punishable, what is celebrated, and what must be silenced. Over time, policy becomes liturgy, repeated civic rituals that train consciences, reshape language, and establish new moral altars. The modern temptation is to treat this as neutral governance: a clash of rights claims, voting blocs, and court precedents. But Scripture does not permit that sterile reading of human life. When a people enthrone the self as the final authority, they will eventually build institutions that enforce that worship. Idolatry is not primarily a primitive mistake; it is a sophisticated substitution, *"they exchanged the truth about God for a lie and worshiped and served the creature rather than the Creator."* (Romans 1:25).[724] The prophets understood this: public sin is never only private preference. It becomes a system, and systems become strongholds.

That is why the Church cannot evaluate a nation's moral architecture by asking what is legal, popular, or constitutionally defensible. The Church must ask what is being worshiped, what is being sacrificed, and what must be confessed to belong. Scripture frames cultural drift as covenant drift: a people abandons the fear of God, and then their public order begins to reflect the new god they have chosen. That is why biblical warnings are so often corporate and national in scope. When the prophets condemn "high places," they condemn institutionalized rebellion and structures of worship that reshape the habits of an entire people. The modern age has its own high places. They are not made of stone and wood; they are made of courts, clinics, classrooms, entertainment pipelines, and regulatory regimes. And they do not permit evil; they normalize it, fund it, celebrate it, and eventually punish anyone who will not participate.

The Bible speaks with disturbing clarity about what happens when a culture baptizes the shedding of innocent blood. *"They sacrificed their sons and their daughters to the demons... they poured out innocent blood."* (Psalm 106:37–38).[725] That language is not metaphor. It is a diagnosis. The text does not say "they did wrong"; it says the worship was demonic, the blood was real, and the pollution was national. The Torah forbids child sacrifice explicitly: *"You shall not give any of your children to offer them to Molech."* (Leviticus 18:21).[726] Deuteronomy repeats the horror: *"they even burn their sons and their daughters in the fire to their gods."* (Deuteronomy 12:31).[727] The sin is framed not only as cruelty toward children but also as profanation against God, because it turns image-bearers into offerings to a false god. When a culture normalizes the killing of the unborn, it may insist it is "healthcare," but the spiritual signature resembles ancient patterns: a sacrificial logic dressed in moral vocabulary. The point is not that modern people are consciously chanting to Molech; the point is that the same demonic bargain reappears, life exchanged for autonomy, inconvenience removed through blood, and guilt managed through euphemism.

This is where the language of "rights" becomes a camouflage mechanism rather than a moral safeguard. Rights language can be used righteously, but it can also be used to disguise a ritual: the strong preserving comfort by eliminating the weak. Scripture names that pattern without apology. It depicts a people who *"sold themselves"* to evil and *"burned their sons and their daughters as offerings."* (2 Kings 17:17).[728] Jeremiah calls it an *"abomination"* that did not come from God's command (Jeremiah 32:35).[729] Isaiah depicts the same slaughter as a fruit of lustful idolatry: *"you... slaughter your children in the valleys."* (Isaiah 57:5).[730] The biblical point is not "don't do that." The point is that such practices reveal what the people love and who they serve.

That is why abortion is not one policy among many. It functions as a national altar. It enshrines the principle that personhood is conditional, granted by choice, sustained by convenience, and revoked by will. It teaches the public to believe that dependence makes you killable, that invisibility makes you disposable, and that the strong may define the value of the weak. Scripture reverses that logic. The unborn are not raw material waiting to become human by permission; they are already under God's intimate regard: *"you... knitted me together in my mother's womb."* (Psalm 139:13–14).[731] When the culture insists that the unborn are "potential life," it is not making a philosophical claim; it is performing spiritual anesthesia. It dulls the conscience so that what would otherwise feel like violence can be reframed as compassion. That moral reframing is not accidental. It is necessary because a culture cannot keep shedding innocent blood without either repenting or hardening.

John Piper's framing lands here with prophetic bluntness: abortion functions as a modern form of child sacrifice, *"pouring out innocent blood"* to idols of autonomy and convenience, with spiritual consequences for a nation that legalizes and normalizes it.[732] He pushes further into the spiritual logic: demonic forces are content to *"send millions of babies to heaven"* if they can make *"millions of murderers on earth,"* particularly mothers and fathers, because guilt and bloodshed become chains.[733] Whether one agrees with every rhetorical edge, the underlying theological point is consistent with Scripture's worldview: principalities seek to bind consciences, invert moral categories, and normalize practices that harden a society against repentance. When the culture says "this is compassion" while the act is the intentional destruction of a child, it is not confused; it is catechized into an inversion.

The early Church recognized this pattern long before modern courts or party platforms. Tertullian called abortion *"accelerated murder,"* arguing that what will be a human is already human in kind, the fruit already present in the seed.[734] He condemned the use of instruments to dissect and extract the fetus, treating it as furtive infanticide and insisting that the unborn are living beings rather than disposable tissue.[735] He grounded the moral claim in theological anthropology: life and soul begin at conception, making abortion the destruction of a human from its commencement.[736] Basil treated those who procure abortion as murderers, guilty of willful destruction, requiring penance *"as for murder,"* whether the embryo is formed or not.[737] Chrysostom's indictment was even more severe: abortion turns the chamber of procreation into a chamber of murder, an abuse of God's gift and a war against His laws.[738] These are not modern "culture war" positions. They are historic Christian moral reasoning: image-bearing life is sacred because God assigns its value, not because the mother, father, or state is pleased to grant it.

Policy turns this into liturgy when the state protects, funds, or celebrates what God condemns. The result is not access; it is institutionalized permission to shed blood with moral approval. That is why the language surrounding abortion is so aggressive in its moral claims. It cannot argue for legality but must demand celebration; it cannot permit but must canonize. Spiritually, that makes sense. A culture that has normalized bloodshed must either repent or justify itself. Since repentance would require admitting sin, justification becomes the civic reflex. Conscience is retrained by repetition: slogans, "care" narratives, clinical language, and legal protections that tell the public, again and again, that the act is righteous.

Scripture's moral clarity is severe: *"There are six things that the LORD hates... hands that shed innocent blood."* (Proverbs 6:16–17).[739] A people that turns what God hates into a protected right has not drifted politically; it has inverted worship. And once worship is inverted, the next step is predictable: the culture demands that everyone treat the altar as sacred. That is why institutions that facilitate abortion often function like a priesthood of the secular sacrament, administering the rites of autonomy, promising relief, and collecting cultural reverence as they remove inconvenient life. The deeper spiritual danger is not the act; it is the formation of a people who learn to call evil good and good evil, then punish anyone who refuses to speak in the approved vocabulary.

But principalities do not build only one altar. Molech's logic spreads because idolatry is rarely isolated; it metastasizes. The same spiritual powers that demand blood also demand the desecration of embodied design. Genesis does not present sex as a social construct; it presents it as creation order: *"male and female he created them."* (Genesis 1:27).[740] Jesus repeats the appeal to creation as normative reality, not negotiable tradition: *"he who created them from the beginning made them male and female."* (Matthew 19:4).[741] These are not peripheral details in Scripture; they are foundational claims about what a human being is. That is why gender ideology is not "diversity." It is defiance, an attempt to sever identity from the body and treat the self as sovereign over nature.

The cultural catechism here is straightforward: "I am what I feel; my body is a canvas; my identity is self-authored; anyone who disagrees is harming me." But that catechism is a metaphysical revolt. It does not request accommodation; it demands that reality bend. And because the body is a stubborn witness, male and female are not linguistic categories; the ideology must be enforced through institutions. That is why policy again becomes liturgy. Language is compelled. Definitions are rewritten. Dissent is stigmatized. And the public learns, through repetition, that to deny the self's sovereignty is a moral crime.

Nancy Pearcey's analysis is useful here because it traces how modern thought denigrates the body and fragments the human person: inner feelings become moral authority, while biological reality becomes morally irrelevant.[742] The result is not liberation; it is a new kind of bondage, because the self becomes its own god and therefore must continually protect its identity claims from contradiction. When identity is built on a fragile speech act rather than a created reality, it requires constant social reinforcement. That is why compelled affirmation becomes central. Not "let me live," but "you must say," "you must agree," "you must celebrate," "you must discipline dissent." That coercive impulse is not an accident. It is a hallmark of idolatry: false gods are jealous, and counterfeit worship always seeks public loyalty.

This is where Jezebel's pattern becomes a biblical lens, if used precisely rather than rhetorically. Jezebel was not immoral; she institutionalized rebellion, weaponized intimidation, and sought to silence prophets (1 Kings 18:4; 1 Kings 19:1–2).[743] She replaced true worship with regime-backed idolatry, and she used power to enforce it. Modern ideological enforcement often works the same way: it is not satisfied with tolerance; it demands submission. It does not request space; it seeks to make dissent socially and professionally unlivable. It uses intimidation, reputational threats, licensing pressures, and institutional penalties to neutralize prophetic speech. The spirit is coercive. It is not content until the prophets are silent.[744]

The culture's sexual liturgies increasingly function as initiation rites rather than mere "expression." When sexualized spectacles are brought near children, the public claim is "inclusion," but the deeper function is consecration: training a generation to treat modesty as oppression and boundary as bigotry. Mohler's warnings about the moral insanity of sexualizing children are framed as cultural critique. Still, the spiritual logic is older: innocence must be defiled because defilement creates allegiance, and allegiance creates a new moral order.[745] Scripture's categories for this are not "progress" but corruption and works of the flesh, which the age is commanded not to celebrate (Galatians 5:19–21).[746] A culture cannot normalize confusion without first making confusion virtuous, and it cannot make confusion virtuous without punishing anyone who insists on clarity.

Scripture repeatedly ties sexual disorder to idolatry. Paul calls covetousness idolatry (Colossians 3:5),[747] and he warns that societies that exchange the Creator for the creature are given over to dishonorable passions (Romans 1:25).[748] The biblical point is not that sin exists; it is that sin reorganizes a culture. When the self becomes sovereign, the body becomes negotiable, and the moral order becomes inverted. In that moment, law becomes an enforcement tool for the new worship order, and conscience becomes an enemy.

This brings the argument to the Equality Act and the broader institutional battlefronts. The Equality Act matters because it is not a symbolic statement; it is a legal mechanism designed to subordinate religious liberty to sexual identity claims and to redefine orthodox Christian teaching as discriminatory behavior. Albert Mohler argues that the Equality Act poses a severe threat to religious liberty by allowing the state to define legitimate Christian teaching and by denying appeal to RFRA protections, thereby pressuring Christian institutions to operate against their convictions.[749] The key spiritual question is not whether the bill sounds compassionate; the key question is whether it seeks to force the Church to bless what God forbids and to punish the Church when it refuses. When the state claims authority to judge whether Christian organizations are "legitimately Christian," it effectively abolishes religious liberty because government becomes the arbiter of faithfulness. That is not a neutral administrative tweak. It is a theological claim dressed in legal garb: Caesar defines orthodoxy.

This is what it means to say policy becomes liturgy: laws function as civic sacraments, teaching the public what must be honored and what must be exiled. Scripture affirms the reality and significance of civil authority (Romans 13:1–4).[750] But it also shows that civil authority becomes beastly when it claims ultimate moral authority and demands worship. When law is used to compel speech, punish conscience, and redefine created reality, it becomes a worship tool. The Church must be able to see that shift. Otherwise, it will debate procedural details while missing the altar being built in the public square.

Pride Month illustrates how these liturgies become seasonal and public. It functions as a civic religious calendar, processions, symbols, corporate sacraments, mandated affirmations, and enforced speech. Carl Trueman's critique is pointed: the rainbow, a biblical sign of God's covenant faithfulness, is inverted into an emblem of sexual autonomy and cultural ownership, and dissenters are treated as moral outsiders unfit for full participation.[751] The issue is not pigment. It is inversion. A symbol of God's mercy becomes a banner of self-sovereignty over the body. That is desecration, not neutrality. And liturgy works precisely because it forms imagination through repetition until resistance feels like blasphemy against the new god.

This is where Babylon becomes more than an ancient city and more than a metaphor. Babylon in Scripture represents a system, an ordering of life built on pride, exploitation, sexual corruption, and idolatrous commerce, all sustained by seductive power. Babylon does not only persecute; it seduces. It offers status, safety, wealth, and belonging on the condition that you bow. Revelation's command is not to manage

Babylon's reputation but to separate from her worship: *"Come out of her, my people, lest you take part in her sins."* (Revelation 18:4).[752] That is a spiritual directive, not a partisan slogan. It tells the Church that there are systems so corrupted that participation becomes contamination. It also tells the Church that judgment comes, not because God is petty, but because the system is built on rebellion that harms image-bearers and defies the Creator.

Idolatry always requires imaginative work because idolatry is not sustained by logic alone; it is sustained by desire. A.W. Tozer warned that idolatry begins with unworthy thoughts about God, meaning the downgrade of God's holiness and authority in the mind, which then produces a downgrade of obedience in life.[753] John Calvin's line that the human heart is a perpetual idol factory explains why modernity's idols are not limited to statues; they are ideologies, institutions, and self-definitions that demand ultimate loyalty.[754] When the sovereign self becomes the central idol, everything downstream begins to serve it: abortion becomes the sacrament that preserves autonomy, gender ideology becomes the liturgy that enthrones inner desire, and laws like the Equality Act become enforcement mechanisms that punish conscience. The public story is always "rights" and "inclusion"; the spiritual reality is worship and coercion.

This is why the Church's role cannot be reduced to commentary. The Church is not called to be the regime's chaplain or the age's therapist. It is called to be prophetic, naming the spirits behind the symptoms and refusing to bless what God condemns. Derek Prince emphasizes that principalities embed themselves in cultures and institutions and that the Church must engage in spiritual warfare with clarity rather than naïve reductionism.[755] Francis Schaeffer's insistence that the Church must confront rather than accommodate applies directly: the loss is not political defeat but the collapse of truth as truth, which leaves the Church pliable and easily managed.[756] Accommodation does not buy safety; it buys surrender. And surrender never satisfies the powers demanding it.

At this point, the Church faces a crucial choice: will it name the spirits, or will it disagree with the symptoms? If it only debates policy outcomes while refusing the Bible's vocabulary of sin, idolatry, judgment, and repentance, it will lose the battle of meaning. Scripture does not speak about child sacrifice in polite abstractions; it calls it an abomination (Deuteronomy 12:31).[757] Scripture does not treat the burning of children as "private choice"; it treats it as demonic worship (Psalm 106:37–38; 1 Corinthians 10:20).[758] Scripture does not speak about sexual disorder as identity; it calls it sin and warns that the unrepentant will not inherit the kingdom: "*Do not be deceived.*" (1 Corinthians 6:9–10).[759] Scripture does not treat idolatry as lifestyle variety; it treats it as adultery against God: "*You shall have no other gods before me.*" (Exodus 20:3–5).[760] Scripture even warns against moral herd instinct: "*You shall not fall in with the many to do evil.*" (Exodus 23:2).[761] The prophetic call is not to be cruel; it is to be clear, because clarity is mercy when the culture is being catechized into destruction.

Modern idolatry always offers itself as compassion. It claims to protect women, affirm identity, include the marginalized, and reduce harm. But the spiritual test is not whether the slogans feel kind; it is whether the policies honor God's created order and God's moral law. When compassion is severed from truth, it becomes a counterfeit virtue that demands affirmation where Scripture demands repentance and demands silence where Scripture demands speech. That is why the demonic logic often presents itself as inclusion: not dialogue, but submission. Not persuasion, but coercion. Not tolerance, but compelled celebration.

And here is the sobering synthesis: these issues are linked because they flow from the same idol, self-sovereignty. When the self becomes god, children become optional, bodies become negotiable, and conscience becomes a threat. Molech's altar reappears wherever innocent blood is justified for the sake of autonomy. Baal's logic reappears wherever fertility, sex, and pleasure become sacred claims against God's boundaries. Jezebel's pattern reappears wherever institutions use intimidation to silence prophets and punish dissent. Babylon's architecture reappears wherever education, media, courts, and corporate power coordinate to enforce a new worship order. The principalities behind such policies do not demand tolerance; they demand submission.

So the Church must reject the false framing that these are isolated policy questions. They are worship questions. They are discipleship questions. They are questions of authority: who defines the human person, who owns the body, who speaks final truth, who sets the moral law, who has the right to name good and evil. If the Church cannot speak with biblical precision here, it will slowly lose its ability to speak at all. But if the Church regains prophetic clarity, naming sin as sin, mercy as mercy, repentance as life, it will be able to confront without hatred and love without surrender. The call is not to panic. The call is to refuse participation in liturgies of rebellion, to speak with theological accuracy, and to confront with prophetic love, because mercy without truth is not mercy and love without repentance is not love.

Section III: Discernment Lost: When the Church Forgets How to See

The defining crisis facing the modern Church is not persecution from without but blindness from within. Opposition has always clarified the Church; comfort has often corrupted it. What is unusual about the present moment is not that the world resists Christian truth but that large portions of the Church struggle to recognize falsehood when it arrives wearing religious vocabulary, a therapeutic tone, and "Christ-centered" branding. Discernment has not weakened; it has been redefined until it resembles personal preference rather than spiritual obedience. The New Testament does not frame discernment as optional sophistication for the theologically curious; it frames it as commanded vigilance for the faithful. *"Beloved, do not believe every spirit, but test the spirits to see whether they are from God."* (1 John 4:1).[762] The command assumes danger, deception, and consequence. Yet much of the contemporary Church behaves as though truth is self-evident, error is rare, and unity is best preserved by avoiding judgment altogether. In that environment, blindness is not accidental.

It is cultivated by habit: treating clarity as cruelty, rebuke as arrogance, and doctrinal edges as unnecessary "negativity." A Church trained to avoid discomfort will inevitably avoid discernment, because discernment requires distinction, and distinction produces friction. But the gospel was never designed to protect us from friction; it was designed to conform us to Christ, who Himself warned that deception would be persuasive enough to endanger many and that false christs and false prophets would arise to mislead, if possible, even the elect (Matthew 24:24).[763] When the Church forgets how to test, it does not become less "sharp." It becomes less safe.

The collapse of discernment becomes visible first in what the Church now platforms. False teachers are not operating from the margins, whispering strange doctrines in obscure corners; they are published, promoted, invited, streamed, and celebrated. Their language is calibrated to sound compassionate, reasonable, and "gospel-adjacent," while quietly evacuating the gospel of its offense. This is not the crude heresy of denying Christ outright; it is the more effective deception of reframing Him. Scripture warned that wolves would not announce themselves as wolves but would dress for the occasion (Matthew 7:15).[764] The danger is not that error exists, but that it is curated by trusted institutions and rewarded by Christian audiences trained to prioritize tone over truth. The Church becomes conditioned to ask, "Was it uplifting?" more readily than "Was it true?" and to ask, "Did it help me?" more readily than "Did it call me to obey?" Yet the apostolic standard for leaders is the opposite of modern platform logic: *"He must hold firm to the trustworthy word as taught so that he may be able to give instruction in sound doctrine and also to rebuke those who contradict it."* (Titus 1:9).[765] Rebuke is not an optional "personality type." It is part of faithful shepherding. When Christian gatekeepers treat rebuke as inherently toxic, they do not produce unity; they create a culture in which contradiction becomes taboo, and taboo becomes the perfect hiding place for deception. A Church that refuses to rebuke will eventually refuse to discern, because discernment inevitably reaches a point where it must say, "This is not the gospel."

One reason deception thrives is that Scripture itself has been demoted from governing authority to inspirational resource. The sentence "we believe the Bible" stays on the sign. Still, the Bible is quietly repositioned as background music: quoted when it comforts, negotiated when it confronts, and ignored when it collides with the moral mood of the age. The result is a Church that can remain busy and still become blind. Activity becomes anesthesia. Programs multiply, production improves, language grows smoother, and the people lose the reflex to tremble. When the fear of God disappears, discernment does not weaken; it becomes socially unacceptable. The congregation learns that clarity is "harsh," that warning is "fear-based," and that naming sin is "unpastoral." Yet Scripture repeatedly frames the danger differently: the threat is not intensity but deception, not persecution but seduction, and not the loss of comfort but the loss of truth. *"But test everything; hold fast what is good."* (1 Thessalonians 5:21).[766] That command is not compatible with a culture that treats testing as unloving. It assumes the Church must sift, weigh, and reject because some things presented in religious packaging must be refused. Discernment must be recovered, not as a mood, but as obedience.

Once the Word is sidelined, a vacuum forms, and vacuums never remain empty. In the modern Church, that space is filled with cultural intuition: what the age labels compassionate, inclusive, or reasonable becomes the moral compass, even when it contradicts Scripture. At that point, sermons can still mention Jesus while functioning as moral therapy rather than apostolic proclamation. It becomes possible to preach "hope" while evacuating repentance, to preach "love" while refusing truth, and to preach "peace" while avoiding holiness. This is why the gospel of comfort without crucifixion is not a doctrinal error; it is a spiritual narcotic. Whitefield warned that the most dangerous congregation is one that has the form of godliness without its power, hearers who feel religious, who attend faithfully, and who call themselves Christians, while the new birth has never touched them and repentance has never broken them.[767] If grace is preached as permission rather than power, the Church can feel spiritually safe while remaining spiritually unchanged. Costly grace does not reassure; it calls, it confronts, it commands, it kills the old man and raises the new.[768] The tragedy of a therapeutic gospel is not that it speaks about pain; it is that it makes peace with sin by refusing to name it as rebellion. When rebellion is reframed as "brokenness" without responsibility, the conscience is not healed; it is muted.

This therapeutic turn reshapes preaching itself. Theology is displaced by psychology, and the pulpit begins to resemble a counseling session rather than a proclamation. Sin is discussed primarily in terms of wounds and shame, rarely in terms of guilt and accountability. Grace is offered as reassurance rather than a pardon. The result is a congregation trained to interpret every biblical demand through the lens of personal well-being. Scripture is consulted not to reveal God's will but to confirm existing feelings. The inversion is subtle but devastating: the Bible becomes a mirror rather than a sword. Yet Scripture presents itself as an instrument that pierces, exposes, and trains. *"But solid food is for the mature, for those who have their powers of discernment trained by constant practice to distinguish good from evil."* (Hebrews 5:14).[769] Discernment is not a vibe. It is a trained capacity, developed by constant practice under the Word. If preaching avoids confrontation as a matter of policy, the people are trained to interpret conviction as harm. Then, when the Bible confronts them directly, they instinctively treat the Bible as the problem. At that point, the Church is not underfed; it is being re-formed into an audience that cannot tolerate the very medicine that would heal it.

Compounding the problem is a redefinition of love. Love, in contemporary church language, is increasingly framed as affirmation without confrontation and unity without holiness. Any insistence on truth that disrupts emotional comfort is labeled unloving. Yet Scripture refuses that dichotomy: love does not celebrate falsehood; it rejoices with the truth (1 Corinthians 13:6).[770] To remove truth from love is not compassion; it is cowardice in religious costume. The Church is explicitly commanded not to treat darkness as a neutral option: *"Take no part in the unfruitful works of darkness, but instead expose them."* (Ephesians 5:11).[771] Exposure is not hatred; exposure is mercy when deception is killing people slowly. The modern Church often wants the fruit of love without the labor of exposure, because exposure creates conflict and conflict threatens comfort. But love without truth does not protect the sheep; it leaves the sheep with wolves while insisting, with a soft voice, that everyone is safe. That is not kindness. That is negligence with good branding.

The pursuit of unity has likewise been detached from biblical holiness. Unity is now treated as an end in itself rather than a fruit of shared submission to truth. The result is a fragile togetherness that depends on silence. Disagreement is framed as division, and doctrinal clarity is treated as arrogance. But biblical unity is not agreement to avoid conflict; it is shared obedience to Christ. When unity is treated as the highest virtue, discernment becomes a threat, because discernment forces decisions: this is true, that is false; this teacher is faithful, that teacher is twisting; this gospel saves, that "gospel" sedates. Scripture will not permit the Church to preserve togetherness by suspending judgment. *"Let two or three prophets speak, and let the others weigh what is said."* (1 Corinthians 14:29).[772] When a Church culture treats evaluation as "unspiritual," it has already surrendered the ground on which discernment stands. A Church that refuses to weigh is a Church that will be carried.

Leadership failure accelerates this collapse. Pastors, publishers, and influencers increasingly function as brand managers rather than shepherds. Decisions about what to preach, endorse, or confront are governed by metrics: attendance, engagement, giving, and reputation. Courage is quietly redefined as imprudence, while silence is baptized as wisdom. Yet Scripture frames negligent silence as culpable. The Church ends up with shepherds who can organize, inspire, and soothe, but who will not fight. Over time, the people learn what their leaders reward: ambiguity is safest, clarity is "too intense," and rebuke is "not our style." But a style that refuses to warn is not a style; it is a surrender. Ravenhill named the price of settling for religious motion without spiritual fire: revival tarries because we are willing to live without it.[773] A Church that will not repent cannot discern, because discernment requires moral seriousness, and moral seriousness requires the fear of God.

Social media intensifies this dynamic by rewarding visibility over fidelity. Platforms amplify voices that are affirming, ambiguous, and adaptable, while marginalizing those who insist on doctrinal clarity. The result is a celebrity culture that values reach more than righteousness. Influence becomes a substitute for authority, and popularity masquerades as fruitfulness. Scripture warns that deception often travels through impressive channels. *"Having the appearance of godliness, but denying its power. Avoid such people."* (2 Timothy 3:5).[774] The danger is not always the obvious apostate; the danger is the religious counterfeit that looks like life while operating as death. Martyn Lloyd-Jones warned that discernment is commanded because religious language and religious experience can be counterfeit.[775] In a media age, the Church can confuse energy for anointing, a platform for calling, and emotional resonance for truth, then call the result "revival" while holiness quietly disappears.

This is why entertainment is not a side issue; it is a spiritual indicator. Wilkerson warned that when the fear of God departs the church, entertainment rushes in to fill the silence, and a leadership that cannot bring people into genuine worship will inevitably resort to spectacle to hold the crowd.[776] That substitution matters because worship calibrates reality. Worship teaches the soul what God is like: holy, weighty, authoritative, and not manageable. When worship is replaced with spectacle, the congregation is trained to evaluate the church the same way it evaluates everything else: by preference, vibe, and personal benefit. In that environment, discernment becomes nearly impossible, as it requires a soul trained to prize truth above comfort. The moment worship is reduced to emotional stimulation, the people become vulnerable to counterfeit "spirituality": experiences that feel powerful but do not produce holiness. Then, when deception presses the Church to soften doctrine and blur repentance, the people lack the categories to resist. They have been trained to crave a feeling, not to obey a Lord.

Compromise is curated. False teaching is not hidden in the shadows; it is marketed, endorsed, and placed on stages under bright lights. Spurgeon's grief was not only over error outside the Church but also over enemies of the cross walking openly among the professing people of God.[777] The Church can grow allergic to doctrinal edges because doctrinal edges cost money, cost attendance, and cost respectability. Ryle warned that worldliness hollows out the church, leaving respectability to replace spiritual force.[778] In that state, leaders may not experience themselves as compromisers; they experience themselves as wise administrators. They call their drift "strategy" and their dilution "winsomeness." They intend to keep the doors open. But a Church can keep its doors open while closing its eyes. The irony is that the very effort to preserve influence often destroys the thing that made influence meaningful: truth as truth, proclaimed with fear of God.

At the center of the blindness is the rise of false gospels, not false emphases but alternate messages that retain Christian vocabulary while removing Christian demands. The apostles did not treat "another gospel" as a harmless variant. Paul's warning is severe: *"If anyone is preaching to you a gospel contrary to the one you received, let him be accursed."* (Galatians 1:6–9).[779] That is an apostolic emergency. Paul is not policing stylistic differences; he is defending the actual message that saves. A false gospel does not confuse people; it damns them. The Church's first act of love, therefore, is not to preserve everyone's emotional comfort. It is to protect the gospel itself because the gospel is the only remedy for sin, death, judgment, and eternal separation from God.

The modern counterfeit gospels rarely deny Jesus by name; they redefine Him by function. Jesus becomes therapist, not Lord. The cross becomes reassurance, not execution. Grace becomes permission, not power. Repentance becomes "processing," not turning. Holiness becomes "growth at your own pace," not obedience under authority. And discipleship becomes "finding your purpose" rather than losing your life to follow Christ. Yet Jesus' terms do not allow that trade: *"If anyone would come after me, let him deny himself and take up his cross daily and follow me."* (Luke 9:23).[780] A church can preach "Jesus" weekly while removing the doorway of self-denial and then wonder why its people cannot see the gospel they are hearing is not forming them to discern because it is not forming them to obey.

This is why the Church must recover discernment as practiced submission to Scripture as the final authority. Discernment is not cynicism. It is not a suspicious personality. It is the discipline of testing teaching by the apostolic gospel, not by emotional effect. It is the willingness to ask the following: Does this message exalt Christ as Lord or reduce Him to a mascot for personal well-being? Does it command repentance or offer reassurance? Does it treat sin as deadly or as "struggle"? Does it produce holiness or produce vibes? Discernment is what happens when a soul has been trained, by constant practice, to prize truth above social approval (Hebrews 5:14).[781] That's why discernment requires the fear of God. Without the fear of God, you will always trade truth for comfort when the pressure rises.

And that brings us back to the internal collapse you're diagnosing: the church forgetting how to see is the church forgetting how to tremble. Isaiah gives the posture in one line: *"But this is the one to whom I will look: he who is humble and contrite in spirit and trembles at my word."* (Isaiah 66:2).[782] Trembling is moral seriousness under authority. It is the recognition that God speaks; therefore, we obey. That posture is incompatible with the modern instinct to negotiate

Scripture. When trembling disappears, discernment becomes an aesthetic preference, something you do if you're "into theology." But when trembling returns, discernment becomes normal Christianity: You test spirits, reject counterfeits, and pursue holiness because God told you to.

Recovery is not complex. It is costly, but it is clear. Return to the Word as governing authority, not decorative inspiration. Restore the cross as death to self, not a symbol of emotional validation. Reclaim repentance as the doorway of grace, not an optional upgrade. Refuse false unity that requires silence about sin. Train leaders who fear God more than backlash. Teach believers that testing is commanded, not elitist. And reestablish the truth that love and truth are not rivals but companions: truth without love becomes cruelty, but love without truth becomes betrayal. When discernment is recovered, the Church regains what it was always meant to be: a people under the Word, purified by repentance, anchored in holiness, and courageous enough to stand when the age demands surrender.

CONVICTION IN ACTION
"Behind the Curtain"

Chapter 8: The Spirit Driving the Democratic Agenda

CONVICTION

The conflict beneath the cultural chaos is not primarily political. It is spiritual. When the Church interprets principalities as policy debates and confusion as mere incompetence, she has already lost the war she refuses to see.

REALITY CHECK

Scripture does not permit a clean split between spiritual reality and public life. The world is an arena of allegiance, and visible conflict is downstream of invisible powers. Abortion is not bad policy; it functions as a national altar, enshrining the principle that personhood is conditional and the weak are disposable. Gender ideology is not confused anthropology; it is a desecration of embodied design. And the confusion that makes the age feel irrational is not accidental. Confusion is a spiritual tactic. The enemy does not need to abolish the Church to neutralize her. He only needs to capture her vocabulary, soften her categories, and train her to call discernment "unkind." A Church that will not name the spirits will eventually bless them.

FAITHFULNESS NOW LOOKS LIKE

Personal: Recover the biblical categories you have surrendered to cultural pressure. The armor of God is not decorative language; it is practical instruction for a Church living in contested territory. Sobriety and watchfulness are commanded because the adversary seeks to destroy through stealth, not spectacle. Test what you are told is compassionate against what Scripture calls holy.

Church: Recover the prophetic function the pulpit abandoned when it traded proclamation for diplomacy. Name the spirits behind the symptoms. Preach on spiritual warfare as the New Testament commands. Train the congregation to recognize moral rhetoric that conceals moral inversion, and restore the biblical categories of sin, idolatry, judgment, and repentance as the vocabulary needed to interpret what the culture is actually doing.

Public: Refuse the framing that abortion, gender ideology, and the assault on conscience are isolated policy questions. They are worship questions. They reveal what a culture sacrifices to, what it protects, and what it punishes. Speak with the clarity of a watchman, not the caution of a diplomat. The Church is not called to be the regime's chaplain. She is called to be prophetic.

COMMITMENTS

☐ Identify one area where you have been interpreting spiritual conflict with only political or sociological tools. This week, read one New Testament passage on spiritual warfare and apply it to something you are watching in the culture.

☐ Take one policy or cultural trend you have treated as political and ask the worship question: what is being sacrificed here, what is being protected, and what spirit is being served?

☐ Remove one source of spiritual fog from your life, whether content, voices, or habits, that has trained you to treat moral clarity as unkind and confusion as sophistication.

☐ Pray specifically and by name this week for the principalities at work in your city, your school district, and your government, asking God to expose what is hidden and strengthen what remains.

PRAYER

Lord Jesus, open our eyes to what is actually happening. Forgive us for calling spiritual warfare politics and for treating the enemy's tactics as mere policy disagreements. Forgive us for losing the biblical categories that make the conflict visible. Restore in Your Church the fear of the Lord that produces discernment, the sobriety that resists deception, and the prophetic courage to name what You have already named. Expose the principalities behind the policies. Break the altars built on innocent blood and broken design. Raise up a Church that sees clearly, speaks plainly, and refuses to bless what You have condemned. Let us be watchmen who warn, not chaplains who comfort the rebellion. Amen.

Chapter 9: Stop Playing Defense—Christians Must Reclaim Boldness

Section I: Silence Is Surrender

The drift rarely announces itself. It does not arrive with sirens; it arrives with fog, softened language, delayed clarity, sermons that soothe more than they confront, and conversations that avoid names. A church can remain busy, friendly, and "healthy" and yet quietly slide into a posture where the highest goal becomes staying unobjectionable. Then fog becomes policy. Policy becomes enforcement. Enforcement becomes an atmosphere, a moral oxygen, where Christians learn, slowly and almost unconsciously, that it is safer to be vague than to be faithful. In a nation under judgment, the first sign is not always catastrophe; it is confusion. The second sign is cowardice rebranded as wisdom. That is where we are.

And if the Church does not repent, we will not lose influence; we will lose sight. We will lose the ability to recognize sin as sin because we have trained our mouths to speak around it. The most dangerous thing that can happen to a people is not that wickedness attacks them but that they become trained to tolerate wickedness as "normal," to treat rebellion as a lifestyle preference, and to speak of God's commands as if they were optional suggestions. When that happens, the battle is no longer "out there." It is inside the conscience. And the Lord does not weigh cultures first. He weighs His people. He weighs what we fear. He weighs what we love. He weighs what we refused to say and then calls it what it is.

Scripture does not treat silence as a neutral posture when the sword is coming. It treats silence as guilt. *"But if the watchman sees the sword coming and does not blow the trumpet... his blood I will require at the watchman's hand."* (Ezekiel 33:6).[783] That is covenant accountability for omission. The watchman is condemned not for creating the danger, but for refusing the warning. America loves to frame everything as "tone," "tribe," and "opinions," but God frames it as obedience. In a moral crisis, you do not become clean by stepping back or wash your hands by getting quiet. Scripture assigns responsibility not only for actions taken but also for duty neglected. That should sober pastors who prefer comfort to clarity, fathers who outsource formation, and citizens who watch evil get institutionalized and tell themselves it is "not my lane." The watchman category means there is a moment when silence itself becomes sin because silence becomes consent by omission.

And the Word will not let you hide behind passivity: *"So whoever knows the right thing to do and fails to do it, for him it is sin."* (James 4:17).[784] That verse kills the fantasy that innocence can be preserved by doing nothing. In a moral crisis, doing nothing is doing something: it is yielding ground, permitting lies to stabilize, and letting your conscience learn disobedience as a habit while you still call yourself faithful.

This is where the illusion of neutrality dies. Neutrality is a luxury only available when the moral order is stable. But when the moral order is being rewritten, neutrality becomes surrender because it yields the definition of good and evil to whoever is loudest and least restrained. Evil does not require your applause; it requires your permission. Silence provides that permission. Christians often say, "I don't want to get political." But the issue is not politics first; it is lordship. If

Christ is Lord, His commands do not stop at private sentiment. The claim that Jesus reigns is not a hobby claim; it is a public claim with consequences. When the Church retreats into privacy, it does not end the world's discipleship; it accepts it. And the world's discipleship will not remain "neutral." It will catechize your children. It will shape your workplace. It will redefine compassion. It will punish conscience. It will demand confession. In time, it will treat biblical speech as "harmful information" and biblical morality as "extremism," not because Scripture changed, but because the culture's conscience is being trained to hate any standard above the self. That is why silence is not personal; it is formative. It trains the body to treat obedience as optional, then wonders why the town burns when the trumpet is quiet.

The engine behind this retreat is fear of man, fear that often masquerades as maturity. It rarely sounds like cowardice; it sounds like strategy: "If we say that, we'll lose people." "If we press that, we'll get labeled." "If we speak plainly, we'll invite backlash." Scripture calls fear of man what it is: a snare. "The fear of man lays a snare, but whoever trusts in the Lord is safe." (Proverbs 29:25)[785] A snare doesn't warn you; it catches you by offering a trade: trade obedience for belonging, trade clarity for approval, trade truth for comfort. Repeated trades become reflex. Jesus named this among leaders who believed yet stayed quiet: *for fear... they did not confess it... for they loved the glory that comes from man more than the glory that comes from God."* (John 12:42–43).[786] Fear reveals what glory you prefer. This is why repentance must go deeper than "tone" or "approach." Fear of man is worship disorder. It treats human opinion as a god that can reward or destroy you.[787] If we will not repent of that idolatry, we will keep calling surrender "wisdom" while heaven calls it sin, and we will train our children to fear labels more than they fear the Lord.

Fear spreads because institutions reward it. Institutions prefer stability. They preserve budgets, reputations, partnerships, accreditation, donor bases, and legal safety. These realities are not automatically evil, but they become a test. The moment a church begins to treat truth as "risk," it is drifting. The moment leaders measure obedience by "what will happen," they have replaced fear of the Lord with fear of consequences. Scripture gives the Church no permission to be governed by intimidation: *"For God gave us a spirit not of fear but of power and love and self-control."* (2 Timothy 1:7).[788] That verse is governance. Power, love, self-control, courage without cruelty, clarity without chaos. A fearful church becomes a therapeutic church. It replaces warning with reassurance, discipline with accommodation, and doctrine with atmosphere. It becomes soft where it must be sharp and sharp where it should be gentle. And when coercion rises, it collapses because it has trained its people to avoid cost rather than endure it. Metaxas has warned that the church can be negotiated into irrelevance by a thousand small concessions, each defended as "pragmatic," until conviction weakens and clarity becomes embarrassment.[789] Negotiation usually begins with silence because silence feels like a painless compromise until the pain arrives later, multiplied.

The culture then weaponizes language to accelerate retreat. It does not debate Christians; it reframes Christian clarity as "harm." It calls repentance "violence." It defines love as affirmation and then criminalizes biblical love as hate. This is not random; it is systematic. The age cannot tolerate moral authority above the self, so it must remove the social permission to speak biblical categories. Scripture commands the opposite: *"Take no part in the unfruitful works of darkness, but instead expose them."* (Ephesians 5:11).[790] Exposure is not cruelty; it is mercy because it interrupts deception before it hardens into policy and policy hardens into coercion. Scripture also commands preaching that includes confrontation, not consolation: *"Preach the word... reprove, rebuke, and exhort, with complete patience and teaching."* (2 Timothy 4:2).[791] The verbs matter. Reprove, rebuke, and exhort, done with patience and done with teaching. The Church is being pressured to delete these verbs and replace them with vocabulary that never reaches "repentance." Dreher describes the modern pressure as "soft totalitarianism," not always prison, but coordinated social and economic penalties that train dissenters to self-censor.[792] Punish speech, produce silence, secure surrender. The culture does not need to win the argument if it can make truth too expensive to say.

This pressure lands with unusual force today because the modern world has redefined the human person. When desire becomes identity and identity becomes sacred, moral boundaries feel like violence. Correction becomes "harm." Repentance becomes "self-erasure." The Church is warned that compassion requires affirmation. But affirmation without repentance is not compassion; it is abandonment. Trueman's analysis of expressive individualism explains why biblical speech is increasingly treated not as disagreement but as threat: the self has been enthroned, and any external authority is experienced as oppression.[793] The modern self does not want a Savior who forgives and transforms; it wants a priest who blesses and validates. It does not want a Lord; it wants permission. And once those assumptions are installed, the culture will not be satisfied with your private belief. It will demand public compliance because the new religion is institutional. It requires corporate confession, schools, businesses, hospitals, churches, families, and governments to participate. When Christians refuse, they are accused of cruelty because the culture's definition of love has been severed from truth. This is why politeness will not save you. The issue is not your tone; it is your King.

At that point many Christians retreat into a phrase that sounds spiritual: "Just preach Jesus." If it means preaching the real Jesus, Lord, Savior, Judge, and King, the One who commands repentance, it is the cure. But if it means preaching a reduced Jesus who comforts without commanding, welcomes without cleansing, and heals without ruling, then it is evasion. Jesus demands confession. *"So everyone who acknowledges me before men, I also will acknowledge before my Father who is in heaven, but whoever denies me before men, I also will deny before him."* (Matthew 10:32–33).[794] That is a crisis-era text. Scripture does not treat cowardice as harmless. *"But as for the cowardly... their portion will be in the lake that burns with fire and sulfur."* (Revelation 21:8).[795] Here is the higher-heat warning we avoid at our peril: if you train your soul to deny Christ by omission now, by habitual silence when obedience requires speech, you are training yourself for denial when the cost becomes higher. You are not remaining "safe"; you are becoming numb.

Accountability is layered. Every Christian will answer to God for obedience, and leaders will answer with heavier responsibility. Ezekiel's watchman imagery is not an honorary title; it is a burden. And long before our age learned to market cowardice as "prudence," the Church warned that a shepherd who fears to speak what is right turns his back through silence.[796] If a shepherd refuses to confront wolves because it makes people uncomfortable, he is not gentle; he is negligent. If a pastor refuses to name sin because it might divide, he is not unifying; he is disarming. The crisis does not create compromise; it reveals it. It exposes what was already governing the church: fear, comfort addiction, and reputation management. And here is the second higher-heat warning: God will not accept religious vocabulary as a cover for disobedience. He weighs hearts. He knows when "discernment" is camouflage for cowardice. He knows when "unity" is a euphemism for silence. Judgment begins with the household of God. If we do not repent, we will be disciplined, not because God hates His Church, but because He refuses to let His Church masquerade as faithful while serving another master.

Silence has downstream consequences that are predictable. What is tolerated becomes celebrated; what is celebrated becomes enforced. First, you're told you don't have to participate, just be quiet. Then you're told you can believe whatever you want, but just don't say it publicly. Then you're told you can say it privately; just don't act on it. Finally you're told to celebrate the lie, or lose your job, your license, your platform, your social standing. The Church is tempted at each stage to accept terms for temporary calm. But temporary calm is purchased with surrender. Scripture refuses plausible deniability: *"Rescue those who are being taken away to death... If you say, "Behold, we did not know this,' does not he who weighs the heart perceive it?"* (Proverbs 24:11–12).[797] God weighs hearts. He sees when "I didn't know" is a cover for "I didn't want the cost." When the Church buys peace through silence, it does not eliminate conflict; it transfers cost to children, to the weak, to the unprotected. Murray has argued that civilizations weaken when they lose confidence in truth and refuse to defend it publicly; the vacuum is then filled by aggressive ideologies.[798] Whatever the label, the mechanism is the same: weakness invites coercion; silence invites enforcement; surrender invites further demands.

Formation never pauses. If the Church will not disciple, someone else will. Families will be catechized by screens. Children will be discipled by institutions. Conscience will be trained by policies. Then Christians will ask why the next generation finds biblical categories offensive. Because we trained them to. We taught them the trumpet was optional. We taught them Scripture was "private." We taught them the safest posture was silence. Pearcey's point about formation is a warning: human beings are shaped by repeated practices and story-worlds, and if the Church does not provide counter-formation, the age will form its people in rival worship.[799] That is why silence is not "not speaking." Silence is the surrender of formation. It is letting the age define love, justice, harm, identity, and virtue while the Church whispers about comfort. It is spiritual malpractice. It also carries a personal cost: if you repeatedly silence yourself when you should speak, you train your conscience to go numb. Numbness becomes normal. Normal becomes identity. And then, when the moment demands courage, you discover you no longer possess it.

So the indictment comes home. Where have you been quiet to keep comfort? Where have you withheld truth to preserve your reputation? Where have you watched institutions lie to children and said nothing because you feared labels? Where have you avoided naming sin because you feared consequences more than you feared God? Repentance begins when we stop blaming "the culture" as if culture is an external force we cannot resist. Culture is downstream of worship, what people worship, what they reward, what they punish, and what they refuse to say. If you have learned to call cowardice "wisdom," repent. If you have learned to call silence "love," repent. If you have learned to treat obedience as optional when it is costly, repent. The apostles did not pray for safe lives; they prayed for faithful speech. *"grant to your servants to continue to speak your word with all boldness."* (Acts 4:29).[800] They assumed threat. They asked for obedience under threat. That is what God is demanding now: not theatrics, not performative outrage, not fleshly rage, but obedience. Because a crisis era does not test what you believe; it tests what you will do with what you claim to believe.

And obedience requires warning. Scripture does not call God's people to retreat from public life; it calls them to establish justice where decisions are made. *"Hate evil, and love good, and establish justice in the gate."* (Amos 5:15)[801] The gate is public. God's people are not told to flee the gate; they are told to establish righteousness there. Scripture also speaks of watchmen who refuse silence as faithfulness: *"On your walls... I have set watchmen... they shall never be silent."* (Isaiah 62:6).[802] "Never silent" does not mean always loud; it means never surrendering duty when warning is required. When God speaks to His servants in crisis seasons, He does not say, "keep quiet so you can survive." He says, *"Do not be afraid, but go on speaking and do not be silent."* (Acts 18:9).[803] That command is mercy. Silence feels safe only briefly. Then the lie consolidates, the conscience hardens, and the cost grows. If you won't speak when it is uncomfortable; you will not speak when it becomes expensive. That is why God is calling His people to repent now, before pressure becomes enforcement, before cowardice becomes identity, before silence becomes a habit that hardens the heart.

This is why silence is surrender. Not because Christians are called to chase every headline, but because the age is discipling the nation with rival definitions of love, harm, justice, and human identity, and it is demanding the Church's quiet cooperation. The Lord is not calling His people to panic; He is calling them to repentance: return to the fear of the Lord, reject the fear of man, and pick up the trumpet before judgment falls heavier. If you will not repent of silence now, you will interpret obedience later as extremism, because fear always rewires the conscience to justify itself. The question becomes immediate: when you speak, how do you speak in a way that honors Christ, truthfully, courageously, and lovingly, without becoming harsh, reckless, or captured by the enemy's dictionary? That is what Section II will govern.

Section II: Truth in Love, Not Love Without Truth

The command to speak the truth in love is not a suggestion for temperamentally gentle Christians; it is a moral obligation bound to the nature of God Himself. Scripture never treats truth and love as competing virtues that must be balanced to avoid offense. They are inseparable because God is both truthful and loving without contradiction. When love is detached from truth, it becomes indulgence, affirming what destroys in the name of compassion. When truth is detached from love, it becomes brutality, accurate words wielded without regard for the soul receiving them. The modern Church has normalized this false dichotomy, as if faithfulness requires choosing which attribute to abandon. Scripture refuses that choice. *"Love does not rejoice at wrongdoing but rejoices with the truth."* (1 Corinthians 13:6).[804] Love does not coexist neutrally with falsehood; it celebrates reality, even when reality wounds.

Love that refuses to tell the truth is not gentleness; it is deception with a smile. The gospel does not rescue by affirming lies; it rescues by exposing them and then offering forgiveness, restoration, and new obedience. Edwards warned that true religion is measured not by warmth of feeling but by the soul's submission to God's moral excellency, so love that refuses truth is not tenderness; it is counterfeit piety.[805]

Truth spoken in love is ordered toward formation, not catharsis. Scripture frames correction as an instrument of growth, not relational sabotage. *"Speaking the truth in love, we are to grow up in every way into him who is the head, into Christ."* (Ephesians 4:15).[806] Maturity does not occur where no one is ever challenged. Growth requires friction; discipleship requires resistance. Jonathan Edwards observed that genuine spiritual affections incline the soul toward obedience and holiness, not toward emotional warmth or religious sentiment.[807] When churches prioritize atmosphere over formation, they may preserve peace in the room while producing instability in the soul. The gospel is not therapeutic affirmation; it is transformative truth. Peace is not the highest virtue; righteousness is. Peace is the fruit of truth embraced, not the substitute for truth that is avoided.

The Church's retreat into euphemism has not made it more loving; it has made it less honest. Sin is renamed to avoid discomfort, rebellion is reframed as identity, and repentance is replaced with "journey language" that never arrives anywhere. Scripture forbids silence masquerading as kindness. *"You shall not hate your brother in your heart, but you shall reason frankly with your neighbor, lest you incur sin because of him.*" (Leviticus 19:17).[808] According to God, refusing frankness in the face of moral danger is not love; it is hatred expressed politely. Trueman has traced how modern expressive individualism elevates inner feelings as the highest authority, demanding social affirmation as a moral right.[809]

When the Church adopts that framework, it stops naming sin as sin and starts managing emotions instead. Clear speech is not cruelty; it is protection, because repentance cannot begin where sin cannot be named.

Scripture gives an ordered pattern for confrontation to guard against chaos and cruelty, not to authorize perpetual silence. *"If your brother sins against you, go and tell him his fault between you and him alone."* (Matthew 18:15).[810] This is not a loophole for avoidance but a mandate for responsibility. Correction begins privately to preserve dignity, not to escape duty. Baxter insisted that private admonition is an essential act of pastoral love, not an optional courtesy.[811]

Yet the modern Church weaponizes this passage as a gag order, insisting that no sin may be addressed publicly, even when it is already public, celebrated, and formative. Order without courage becomes paralysis. Discipline delayed indefinitely is discipline denied.

The cultural redefinition of correction as violence has discipled the Church. Disagreement is framed as harm, warning is labeled trauma, and moral clarity is treated as danger. Scripture anticipated this reaction. *"Have I then become your enemy by telling you the truth?"* (Galatians 4:16).[812]

And Paul does not apologize for the offensive truth he creates; he exposes the lie that equates discomfort with betrayal. Lukianoff and Haidt describe how a culture of safetyism trains people to treat emotional distress as injury, producing fragility rather than resilience.[813] The Church has absorbed that mindset and baptized it as compassion. But Scripture never treats offense as proof of wrongdoing. Often, offense is the cost of rescue. Love that refuses that cost is not love; it is abdication.

Biblical correction is oriented toward restoration, not domination. *"If your brother sins, rebuke him, and if he repents, forgive him."* (Luke 17:3).[814] Rebuke without forgiveness becomes tyranny; forgiveness without repentance becomes deception. Scripture holds both together because God holds both together. Watson wrote that true repentance involves hatred of sin itself, not regret over consequences.[815] When churches rush to reassure without calling for repentance, they offer relief without transformation, a counterfeit grace that soothes consciences while leaving chains intact. Correction that leads to repentance is not cruelty but rescue; silence that leaves people enslaved to falsehood is not mercy but abandonment.

There are two equal and opposite failures in truth-telling, and both destroy credibility. One is brutality, truth delivered with contempt, driven by ego, outrage, or tribal dominance, and more interested in winning than healing. The other is betrayal, love reduced to affirmation, and an unwillingness to wound even when wounds are required. *"Faithful are the wounds of a friend; profuse are the kisses of an enemy."* (Proverbs 27:6).[816] Truth must be wielded like a scalpel, not a sledgehammer, precise and intentional, and governed by diagnosis rather than impulse. But refusing to cut when infection spreads is not compassion; it is malpractice. Owen warned that sin left unopposed does not weaken; it strengthens.[817] Discipline without courage becomes cowardice; courage without discipline becomes recklessness. Scripture demands both because souls are at stake.

The slogan "preach Jesus" has become a sanctuary for leaders who want the safety of spiritual language without the risk of spiritual authority. It sounds humble, but it often functions like a muzzle. Jesus is preached as comforter but not commander, healer but not judge, and friend but not King. That is not Christ; it is a culturally acceptable silhouette wearing His name. When Scripture commands ministers to confront, it assumes confrontation will touch real sins, real ideologies, and real deceptions, not offer vague encouragement.

The moment Jesus is detached from repentance, the cross becomes therapy instead of atonement, and grace becomes permission instead of power. Gregory the Great understood that the pastor who withholds correction from those in his care has not spared them pain; he has chosen his own comfort over their souls, and God will require an account for that silence.[818] Love does not hide Christ's warnings or strip the gospel down until it fits the world's comfort standards. What gets called "winsome" is frequently fear dressed up as tone.

A clear test of whether truth is being spoken in love is whether it is being spoken with moral clarity rather than moral fog. Scripture is not ashamed of directness: *"Better is open rebuke than hidden love."* (Proverbs 27:5).[819] Hidden love is what the modern Church calls "being nice," and it is often a cowardly substitute for actual charity. Open rebuke is not public humiliation; it is visible, honest correction when truth is required and silence becomes betrayal. That verse does not authorize harshness; it destroys the lie that love must always be quiet. "Rutherford understood that silence before sin is not diplomacy but desertion, and that the minister who withholds rebuke to preserve his comfort has not loved his people but abandoned them to their ruin."[820] Watson's insistence that repentance requires a real turning from sin exposes why hidden love fails: repentance cannot begin where sin cannot be named.[821] The modern demand for "non-judgment" is not virtue; it is an anti-repentance ethic. And falsehood is never love, no matter how calm the voice sounds.

Truth in love requires the ability to distinguish between correction that restores and correction that performs. Some Christians have been discipled by outrage more than by Scripture; they speak as if volume is virtue and sarcasm is courage. That is not prophetic courage; it is flesh dressed in righteousness language. Sibbes knew the difference between holy severity and fleshly anger: one grieves over sin while piercing it; the other enjoys the piercing.[822] Owen warned that sin thrives where it is not mortified daily, including the sins of the tongue: pride, bitterness, impatience, and the desire to punish rather than heal.[823] If the goal is rescue, the speaker must be governed by humility. The Church's credibility is damaged when truth is delivered with contempt because it confirms the world's accusation that Christians want control. Love aims its speech at the other person's good, not at the speaker's emotional release. The moment correction becomes performance, it stops being love.

Truth-telling has become difficult in part because the culture has redefined personhood so that moral boundaries feel like personal attacks. Paul Kingsnorth has observed that when identity becomes sacred, any challenge to it functions as blasphemy, and blasphemy in any religion is met not with argument but with punishment.[824] Once that framework takes hold, the moral universe is inverted. Repentance becomes "self-hatred," correction becomes "harm," and truth becomes "oppression." Christians who do not understand this dynamic will either retreat into silence or respond with frustration that only deepens conflict.

Love requires discernment about what the other person has been trained to believe about reality. Pearcey argues that biblical love honors the whole person, body and soul, as an integrated unity, cutting against the modern split that treats the body as morally neutral material to be reshaped for inner psychological desire.[825] Speaking truth in love is not about tone; it is about refusing a counterfeit anthropology. The Church must speak as if creation is real and God's design has authority, because it does.

Truth in love also requires refusing to be discipled by fear of institutional consequences. The modern world regulates speech through policies, HR codes, professional reputations, and social punishment, not to silence Christians, but to train them to self-censor before anyone asks. MacArthur has observed that the church which measures its faithfulness by institutional tolerance has already surrendered its independence to the very system it was called to confront.[826]

And that is the trap: when the Church absorbs this environment, it starts treating moral clarity as "unwise" and baptizes fear as prudence. Love cannot be governed by an institution's comfort rules when those rules contradict God. This is not a call to recklessness; it is a call to priority. When leaders choose institutional peace over truth, they justify it as strategy, but strategy that requires betrayal is surrender wearing a tie. Love speaks because love protects.

The ordered nature of biblical correction also means knowing when private speech is sufficient and when public clarity is required. Private admonition is often the first duty, but public deception creates public casualties. Whitefield did not reserve his rebukes for private correspondence when error was preached from public pulpits, for he understood that when the disease is public, the remedy must be equally visible.[827]

Today's falsehoods are not personal; they are institutional. When schools, corporations, and public institutions catechize people into moral inversion, the Church cannot pretend that "quiet discipleship" alone will counteract what is taught loudly, constantly, and authoritatively. Lukianoff and Haidt show how institutions can train people to interpret disagreement as danger; when that lens dominates, public clarity becomes necessary to keep reality intelligible.[828] This is where many Christians collapse into a false dilemma: either stay silent or become harsh. Scripture requires neither. It requires ordered courage, clarity without slander, firmness without theatrics, and correction without contempt. Love speaks to the person, and it warns the community. Love protects the weak from confusion. Love refuses to let deception present itself as virtue without resistance.

The end of this method is not argument-winning; it is soul-rescuing and church-strengthening. Truth in love refuses to treat people as enemies to defeat but as neighbors to warn, and refuses to equate kindness with silence or courage with rage. When correction is shaped by Scripture and anchored in humility, it becomes a form of mercy the world cannot imitate because the world has no category for repentance. It can only affirm or cancel. The Church must do neither. It must call for repentance and then open the door to restoration. That is why the Church cannot surrender its vocabulary to the culture. If love is redefined as affirmation, repentance becomes "hate," and the gospel becomes unintelligible. Winslow understood that the most powerful corrective the Church possesses is not argument but the visible reality of a love that endures the cost of truth-telling, a love the world has no category for because it receives nothing in return.[829] The Church must keep the biblical meaning of love intact so sinners can be saved from sin rather than comforted inside it.

Discernment is not the ability to spot error; it is the discipline of prioritizing what must be said now. Many churches have learned to argue loudly about secondary matters while whispering about primary rebellions, and then they call the whisper "wisdom." Scripture commands the opposite: *"Let the word of Christ dwell in you richly, teaching and admonishing one another in all wisdom."* (Colossians 3:16).[830] Wisdom is not cowardice with a diploma. It is the capacity to recognize what lies do to people and to intervene with timely clarity. When leaders treat every issue as equally debatable, they create moral fog that benefits the boldest rebels and punishes the quietest saints. This is how the Church becomes confused without realizing it: it cannot tell the difference between a preference and a prohibition, between a tension among brothers and a direct assault on God's design. Adrian Rogers said plainly what most pulpits now refuse to say: a church that has learned to shout about preferences and whisper about sin has reversed the order of heaven, and God will not honor that inversion.[831] But Scripture does not grant that freedom. It calls the Church to speak with hierarchy, not hysteria.

Speaking truth in love also means refusing the modern lie that love must affirm what God calls sin to be "safe." The culture treats emotional comfort as sacred and then demands everyone protect it. Sproul insisted that the fear of God is the only fear that liberates a man from every other fear, and that the church which has lost its reverence for God will inevitably become enslaved to the reverence of man.[832] John Stott insisted that the Church's first obligation is not to make people feel accepted but to tell them the truth, and that a love which withholds truth to protect feelings has confused kindness with cowardice.[833] The Church cannot operate under that moral regime without becoming cowardly. Scripture commands frankness precisely so the Church will not be trapped by the other person's feelings. *"Pay attention to yourselves! If your brother sins, rebuke him, and if he repents, forgive him."* (Luke 17:3).[834] Rebuke is an act of attention, not aggression; it is spiritual care, not hostility. Love pays attention. Love refuses to let a brother drift toward destruction because speaking would be uncomfortable. But love watches itself, guarding against pride, harshness, and the itch to punish.

The Church must recover the courage to name sin as sin without adopting the world's theatrical methods. The world uses speech either to dominate or to flatter, to humiliate or to seduce. The Church has imitated both. David Wilkerson warned that the Church that borrows the world's tools to do God's work will produce the world's results, and that a generation trained on spectacle will not be moved by substance.[835] That warning lands because many believers are not tolerating sin; they are being trained to celebrate it, and churches are afraid to confront the training. Yet Scripture teaches correction is a function of love, not temperament. *"Those whom I love, I reprove and discipline, so be zealous and repent."* (Revelation 3:19).[836] Christ does not outsource confrontation. He reproves and disciplines. Calvin understood that the human heart is an idol factory precisely because it will not tolerate an authority above itself, and that a church which stops naming sin has simply agreed to let the factory run unopposed.[837] If a church has lost the ability to correct, it has not become more loving. It has become less holy, and therefore less safe for its people.

Truth in love demands a biblical anthropology, because modern moral confusion is rooted in a modern view of the human person. When the culture detaches identity from creation and grounds it in inner feeling, moral boundaries become "oppression," and the body becomes raw material for self-definition. John Lennox argues that the biblical account of the human person is not a religious preference but a rational necessity, and that once the body is severed from moral meaning, no coherent account of human dignity survives.[838] That matters because the Church cannot speak truthfully about love if it cannot speak truthfully about what a human is. When Christians adopt the culture's anthropology, they treat moral instruction as harm and discipline as abuse. But Scripture grounds love in truth about reality. *"You shall reason frankly with your neighbor, lest you incur sin because of him."* (Leviticus 19:17).[839] Frank reasoning assumes an objective moral order, the possibility of being wrong, and the necessity of repentance. The Church must speak as if creation is real and God's design is authoritative, because if it does not, it cannot speak lovingly; it can only speak sentimentally.

The ethic of truth-telling requires patience, because restoration is often slower than rebuke. The Church fails when it either refuses to confront or confronts and then abandons. Love does neither. Flavel understood that the work of grace in a soul is not a transaction but a campaign, and that the minister who abandons a soul because progress is slow has mistaken his own impatience for discernment.[840] That means pastoral correction is rarely a single conversation. It is a process, repeated warnings, patient teaching, and, when necessary, firm boundaries.

Scripture commands urgency with endurance: truth must be spoken "in season and out of season," with patience and teaching (2 Timothy 4:2).[841] Patience is not weakness; it is the refusal to treat souls as disposable when sanctification is messy. Yet patience is not permission. The Church must reject counterfeit patience that is avoidance. Love bears the awkwardness of repeated confrontation if that is what it takes to rescue someone from the slow drift into destruction. The ethic is simple: do not wound for sport, and do not withhold the wound that heals.

The point of speaking truth in love is not to create a church full of combative people; it is to form a church full of clear, courageous, disciplined saints who can withstand deception without becoming cruel. That requires leaders who refuse both the soft lie and the hard sin, leaders who will not affirm what God condemns and will not condemn without opening the path of repentance and restoration. The modern Church is tempted to treat truth as optional and love as tone. Scripture reverses that: truth is obedience, and love is covenantal action aimed at the other person's eternal good.

This is why the Church must keep the biblical definition of love intact. If love is reduced to affirmation, repentance becomes "harm," and the gospel becomes unintelligible. Bonar pressed the same indictment the modern Church refuses to hear: repentance is not regret dressed in religious language but a complete reversal of direction, costly, concrete, and visible in changed living.[842] M'Cheyne confirmed what every honest pastor eventually learns: where true religion lives, obedience follows as naturally as fruit follows root, and where obedience is absent, the profession of faith is a performance, not a reality.[843] Truth in love wounds faithfully and then heals patiently. It speaks clearly and then walks with people through repentance. Anything else is either brutality or betrayal. And neither is the way of Christ.

Section III: The Remnant Who Won't Bow

Faithfulness has never belonged to the majority. Scripture consistently presents obedience as something preserved through narrowing rather than expansion. When Elijah fled into the wilderness, convinced that he alone remained faithful, God did not correct him by pointing to influence or visibility but by revealing preservation: *"Yet I will leave seven thousand in Israel, all the knees that have not bowed to Baal, and every mouth that has not kissed him."* (1 Kings 19:18).[844] The remnant is not loud, dominant, or culturally secure; it is hidden, obedient, and sustained by God rather than validated by numbers. Paul later retrieves this same category to explain why faithfulness often looks like failure from the outside: *"So too at the present time there is a remnant, chosen by grace."* (Romans 11:5).[845] Remnant theology is not pessimism; it is realism anchored in covenant history. Truth divides because allegiance divides. The remnant exists not because God has failed to persuade the masses, but because obedience is costly, and cost filters loyalty. Ryle knew that the distinguishing mark of real Christianity is not profession but endurance; that the true believer is known not by what he claims in safety but by what he holds in the hour of cost.[846]

The modern Church often treats cultural hostility as an aberration rather than an expectation, as if faithfulness should naturally produce affirmation if only it were framed winsomely enough. Scripture prepares believers for the opposite. Jesus does not promise relevance; He promises resistance: *"If the world hates you, know that it has hated me before it hated you."* (John 15:18).[847] Pressure is not an interruption to the Christian life; it is the environment in which allegiance is clarified. Where belief carries no cost, conviction remains shallow. Where obedience invites loss, the heart is exposed. Christians today must prepare to live as a creative minority, learning from those who resisted communism how to maintain identity and truth under pressure.[848] The remnant is formed not by outrage but by endurance. It is not animated by panic but by settled obedience that continues when applause disappears. Faith that survives only in safety is preference, not conviction.

Throughout history, prosperity has diluted the Church more effectively than persecution ever did. Comfort blurs moral edges; constraint sharpens them. The early Church did not grow because it was protected, but because it refused to bow when pressure demanded accommodation. *"We must obey God rather than men."* (Acts 5:29).[849] Pressure makes neutrality impossible. Indeed, *"all who desire to live a godly life in Christ Jesus will be persecuted."* (2 Timothy 3:12).[850] Under such conditions, the remnant emerges wherever obedience continues when disobedience would be safer, quieter, and more rewarded. This is not heroism; it is fidelity. Polycarp refused the proconsul's offer of safety and walked to his death confessing Christ, not because he sought martyrdom, but because he had already settled the question of whom he served.[851] God does not preserve His people by insulating them from pressure but by sustaining them through it.

Formation is the decisive battleground in every generation, and pressure exposes who has taken responsibility for it and who has abdicated. Children are not neutral vessels waiting to choose; they are being catechized constantly by schools, screens, peers, institutions, and narratives that interpret reality long before critical thinking develops. *"Train up a child in the way he should go; even when he is old he will not depart from it."* (Proverbs 22:6).[852] Silence in the name of peace does not preserve innocence; it cedes formation to other authorities. The church must build thick communities of virtue, including education and work, to sustain the remnant across generations.[853] The remnant is forged where families and churches reclaim formation under pressure, teaching truth even when it isolates and discipling deeply even when it costs attendance, reputation, or security.

Formation does not stop at the church door, and pressure intensifies where authority structures overlap. Education has never been neutral, because it always answers prior questions about reality, authority, and meaning. When schools redefine the human person, they are not transmitting information; they are demanding allegiance. Scripture treats this dynamic with sobriety, not surprise. *"The fear of the Lord is the beginning of knowledge."* (Proverbs 1:7).[854] Voddie Baucham has pressed the point with urgency: the family that surrenders its children to rival discipleship has not avoided the culture war; it has simply chosen to lose it without a fight.[855] Under such conditions, parents who imagine that silence will preserve access or protect opportunity misunderstand how formation works. The remnant is not created by withdrawal from the world but by discernment within it, knowing where participation requires compromise and where resistance becomes obedience.

Pressure reveals itself when institutions move from persuasion to compulsion. Persuasion invites agreement; compulsion demands affirmation. Scripture consistently treats forced speech as a test of allegiance. When the king demanded not outward compliance but submission of conscience, faithful refusal became the line between obedience and idolatry: *"But if not, be it known to you, O king, that we will not serve your gods or worship the golden image that you have set up."* (Daniel 3:18).[856] Compelled affirmation trains the soul to bow internally even when outward resistance remains minimal. Knox understood that when a government demands the Church bless what God has cursed, silence is not neutrality; it is complicity, and complicity is the beginning of captivity.[857] The remnant recognizes this pattern and refuses to treat language as inconsequential. Words shape loyalty. Silence under coercion does not preserve peace; it prepares surrender.

History confirms that systems do not begin by demanding belief; they begin by regulating speech and punishing dissent until self-censorship becomes habit. Scripture exposes what this pressure is doing at the level of worship: *"They exchanged the truth about God for a lie and worshiped and served the creature rather than the Creator."* (Romans 1:25).[858] The remnant is not marked by noise but by refusal, refusal to speak what is false to belong. This refusal often appears unspectacular. It does not seek martyrdom, but it does not flee it either. Ignatius understood that the Christian who bargains with the world's definitions to preserve his standing has not saved his witness, he has surrendered it, and what remains is a shell that wears the name of Christ without bearing His cross.[859] Faithfulness that is performative burns quickly; faithfulness that is obedient endures quietly.

Legal and professional pressure intensifies this test because it arrives clothed in legitimacy. Policies, accreditation standards, and compliance language create the illusion that conscience objections are personal preferences obstructing progress. Scripture anticipates this inversion. *"Woe to those who call evil good and good evil."* (Isaiah 5:20).[860] When participation requires affirmation of what God forbids, withdrawal becomes witness rather than retreat. Bonhoeffer's stand against the compromised German church demonstrates that true discipleship refuses alignment with evil powers.[861] The remnant does not seek conflict, but it refuses to pretend that obedience is negotiable. Faithfulness that survives only within permissive structures is fragile. The Church's calling has never depended on institutional favor; it has depended on covenant loyalty sustained under cost.

Witnesses have always been authenticated by cost rather than by volume. Scripture never equates faithfulness with visibility or numerical success; it equates it with endurance under pressure. *"And they have conquered him by the blood of the Lamb and by the word of their testimony, for they loved not their lives even unto death."* (Revelation 12:11).[862] The remnant bears witness precisely because it refuses to treat survival as the highest good. The ten Boom family risked and lost everything to hide Jews, yet maintained faith and forgiveness in Ravensbrück.[863] The remnant does not wait for permission to be faithful. It understands that delay often disguises disobedience. Where the Church conditions obedience on safety, it teaches believers that conviction is optional. But where obedience persists despite loss, the gospel becomes visible as something more than a preference; it becomes a claim on life itself.

Outrage-driven resistance often masquerades as courage, but it rarely endures. Scripture calls the faithful to steadiness rather than spectacle. *"Be watchful; stand firm in the faith, act like men, and be strong."* (1 Corinthians 16:13).[864] Performative defiance tends to exhaust itself quickly, while disciplined communities quietly build habits capable of surviving sustained pressure. Lloyd-Jones warned that the church formed by emotion rather than doctrine will collapse when emotion fades, because it has trained its people to feel conviction rather than hold it.[865] The remnant is not sustained by adrenaline but by formation, daily obedience repeated when no one is watching. Noise attracts attention, but endurance shapes legacy. The Church's credibility has never rested on its ability to shout but on its refusal to abandon truth when silence would be rewarded. Faithfulness measured by volume confuses reaction with resolve. The remnant understands that obedience practiced slowly is more threatening to false systems than anger expressed briefly.

Endurance requires a different imagination than resistance framed around victory or defeat. Scripture consistently directs the faithful to think in terms of inheritance rather than outcomes. *"For here we have no lasting city, but we seek the city that is to come."* (Hebrews 13:14).[866] Suffering loses its terror when obedience is anchored to eternity rather than to comfort or reputation. Bunyan wrote from a prison cell not as a man defeated by his circumstances but as a man who had already chosen his citizenship, and that settled choice made the cell irrelevant to his faithfulness.[867] This orientation frees the remnant from panic. It does not need to win every battle to remain faithful. It needs only to refuse to bow. When believers expect faithfulness to feel victorious, disappointment leads to compromise. But when faithfulness is understood as loyalty regardless of outcome, courage becomes sustainable. The remnant survives because it does not measure success by immediate relief but by covenant alignment.

Under prolonged pressure, despair and triumphalism become twin temptations. Despair whispers that resistance is futile; triumphalism insists that faithfulness guarantees dominance. Scripture rejects both. *"Do not be conformed to this world, but be transformed by the renewal of your mind, so that by testing you may discern what is the will of God, what is good and acceptable and perfect."* (Romans 12:2).[868] Remnant theology guards against confusion by restoring proportion: narrowing does not necessarily mean defeat; it often means filtration. Tozer observed that God does not measure His church by its size but by its purity, and that a shrinking remnant walking in holiness is more powerful before heaven than a swelling crowd walking in compromise.[869] God preserves His people not by ensuring cultural dominance but by sustaining obedience across generations. Faithfulness that outlives its context testifies to a kingdom not dependent on platforms or power.

Discernment under pressure is not instinctive; it is cultivated. Scripture does not call the faithful to courage alone but to wisdom that knows when clarity must be public and when faithfulness is borne quietly. *"The wise heart will know the proper time and the just way."* (Ecclesiastes 8:5).[870] The remnant learns to distinguish between moments that demand declaration and moments that require endurance without explanation. This distinction is not cowardice; it is stewardship of witness. Where every provocation is answered publicly, the soul becomes exhausted and the witness diluted.

Discernment preserves strength for the moments that truly require refusal.

Public clarity becomes unavoidable when deception is institutionalized, and silence would imply consent. Scripture records moments when quiet obedience was sufficient and moments when public refusal became necessary for the sake of others. *"We cannot but speak of what we have seen and heard."* (Acts 4:20).[871] When lies are taught authoritatively, especially to the young or the vulnerable, withdrawal alone no longer protects conscience; it abandons neighbors to confusion. Wilberforce understood that the man who sees injustice being normalized and says nothing to preserve his comfort has not remained neutral, he has chosen the side of the oppressor by his silence.[872] The remnant does not seek exposure, but it refuses invisibility when truth itself is under assault. Public clarity, when required, is not aggression; it is love that refuses to let deception go unchallenged.

This balance, between quiet endurance and visible refusal, cannot be reduced to formulas. It requires leaders and families who are spiritually formed rather than informed. Scripture warns against mistaking confidence for wisdom, because zeal unshaped by obedience fractures community. *"Let your reasonableness be known to everyone."* (Philippians 4:5).[873] Embodied faithfulness, how believers live, teach, and suffer, often speaks more powerfully than slogans, especially in cultures suspicious of moral claims.[874] The remnant understands that credibility is cumulative. It is earned through consistency over time, not through moments of defiance disconnected from daily obedience. This kind of courage is quieter, but harder to discredit.

Sustained pressure exposes whether faith is intellectual or fully embodied. Scripture consistently ties perseverance to the formation of character rather than to the preservation of comfort. *"Blessed is the man who remains steadfast under trial..."* (James 1:12).[875] Scripture frames endurance as the path to maturity, not as an unfortunate detour. Wurmbrand testified that believers who survived prolonged persecution were not those who relied on emotional resolve but those whose obedience had been rehearsed long before suffering arrived.[876] The remnant does not improvise faithfulness in crisis; it practices it daily. This is why cultural pressure feels overwhelming to those whose convictions have remained abstract. Embodied obedience, formed through prayer, Scripture, family discipline, and accountable community, creates spiritual muscle memory that pressure cannot instantly manufacture.

Scripture describes this kind of formation as readiness, not improvisation: *"Take up the whole armor of God, that you may be able to withstand in the evil day, and having done all, to stand firm."* (Ephesians 6:13).[877] When the Church trades formation for convenience, it produces believers who can explain truth but cannot withstand coercion. But when the Church trains saints to endure through disciplined worship, habitual repentance, and courageous love, pressure becomes a refining fire rather than a consuming one.

The remnant is sustained by inheritance thinking rather than outcome obsession. Scripture consistently lifts the eyes of the faithful *beyond immediate results and fixes them on what endures. "Therefore, my beloved brothers, be steadfast, immovable, and always abounding in the work of the Lord, knowing that in the Lord your labor is not in vain."* (1 Corinthians 15:58).[878] Faithfulness is not validated by visible success; it is validated by obedience rendered before God.

Bonhoeffer insisted that responsible action must be undertaken without guarantees, because obedience that requires assurance is no longer obedience but calculation.[879] The remnant acts not because victory is assured but because truth is owed allegiance regardless of consequence. This orientation liberates believers from panic when influence wanes and from arrogance when resistance succeeds. The Church does not exist to secure outcomes; it exists to bear witness.

This inheritance-focused posture protects the remnant from the twin deceptions of despair and illusion. Despair claims that narrowing influence means failure; illusion promises that boldness guarantees dominance. Scripture dismantles both. God's promise stands firm: *"The Lord knows those who are his."* (2 Timothy 2:19).[880] That promise grounds confidence not in cultural position but in divine preservation. Adoniram Judson labored seven years in Burma before a single convert. He did not measure faithfulness by counting heads. He measured it by whether he had obeyed the commission and left the outcome where it belongs.[881] Remnant theology steadies the soul by restoring proportion. God has never depended on majorities to accomplish His purposes. He has depended on obedience sustained across generations, often unseen and unrewarded in its own time. The remnant does not panic when numbers shrink, because it understands that faithfulness is not measured by scale but by continuity.

Embodied courage, not rhetorical certainty, is the final measure of remnant faithfulness. Scripture never praises those who affirm truth verbally while surrendering it practically. *"Be doers of the word and not hearers only, deceiving yourselves."* (James 1:22).[882] That command confronts the illusion that conviction can remain abstract under pressure. Wurmbrand observed that in moments of coercion, theology becomes either embodied or exposed as ornamental.[883] The remnant survives because it practices obedience in ordinary rhythms long before extraordinary tests arrive. Prayer, Scripture, family discipline, sacramental life, and community accountability form muscles that crisis cannot instantly build. Courage that appears suddenly under pressure is usually borrowed; courage that endures has been cultivated. The remnant does not wait to see what will happen before deciding how to live. It has already decided.

The Church's task, then, is not to manufacture heroes but to form faithful people who will not bow when bending is rewarded. Scripture closes this call with sober clarity: *"Here is the endurance of the saints, those who keep the commandments of God and their faith in Jesus."* (Revelation 14:12).[884] Endurance, not dominance, is the mark of faithfulness. The remnant does not withdraw from the world, nor does it assimilate into it. It remains present without surrender, engaged without compromise, hopeful without illusion. God preserves His people not by removing pressure, but by sustaining obedience within it. The remnant that will not bow is not preserved by strength of will, clarity of strategy, or certainty of outcome. It is preserved by allegiance, quiet, costly, and unwavering to the Lord, who remains faithful even when His people are few.

CONVICTION IN ACTION
"Boldness Reclaimed"

Chapter 9: Stop Playing Defense; Christians Must Reclaim Boldness

CONVICTION

Boldness is not a personality trait for outspoken Christians. It is commanded allegiance to Christ. When the Church treats silence as wisdom and fear as prudence, it surrenders ground to lies that enslave and gospels that cannot save.

REALITY CHECK

The greatest threat to the Church is not hostility outside her walls. It is the internal habit of self-censorship that grows so normal it begins to feel like maturity. Sin gets renamed. Boundaries blur. Courage gets delayed until the right time. The Church learns to survive by subtraction, removing anything that might cost reputation, attendance, or safety. The result is not gentleness. It is gradual captivity: a congregation that still sings worship songs but cannot withstand coercion.

FAITHFULNESS NOW LOOKS LIKE

Personal: Refuse the false safety of private conviction with public silence. Kill the fear of man at the root by rebuilding your conscience through Scripture and prayer. Identify the lies you've learned to live with in speech, work, relationships, and habits, and repent concretely.

Church: Recover the nerve to form saints, not audiences. Preach the whole counsel of God: sin as sin, grace as power, discipleship as costly, and Christ as Lord. Rebuild a culture where shepherds correct with clarity and compassion and where mature believers are trained to withstand pressure without becoming cruel.

Public: Speak truth with steadiness, without cruelty, and without apology. Refuse compelled speech and ideological intimidation. Defend conscience rights, parental authority, and the moral clarity required to protect children. Public courage is not the gospel, but the absence of public courage often signals that the gospel has been domesticated.

COMMITMENTS

☐ Identify one place where you have stayed silent to preserve comfort or reputation, and take one specific act of obedient speech this week.

☐ Remove one formation pipeline from your life or home that is disciplining you against Scripture, whether content, voices, or habits, and replace it with a better one.

☐ Initiate one direct, measured conversation where you speak biblical truth plainly, with no euphemisms, no hostility, and no retreat.

☐ Establish a household rhythm of Scripture, prayer, and conversation at least three times this week to train courage and discernment where it matters most.

PRAYER

Lord Jesus, deliver me from fear disguised as wisdom and silence disguised as love. Forgive me where I have protected comfort more than I have protected truth, and where I have treated clarity as cruelty instead of as obedience. Rebuild my conscience by Your Word. Make me steady, not reactive; courageous, not cruel; discerning, not suspicious; and uncompromising, not arrogant. Strengthen Your Church to preach repentance, practice discipline, protect the flock, and bear witness without bargaining. Keep us from trading the Cross for applause. Form in us the endurance of the saints, so the next generation receives the real gospel, the real Christ, and real life. Amen.

Chapter 10: Living Unshaken in a Hostile Culture

Section I: Building a Life Grounded in Scripture, Not Systems

The psalmist asks the question our generation refuses to face: *"If the foundations are destroyed, what can the righteous do?"* (Psalm 11:3).[885] That question is not rhetorical. It is prophetic. It assumes the foundations *can* be destroyed and that the righteous must reckon with the consequences when they are. We are living in the consequences. For decades, the West has treated Scripture as a quaint inheritance rather than a governing authority, replacing the eternal Word of God with a constellation of human systems, economic, political, technological, and institutional, each promising stability none of them can deliver. The result is a civilization built on sand, and the rains have already begun. The question is no longer theoretical. It is existential: Will we rebuild on the Rock, or will we be buried in the rubble?

Jesus drew the line without apology. *"Everyone then who hears these words of mine and does them will be like a wise man who built his house on the rock. And the rain fell, and the floods came, and the winds blew and beat on that house, but it did not fall because it had been founded on the rock. But the one who hears and does not act will be like a foolish man who built his house on the sand. And the rain fell, and the floods came, and the winds blew and beat against that house, and it fell, and great was the fall of it."* (Matthew 7:24–27).[886] The parable is not about weather. It is about allegiance. The rock is Christ and His Word. The sand is every

339

system that pretends to offer what only God can give: security, identity, meaning, and salvation. The dividing line of our generation is not between left and right, educated and uneducated, or religious and secular. It is between those who build on the Word and those who build on the world.

Human systems are not fragile; they are spiritually rivalrous. They do not fail; they demand worship before they fall. Government presents itself as provider and protector, conditioning citizens to look to Washington rather than to God for daily bread. Technology presents itself as omniscient, training a generation to consult algorithms for wisdom that only the Holy Spirit can give. The market presents itself as the arbiter of value, teaching men to measure worth in portfolios and productivity rather than in faithfulness and obedience. Entertainment numbs the conscience so the transfer of allegiance goes unnoticed, and by the time the idol is fully installed, the worshiper no longer recognizes that he has changed gods. Scripture diagnoses this rivalry with surgical precision: *"Do not love the world or the things in the world. If anyone loves the world, the love of the Father is not in him."* (1 John 2:15).[887] James sharpens the blade further: *"Do you not know that friendship with the world is enmity with God? Therefore whoever wishes to be a friend of the world makes himself an enemy of God."* (James 4:4).[888] These are not metaphors. They are declarations of war. Every system of man that claims ultimate loyalty is a rival altar, and God does not share His throne.

John Calvin understood this with unnerving clarity. "Man's nature, so to speak, is a perpetual factory of idols."[889] The factory never shuts down. It updates its product line. In the ancient world, the idols were carved from wood and stone. In ours, they are coded in algorithms, denominated in currencies, and legislated into policy. The form changes; the function remains: to offer a substitute for God that is easier to manage and less demanding to obey. What makes the modern idols especially dangerous is that they arrive not as obvious rivals but as necessary utilities: the bank account that promises security, the health-care system that promises life, the social platform that promises community. Each one displaces a trust that belongs to God alone, and each one fails at the precise moment it is most needed.

Augustine mapped the architecture of this rivalry centuries before Calvin named it. Two cities, he wrote, have been formed by two loves, "the earthly by the love of self, even to the contempt of God; the heavenly by the love of God, even to the contempt of self."[890] Every human system belongs to the earthly city. It may produce roads and courts and hospitals, but its foundation is self-love, and self-love cannot bear the weight of eternity. What Rome discovered in its ashes, what every empire since has confirmed, Augustine articulated as theology: temporal systems glorify self and rival God's eternal kingdom.[891] Basil the Great, Augustine's Eastern contemporary, exposed the same idolatry operating through wealth and provision: "The bread which you keep belongs to the hungry; the coat which you preserve in your wardrobe belongs to the naked."[892] The hoarding instinct, whether of resources, comfort, or cultural approval, is the mark of a people who have traded covenant dependence on God for contractual dependence on systems.

History is merciless to civilizations that forget this. Rome did not fall because the barbarians were strong but because Rome was hollow; its bread-and-circuses economy anesthetized its citizens while its moral infrastructure rotted from the core. The grandeur remained long after the substance had departed, and the same is true of any society that mistakes comfort for strength. The parallel to modern America is not subtle. Victor Davis Hanson has documented how elite-driven tribalism and the erosion of shared citizenship are accelerating the decay of the American experiment from within.[893] Douglas Murray, writing from across the Atlantic, observes that Europe "has little desire to reproduce itself, fight for itself or even take its own side in an argument."[894] These are not Christian polemicists sounding alarms from the margins; they are secular historians diagnosing a civilizational exhaustion that Scripture predicted millennia ago. The prophet Jeremiah warned, *"Cursed is the man who trusts in man and makes flesh his strength, whose heart turns away from the Lord."* (Jeremiah 17:5).[895] The curse is not arbitrary punishment. It is the natural consequence of building on a foundation that was never designed to hold.

Systems fail not because their architects are stupid but because their material has fallen. Thomas Sowell captured the honest admission that secular governance cannot make: "There are no solutions; there are only trade-offs."[896] Every political system, every economic model, every technological platform operates within the constraints of human finitude and fallenness. They can manage symptoms but cannot cure the disease. Jordan Peterson, writing from outside the Church, presses the point further: systems without a transcendent anchor inevitably collapse into stagnation or chaos, because order alone, without meaning, cannot sustain a civilization.[897] He is, without knowing it, restating what the psalmist declared three thousand years ago: *"Put not your trust in princes, in a son of man, in whom there is no salvation." (Psalm 146:3).*[898] Princes pass. Platforms crash. Economies correct. Only the Word of God endures.

And here is the contrast that defines everything else in this chapter. Against the fragility of every human system stands the immovable permanence of Scripture. *"The grass withers, the flower fades, but the word of our God will stand forever."* (Isaiah 40:8).[899] *"Forever, O Lord, your word is firmly fixed in the heavens."* (Psalm 119:89).[900] These are not devotional sentiments to cross-stitch on pillows. They are foundational claims about the nature of reality. God's Word does not adjust to opinion polls, market fluctuations, or cultural revolutions. It does not erode under the pressure of elite consensus or popular demand. It does not update when new theories emerge or new movements gain traction. It stands because its author is eternal, and it speaks because its authority is absolute. Every other text on earth is a product of its time; Scripture is a product of eternity, addressed to time. Isaiah announced the cornerstone that would outlast every human foundation: *"Behold, I am the one who has laid as a foundation in Zion, a stone, a tested stone, a precious cornerstone, of a sure foundation: 'Whoever believes will not be in haste.'"* (Isaiah 28:16).[901] The one who trusts in this stone does not scramble when systems shake, because the foundation beneath him cannot move. He does not panic when governments fail or despair when institutions betray, because his trust was never in the institution but in the God who judges all institutions.

The shaking itself is not an accident. It is mercy. The prophet Haggai declared it first: *"Yet once more, in a little while, I will shake the heavens and the earth and the sea and the dry land."* (Haggai 2:6).[902] The writer of Hebrews then interpreted the prophecy with devastating theological precision: *"This phrase, 'Yet once more,' indicates the removal of things that are shaken, that is, things that have been made, in order that the things that cannot be shaken may remain."* (Hebrews 12:26–27).[903] This is not divine tantrum. It is divine surgery. God shakes the systems so that only the unshakable remains. He collapses the economy of idols so that the economy of faith becomes visible. He strips the scaffolding of human confidence so that the Rock beneath it is unmistakable. Every financial crisis, every political upheaval, every cultural convulsion is an act of mercy disguised as disruption. God prying His people's fingers off the things that cannot save, so they will grip the one thing that can. Carl Trueman has shown how this shaking plays out in the modern self. When identity is constructed from psychology rather than Scripture, the entire edifice of personhood becomes fragile, resting on something that shifts with every cultural tide.[904] The shaking is not chaos. It is revelation. And the appropriate response is not panic but worship: *"Therefore, let us be grateful for receiving a kingdom that cannot be shaken, and thus let us offer to God acceptable worship, with reverence and awe."* (Hebrews 12:28).[905] The kingdom of God is not one option among many. It is the only kingdom that survives the fire.

Daniel foresaw this when he interpreted the king's dream: *"In the days of those kings the God of heaven will set up a kingdom that shall never be destroyed, nor shall the kingdom be left to another people. It shall break in pieces all these kingdoms and bring them to an end, and it shall stand forever."* (Daniel 2:44).[906] Every earthly kingdom, Babylon, Persia, Greece, Rome, and every modern empire that imagines itself permanent, will be broken and not reformed and not improved. Broken. Nebuchadnezzar's golden statue, with its head of gold and feet of clay, is the portrait of every civilization that believes its own propaganda. The feet always crack first, because the material closest to the ground is always the weakest. Only the kingdom that God establishes endures, because it is built not from clay or iron or gold but from the eternal decree of an unchanging God. The question is not whether the systems of our age will fall. The question is whether we will be found standing on the Rock when they do.

Yet the modern Church has, to its deep shame, built its life more on systems than on Scripture. This is not an accusation from the outside; it is a confession from within. The evidence is visible in every suburb and city center in America. Nancy Pearcey diagnosed the disease precisely: the sacred-secular divide has privatized faith, reducing Christianity from a total worldview to a compartmentalized preference that the culture tolerates as long as it stays quiet.[907] When faith becomes private, the Church becomes a chaplain, offering spiritual comfort within the system rather than prophetic confrontation against it. The preacher becomes a therapist, the sanctuary becomes a lecture hall, and the congregation becomes an audience. The result, Pearcey argues, is worldview fragmentation that makes the Church a servant of culture rather than its conscience.[908] Carl Trueman deepened this diagnosis: the rise of expressive individualism, the belief that identity is defined by inner feelings rather than objective truth, has not shifted culture; it has destabilized the very concept of the self, untethering identity from creation, covenant, and community.[909] The modern Church absorbed this framework without recognizing it, prioritizing felt needs over revealed truth, therapeutic comfort over doctrinal clarity, and institutional survival over prophetic obedience. The Church did not decide to abandon Scripture. It stopped treating Scripture as the final word, and the systems rushed in to fill the vacuum.

The COVID-19 pandemic exposed this drift with devastating clarity. When governments ordered churches closed, the vast majority complied without protest, not because the orders were just but because the Church had already ceded its authority to the state in all but name. Rod Dreher warned that soft totalitarianism works precisely this way: it "seduces those, even Christians, who do not notice the threat it poses to human dignity."[910] The compliance was not courageous deference; it was trained dependence. For decades, churches had built their identity on programs, facilities, and cultural respectability, all of which depended on the goodwill of the very systems that now demanded their silence. When the state spoke, the Church obeyed, because the Church's foundation was not the Word but the system that permitted the Word to be spoken.

The tragedy was not that churches closed. Prudence in a genuine emergency is not sin. The tragedy was how easily they closed, how little resistance the body of Christ mounted when an earthly authority presumed to determine when and whether God's people could worship. John MacArthur was among the few who refused, insisting that the Church's authority derives solely from Christ, not from temporal powers.[911] His defiance was not political theater. It was a theological declaration: the head of the Church is not the governor, not the health department, and not the cultural consensus. The head of the Church is Christ. And where Christ's authority is acknowledged, no earthly edict can override the command to gather, to worship, and to proclaim.

The drift did not begin with COVID. It began when churches traded the pulpit for the platform, when sermons became self-help talks dressed in religious language, and when the measure of a congregation became attendance rather than obedience. Albert Mohler has described our moment as a "gathering storm" in which secularism does not compete with Christianity but demands its capitulation.[912] The storm is not coming. It has arrived. And the churches that built on cultural relevance rather than biblical revelation are being swept away like houses on the sand. David Platt diagnosed the same sickness from inside the evangelical mainstream: the American dream has become a rival gospel, promising comfort, safety, and success as substitutes for the cross.[913] When the Church promises what the system promises, it has nothing unique to offer when the system fails. John Piper pressed the indictment still further: worldliness seduces by offering counterfeit satisfaction apart from God, and when the Church drinks from that well, it trades its birthright for a bowl of stew.[914] Voddie Baucham has called the captivity by its proper name: the Church no longer shapes culture but echoes it, and the result is a Christianity that is indistinguishable from the world it was sent to redeem.[915] When compliance with rival authorities becomes habitual, resistance becomes unthinkable, not because it is impossible but because the will to resist has been trained out of the body.[916]

The call, then, is not to reform the systems. Systems cannot be reformed into something they were never designed to be. The call is to abandon them as foundations and rebuild on the Rock. The call is to recover what the Church Fathers, the Reformers, and the apostles knew without question: that the Word of God is the only authority that does not bend, the only promise that does not fail, and the only foundation that does not crack under the weight of a fallen world. Homes must be rebuilt on Scripture, not on the credentials the system rewards. Churches must be rebuilt on proclamation, not on the platforms the culture applauds. Identity must be received from Christ, not constructed from the self. And the measure of faithfulness must be obedience to God, not acceptance by the age. David Platt named the cost plainly: "Radical obedience to Christ is not easy ... It's not comfort, not health, not wealth, and not prosperity in this world."[917] Mohler warned that silence amid secular rivalry equates to surrender.[918] The choice is stark, and it is the same choice it has always been: *"Choose this day whom you will serve ... But as for me and my house, we will serve the Lord."* (Joshua 24:15).[919]

The systems are shaking. The foundations men trusted are crumbling beneath their feet. But for those who build on the Word of God, the promise holds. The kingdom we have received cannot be shaken. That is the premise of everything that follows: Scripture alone is the authority; systems alone will fail, and the generation willing to rebuild on the Rock will be the generation that stands when the dust of every human empire has settled. And if that is true, if systems do indeed disciple and if they do shape hearts and minds and loyalties, then the most urgent question is not what we build for ourselves but what we build into the next generation. Because whoever forms the children inherits the future.

Section II: Raising Children Who Aren't Cultural Hostages

Children are not neutral ground. They are discipleship territory, and the question is not whether they will be formed, but who will form them. Scripture makes the stakes explicit. *"Hear, O Israel: The LORD our God, the LORD is one. You shall love the LORD your God with all your heart and with all your soul and with all your might. And these words that I command you today shall be on your heart. You shall teach them diligently to your children and shall talk of them when you sit in your house, and when you walk by the way, and when you lie down, and when you rise."* (Deuteronomy 6:5–7).[920] The rhythm is not occasional. It is continual. Sit, walk, lie down, and rise. The home is the primary arena of formation, and parents are the primary agents. This is not a nice idea for motivated families. It is the mandate.

The culture understands what many Christian parents have forgotten: whoever shapes the children shapes the future. That is why the battle for the next generation is so fierce. Systems compete for formative authority, and they do not compete politely. Schools deliver curriculum that reshapes moral categories. Entertainment normalizes what Scripture condemns. Algorithms curate identities before children have the theological vocabulary to resist. Peers become the primary interpreters of reality, and what they believe is often what culture has taught them. The result is a generation that does not know the Lord, not because they rejected Him but because no one told them who He is (Judges 2:10).[921] The failure is not theirs. It is ours.

Parents who outsource discipleship to schools, youth programs, or even to faithful pastors are handing over the steering wheel while pretending to remain in the driver's seat. The church can equip parents, but it cannot replace them. Voddie Baucham puts it plainly: parents bear the responsibility for their children's spiritual formation under Ephesians 6:4, and nothing can substitute for that mandate.[922] The home is the first church and the first seminary. If it is not functioning as such, no Sunday school curriculum or midweek program will compensate. Sporadic devotions treat church as an excursion rather than a lived reality, and children absorb what is modeled far more than what is taught.[923] When parents delegate spiritual authority, they do not fail to disciple. They actively disciple toward passivity, teaching children that faith is something experts handle while families spectate.

This is not about perfection. It is about presence. The Deuteronomy 6 rhythm assumes that parents are with their children, talking as they walk, answering questions as they rise, embedding the Word into the ordinary flow of life. But modern parenting has professionalized formation, and professionalization always distances authority from intimacy. Jordan Peterson notes that modern parents fear their children's dislike, sacrificing respect for the illusion of friendship.[924] The result is indulgent parenting that allows children to dominate, reversing the proper authority structure that is meant to protect and guide them.[925] Children do not need friends. They need fathers and mothers who love them enough to correct them, who understand that discipline is not cruelty but mercy, a refusal to let impulses that damage relationships go unchecked.[926]

The pressure to abdicate authority comes from multiple directions. Therapeutic culture has reframed correction as trauma and boundaries as oppression. Ferguson argues that when the flesh rather than the Spirit governs formation, children are trained to treat inner desire as sovereign and any external authority as intrusion, producing not authenticity but ungovernable autonomy.[927] Parents who adopt these norms in the name of gentleness are not gentle. They are negligent, leaving children without the moorings they need to navigate a hostile world.

The failure pattern is generational. Judges 2:10 records it with surgical precision: "And all that generation also were gathered to their fathers. And there arose another generation after them who did not know the LORD or the work that he had done for Israel." Neglect leads to amnesia. Amnesia leads to idolatry. The cycle does not take centuries. It takes one generation. The gap between knowing God and not knowing God is not gradual decay. It is a catastrophic rupture that occurs in the space between one generation's death and the next generation's independence. When parents fail to tell the works of God, the next generation does not inherit a neutral void. They inherit the catechesis of competing systems, and those systems are not neutral. They are hostile.

The Judges passage does not describe a slow drift. It describes a complete collapse. One generation served the Lord. The next did not know Him. What happened in between? Parents died without passing on what they knew. The elders who remembered the Exodus were gone, and no one had prepared the young to carry the memory forward. The failure was not theological. It was pedagogical. The content existed. The conviction existed. But the transmission failed. Psalm 78 makes the same point with devastating clarity: *"He established a testimony in Jacob and appointed a law in Israel, which he commanded our fathers to teach to their children, so that the next generation might know them, the children yet unborn, and arise and tell them to their children so that they should set their hope in God and not forget the works of God but keep his commandments."* (Psalm 78:5–7).[928] The chain of remembrance depends on deliberate telling. Break the chain, and you do not get neutrality. You get forgetfulness. And forgetfulness always bows to whatever system fills the void.

Culture catechizes constantly. It does so through the stories children consume, the platforms they scroll, the classrooms they sit in, and the friends they trust. The method is immersive, not instructional. Children do not sit down for a formal lesson in secular anthropology. They absorb it through a thousand micro-exposures, each one reshaping their intuitions about identity, morality, authority, and meaning. Jonathan Haidt and Greg Lukianoff document the results: a generation conditioned to see discomfort as danger, trained to prioritize emotional safety over truth, and taught to fragment identity into fluid categories detached from reality.[929] Overprotection does not shield children from cultural pressure. It renders them fragile under it. Safetyism produces anxiety, not resilience, because it teaches children that the world is hostile and they are incapable of navigating it.

The ideological mechanisms are sophisticated. Curriculum introduces critical frameworks that divide the world into oppressors and the oppressed, rewriting history as a narrative of power rather than providence. Entertainment normalizes moral chaos as liberation, celebrating autonomy detached from consequence. Algorithms curate feeds that confirm cultural assumptions, creating echo chambers where dissent is invisible and conformity feels like discovery. Peer groups function as enforcement mechanisms, rewarding compliance with belonging and punishing deviation with isolation. The combined effect is a discipleship pipeline far more comprehensive than anything most churches attempt. Parents who refuse to discipline out of fear of conflict raise children who collapse under the weight of a world that will not coddle them.[930] The culture that promises liberation through validation delivers captivity through confusion.

The sacred-secular split has trained Christian parents to compartmentalize faith, treating it as a Sunday category rather than a total worldview. Edwards argued that a faith confined to the devotional sphere and disconnected from the whole of life is not genuine faith but a counterfeit that leaves the soul unguarded, producing children who have the form of religion without the integrating power of it.[931] The result is a generation that knows how to be nice but not how to be faithful, that can quote verses but cannot apply a worldview, and that treats Christianity as a hobby rather than a kingdom. Worldview fragmentation turns the church into a cultural chaplain, blessing the status quo rather than challenging it.[932] If parents do not integrate truth into every sphere, children will learn to compartmentalize it out of every sphere.

This is where the home becomes either a fortress or a greenhouse. Rod Dreher argues that Christian families must intentionally reclaim education and formation, building resistance communities that counter the ideological captivity embedded in secular institutions.[933] Classical Christian schools, cooperative homeschool networks, and intergenerational church communities become the infrastructure of faithfulness, equipping children to think Christianly in a post-Christian world.[934] But the infrastructure means nothing if the home is passive. The church equips parents; it does not replace them.[935] If parents delegate discipleship to professionals, the next generation will professionalize faith, turning it into a service industry rather than a way of life.

The alternative is not complicated, but it is costly. It requires parents to stop outsourcing and start shepherding. *"As for me and my house, we will serve the LORD."* (Joshua 24:15).[936] That declaration is not inspirational decor. It is a declaration of war. The home is the frontline, and children are the arrows (Psalm 127:3–4).[937] Arrows are not ornaments. They are weapons, and weapons require preparation. An arrow that is not sharpened, not straightened, and not aimed does not serve its purpose. It becomes decoration or debris. The psalmist's metaphor is military, not sentimental. "Like arrows in the hand of a warrior are the children of one's youth. Blessed is the man who fills his quiver with them!" The blessing is not in having children. The blessing is in having children prepared for battle, children who know the enemy, who recognize deception, who can stand under pressure.

This is where the Deuteronomy 6 rhythm becomes tactical. Sit, walk, lie down, and rise. These are not devotional suggestions. They are formation protocols. When you sit at the table, you are not just feeding bodies. You are shaping worldviews. When you walk through the neighborhood, you are not just passing time. You are interpreting culture. When you lie down at night, you are not just ending the day. You are entrusting your children to the Lord. When you rise in the morning, you are not just beginning another routine. You are reaffirming the centrality of God's commands in everything that follows. Richard Baxter warned parents centuries ago that negligence in instruction serves their children's spiritual enemies and that the primary labor of a parent is to make holiness necessary, honorable, and delightful through daily practice.[938] The father who leads worship is not performing a ritual. He is preparing arrows.

Family worship must be mandatory and participatory, not optional or sporadic. M'Cheyne understood that a father who leads his household in worship is himself formed by the leading; the discipline of bringing others before God shapes the leader's own walk in ways no private devotion alone can replicate.[939] This is not about perfection in execution. It is about consistency in presence. The table becomes a discipleship laboratory. The car becomes a catechism class. Bedtime becomes a moment of Scripture and prayer, not just routine. Deuteronomy 11:19 repeats the rhythm: teach God's words when you sit at home, when you walk along the road, when you lie down, when you get up (Deuteronomy 11:19).[940] The pattern is relentless because the competition is relentless. Culture never takes a day off from catechizing your children. Neither can you.

The model is not mystical. It is liturgical. Rosaria Butterfield describes this as radically ordinary hospitality, home practices that catechize more powerfully than programs, where the gospel is not taught as information but lived as reality.[941] Open homes teach repentance through shared struggle, modeling grace under pressure and faith in tension.[942] Children learn theology not from systematic lectures but from watching how their parents respond to disappointment, conflict, and suffering. When a parent confesses sin at the dinner table, children learn repentance. When a parent prays through fear, children learn trust. When a parent extends hospitality to the difficult neighbor, children learn mission. The gospel becomes plausible not because it was explained well but because it was lived consistently.

This kind of formation requires attention. Effortful attention. Limits on freedom are not oppression. They are socialization. They teach children to share, to wait, to respect boundaries, and to build the citizenship that functional communities require.[943] Without those limits, children do not gain freedom. They gain chaos.

The resistance must be deliberate and communal. Families cannot stand alone against the discipleship machinery of culture. They need the body of Christ functioning as it was designed, equipping parents, not replacing them. The early church understood this. Fathers were responsible for catechizing their children, and the church provided the doctrinal framework and accountability structure to ensure it happened.

But this vision requires parents who are present, engaged, and theologically competent. George Barna's research reveals the crisis: only 2% of American parents have a biblical worldview.[944] Parents who do not know Scripture cannot teach Scripture. Parents who do not practice worship cannot lead worship.

The enemy is not secular curriculum or immoral entertainment. The enemy is passivity. Cultural amnesia erodes the transmission of truth, leaving each generation to reinvent meaning from the fragmented narratives culture offers.[945] When one generation fails to tell the next, the covenant lapses, and the nation becomes Babylon by another name. The Israelites did not lose the land because they lacked military strength. They lost it because they stopped telling their children who God was and what He had done. The prophetic books are filled with this diagnosis. Joel commanded, *"Tell your children of it, and let your children tell their children, and their children to another generation."* (Joel 1:3).[946] The chain of remembrance is the only thing standing between faithfulness and apostasy.

"Do not be conformed to this world, but be transformed by the renewal of your mind." (Romans 12:2).[947] The renewal does not happen in isolation. It happens in community, and the first community is the home. Paul reminds Timothy that he knew the sacred writings from childhood because his mother and grandmother taught him (2 Timothy 3:15).[948]

That is the model. Generational faithfulness does not depend on perfect parents. It depends on present parents, parents who teach diligently, who talk of God's commands when they sit and when they walk, and who embed the Word into the rhythm of ordinary life so that children grow up breathing it in. The failure of one generation to do this does not weaken the next generation. It abandons them to captivity.

The stakes are generational, but the tactics are daily. Malachi closes the Old Testament with this warning: God will raise up godly offspring through faithful families, or He will strike the land with a decree of utter destruction (Malachi 2:15).[949] The connection between family faithfulness and national survival is explicit. Civilizations do not collapse because of bad policy. They collapse because families stop transmitting truth. When parents are silent, children do not remain neutral. They adopt the catechism of whatever system is speaking loudest. The breakfast table is a discipleship moment. The car ride is a worldview lesson. The bedtime routine is a liturgy. If parents do not seize those moments, culture will. And culture's catechism is already written.

Strauch argues that a household practicing open, gospel-shaped hospitality trains children to see faith as a living reality rather than a private conviction, because they watch their parents extend grace, practice repentance, and proclaim Christ in the presence of real people with real needs.[950] When the home is open, children see their parents practice repentance, reconciliation, sacrificial service, and gospel proclamation in real time. They learn that Christianity is not a private belief system but a public way of life. The closed home produces children who think faith is something you whisper about in church but never mention at the dinner table. The open home produces children who understand that the gospel is for strangers, that holiness is lived in community, and that mission begins at the front door.

The alternative to this kind of formation is not neutrality. It is surrender. Ortlund argues that when the church fails to catechize its children with theological depth and clarity, it does not leave them neutral; it leaves them defenseless, and a culture actively hostile to Christian truth will fill that vacuum without hesitation.[951] The public school system, while staffed by many well-meaning teachers, operates under ideological frameworks that contradict Scripture at foundational levels. Gender ideology, critical race theory, and therapeutic moralism are not fringe positions. They are the operating assumptions of contemporary education, and children absorb them not through explicit instruction but through the daily rhythms of classroom life. The Christian parent who sends their child into that system without counter-catechesis at home is sending an unarmed soldier into battle.

But the solution is not withdrawal into isolation. The construction of resistance communities provides an alternative infrastructure for formation. Classical Christian schools and cooperative homeschool networks are not escapes from the world but strategic retreats that allow families to rebuild the intellectual and spiritual resources needed to engage the world faithfully. Ferguson argues that Spirit-wrought formation produces whole-life discipleship rather than compartmentalized religion, equipping believers to bring every domain of thought and practice under the lordship of Christ rather than conceding it to rival frameworks.[952]

This kind of education requires parents who are theologically equipped and relationally present. It cannot be outsourced to professionals, no matter how gifted they are.

The church's role is to equip parents, not to replace them. Pastors are not surrogate fathers. Youth pastors are not substitute shepherds. The most effective youth ministry in the world cannot compensate for a home where God is not discussed, where Scripture is not read, where prayer is not practiced, and where parents model functional atheism six days a week.

The prophetic alarm is sounding. Judges 2:10 is not ancient history. It is a warning. A generation arose that did not know the Lord. Not because the Lord was absent, but because parents were silent. The mandate is not complicated: tell your children. Tell them of God's works. Tell them of His commands. Tell them why you worship, why you repent, why you hope. Make your house a place where the Lord is not a guest but the center. Set the table with Scripture. Walk the streets with conversation. Lie down with prayer. Rise with thanksgiving. Do not delegate. Do not professionalize. Do not assume someone else will handle it.

Culture is raising your children. The only question is whether you will raise them too. Silence is not neutrality. It is surrender. And surrender does not produce heirs. It produces hostages. Choose this day whom you will serve, and let your house serve the Lord (Joshua 24:15).[953] That choice is made daily, in moments so ordinary they seem inconsequential, but those moments are where kingdoms are built, and captives are freed. The generational consequences of neglect are catastrophic, but the generational power of faithfulness is unstoppable. Psalm 34 invites children to come and listen, promising that the fear of the Lord will be taught (Psalm 34:11).[954] Proverbs repeats the promise: train up a child in the way he should go, and when he is old he will not depart from it (Proverbs 22:6).[955] The promise is not automatic. It is covenantal. God honors faithfulness, but faithfulness requires presence. The home is not a retreat from the world. It is the launch point for arrows. Train them well. Aim them true. And do not hand them to Caesar.

Section III: Creating a Legacy That Honors Christ and Resists Compromise

The Warning: Fragile Legacies

Legacy is never neutral. It either magnifies Christ or multiplies compromise. From Genesis to Revelation, Scripture is filled with the rise and fall of men whose legacies turned on a single decision to obey or to yield. Solomon began with divine favor and unmatched wisdom, greater in riches and wisdom than all the other kings of the earth (1 Kings 10:23).[956] Yet time revealed that brilliance cannot substitute for obedience: *"When Solomon was old, his wives turned away his heart after other gods, and his heart was not wholly true to the LORD his God."* (1 Kings 11:4).[957] What began in purity ended in pollution. The kingdom split, and Israel's faith fractured for generations. One man's *compromise* became a nation's catastrophe.

The pattern repeats. Demas, once Paul's trusted laborer, forsook his calling because he loved this present world (2 Timothy 4:10).[958] The tragedy is not that their gifts vanished but that their devotion did. Scripture preserves their failures so that every believer might remember a legacy can be lost faster than it was built. Rutherford understood that a man's legacy is determined not by what he accumulated but by what he loved, and that a soul oriented toward heaven leaves something permanent while a soul oriented toward earth leaves only what the earth will reclaim.[959] The question is not whether you will leave a legacy. The question is which city your legacy will serve.

The drift toward compromise rarely announces itself. It whispers in the language of relevance, convenience, and progress. It offers partial obedience wrapped in persuasive logic. Jesus made the cost unmistakable: *"No one can serve two masters, for either he will hate the one and love the other, or he will be devoted to the one and despise the other."* (Matthew 6:24).[960] A heart divided between God and the world eventually belongs to the world. The human heart is a perpetual factory of idols, and the production never stops.[961] When believers imitate the world to win it, they end up resembling it instead of redeeming it. The Israelites honored God with their lips while worshiping idols with their lives, fulfilling the rebuke: *"These people honor me with their lips, but their hearts are far from me."* (Matthew 15:8).[962] The result was inevitable: a generation outwardly religious but inwardly rebellious.

History confirms that moral erosion always begins in the sanctuary long before it reaches the streets. When truth is diluted for peace, both truth and peace perish. When pulpits surrender conviction for cultural applause, the presence of God departs, and only the echo of religion remains. The Church may retain its architecture and its choirs, but without holiness, it becomes a museum, beautiful, silent, and dead. The house of God, which should be the pillar and ground of the truth, too often becomes a temple for idols when conviction is traded for comfort.

The contagion of compromise spreads through generations. The sins parents tolerate, their children normalize, and their grandchildren celebrate. *"They served the LORD all the days of Joshua... And there arose another generation after them who did not know the LORD or the work that he had done for Israel."* (Judges 2:7, 10).[963] What began as mild neglect ended as national apostasy.[964] When worldliness becomes acceptable, rebellion becomes inevitable. Children raised amid spiritual lukewarmness inherit a faith without fire, a religion of memory, not movement.

The warning stretches beyond pulpits and households to entire nations. Scripture is clear: *"Righteousness exalts a nation, but sin is a reproach to any people."* (Proverbs 14:34).[965] America's founders, though imperfect men, recognized that liberty requires virtue as its guardian. Remove morality, and freedom devours itself. The psalmist asked: *"If the foundations are destroyed, what can the righteous do?"* (Psalm 11:3).[966] Foundations crumble when righteousness is redefined, and sin is celebrated. When truth retreats from the sanctuary, corruption rushes into the Capitol. The health of a nation mirrors the holiness of its pulpits.

When faith is reduced to form and ritual, legacy turns hollow. Parents may leave possessions, and pastors may build platforms, but only obedience leaves a spiritual inheritance. Jesus contrasted the wise and foolish builders: *"Everyone then who hears these words of mine and does them will be like a wise man who built his house on the rock... and everyone who hears these words of mine and does not do them will be like a foolish man who built his house on the sand."* (Matthew 7:24–27).[967] Christ is not valued at all unless He is valued above all.[968] A life anchored in convenience will always collapse when the storm arrives. A life anchored in Christ remains immovable. A generation that measures success by visibility rather than virtue is building on sand, and the tide of history is already rising.

The only cure for fragile legacies is a return to the eternal Word of God. Compromise trades revelation for opinion, eternity for expediency. Isaiah reminded us, *"The grass withers, the flower fades, but the word of our God will stand forever."* (Isaiah 40:8).[969] When Solomon drifted from the Word, his kingdom crumbled. When Josiah rediscovered it, revival swept the land. Scripture alone anchors a generation in truth. Paul charged Timothy: *"What you have heard from me in the presence of many witnesses entrust to faithful men, who will be able to teach others also."* (2 Timothy 2:2).[970] That is the architecture of legacy, truth received, lived, and transmitted. The warning of fragile legacies is not meant to breed despair but to ignite resolve. Every believer, every family, and every church stands at the same crossroads: compromise that corrodes or conviction that endures.

The Foundation: Truth as Anchor

The foundation of every enduring legacy is truth. When the Word of God ceases to be the plumb line of faith, everything else begins to tilt. The Church was never meant to drift with the tides of culture but to stand as a lighthouse guiding through the storm. The Psalmist declared, "Forever, *O LORD, your word is firmly fixed in the heavens."* (Psalm 119:89).[971] Truth is not seasonal. It does not bend with opinion or evolve with ideology. The moment Scripture becomes negotiable, authority collapses. Jesus Himself affirmed this permanence: *"Heaven and earth will pass away, but my words will not pass away."* (Matthew 24:35).[972] The foundation of faith is not the shifting consensus of men but the eternal decree of God. Those who build their convictions on revelation rather than reaction remain anchored when storms come.

Repentance, then, is the act of realignment with that foundation. It is not regret; it is a return. When a person, a church, or a nation drifts from truth, repentance is the only way home. King Josiah understood this. When the Book of the Law was rediscovered, he tore his garments in grief, crying out for mercy, and led an entire people back to obedience. *"Before him there was no king like him, who turned to the LORD with all his heart and with all his soul and with all his might."* (2 Kings 23:25).[973] Repentance restores what rebellion destroys. That is why a revival of the kind of Christianity found in the New Testament is impossible until there is radical repentance, a return to the Lord.[974] The Church's crisis is not that sinners are outside, but that unrepentance is tolerated inside. True reformation will not come through better marketing or music but through brokenness and a renewed fear of the Lord.

The courage to repent publicly and lead faithfully is the mark of a generation that refuses compromise. When Israel faced idolatry, Elijah stood alone on Mount Carmel and declared, *"If the LORD is God, follow him; but if Baal, then follow him."* (1 Kings 18:21).[975] The crowd hesitated, paralyzed by indecision. Yet one man's boldness turned the tide of a nation. Courage is not loud defiance; it is quiet obedience when silence is safer. In every generation, truth demands voices willing to risk comfort for conviction. The Church's greatest need is not more strategists but more soldiers, men and women who will say, "Though none go with me, still I will follow." The hour demands pastors who preach the Word unfiltered, parents who disciple without apology, and believers who speak truth with grace but never retreat.

Yet courage alone is insufficient without conviction rooted in Scripture. Paul warned Timothy, *"Evil people and impostors will go on from bad to worse, deceiving and being deceived. But as for you, continue in what you have learned and have firmly believed."* (2 Timothy 3:13–14).[976] Conviction without knowledge breeds error. Knowledge without courage breeds cowardice. The two must walk hand in hand. When courage flows from intimacy with truth, the believer stands unshaken no matter the opposition. But when courage is severed from Scripture, it becomes mere activism, noise without power. The strength to endure persecution or public rejection comes not from self-confidence but from the indwelling Word of God that cannot be silenced.

The remnant, therefore, stands as the visible proof that truth endures even when institutions fail. God has always preserved a faithful few. When Elijah despaired, believing he was the last righteous prophet left, God replied: *"I have kept for myself seven thousand men who have not bowed the knee to Baal."* (Romans 11:4).[977] There has always been a remnant, men and women who refuse to bend their knees to the idols of the age. They are not defined by numbers but by faithfulness. In every generation, the church is to be the living church of its own age, standing on the Word of God, without compromise.[978] The remnant's existence proves that the Word still has power to separate light from darkness and faith from apostasy.

The anchor of truth must be restored not in pulpits but in homes. Parents who build their households on Scripture are raising the next generation of reformers. Moses commanded Israel: *"You shall teach them diligently to your children and shall talk of them when you sit in your house, and when you walk by the way, and when you lie down, and when you rise."* (Deuteronomy 6:7).[979] The Word must be woven into daily life until it shapes thought, language, and conscience. Modern families outsource discipleship to programs, schools, or churches, but God assigned that responsibility to the home. The Word of God is not a text to be read but a life to be lived. When homes return to the habit of Scripture, reading it aloud, praying it together, and obeying it daily, they become living sanctuaries where truth outlives trends.

A church anchored in the Word becomes a fortress of light in a darkening age. Paul described this foundation: *"Built on the foundation of the apostles and prophets, Christ Jesus himself being the cornerstone."* (Ephesians 2:20).[980] When Christ and Scripture are central, every other stone holds. The church is only strong when it is biblical.[981] The strength of a congregation is not measured by attendance or aesthetics but by fidelity to Scripture. In an era where many pulpits avoid offense to maintain attendance, courage to preach the full counsel of God has become the rarest form of leadership. The Church's foundation is not cultural relevance but divine revelation. To rebuild that foundation is to restore authority, clarity, and conviction to the people of God.

Finally, the foundation of truth demands endurance. Paul urged believers, "Be *steadfast, immovable, and always abounding in the work of the Lord, knowing that in the Lord your labor is not in vain."* (1 Corinthians 15:58).[982] The remnant does not survive by isolation but by perseverance. When storms rise, the anchor does not move; the ship holds because it is tethered to something deeper than itself. The Word of God, well understood and religiously obeyed, is the shortest route to spiritual perfection.[983] To hold fast to that Word is to outlast every cultural collapse. In the end, truth will not need defenders. It will stand when everything built on sand has fallen. Those who anchor their lives in it will find themselves, like the wise builder, unmoved amid the flood.

The Call: Choose This Day

Legacy is transmission. What you entrust determines what endures. Paul instructed, *"And what you have heard from me in the presence of many witnesses entrust to reliable people, who will also be qualified to teach others."* (2 Timothy 2:2).[984] The chain of transmission requires deliberate effort. It does not happen automatically. Multi-generational faithfulness requires intentional teaching against cultural captivity.[985] Silence surrenders legacy to rival masters. The default is drift. The culture catechizes constantly, and if parents are silent, children will be discipled by whatever system speaks loudest.

Strategic withdrawal preserves Christian distinctiveness for long-term legacy.[986] The posture is not isolation but intentional separation from systems that catechize toward compromise.

Expressive individualism politicizes identity, eroding objective truth across generations.[987] Privatized faith surrenders public legacy to rival worldviews.[988] If faith is private and formation is public, then the next generation will learn that God is irrelevant to the spheres that matter.

Moral confusion accelerates civilizational tiredness, leaving a confused inheritance.[989] When a civilization stops believing in its own foundations, it adopts the foundations of whatever system is most aggressive. American comfort rivals radical obedience, yielding a temporal legacy.[990] A legacy built on comfort collapses the moment pressure arrives.

Institutional drift signals broader generational accommodation.[991]

Costly obedience, even unto death, leaves a legacy of surrender to Christ.[992] What you model, your children will normalize. If you model compromise, they will normalize compromise. If you model costly obedience, they will understand that the faith is worth dying for. Repentant hospitality transmits the gospel across generations.[993] The home that practices repentance, hospitality, and costly mission teaches children that the gospel is not theoretical. It is a lived reality.

Scripture commands transmission. *"One generation shall commend your works to another and shall declare your mighty acts."* (Psalm 145:4).[994] *"Let this be recorded for a generation to come, so that a people yet to be created may praise the LORD."* (Psalm 102:18).[995] *"Tell your children of it, and let your children tell their children, and their children to another generation."* (Joel 1:3).[996] The mandate is explicit. Generational faithfulness is not optional. It is commanded. *"But the steadfast love of the LORD is from everlasting to everlasting on those who fear him, and his righteousness to children's children."* (Psalm 103:17).[997] God keeps covenant with those who love him and keep his commandments, to a thousand generations (Deuteronomy 7:9).[998] The righteousness of the parent blesses the children after him (Proverbs 20:7).[999] A good man leaves an inheritance to his children's children (Proverbs 13:22).[1000]

But the inverse is also true. *"Visiting the iniquity of the fathers on the children and the children's children, to the third and the fourth generation."* (Exodus 34:7).[1001] Compromise has generational consequences. The father who bows to Babylon teaches his children that Babylon's gods are worthy of worship. The pulpit that softens truth to avoid offense teaches the congregation that truth is negotiable. What is whispered in private becomes shouted in public, and what one generation tolerates, the next generation celebrates.

"No one can serve two masters, for either he will hate the one and love the other, or he will be devoted to the one and despise the other." (Matthew 6:24).[1002] The principle is binary. There is no middle ground. Lordship is exclusive. The attempt to serve both Christ and culture, both God and mammon, both Scripture and systems, is not balance. It is betrayal. And betrayal does not produce faithful heirs. It produces spiritual orphans, children who know the vocabulary of faith but have never seen it lived without compromise.

Joshua's declaration remains the summons: *"But as for me and my house, we will serve the LORD."* (Joshua 24:15).[1003] That choice is not made once. It is made daily. Choose this day whom you will serve: the false gods your fathers served beyond the River or the God who brought you out of captivity. Choose. And make your house choose with you. The legacy you leave will be determined by the master you serve, and your children will serve the master you modeled.

What does an unshaken legacy look like? It looks like Abel, whose faith still speaks though he is dead (Hebrews 11:4).[1004] It looks like Abraham, whom God chose so that he may command his children and his household after him to keep the way of the LORD (Genesis 18:19).[1005] It looks like Timothy, who knew the sacred writings from childhood because his mother and grandmother taught him (2 Timothy 3:15).[1006] It looks like generations who set their hope in God and are not like their fathers, a stubborn and rebellious generation (Psalm 78:7–8).[1007] It looks like integrity in teaching so that opponents are put to shame (Titus 2:7–8).[1008] It looks like labor in the Lord that is not in vain (1 Corinthians 15:58).[1009] It looks like deeds that follow you beyond the grave (Revelation 14:13).[1010]

The prophetic alarm is not theoretical. It is urgent. *"Watch your life and doctrine closely. Persevere in them, because if you do, you will save both yourself and your hearers."* (1 Timothy 4:16).[1011] The stakes are not personal. They are generational. *"The promise is for you and for your children and for all who are far off."* (Acts 2:39).[1012] The covenant extends beyond you, but only if you transmit it faithfully. *"Train up a child in the way he should go; even when he is old, he will not depart from it."* (Proverbs 22:6).[1013] Seek godly offspring through faithful covenant (Malachi 2:15).[1014] *"Blessed is the man who fears the LORD, who greatly delights in his commandments! His offspring will be mighty in the land."* (Psalm 112:1–2).[1015]

Culture is raising your children. Systems are catechizing them. Babylon is bidding for their allegiance. The only question is whether you will raise them for Christ or surrender them to Caesar. Silence is not neutrality. It is capitulation. Compromise is not balance. It is betrayal. And betrayal does not produce a legacy that honors Christ. It produces a legacy of drift, confusion, and eventual apostasy.

The heavenly city endures. The earthly city crumbles. Choose which city you will build, and build it deliberately, daily, without compromise. Your legacy depends on it. So does the faith of your children, your grandchildren, and generations yet unborn. The time is now. The choice is clear. Choose this day whom you will serve.

CONVICTION IN ACTION
"Unshaken"

Chapter 10: Living Unshaken in a Hostile Culture

CONVICTION

Legacy is never neutral. It either magnifies Christ across generations or multiplies compromise until the faith collapses. When the Church mistakes cultural accommodation for wisdom and treats discipleship as optional, it leaves no sustainable inheritance, only spiritual orphans who know religious vocabulary but have never seen costly obedience lived out.

REALITY CHECK

The greatest threat to generational faithfulness is not outright persecution. It is the slow drift that begins with whispered convenience and ends with normalized rebellion. What parents tolerate, children normalize. What the pulpit avoids, the pew celebrates. And what one generation whispers, the next generation shouts. Systems understand what many Christian families have forgotten: whoever shapes the children shapes the future.

FAITHFULNESS NOW LOOKS LIKE

Personal: Refuse the false gospel of comfortable Christianity. Rebuild your life on Scripture as the plumb line, not culture, not comfort, and not consensus. Practice daily obedience in small things so you are not improvising faithfulness when pressure rises.

Family: Reclaim the home as the first church and the first seminary. Stop outsourcing discipleship to schools, youth programs, or screens. Teach the Word diligently when you sit, when you walk, when you lie down, and when you rise. What you model, they will normalize. Model costly obedience.

Church: Recover the courage to form saints, not audiences. Equip parents to disciple their children, but do not replace them. Build resistance communities, whether classical schools, homeschool networks, or intergenerational fellowships, that preserve Christian distinctiveness for long-term transmission.

Public: Defend the foundations required for generational faithfulness. Protect parental rights. Resist ideological indoctrination in public education. Oppose compelled speech and ideological coercion. When the Church retreats from public witness, darkness fills the void.

COMMITMENTS

☐ Identify one area where you have outsourced discipleship, whether to schools, programs, or screens, and reclaim responsibility this week by implementing one concrete family discipleship practice.

☐ Establish or restore a household rhythm of Scripture, prayer, and conversation at least four times this week, embedding the Word into daily life.

☐ Repent of one tolerated compromise in your life or home, whether it's a renamed sin, blurred boundary, or delayed obedience, and replace it with obedience.

☐ Have one direct conversation with your children this week about costly faithfulness, using a biblical example to teach that following Christ may cost everything but is worth it.

PRAYER

Lord Jesus, forgive me where I have built on sand, prioritizing comfort over conviction, safety over faithfulness, and approval over obedience. Forgive me for tolerating compromise, outsourcing discipleship, and modeling selective obedience to my children. Rebuild my life and my home on the foundation of Your Word. Make me a faithful steward of the legacy You have entrusted to me not wealth or reputation, but truth received, lived, and transmitted. Strengthen Your Church to preach without apology, discipline with love, and equip families to disciple the next generation. Raise up a remnant who will not bow, who will choose You over comfort, and who will leave a legacy that magnifies Christ across generations. Amen.

About the Author

Drew Reitzel holds a degree in theology and spent several years in pastoral ministry before entering the marketplace, where he has worked for the past twenty-five years. He writes as someone who has lived on both sides of the pulpit and the pew — who has known the mountaintop and the valley, carried his own cross, and understands what it means to love God and still struggle to obey Him.

This book was not written from a place of arrival. It was written from a place of conviction — forged through personal failure, sustained by God's mercy, and driven by an unshakable belief that the Church still has time to turn.

His prayer is that these pages do not sit on a shelf. That they disturb, convict, and ultimately drive you back to your knees — and back to the God who is still waiting, still merciful, and still able to rebuild what compromise has broken. That you leave these pages with the courage to speak where you have been silent, to stand where you have been retreating, and to carry truth into every room you enter — your home, your workplace, your community, and your nation. The healing of this nation will not come from Washington. It will not come from a platform or a movement. It will come when the people of God decide that His Word is the final authority on every question, in every arena, without apology and without retreat. You are not called to be comfortable. You are called to be faithful. And faithfulness, sustained by repentance and fueled by grace, is still the most dangerous force on earth.

"The remnant is rising. The only question is whether you will be counted among them."

Endnotes

1. Christian Smith with Melinda Lundquist Denton, *Soul Searching: The Religious and Spiritual Lives of American Teenagers* (New York: Oxford University Press, 2005), 162–163.

2. ESV, 2 Timothy 3:5.

3. Carl R. Trueman, *The Rise and Triumph of the Modern Self: Cultural Amnesia, Expressive Individualism, and the Road to Sexual Revolution* (Wheaton: Crossway, 2020), 38.

4. Thomas Watson, *A Body of Divinity* (1692; repr., Edinburgh: Banner of Truth Trust, 1958), 47–49.

5. ESV, Proverbs 9:10.

6. Tertullian, *Apology*, trans. S. Thelwall, in *Ante-Nicene Fathers*, vol. 3, ed. Alexander Roberts and James Donaldson (Buffalo: Christian Literature Publishing, 1885), 42.

7. R. C. Sproul, *The Holiness of God* (Wheaton: Tyndale House, 1985), 25–27.

8. Tertullian, *Apology*, 44.

9. Jordan B. Peterson, *12 Rules for Life: An Antidote to Chaos* (Toronto: Random House Canada, 2018), 147–149.

10. Douglas Murray, *The Madness of Crowds: Gender, Race and Identity* (London: Bloomsbury Continuum, 2019), 12.

11. Grey Matter Research & Consulting, "The State of American Theology Study 2020," Ligonier Ministries and LifeWay Research, September 8, 2020, accessed January 15, 2025, https://thestateoftheology.com.

12. ESV, Galatians 2:20.

13. Jonathan Edwards, "Sinners in the Hands of an Angry God," sermon delivered July 8, 1741, in *The Works of Jonathan Edwards*, vol. 2 (Edinburgh: Banner of Truth Trust, 1974), 10.

14. ESV, Matthew 10:38.

15. Charles Haddon Spurgeon, "Spiritual Revival the Want of the Church," Sermon No. 293, *Metropolitan Tabernacle Pulpit*, February 1, 1863, in *Metropolitan Tabernacle Pulpit*, vol. 9 (London: Passmore & Alabaster, 1863), 73.

16. ESV, Luke 6:46.

17. ESV, Matthew 7:19.

18. Grey Matter Research & Consulting, "The Scandal of Biblical Illiteracy: It's Our Problem," *Christianity Today*, October 2016, accessed January 20, 2025, https://www.christianitytoday.com/ct/2016/october-web-only/scandal-of-biblical-illiteracy-its-our-problem.html.

19. Grey Matter Research & Consulting, "The State of American Theology Study 2020," Ligonier Ministries and LifeWay Research, September 8, 2020, accessed January 15, 2025, https://thestateoftheology.com.

20   ESV, Isaiah 66:2.

21   ESV, 1 Peter 4:17.

22   Eugene H. Peterson, *The Pastor: A Memoir* (New York: HarperOne, 2011), 57.

23   ESV, Luke 9:23.

24   Dietrich Bonhoeffer, *The Cost of Discipleship* (New York: Macmillan, 1959), 45.

25   James K. A. Smith, *You Are What You Love: The Spiritual Power of Habit* (Grand Rapids: Brazos Press, 2016), 11.

26   Bonhoeffer, *The Cost of Discipleship*, 47.

27   Bret Weinstein and Heather Heying, *A Hunter-Gatherer's Guide to the 21st Century: Evolution and the Challenges of Modern Life* (New York: Portfolio/Penguin, 2021), 53.

28   Rosaria Champagne Butterfield, *The Gospel Comes with a House Key: Practicing Radically Ordinary Hospitality in Our Post-Christian World* (Wheaton: Crossway, 2018), 23.

29   ESV, Luke 14:27.

30   Carl R. Trueman, *Strange New World: How Thinkers and Activists Redefined Identity and Sparked the Sexual Revolution* (Wheaton: Crossway, 2022), 29.

31   Richard Sibbes, *The Bruised Reed* (1630; repr., Edinburgh: Banner of Truth Trust, 1998), 38–40.

32   ESV, Acts 14:22.

33   Mark Dever, *Nine Marks of a Healthy Church*, 3rd ed. (Wheaton: Crossway, 2013), 155–157.

34   ESV, 1 Peter 1:16.

35   John Owen, *The Works of John Owen*, ed. William H. Goold, vol. 6 (Edinburgh: Banner of Truth Trust, 1967), 4–7.

36   ESV, Matthew 7:14.

37   Richard Baxter, *The Reformed Pastor* (1656; repr., Edinburgh: Banner of Truth Trust, 1974), 53–55.

38   ESV, 2 Timothy 3:16.

39   William Wilberforce, *A Practical View of Christianity* (1797; repr., Peabody, MA: Hendrickson, 1996), 89–91.

40   ESV, Ezekiel 33:8.

41   ESV, Matthew 13:5–6.

42   ESV, 1 Corinthians 3:12.

43   ESV, Judges 21:25.

44   ESV, Matthew 10:37.

45   ESV, Luke 9:23.

46   Augustine of Hippo, *Confessions*, trans. Henry Chadwick (Oxford: Oxford University Press, 1991), 3.

47   Kevin DeYoung, *The Hole in Our Holiness: Filling the Gap between Gospel Passion and the Pursuit of Godliness* (Wheaton: Crossway, 2012), 31–33.

48   Eric Metaxas, *Letter to the American Church* (Washington, DC: Salem Books, 2022), 47–49.

49 ESV, Jeremiah 17:9.
50 John Calvin, *Institutes of the Christian Religion*, ed. John T. McNeill, trans. Ford Lewis Battles (Philadelphia: Westminster Press, 1960), 1:108–109.
51 ESV, Leviticus 11:44.
52 Peterson, *12 Rules for Life*, 148.
53 ESV, 2 Corinthians 10:5.
54 Murray, *The Madness of Crowds*, 256–259.
55 Jonathan Haidt, *The Righteous Mind: Why Good People Are Divided by Politics and Religion* (New York: Pantheon Books, 2012), 153–155.
56 Smith, *You Are What You Love*, 22.
57 Charlie Kirk, *The College Scam* (Washington, DC: Regnery Publishing, 2023), 178–180.
58 Butterfield, *The Gospel Comes with a House Key*, 39.
59 Thomas Sowell, *The Vision of the Anointed: Self-Congratulation as a Basis for Social Policy* (New York: Basic Books, 1995), 2–4.
60 ESV, Genesis 1:27.
61 ESV, 2 Corinthians 5:17.
62 ESV, Romans 5:3–4.
63 John Piper, *Desiring God: Meditations of a Christian Hedonist* (Colorado Springs: Multnomah, 2011), 50.
64 William Wilberforce, *A Practical View of Christianity* (1797; repr., Peabody, MA: Hendrickson, 1996), 44–46.
65 ESV, Romans 6:18.
66 Bari Weiss, *How to Fight Anti-Semitism* (New York: Crown, 2019), 44–46.
67 Paul Kingsnorth, *The Wake* (Minneapolis: Graywolf Press, 2015), 311–313.
68 ESV, 1 Peter 4:17.
69 Leonard Verduin, *The Reformers and Their Stepchildren* (Grand Rapids: Eerdmans, 1964), 23–25.
70 Albert Mohler, *The Gathering Storm: Secularism, Culture, and the Church* (Nashville: Nelson Books, 2020), 89.
71 ESV, Matthew 5:13.
72 D. Martyn Lloyd-Jones, *Revival* (Wheaton: Crossway Books, 1987), 99–101..
73 ESV, 1 Samuel 16:7.
74 Albert Mohler, *The Gathering Storm: Secularism, Culture, and the Church* (Nashville: Nelson Books, 2020), 89.
75 ESV, Jeremiah 23:29.
76 ESV, Acts 2:42.
77 Charles Haddon Spurgeon, "Feeding Sheep or Amusing Goats," sermon circa 1890, reprinted in *The Sword and the Trowel* (London: Passmore & Alabaster, 1890), 397.
78 David Platt, *Radical: Taking Back Your Faith from the American Dream* (Colorado Springs: Multnomah Books, 2010), 18.

79 Victor Davis Hanson, *The Dying Citizen: How Progressive Elites, Tribalism, and Globalization Are Destroying the Idea of America* (New York: Basic Books, 2021), 167–169.

80 ESV, Matthew 23:27.

81 David Platt, *Radical: Taking Back Your Faith from the American Dream* (Colorado Springs: Multnomah Books, 2010), 24.

82 Andrew Murray, *The Ministry of Intercession* (1897; repr., New Kensington, PA: Whitaker House, 1982), 11–13.

83 ESV, Matthew 15:8.

84 Pliny the Younger, *Letters*, Book X, Letter 96, trans. Betty Radice (Cambridge, MA: Harvard University Press, 1969), 285.

85 Baucham, *Expository Apologetics*, 27.

86 ESV, 2 Timothy 3:5.

87 Baucham, *Expository Apologetics*, 33.

88 ESV, 1 Corinthians 1:18.

89 ESV, Ezekiel 33:7.

90 D. Martyn Lloyd-Jones, *Spiritual Depression: Its Causes and Cure* (Grand Rapids: Eerdmans, 1965), 20.

91 ESV, Isaiah 66:2.

92 Os Guinness, *The Dust of Death: A Critique of the Establishment and the Counter Culture* (Downers Grove: InterVarsity Press, 1973), 19–21.

93 ESV, Proverbs 1:7.

94 ESV, Malachi 3:7.

95 ESV, Matthew 3:2.

96 ESV, Matthew 4:17.

97 Adrian Rogers, *Adrianisms: The Wit and Wisdom of Adrian Rogers* (Memphis: Love Worth Finding Ministries, 2006), 47.

98 Samuel Rutherford, *Letters of Samuel Rutherford*, ed. Andrew Bonar (Edinburgh: Oliphant, Anderson & Ferrier, 1891), 112–113.

99 ESV, Revelation 3:16.

100 Charles G. Finney, *Lectures on Revivals of Religion* (1835; repr., Virginia Beach: CBN University Press, 1978), 9–11.

101 ESV, Luke 6:46.

102 Walter Marshall, *The Gospel Mystery of Sanctification* (1692; repr., Grand Rapids: Reformation Heritage Books, 1999), 17–19.

103 ESV, Joel 2:12–13.

104 John Knox, *The Works of John Knox*, ed. David Laing, vol. 3 (Edinburgh: Wodrow Society, 1854), 83–85.

105 ESV, Hosea 4:6.

106 ESV, 1 Peter 4:17.

107 ESV, Matthew 3:8.

108 ESV, Matthew 13:24–30.

109 Samuel Rutherford, *Letters of Samuel Rutherford*, ed. Andrew Bonar (Edinburgh: Oliphant, Anderson & Ferrier, 1891), 87–88.

110 ESV, Revelation 3:14–22.

111 ESV, Revelation 3:19.

112 ESV, Malachi 3:7.

113 ESV, Matthew 7:21–23.

114 ESV, 2 Chronicles 7:14.

115 ESV, Isaiah 44:22.

116 C.S. Lewis, *The Abolition of Man* (New York: HarperOne, 2001), 26.

117 2 Timothy 3:16–17 (ESV).

118 Psalm 119:89 (ESV).

119 Isaiah 40:8 (ESV).

120 Matthew 6:24 (ESV).

121 Matthew 5:17–18 (ESV).

122 Nancy Pearcey, *Total Truth: Liberating Christianity from Its Cultural Captivity* (Wheaton: Crossway, 2005), 23–32.

123 Hebrews 4:12 (ESV).

124 Psalm 119:105 (ESV).

125 Carl Trueman, *The Rise and Triumph of the Modern Self: Cultural Amnesia, Expressive Individualism, and the Road to Sexual Revolution* (Wheaton: Crossway, 2020), 48–56.

126 John 17:17 (ESV).

127 Deuteronomy 4:2 (ESV).

128 James K.A. Smith, *You Are What You Love: The Spiritual Power of Habit* (Grand Rapids, MI: Brazos Press, 2016), 21–32.

129 Jeremiah 17:9 (ESV).

130 Francis A. Schaeffer, *How Should We Then Live? The Rise and Decline of Western Thought and Culture* (Wheaton: Crossway, 2005), 205–227.

131 Jeremiah 17:5 (ESV).

132 Romans 1:25 (ESV).

133 Isaiah 40:8 (ESV).

134 Isaiah 5:20 (ESV).

135 1 Corinthians 13:6 (ESV).

136 John 8:36 (ESV).

137 Douglas Wilson, *Rules for Reformers* (Moscow, ID: Canon Press, 2014), 67–75.

138 John 17:17 (ESV).

139 G.K. Chesterton, *The Thing: Why I Am a Catholic* (San Francisco: Ignatius Press, 2002), 38–39.

140 Colossians 2:8 (ESV).

141 John 14:6 (ESV).

142 Democratic Platform 2020, Democratic National Committee, accessed February 14, 2026, https://democrats.org/where-we-stand/party-platform/, 34–37.

143 U.S. Department of Education, "Nondiscrimination on the Basis of Sex in Education Programs or Activities Receiving Federal Financial Assistance," Federal Register 89, no. 83 (April 29, 2024): 33474–33809.

144 Romans 1:25 (ESV).

145 Douglas Murray, *The Madness of Crowds: Gender, Race and Identity* (London: Bloomsbury Continuum, 2019), 1–18.

146 Francis A. Schaeffer, *How Should We Then Live? The Rise and Decline of Western Thought and Culture* (Wheaton: Crossway, 2005), 205–227.

147 John 17:17 (ESV).

148 Leviticus 19:2 (ESV).

149 H.R. 5, Equality Act, 117th Congress (2021).

150 Obergefell v. Hodges, 576 U.S. 644 (2015).

151 Isaiah 5:20 (ESV).

152 Rosaria Champagne Butterfield, *The Gospel Comes with a House Key: Practicing Radically Ordinary Hospitality in Our Post-Christian World* (Wheaton: Crossway, 2018), 23–37.

153 1 Peter 1:15–16 (ESV).

154 Voddie Baucham Jr., *Fault Lines: The Social Justice Movement and Evangelicalism's Looming Catastrophe* (Washington, DC: Salem Books, 2021), 87–104.

155 Genesis 1:27 (ESV).

156 Psalm 139:13 (ESV).

157 Bostock v. Clayton County, 590 U.S. ____ (2020).

158 Andrew Chung and John Kruzel, "US Supreme Court conservatives lean toward allowing transgender sports bans," Reuters, January 13, 2026, https://www.reuters.com/legal/government/us-supreme-court-hears-challenge-transgender-sports-bans-2026-01-13/.

159 U.S. Department of Education, Office for Civil Rights, "Regulations Enforced by the Office for Civil Rights," accessed February 14, 2026, https://www.ed.gov/about/ed-offices/ocr/regulations-enforced-by-the-office-for-civil-rights.

160 Associated Press, "Virginia school board to pay $575K to a teacher fired for refusing to use trans student's pronouns," October 1, 2024, https://apnews.com/article/virginia-teacher-fired-transgender-student-pronouns-8fce2e788ecb5db6f2ea6250ea0d5adf; Meriwether v. Hartop, No. 20-3289, 992 F.3d 492 (6th Cir. Mar. 26, 2021), https://www.opn.ca6.uscourts.gov/opinions.pdf/21a0071p-06.pdf.

161 Democratic Platform 2024, Democratic National Committee, accessed February 14, 2026, https://democrats.org/where-we-stand/party-platform/.

162 Carl Trueman, *The Rise and Triumph of the Modern Self: Cultural Amnesia, Expressive Individualism, and the Road to Sexual Revolution* (Wheaton: Crossway, 2020), 171–187.

163 Rod Dreher, *Live Not by Lies: A Manual for Christian Dissidents* (New York: Sentinel, 2020), 3–18.

164 James K.A. Smith, *You Are What You Love: The Spiritual Power of Habit* (Grand Rapids, MI: Brazos Press, 2016), 47–63.

165 Deuteronomy 32:4 (ESV).

166 Democratic Platform 2020, Democratic National Committee, accessed February 14, 2026, https://democrats.org/where-we-stand/party-platform/, 21–28.

167 Voddie Baucham Jr., *Fault Lines: The Social Justice Movement and Evangelicalism's Looming Catastrophe* (Washington, DC: Salem Books, 2021), 187–206.

168 H.R. 5, Equality Act, 117th Congress (2021).

169 Psalm 89:14 (ESV).

170 Thaddeus Williams, *Confronting Injustice without Compromising Truth: 12 Questions Christians Should Ask About Social Justice* (Grand Rapids, MI: Zondervan, 2020), 31–47.

171 Thomas Sowell, *The Quest for Cosmic Justice* (New York: Free Press, 1999), 1–18.

172 Rod Dreher, *Live Not by Lies: A Manual for Christian Dissidents* (New York: Sentinel, 2020), 67–84.

173 Douglas Murray, *The Madness of Crowds: Gender, Race and Identity* (London: Bloomsbury Continuum, 2019), 89–107.

174 Jordan B. Peterson, *12 Rules for Life: An Antidote to Chaos* (Toronto: Random House Canada, 2018), 203–220.

175 Matthew 7:21 (ESV).

176 Dietrich Bonhoeffer, *The Cost of Discipleship*, trans. R.H. Fuller (New York: Touchstone, 1995), 43–56.

177 A.W. Tozer, *The Pursuit of God* (Chicago: Moody Publishers, 2015), 89–103.

178 James 1:22 (ESV).

179 2 Timothy 4:3–4 (ESV).

180 J.C. Ryle, *Holiness: Its Nature, Hindrances, Difficulties, and Roots* (Moscow, ID: Charles Nolan Publishers, 2001), 134–147.

181 David Platt, *Radical: Taking Back Your Faith from the American Dream* (Colorado Springs: Multnomah Books, 2010), 3–18.

182 Revelation 3:15–16 (ESV).

183 Francis Chan, *Crazy Love: Overwhelmed by a Relentless God*, rev. ed. (Colorado Springs: David C Cook, 2013), 67–83.

184 Barna Group, "The State of the Bible 2023," accessed February 14, 2026, https://www.barna.com/research/sotb-2023/.

185 Luke 9:23 (ESV).

186 Kevin DeYoung, *The Hole in Our Holiness: Filling the Gap between Gospel Passion and the Pursuit of Godliness* (Wheaton, IL: Crossway, 2012), 17–31.

187 Galatians 1:10 (ESV).

188 Pew Research Center, "Religious Landscape Study," accessed February 14, 2026, https://www.pewresearch.org/religion/religious-landscape-study/.

189 2 Corinthians 5:11 (ESV).

190 1 Timothy 3:15 (ESV).

191 D. Martyn Lloyd-Jones, *Preaching and Preachers* (Grand Rapids, MI: Zondervan, 2011), 53–68.

192 Presbyterian Church (U.S.A.), "Amendment 14-F: Marriage Redefinition," June 19, 2014, https://www.pcusa.org/site_media/media/uploads/oga/pdf/amendment-14-f.pdf.

193 United Methodist Church, "Protocol of Reconciliation & Grace Through Separation," January 3, 2020, https://www.resourceumc.org/en/content/protocol-of-reconciliation-grace-through-separation.

194 Revoice, "Supporting, Encouraging, and Empowering Gay, Lesbian, Same-Sex-Attracted, and Other LGBTQ+ Christians," accessed February 14, 2026, https://www.revoice.us/.

195 Ezekiel 33:6 (ESV).

196 Acts 20:27 (ESV).

197 Matthew 28:18–20 (ESV).

198 R.C. Sproul, *The Holiness of God*, rev. ed. (Carol Stream, IL: Tyndale House, 2000), 113–128.

199 Sinclair B. Ferguson, *Devoted to God: Blueprints for Sanctification* (Edinburgh: Banner of Truth Trust, 2016), 11–26.

200 Hebrews 12:28–29 (ESV).

201 Genesis 1:27 (ESV).

202 Exodus 20:13 (ESV).

203 Psalm 139:13 (ESV).

204 Basil the Great, On Social Justice, trans. C. Paul Schroeder (Crestwood, NY: St. Vladimir's Seminary Press, 2009), 69–71.

205 Jeremiah 1:5 (ESV).

206 Francis Schaeffer, How Should We Then Live? The Rise and Decline of Western Thought and Culture (Wheaton: Crossway, 1976), 205–207.

207 Didache 2.2, in The Apostolic Fathers, trans. Bart D. Ehrman, Loeb Classical Library 24 (Cambridge, MA: Harvard University Press, 2003), 417.

208 Tertullian, Apology, trans. T. R. Glover, Loeb Classical Library 250 (Cambridge, MA: Harvard University Press, 1931), 151.

209 Democratic Platform 2024, Democratic National Committee, accessed February 14, 2026, https://democrats.org/where-we-stand/party-platform/.

210 Roe v. Wade, 410 U.S. 113 (1973).

211 Dobbs v. Jackson Women's Health Organization, 597 U.S. ____ (2022).

212 Hillary Clinton, interview with Chuck Todd, Meet the Press, NBC, April 3, 2016.

213 C.S. Lewis, The Abolition of Man (New York: HarperOne, 2001), 73–77.

214 Psalm 8:4–5 (ESV).

215 Luke 1:44 (ESV).

216 Romans 1:25 (ESV).
217 John Calvin, Institutes of the Christian Religion, ed. John T. McNeill, trans. Ford Lewis Battles (Louisville: Westminster John Knox, 1960), 1:108.
218 Augustine, Confessions, trans. Henry Chadwick (Oxford: Oxford University Press, 1991), 29–30.
219 Psalm 106:37–38 (ESV).
220 Thomas Sowell, A Conflict of Visions: Ideological Origins of Political Struggles, rev. ed. (New York: Basic Books, 2007), 26–28.
221 Victor Davis Hanson, The Dying Citizen: How Progressive Elites, Tribalism, and Globalization Are Destroying the Idea of America (New York: Basic Books, 2021), 14–16.
222 Isaiah 1:16–17 (ESV).
223 R. C. Sproul, The Holiness of God (Carol Stream, IL: Tyndale House, 1985), 55–56.
224 Deuteronomy 30:19 (ESV).
225 Genesis 3:5 (ESV).
226 National Right to Life Committee, "Abortion Statistics: United States Data and Trends," accessed February 14, 2026, https://www.nrlc.org/uploads/factsheets/FS01AbortionintheUS.pdf.
227 Guttmacher Institute, "Abortion Incidence and Service Availability in the United States, 2020," February 2022, https://www.guttmacher.org/report/abortion-incidence-service-availability-us-2020.
228 Centers for Disease Control and Prevention, "Abortion Surveillance, United States, 2020," Morbidity and Mortality Weekly Report 71, no. SS-10 (November 25, 2022): 1–27.
229 Guttmacher Institute, "Monthly Abortion Provision Study," March 2024, https://www.guttmacher.org/monthly-abortion-provision-study.
230 Democratic Platform 2024, Democratic National Committee, accessed February 14, 2026, https://democrats.org/where-we-stand/party-platform/.
231 Ibid.
232 Ibid.
233 Ephesians 6:12 (ESV).
234 George Orwell, 1984 (London: Secker & Warburg, 1949), 6.
235 Ephesians 5:6 (ESV).
236 Psalm 139:13-14 (ESV).
237 Roe v. Wade, 410 U.S. 113 (1973).
238 Roe v. Wade, 410 U.S. 113, 221 (1973) (White, J., dissenting).
239 Planned Parenthood, "2021-2022 Annual Report," accessed February 14, 2026, https://www.plannedparenthood.org/uploads/filer_public/2022/annual-report.pdf.

240 Dobbs v. Jackson Women's Health Organization, 597 U.S. ____ (2022).

241 Ibid., at 6.

242 Joseph R. Biden Jr., "Statement by President Joe Biden on the Supreme Court Decision in Dobbs v. Jackson Women's Health Organization," June 24, 2022, https://www.whitehouse.gov/briefing-room/statements-releases/2022/06/24/statement-by-president-biden-on-the-supreme-court-decision-in-dobbs-v-jackson-womens-health-organization/.

243 Genesis 11:1-9 (ESV).

244 Isaiah 1:15 (ESV).

245 Jeremiah 19:4 (ESV).

246 Jeremiah 21:14 (ESV).

247 Romans 1:28 (ESV).

248 Isaiah 5:20 (ESV).

249 Death with Dignity National Center, "Death with Dignity Acts," accessed February 14, 2026, https://deathwithdignity.org/learn/death-with-dignity-acts/.

250 Matthew 23:27 (ESV).

251 John 2:15 (ESV).

252 Matthew 18:6 (ESV).

253 Genesis 4:10 (ESV).

254 Proverbs 6:16-17 (ESV).

255 New York State Senate Bill S240, Reproductive Health Act, signed January 22, 2019.

256 U.S. Food and Drug Administration, "Mifepristone U.S. Post-Marketing Adverse Events Summary through 12/31/2018," January 2023, https://www.fda.gov/drugs/postmarket-drug-safety-information-patients-and-providers/mifeprex-mifepristone-information.

257 Ezekiel 18:23 (ESV).

258 2 Chronicles 7:14 (ESV).

259 1 Peter 4:17 (ESV).

260 Acts 20:27 (ESV).

261 1 John 1:9 (ESV).

262 Galatians 6:2 (ESV).

263 Ezekiel 33:6 (ESV).

264 Southern Baptist Convention, "Resolution on Abortion," June 1971, accessed February 14, 2026, https://www.sbc.net/resource-library/resolutions/resolution-on-abortion/.

265 Southern Baptist Convention, "Resolution on Abortion," June 1980, accessed February 14, 2026, https://www.sbc.net/resource-library/resolutions/resolution-on-abortion-2/.

266 Various mainline Protestant denominational statements on abortion, 1970s, documented in diverse church archives and historical records.

267 Randall Balmer, Thy Kingdom Come: How the Religious Right Distorts Faith and Threatens America (New York: Basic Books, 2006), 13–28.

268 Dietrich Bonhoeffer, attributed, widely cited in Bonhoeffer biographies and ethical works.

269 LifeWay Research, "Pastors' Views on Abortion," September 2019, accessed February 14, 2026, https://lifewayresearch.com/2019/09/10/pastors-views-on-abortion/.

270 Ed Stetzer, "The Church and Abortion: Why We've Been Silent," Christianity Today, January 22, 2019, accessed February 14, 2026, https://www.christianitytoday.com/edstetzer/2019/january/church-and-abortion-why-weve-been-silent.html.

271 Carl Trueman, The Rise and Triumph of the Modern Self: Cultural Amnesia, Expressive Individualism, and the Road to Sexual Revolution (Wheaton: Crossway, 2020), 23–41.

272 Rosaria Butterfield, The Gospel Comes with a House Key: Practicing Radically Ordinary Hospitality in Our Post-Christian World (Wheaton: Crossway, 2018), 67–82.

273 Barna Group, "What Do Christians Really Believe About Abortion?" January 2020, accessed February 14, 2026, https://www.barna.com/research/what-do-christians-really-believe-about-abortion/.

274 James K. A. Smith, You Are What You Love: The Spiritual Power of Habit (Grand Rapids: Brazos Press, 2016), 2.

275 1 Peter 4:17 (ESV).

276 Matthew 7:21 (ESV).

277 1 John 1:9 (ESV).

278 Dietrich Bonhoeffer, The Cost of Discipleship, trans. R. H. Fuller (New York: Macmillan, 1937), 89.

279 1 Corinthians 5:6-7 (ESV).

280 Genesis 1:27 (ESV).

281 Democratic National Committee, "2024 Democratic Party Platform," accessed February 17, 2026, https://democrats.org/where-we-stand/party-platform/.

282 Democratic National Committee, "2024 Democratic Party Platform," accessed February 17, 2026, https://democrats.org/where-we-stand/party-platform/.

283 Acts 5:29 (ESV).

284 Genesis 3:1 (ESV).

285 U.S. Department of Education, Office for Civil Rights, "Notice of Interpretation: Enforcement of Title IX of the Education Amendments of 1972 with Respect to Discrimination Based on Sexual Orientation and Gender Identity in Light of Bostock v. Clayton County," Federal Register 86, no. 106 (June 4, 2021): 30574-30579.

286 California Legislature, Assembly Bill No. 2218, Chapter 182, Statutes of 2020 (approved September 26, 2020).

287 American Academy of Pediatrics, "Ensuring Comprehensive Care and Support for Transgender and Gender-Diverse Children and Adolescents," Pediatrics 142, no. 4 (October 2018): e20182162.

288 Proverbs 12:10 (KJV).

289 John Calvin, Institutes of the Christian Religion, ed. John T. McNeill, trans. Ford Lewis Battles (Louisville: Westminster John Knox Press, 1960), 2.1.8.

290 Chloe Cole and other detransitioners have testified before state legislatures and in public forums about irreversible medical harm from pediatric gender transition. See testimony before the Ohio House of Representatives, March 2023, and widespread media coverage of detransitioner advocacy organizations, including the Detransition Advocacy Network.

291 Dietrich Bonhoeffer, The Cost of Discipleship, trans. R. H. Fuller (New York: Touchstone, 1995), 43-45.

292 Matthew 28:19-20 (ESV).

293 Charles Spurgeon, Lectures to My Students (Grand Rapids: Zondervan, 1954), 76-77.

294 Ezekiel 33:1-6 (ESV).

295 Leonard Ravenhill, Why Revival Tarries (Minneapolis: Bethany House, 1959), 18-20.

296 Isaiah 5:20 (ESV).

297 Ephesians 6:12 (ESV).

298 2 Kings 17:7-23 (ESV).

299 Douglas Murray, The Madness of Crowds: Gender, Race and Identity (London: Bloomsbury Continuum, 2019), 16-18.

300 Romans 1:26-28 (ESV).

301 Daniel 1:8 (ESV).

302 Galatians 6:7 (ESV).

303 1 John 4:8 (ESV).

304 Augustine, The City of God, trans. Marcus Dods (New York: Modern Library, 1950), 477.

305 1 Corinthians 13:6 (ESV).

306 Democratic National Committee, "2024 Democratic Party Platform," accessed February 17, 2026, https://democrats.org/where-we-stand/party-platform/.

307 1 Corinthians 6:9-10 (ESV).

308 Genesis 1:27 (ESV).

309 Carl R. Trueman, The Rise and Triumph of the Modern Self: Cultural Amnesia, Expressive Individualism, and the Road to Sexual Revolution (Wheaton, IL: Crossway, 2020), 23.

310 U.S. Department of Education, Office for Civil Rights, "Notice of Interpretation: Enforcement of Title IX of the Education Amendments of 1972 with Respect to Discrimination Based on Sexual Orientation and Gender Identity in Light of Bostock v.

Clayton County," Federal Register 86, no. 106 (June 4, 2021): 30574-30579.

311 California Legislature, Assembly Bill No. 2218, Chapter 182, Statutes of 2020 (approved September 26, 2020).

312 American Academy of Pediatrics, "Ensuring Comprehensive Care and Support for Transgender and Gender-Diverse Children and Adolescents," Pediatrics 142, no. 4 (October 2018): e20182162.

313 Abigail Shrier, Irreversible Damage: The Transgender Craze Seducing Our Daughters (Washington, DC: Regnery Publishing, 2020), xvi.

314 Matthew 18:6 (ESV).

315 Romans 1:26, 28 (ESV).

316 Mary Eberstadt, Adam and Eve After the Pill: Paradoxes of the Sexual Revolution (San Francisco: Ignatius Press, 2012), 17.

317 2 Timothy 4:2 (ESV).

318 Ross Douthat, Bad Religion: How We Became a Nation of Heretics (New York: Free Press, 2012), 198.

319 2 Timothy 4:3-4 (ESV).

320 Matthew 7:15-16 (ESV).

321 Jordan B. Peterson, 12 Rules for Life: An Antidote to Chaos (Toronto: Random House Canada, 2018), 188.

322 C. S. Lewis, The Four Loves (New York: Harcourt Brace Jovanovich, 1960), 169.

323 Jonathan Edwards, Religious Affections, ed. John E. Smith, vol. 2 of The Works of Jonathan Edwards (New Haven: Yale University Press, 1959), 383.

324 A. W. Tozer, The Knowledge of the Holy (New York: Harper & Row, 1961), 105.

325 Elisabeth Elliot, Shadow of the Almighty: The Life and Testament of Jim Elliot (New York: Harper & Brothers, 1958), 247.

326 1 Kings 18:21 (ESV).

327 Matthew 6:24 (ESV).

328 Matthew 10:33 (ESV).

329 William Wilberforce, Real Christianity, ed. James M. Houston (Portland, OR: Multnomah Press, 1982), 79.

330 1 John 1:5 (ESV).

331 John 14:6 (ESV).

332 Romans 1:18 (ESV).

333 Romans 1:24 (ESV).

334 Romans 1:26 (ESV).

335 Romans 1:28 (ESV).

336 Ronald Bayer, Homosexuality and American Psychiatry: The Politics of Diagnosis (New York: Basic Books, 1981), 3-4.

337 American Psychiatric Association, Diagnostic and Statistical Manual of Mental Disorders, 3rd ed., revised (Washington, DC: American Psychiatric Association, 1987), 296.

338 American Psychiatric Association, Diagnostic and Statistical Manual of Mental Disorders, 4th ed. (Washington, DC: American Psychiatric Association, 1994), 532-538; American Psychiatric Association, Diagnostic and Statistical Manual of Mental Disorders, 5th ed. (Washington, DC: American Psychiatric Association, 2013), 451-459; World Health Organization, International Classification of Diseases, 11th ed. (Geneva: World Health Organization, 2019).

339 American Psychiatric Association, Diagnostic and Statistical Manual of Mental Disorders, 5th ed., text revision (Washington, DC: American Psychiatric Association, 2022), 511.

340 American Psychiatric Association, Diagnostic and Statistical Manual of Mental Disorders, 5th ed. (Washington, DC: American Psychiatric Association, 2013), 50-59.

341 American Psychiatric Association, Diagnostic and Statistical Manual of Mental Disorders, 5th ed. (Washington, DC: American Psychiatric Association, 2013), 315-318.

342 Cecilia Dhejne et al., "Long-Term Follow-Up of Transsexual Persons Undergoing Sex Reassignment Surgery: Cohort Study in Sweden," PLoS ONE 8, no. 2 (2013): e56885.

343 The Trevor Project, 2022 National Survey on LGBTQ Youth Mental Health (West Hollywood, CA: The Trevor Project, 2022), 5.

344 Jeremiah 6:14 (ESV).

345 Chloe Cole, testimony before Ohio House of Representatives, March 8, 2023.

346 Helena Kerschner, "By Any Other Name," Pitt Magazine, University of Pittsburgh, Winter 2023.

347 Proverbs 12:10 (KJV).

348 Ephesians 6:12 (ESV).

349 Genesis 1:27 (ESV).

350 Genesis 3:1 (ESV).

351 2 Corinthians 4:4 (ESV).

352 Leviticus 18:21 (ESV).

353 Jeremiah 32:35 (ESV).

354 Daniel 3:6 (ESV).

355 Daniel 3:18 (ESV).

356 Episcopal Church, Journal of the General Convention of The Episcopal Church, Minneapolis, 2003 (New York: General Convention, 2003).

357 Evangelical Lutheran Church in America, "Human Sexuality: Gift and Trust," A Social Statement adopted by the 2009 Churchwide Assembly, August 2009.

358 United Church of Christ, General Synod Resolution, "In Support of Equal Marriage Rights for All," July 2005.

359 A. W. Tozer, The Root of the Righteous (Chicago: Moody Publishers, 1955), 56.

360 Dietrich Bonhoeffer, attributed statement, widely cited in various sources.

361 Charles Spurgeon, The Soul Winner (New Kensington, PA: Whitaker House, 1995), 32.

362 Ezekiel 33:7 (ESV).

363 Ezekiel 33:6 (ESV).

364 Proverbs 14:34 (ESV).

365 Victor Davis Hanson, The Dying Citizen: How Progressive Elites, Tribalism, and Globalization Are Destroying the Idea of America (New York: Basic Books, 2021), 3-7.

366 Malachi 3:7 (ESV).

367 1 John 1:9 (ESV).

368 Isaiah 58:1 (ESV).

369 2 Kings 22-23 (ESV).

370 Matthew 12:30 (ESV).

371 Philippians 2:10-11 (ESV).

372 1 Kings 19:18 (ESV).

373 Daniel 1:8 (ESV).

374 Joshua 24:15 (ESV).

375 Matthew 10:33 (ESV).

376 1 Corinthians 16:13 (ESV).

377 Isaiah 5:20 (ESV).

378 Romans 5:8 (ESV).

379 Isaiah 53:10 (ESV).

380 1 Corinthians 13:6 (ESV).

381 Genesis 3:1 (ESV).

382 John Calvin, 'Institutes of the Christian Religion,' ed. John T. McNeill, trans. Ford Lewis Battles (Louisville: Westminster John Knox Press, 1960), 1.11.8.

383 Matthew 10:34 (ESV).

384 Tertullian, De Spectaculis, trans. T. R. Glover, Loeb Classical Library (Cambridge, MA: Harvard University Press, 1931), 10.

385 2 Timothy 3:5 (ESV).

386 Revelation 3:19 (ESV).

387 Matthew 7:13–14 (ESV).

388 Ezekiel 33:6 (ESV).

389 U.S. Congress, House, Equality Act of 2021, H.R. 5, 117th Cong., 1st sess., introduced in House February 18, 2021.

390 Rosaria Butterfield, The Gospel Comes with a House Key: Practicing Radically Ordinary Hospitality in Our Post-Christian World (Wheaton, IL: Crossway, 2018), 147.

391 Luke 9:23 (ESV).

392 Martin Luther, quoted in Roland H. Bainton, Here I Stand: A Life of Martin Luther (Nashville: Abingdon Press, 1950), 185.

393 Jeremiah 17:9 (ESV).

394 John 3:20 (ESV).

395 Francis A. Schaeffer, The Great Evangelical Disaster (Wheaton, IL: Crossway Books, 1984), 37.

396 Luke 13:3 (ESV).

397 Romans 1:16 (ESV).

398 Amos 5:10 (ESV).

399 Matthew 12:30 (ESV).

400 Abington School District v. Schempp, 374 U.S. 203 (1963).

401 G. K. Chesterton, Orthodoxy (New York: Dodd, Mead and Company, 1908), 30.

402 Douglas Murray, The Madness of Crowds: Gender, Race and Identity (London: Bloomsbury Continuum, 2019), 14.

403 Vance Havner, quoted in Leonard Ravenhill, Why Revival Tarries (Minneapolis: Bethany House Publishers, 1959), 83.

404 Luke 17:2 (ESV).

405 Matthew 11:21 (ESV).

406 Romans 12:2 (ESV).

407 Leonard Ravenhill, Why Revival Tarries (Minneapolis: Bethany House Publishers, 1959), 29.

408 Exodus 32:4 (ESV).

409 Exodus 32:22 (ESV).

410 Miriam Grossman, You're Teaching My Child What? A Physician Exposes the Lies of Sex Education and How They Harm Your Child (Washington, DC: Regnery Publishing, 2009), 127.

411 Jordan B. Peterson, 12 Rules for Life: An Antidote to Chaos (Toronto: Random House Canada, 2018), 295.

412 Galatians 1:10 (ESV).

413 1 Kings 18:21 (ESV).

414 2 Corinthians 6:17 (ESV).

415 Amos 1:2 (ESV).

416 Amos 3:6 (ESV).

417 Luke 19:42 (ESV).

418 2 Peter 2:5 (ESV).

419 Jeremiah 38:6 (ESV).

420 Amos 4:12 (ESV).

421 Matthew 11:20–24 (ESV).

422 John 8:11 (ESV).

423 Mark 10:21–22 (ESV).

424 Matthew 25:30 (ESV); Mark 9:48 (ESV).

425 1 Peter 4:17 (ESV).

426 Luke 5:37–38 (ESV).

427 Jeremiah 6:14 (ESV).

428 Thomas Sowell, A Conflict of Visions: Ideological Origins of Political Struggles, rev. ed. (New York: Basic Books, 2007), 18–22.

429 Rod Dreher, Live Not by Lies: A Manual for Christian Dissidents (New York: Sentinel, 2020), 6–11.

430 Ezekiel 18:23 (ESV).

431 Psalm 103:8 (ESV).

432 Luke 12:49 (ESV).

433 John 2:17 (ESV).

434 Matthew 23:14–15 (ESV).

435 Matthew 12:25 (ESV).

436 Matthew 12:36 (ESV).

437 Romans 1:24 (ESV).

438 Romans 1:26 (ESV).

439 Romans 1:28 (ESV).

440 Joel 2:17 (ESV).

441 Revelation 3:19 (ESV).

442 Ezekiel 33:6 (ESV).

443 Jeremiah 7:3 (ESV).

444 Isaiah 59:14 (ESV).

445 Proverbs 9:10 (ESV).

446 1 Kings 18:38–40 (ESV).

447 2 Timothy 4:3 (ESV).

448 2 Timothy 3:13 (ESV).

449 2 Samuel 12:7 (ESV).

450 1 Kings 17:1 (ESV).

451 Mark 6:18–28 (ESV).

452 Judges 21:25 (ESV).

453 Lifeway Research, "State of Theology 2022: Evangelical Beliefs in America," Lifeway Research, 2022, https://lifewayresearch.com/2022/09/20/state-of-theology-2022/.

454 Charles H. Spurgeon, Lectures to My Students (Grand Rapids, MI: Zondervan, 1954), 42.

455 Acts 5:29 (ESV).

456 John Flavel, The Mystery of Providence (Edinburgh: Banner of Truth Trust, 1678; repr. 1963), 194–197.

457 John Knox, quoted in Thomas M'Crie, The Life of John Knox (Edinburgh: William Blackwood, 1813), 284.

458 Joel 2:15 (ESV).

459 Joshua 24:15 (ESV).

460 John 8:11 (ESV).

461 John 3:7 (ESV).

462 Jordan B. Peterson, Maps of Meaning: The Architecture of Belief (New York: Routledge, 1999), 264–287.

463 Douglas Murray, The War on the West (New York: Broadside Books, 2022), 89–112.

464 2 Timothy 4:3 (ESV).

465 A. W. Tozer, The Radical Cross: Living the Passion of Christ (Camp Hill, PA: WingSpread Publishers, 2009), 47.

466 2 Corinthians 5:17 (ESV).

467 Psalm 89:14 (ESV).

468 Matthew 4:17 (ESV).

469 Rod Dreher, Live Not by Lies: A Manual for Christian Dissidents (New York: Sentinel, 2020), 34–58.

470 Os Guinness, Prophetic Untimeliness: A Challenge to the Idol of Relevance (Grand Rapids, MI: Baker Books, 2003), 72.

471 A. W. Tozer, The Root of the Righteous (Camp Hill, PA: WingSpread Publishers, 1955), 56.

472 Matthew 11:6 (ESV).

473 Malachi 3:7 (ESV).

474 Mark 1:15 (ESV).

475 The Holy Bible: English Standard Version (Wheaton, IL: Crossway, 2016), Mark 1:15.

476 ESV, Romans 13:3.

477 ESV, Genesis 2:15.

478 ESV, 2 Thessalonians 3:10.

479 ESV, 1 Thessalonians 4:11–12.

480 ESV, Exodus 20:15.

481 ESV, Exodus 20:17.

482 ESV, Leviticus 23:22.

483 ESV, Deuteronomy 14:28–29.

484 ESV, Leviticus 25:10.

485 ESV, Matthew 14:16.

486 ESV, 1 Timothy 3:15.

487 ESV, 1 Peter 4:17.

488 ESV, 1 Timothy 5:8.

489 U.S. Congress, H.R. 5 (117th): Equality Act, sec. 1107, Congress.gov, accessed January 28, 2026.

490 Basic Income Earth Network, "What Is Basic Income?" Basic Income Earth Network, accessed January 28, 2026.

491 Internal Revenue Service, "2021 Child Tax Credit and Advance Child Tax Credit Payments—Topic A," IRS.gov, accessed January 28, 2026.

492 U.S. Department of Labor, Employment and Training Administration, Unemployment Insurance Program Letter (UIPL) No. 14-21, "Important Dates for the American Rescue Plan Act of 2021 Benefit Programs," accessed January 28, 2026.

493 Becker Friedman Institute for Economics at the University of Chicago, "U.S. Unemployment Insurance Replacement Rates During the Pandemic," accessed January 28, 2026.

494 ESV, Isaiah 31:1.

495 ESV, 1 Samuel 8:20.

496 John Chrysostom, On Wealth and Poverty, trans. Catharine P. Roth (Crestwood, NY: St. Vladimir's Seminary Press, 1984), 55.

497 A. W. Tozer, The Knowledge of the Holy: The Attributes of God, Their Meaning in the Christian Life (New York: HarperOne, 1978), 1.

498 Dietrich Bonhoeffer, The Cost of Discipleship, trans. R. H. Fuller (New York: Touchstone, 1995), 43.

499 Francis A. Schaeffer, How Should We Then Live? The Rise and Decline of Western Thought and Culture (Old Tappan, NJ: Fleming H. Revell, 1976), 205.
500 ESV, James 1:27.
501 ESV, Psalm 119:67.
502 ESV, 2 Corinthians 3:17.
503 Friedrich A. Hayek, The Road to Serfdom: Text and Documents—The Definitive Edition, ed. Bruce Caldwell (Chicago: University of Chicago Press, 2007), 112–124.
504 George Orwell, "Politics and the English Language," in All Art Is Propaganda: Critical Essays, ed. George Packer (New York: Mariner Books, 2009), 270–286.
505 ESV, Isaiah 5:20.
506 Helen Pluckrose and James A. Lindsay, Cynical Theories: How Activist Scholarship Made Everything about Race, Gender, and Identity—and Why This Harms Everybody (Durham, NC: Pitchstone Publishing, 2020), 47–80.
507 Carl R. Trueman, The Rise and Triumph of the Modern Self: Cultural Amnesia, Expressive Individualism, and the Road to Sexual Revolution (Wheaton, IL: Crossway, 2020), 221–300.
508 Christopher Watkin, Biblical Critical Theory: How the Bible's Unfolding Story Makes Sense of Modern Life and Culture (Grand Rapids: Zondervan Academic, 2022), 345–367.
509 ESV, Colossians 2:20–22.
510 Rod Dreher, Live Not by Lies: A Manual for Christian Dissidents (New York: Sentinel, 2020), 3–90.
511 ESV, Proverbs 29:25.
512 U.S. Department of Labor, Employee Benefits Security Administration, "Prudence and Loyalty in Selecting Plan Investments and Exercising Shareholder Rights," Federal Register 87, no. 230 (December 1, 2022): 73822–73826.
513 ESV, James 4:12.
514 U.S. Department of Labor, Employment and Training Administration, Unemployment Insurance Program Letter No. 14-21: American Rescue Plan Act of 2021 (ARPA) – Key Unemployment Insurance (UI) Provisions (Washington, DC: U.S. Department of Labor, March 15, 2021), 1–4.
515 Robert D. Lupton, Toxic Charity: How Churches and Charities Hurt Those They Help (And How to Reverse It) (New York: HarperOne, 2011), 8.
516 Steve Corbett and Brian Fikkert, When Helping Hurts: How to Alleviate Poverty Without Hurting the Poor... and Yourself (Chicago: Moody Publishers, 2009), 105–115.
517 Marvin Olasky, The Tragedy of American Compassion (Washington, DC: Regnery Gateway, 1992), 167–200.
518 ESV, Romans 14:23.

519 The Heritage Foundation, ESG, DEI, and What to Do About Them, Special Report no. 307 (Washington, DC: The Heritage Foundation, December 31, 2024), 8–12.

520 Vivek Ramaswamy, Woke, Inc.: Inside Corporate America's Social Justice Scam (New York: Center Street, 2021), 149–210.

521 ESV, James 1:26.

522 ESV, Daniel 3:4–5.

523 John F. Walvoord, Daniel: The Key to Prophetic Revelation (Chicago: Moody Press, 1971), 82–91.

524 Sinclair B. Ferguson, Daniel: The Master, the Servants, and the King (Fearn, Ross-shire: Christian Focus, 1998), 65–78.

525 U.S. Equal Employment Opportunity Commission, "Section 12: Religious Discrimination," accessed January 30, 2026, https://www.eeoc.gov/laws/guidance/section-12-religious-discrimination.

526 ESV, Acts 5:29.

527 Martin Luther, The Freedom of a Christian, trans. Mark D. Tranvik (Minneapolis: Fortress Press, 2008), 50–65.

528 ESV, Galatians 5:1.

529 Timothy George, Galatians, New American Commentary, vol. 30 (Nashville: Broadman & Holman, 1994), 354–362.

530 C. S. Lewis, The Abolition of Man (New York: HarperOne, 2015), 1–15.

531 ESV, Matthew 12:30.

532 ESV, Isaiah 8:12.

533 ESV, 1 Corinthians 7:23.

534 C. K. Johnson, "Christian Charity vs. Government Welfare," Foundation for Economic Education, April 1, 1970.

535 ESV, 2 Corinthians 9:7.

536 Charles Haddon Spurgeon, "The Churl and the Bountiful," Metropolitan Tabernacle Pulpit 13 (1867): 545–553, at 548.

537 ESV, Leviticus 19:15.

538 Samuel Gregg, "Edmund Burke's Case for Private Charity over the Welfare State," Acton Institute, April 16, 2014.

539 Stephen McDowell, "Socialism Undermines Charity," TrueCharity, June 13, 2018.

540 ESV, Luke 12:14.

541 J. C. Ryle, Practical Religion (Oak Harbor, WA: Baptist Standard Bearer, 2001), 39.

542 ESV, Matthew 19:21.

543 David Platt, Radical: Taking Back Your Faith from the American Dream (Colorado Springs, CO: Multnomah, 2010), 72–73.

544 Frédéric Bastiat, The Law (Irvington-on-Hudson, NY: Foundation for Economic Education, 1950), 18.

545 Bastiat, The Law, 18.

546 Alexis de Tocqueville, Memoir on Pauperism, trans. Seymour Drescher (New York: The Free Press, 1997), 25–28.

547 Arthur C. Brooks, Who Really Cares: The Surprising Truth About Compassionate Conservatism (New York: Basic Books, 2006), 23–27.

548 ESV, 2 Thessalonians 3:10.

549 Charles Murray, Losing Ground: American Social Policy, 1950–1980 (New York: Basic Books, 1984), 154–180.

550 ESV, Ephesians 4:28.

551 ESV, Ephesians 4:28; cf. 2 Corinthians 9:7.

552 ESV, Galatians 6:10.

553 McDowell, "Socialism Undermines Charity," TrueCharity.

554 Basil the Great, "I Will Tear Down My Barns," in On Social Justice, trans. C. Paul Schroeder (Crestwood, NY: St. Vladimir's Seminary Press, 2009), 42–44.

555 John Chrysostom, On Wealth and Poverty, trans. Catherine P. Roth (Crestwood, NY: St. Vladimir's Seminary Press, 1984), 49–50.

556 Basil the Great, On Social Justice, 42–48; Chrysostom, On Wealth and Poverty, 49–60.

557 ESV, 1 Timothy 5:8.

558 Joel J. Miller, "Should Government Coerce Charity?," Patheos, April 12, 2019.

559 ESV, 1 Timothy 5:16.

560 Miller, "Should Government Coerce Charity?"; McDowell, "Socialism Undermines Charity."

561 Murray, Losing Ground, 154–180.

562 Tocqueville, Memoir on Pauperism, 25–28.

563 ESV, 1 Thessalonians 4:11–12.

564 Murray, Losing Ground, 154–180; Miller, "Should Government Coerce Charity?"

565 Brooks, Who Really Cares, 23–27.

566 Marvin Olasky, The Tragedy of American Compassion (Washington, DC: Regnery Publishing, 1992), 108–112.

567 James Madison, quoted in Gregg, "Edmund Burke's Case for Private Charity over the Welfare State."

568 ESV, Acts 20:35.

569 Steve Corbett and Brian Fikkert, When Helping Hurts: How to Alleviate Poverty Without Hurting the Poor and Yourself (Chicago: Moody Publishers, 2009), 52–56.

570 Gregg, "Edmund Burke's Case for Private Charity over the Welfare State."

571 Thomas Sowell, A Conflict of Visions: Ideological Origins of Political Struggles, rev. ed. (New York: Basic Books, 2007), 32–38.

572 ESV, Proverbs 19:17.

573 ESV, 2 Corinthians 9:7; Platt, Radical, 72–73.

574 ESV, James 2:15–16.

575 Robert D. Lupton, Toxic Charity: How Churches and Charities Hurt Those They Help (And How to Reverse It) (New York: HarperOne, 2011), 38–42.

576 A. W. Tozer, The Knowledge of the Holy (New York: Harper & Row, 1961), 8–12.

577 ESV, Matthew 6:24.

578 C. K. Johnson, "Christian Charity vs. Government Welfare"; Brooks, Who Really Cares, 23–27.

579 John Flavel, The Mystery of Providence (Edinburgh: Banner of Truth Trust, 1678; repr. 1963), 174–178.

580 The Holy Bible: English Standard Version (Wheaton, IL: Crossway, 2016), Matthew 16:24.

581 ESV, 2 Timothy 3:5.

582 Carl R. Trueman, The Rise and Triumph of the Modern Self: Cultural Amnesia, Expressive Individualism, and the Road to Sexual Revolution (Wheaton, IL: Crossway, 2020), 38–39.

583 Jonathan Haidt and Greg Lukianoff, The Coddling of the American Mind: How Good Intentions and Bad Ideas Are Setting Up a Generation for Failure (New York: Penguin Press, 2018), 29.

584 ESV, Romans 12:2.

585 John F. MacArthur Jr., Ashamed of the Gospel: When the Church Becomes Like the World, 3rd ed. (Wheaton, IL: Crossway, 2010), 65.

586 Cultural Research Center at Arizona Christian University, "American Worldview Inventory 2022 Release #5: The Worldview Deficit in the Pulpits" (PDF, May 10, 2022), 2–3, accessed February 3, 2026.

587 ESV, Acts 20:28–31.

588 Barna Group, "Pastors Face Communication Challenges in a Divided Culture," Barna, January 29, 2019, accessed February 3, 2026.

589 Lifeway Research, "Pastors' Views on Fear within Their Congregation" (PDF; survey September 6–30, 2022; published September 6, 2022), accessed February 3, 2026.

590 ESV, Matthew 28:18–20.

591 Dietrich Bonhoeffer, The Cost of Discipleship (New York: Touchstone, 1995), 44–45.

592 Voddie T. Baucham Jr., Fault Lines: The Social Justice Movement and Evangelicalism's Looming Catastrophe (Washington, DC: Salem Books, 2021), 5–6.

593 Oswald Chambers, My Utmost for His Highest (New York: Dodd, Mead & Company, 1935), 187–189.

594 Rosaria Butterfield, Five Lies of Our Anti-Christian Age (Wheaton, IL: Crossway, 2023), 28.

595 ESV, James 4:4.

596 Francis A. Schaeffer, The Great Evangelical Disaster (Wheaton, IL: Crossway, 1984), 37.

597 ESV, Colossians 2:8.

598 Nancy R. Pearcey, Love Thy Body: Answering Hard Questions about Life and Sexuality (Grand Rapids, MI: Baker Books, 2018), 21.

599 ESV, 1 Peter 2:9.

600 J. C. Ryle, Holiness (London: William Hunt, 1879), 256.

601 Barna Group, "Pastors Face Communication Challenges in a Divided Culture," Barna, January 29, 2019, accessed February 3, 2026.

602 ESV, Genesis 3:1.

603 Bonhoeffer, Cost of Discipleship, 47.

604 Charles H. Spurgeon, "The Best Donation," Metropolitan Tabernacle Pulpit 33 (1887): 214–15.

605 Ryle, Holiness, 258.

606 ESV, Revelation 3:1–2.

607 ESV, Revelation 3:15–16.

608 ESV, Revelation 2:4–5.

609 ESV, Hebrews 13:13.

610 ESV, 2 Timothy 3:5.

611 ESV, 2 Timothy 4:3–4.

612 James K. A. Smith, You Are What You Love: The Spiritual Power of Habit (Grand Rapids, MI: Brazos Press, 2016), 41–45.

613 ESV, Isaiah 5:20.

614 ESV, Psalm 51:4.

615 R. C. Sproul, The Holiness of God (Wheaton, IL: Tyndale House, 1985), 116.

616 ESV, Romans 1:18–25.

617 John Calvin, Institutes of the Christian Religion, trans. Henry Beveridge (Edinburgh: Calvin Translation Society, 1845), 1:47 (1.11.8).

618 ESV, Mark 7:20–23.

619 John Owen, The Mortification of Sin (Edinburgh: Banner of Truth, 2000), 52.

620 ESV, Colossians 3:5.

621 Richard Sibbes, The Bruised Reed (Edinburgh: Banner of Truth Trust, 1630; repr. 1998), 37–40.

622 Sproul, The Holiness of God, 138.

623 ESV, Mark 1:15.

624 ESV, Leviticus 19:15.

625 Douglas Murray, The Madness of Crowds: Gender, Race and Identity (London: Bloomsbury Continuum, 2019), 11.

626 ESV, Ephesians 4:15.

627 Jonathan Haidt and Greg Lukianoff, The Coddling of the American Mind: How Good Intentions and Bad Ideas Are Setting Up a Generation for Failure (New York: Penguin Press, 2018), 29.

628 John Flavel, The Fountain of Life (London: printed by R. Roberts, 1673; repr. Edinburgh: Banner of Truth Trust, 2016), 44–48.

629 ESV, Colossians 2:8.

630 ESV, Titus 2:11–14.

631 Baucham, Fault Lines, 222.

632 ESV, John 14:6.

633 Rosaria Butterfield, Five Lies of Our Anti-Christian Age (Wheaton, IL: Crossway, 2023), 134.

634 ESV, John 8:34.

635 Rod Dreher, Live Not by Lies: A Manual for Christian Dissidents (New York: Sentinel, 2020), 18.

636 ESV, Galatians 1:8–9.

637 Francis A. Schaeffer, The Great Evangelical Disaster (Wheaton, IL: Crossway, 1984), 37.

638 ESV, 2 Corinthians 7:10.

639 ESV, Galatians 1:6–7.

640 ESV, 2 Corinthians 11:3–4.

641 ESV, Genesis 3:1–6.

642 ESV, 2 Corinthians 11:3.

643 ESV, Mark 1:15.

644 Kevin DeYoung, What Does the Bible Really Teach about Homosexuality? (Wheaton, IL: Crossway, 2015), 138–141.

645 Nancy Pearcey, Love Thy Body: Answering Hard Questions about Life and Sexuality (Grand Rapids, MI: Baker Books, 2018), 31–36.

646 ESV, 2 Timothy 4:3–4.

647 Sinclair B. Ferguson, The Holy Spirit (Downers Grove, IL: InterVarsity Press, 1996), 189.

648 ESV, 1 John 4:1–3.

649 John F. MacArthur Jr., The Gospel According to Jesus: What Does Jesus Mean When He Says "Follow Me"?, rev. and exp. ed. (Grand Rapids: Zondervan, 2008), 204.

650 ESV, Mark 8:34.

651 Irenaeus, "Against Heresies," in Ante-Nicene Fathers, vol. 1, ed. Alexander Roberts and James Donaldson (Buffalo, NY: Christian Literature, 1885), 331 (1.1).

652 ESV, Galatians 1:6–9.

653 Athanasius, On the Incarnation, trans. John Behr (Crestwood, NY: St. Vladimir's Seminary Press, 2011), 57.

654 ESV, John 14:6.

655 Jonathan Edwards, Religious Affections, ed. John E. Smith, Works of Jonathan Edwards, vol. 2 (New Haven: Yale University Press, 1959), 254–258.

656 ESV, James 4:4.

657 ESV, 1 John 3:8.

658 John Owen, The Mortification of Sin (Edinburgh: Banner of Truth, 2000), 52.

659 Douglas Murray, The Madness of Crowds: Gender, Race and Identity (London: Bloomsbury Continuum, 2019), 147.

660 Bret Weinstein and Heather Heying, A Hunter-Gatherer's Guide to the 21st Century: Evolution and the Challenges of Modern Life (New York: Portfolio/Penguin, 2021), 68–72.

661 ESV, Jude 3.

662 Victor Davis Hanson, The Dying Citizen: How Progressive Elites, Tribalism, and Globalization Are Destroying the Idea of America (New York: Basic Books, 2021), 187–192.

663 ESV, Colossians 2:8.

664 ESV, Titus 2:11–12.

665 ESV, Jude 4.

666 ESV, Galatians 1:8–9.

667 ESV, Revelation 19:11–16.

668 ESV, Hebrews 12:28–29.

669 ESV, Matthew 7:21–23.

670 The Holy Bible: English Standard Version (Wheaton, IL: Crossway, 2016), Genesis 1:27–28; Genesis 2:24.

671 Augustine, Confessions, trans. Henry Chadwick (Oxford: Oxford University Press, 1991), 21 (2.1).

672 ESV, Genesis 2:24; ESV, Ephesians 5:31–32.

673 Os Guinness, The Call: Finding and Fulfilling the Central Purpose of Your Life (Nashville: Thomas Nelson, 1998), 44–48.

674 ESV, Malachi 2:14–16; ESV, Matthew 19:4–6.

675 ESV, Mark 1:15; ESV, Matthew 28:18–20.

676 John Bunyan, Grace Abounding to the Chief of Sinners (Edinburgh: Banner of Truth Trust, 1666; repr. 1987), 14–18.

677 Thomas Watson, The Doctrine of Repentance (Edinburgh: Banner of Truth Trust, 1668; repr. 1987), 18–21.

678 ESV, Deuteronomy 6:6–9; ESV, Proverbs 1:8–9; ESV, Ephesians 6:4.

679 Jordan B. Peterson, 12 Rules for Life: An Antidote to Chaos (Toronto: Random House Canada, 2018), 122–127.

680 ESV, Hebrews 12:5–11.

681 ESV, Psalm 139:13–16; ESV, 1 Corinthians 6:19–20.

682 Rod Dreher, Live Not by Lies: A Manual for Christian Dissidents (New York: Sentinel, 2020), 92.

683 ESV, Genesis 1:27.

684 John Calvin, Institutes of the Christian Religion, trans. Henry Beveridge (Edinburgh: Calvin Translation Society, 1845), 1:48 (1.11.9).

685 Trueman, Rise and Triumph of the Modern Self, 308.

686 Paul Kingsnorth, Confessions of a Recovering Environmentalist and Other Essays (Minneapolis: Graywolf Press, 2017), 112–116.

687 ESV, 1 Kings 19:18; ESV, Romans 11:5.

688 ESV, Joshua 24:15; ESV, Colossians 3:12–17.

689 Octavius Winslow, Personal Declension and Revival of Religion in the Soul (Edinburgh: Banner of Truth Trust, 1841; repr. 2011), 34–38.

690 John Piper, Desiring God: Meditations of a Christian Hedonist (Sisters, OR: Multnomah Books, 1986), 31–35.

691 D. Martyn Lloyd-Jones, Preaching and Preachers (Grand Rapids: Zondervan, 1971), 28.

692 ESV, Psalm 127:1.

693 The Holy Bible: English Standard Version (Wheaton, IL: Crossway, 2016), 1 Peter 5:8.

694 D. A. Carson, The Gagging of God (Grand Rapids: Zondervan, 1996), 345.

695 ESV, Luke 9:23.

696 Dietrich Bonhoeffer, The Cost of Discipleship, trans. R. H. Fuller (New York: Touchstone, 1995), 47.

697 ESV, Ephesians 6:12.

698 ESV, James 4:4.

699 A. W. Tozer, Man: The Dwelling Place of God (Chicago: Moody, 1966), 112.

700 ESV, 1 Thessalonians 5:21–22.

701 ESV, 1 John 4:1.

702 Leonard Ravenhill, Why Revival Tarries (Minneapolis: Bethany House, 1959), 34.

703 Francis A. Schaeffer, The Great Evangelical Disaster (Wheaton: Crossway, 1984), 37.

704 Jonathan Haidt, The Righteous Mind (New York: Pantheon, 2012), 366.

705 Rod Dreher, Live Not By Lies (New York: Sentinel, 2020), 134.

706 ESV, Proverbs 29:25.

707 Carl R. Trueman, The Rise and Triumph of the Modern Self (Wheaton: Crossway, 2020), 46.

708 William Gurnall, The Christian in Complete Armour (London: Ralph Smith, 1655; repr. Edinburgh: Banner of Truth Trust, 1964), vol. 1, 71–74.

709 ESV, John 8:44.

710 ESV, Matthew 24:4.

711 ESV, 2 Corinthians 4:4.

712 Jordan Peterson, 12 Rules for Life (Toronto: Random House, 2018), 45.

713 Martyn Lloyd-Jones, The Christian Warfare (Edinburgh: Banner of Truth, 1976), 118.

714 ESV, Ezekiel 33:6.

715 ESV, 1 John 4:1.

716 ESV, Colossians 2:4.

717 ESV, Ephesians 6:11.

718 ESV, Ephesians 6:14.

719 Samuel Rutherford, Letters of Samuel Rutherford, ed. Andrew Bonar (Edinburgh: Banner of Truth Trust, 1664; repr. 1984), 112–114.

720 ESV, Ephesians 6:13–14.

721 William Wilberforce, Real Christianity (1797; repr. Vancouver: Regent College Publishing, 1997), 88–91.

722 ESV, 1 Thessalonians 5:6.

723 Dreher, Live Not By Lies, 102.

724 ESV, Romans 1:25.

725 ESV, Psalm 106:37–38; 1 Corinthians 10:20.

726 ESV, Leviticus 18:21.

727 ESV, Deuteronomy 12:31.

728 ESV, 2 Kings 17:17.

729 ESV, Jeremiah 32:35.

730 ESV, Isaiah 57:5.

731 ESV, Psalm 139:13–14.

732 John Piper, "Why I Am Pro-Life," Desiring God, January 13, 2012, accessed February 6, 2026, https://www.desiringgod.org/articles/why-i-am-pro-life.

733 John Piper, "Why I Am Pro-Life," Desiring God, January 13, 2012.

734 Tertullian, Apology, 9.8, in Ante-Nicene Fathers, vol. 3, ed. Alexander Roberts and James Donaldson (Peabody, MA: Hendrickson, 1994), 25.

735 Tertullian, On the Soul, 25, in Ante-Nicene Fathers, vol. 3, 216–17.

736 Tertullian, On the Soul, 27, in Ante-Nicene Fathers, vol. 3, 218.

737 Basil of Caesarea, First Canonical Letter, canons 2 and 8, in Nicene and Post-Nicene Fathers, Second Series, vol. 8, ed. Philip Schaff and Henry Wace (Peabody, MA: Hendrickson, 1994), 188–89.

738 John Chrysostom, Homilies on Romans, Homily 24, in Nicene and Post-Nicene Fathers, First Series, vol. 11 (Peabody, MA: Hendrickson, 1994), 463.

739 ESV, Proverbs 6:16–17.

740 ESV, Genesis 1:27.

741 ESV, Matthew 19:4.

742 Nancy R. Pearcey, Love Thy Body: Answering Hard Questions about Life and Sexuality (Grand Rapids: Baker Books, 2018), 39–41.

743 ESV, 1 Kings 18:4.

744 ESV, 1 Kings 19:1–2.

745 R. Albert Mohler Jr., "The Moral Insanity of Drag Queen Story Hour," AlbertMohler.com, accessed February 6, 2026, https://albertmohler.com.

746 ESV, Galatians 5:19–21.

747 ESV, Colossians 3:5.

748 ESV, Romans 1:25.

749 R. Albert Mohler Jr., "The Equality Act and the Future of Religious Liberty," AlbertMohler.com, 2021, accessed February 6, 2026, https://albertmohler.com.

750 ESV, Romans 13:1–4.

751 Carl R. Trueman, The Rise and Triumph of the Modern Self (Wheaton, IL: Crossway, 2020), 38–39.

752 ESV, Revelation 18:4.

753 A. W. Tozer, The Knowledge of the Holy (New York: Harper & Row, 1961), 11–13.

754 John Calvin, Institutes of the Christian Religion, trans. Henry Beveridge (Edinburgh: Calvin Translation Society, 1845), 1.11.8.

755 Derek Prince, Blessing or Curse: You Can Choose (Fort Lauderdale, FL: Derek Prince Ministries, 1987), 135–38.

756 Francis A. Schaeffer, A Christian Manifesto (Westchester, IL: Crossway, 1981), 33–35.

757 ESV, Deuteronomy 12:31.

758 ESV, Psalm 106:37–38; 1 Corinthians 10:20.

759 ESV, 1 Corinthians 6:9–10.

760 ESV, Exodus 20:3–5.

761 ESV, Exodus 23:2.

762 ESV, 1 John 4:1.

763 ESV, Matthew 24:24.

764 ESV, Matthew 7:15.

765 ESV, Titus 1:9.

766 ESV, 1 Thessalonians 5:21.

767 George Whitefield, Sermons of George Whitefield, ed. Lee Gatiss (Wheaton, IL: Crossway, 2012), 78–82.

768 Octavius Winslow, Personal Declension and Revival of Religion in the Soul (Edinburgh: Banner of Truth Trust, 1841; repr. 2011), 44–48.

769 ESV, Hebrews 5:14.

770 ESV, 1 Corinthians 13:6.

771 ESV, Ephesians 5:11.

772 ESV, 1 Corinthians 14:29.

773 Leonard Ravenhill, Why Revival Tarries (Minneapolis: Bethany House Publishers, 1959), 25.

774 ESV, 2 Timothy 3:5.

775 D. Martyn Lloyd-Jones, Preaching and Preachers (Grand Rapids: Zondervan, 1987), 20.

776 David Wilkerson, Revival on Broadway (New York: World Challenge, 1996), 54–58.

777 Charles Spurgeon, "The Wailing of Risca," sermon no. 120, preached July 20, 1856, on Luke 19:41–42.

778 J. C. Ryle, Holiness (Boston: James R. Osgood and Company, 1877), 326.

779 ESV, Galatians 1:6–9.

780 ESV, Luke 9:23.

781 ESV, Hebrews 5:14.

782 ESV, Isaiah 66:2.

783 The Holy Bible: English Standard Version (Wheaton, IL: Crossway, 2016), Ezekiel 33:6.

784 ESV, James 4:17.

785 ESV, Proverbs 29:25.

786 ESV, John 12:42–43.
787 William Gurnall, The Christian in Complete Armour, abridged ed. (Edinburgh: Banner of Truth Trust, 1964), 12–25.
788 ESV, 2 Timothy 1:7.
789 Eric Metaxas, Bonhoeffer: Pastor, Martyr, Prophet, Spy (Nashville: Thomas Nelson, 2010), 293–300.
790 ESV, Ephesians 5:11.
791 ESV, 2 Timothy 4:2.
792 Rod Dreher, Live Not by Lies: A Manual for Christian Dissidents (New York: Sentinel, 2020), xvii–xx.
793 Carl R. Trueman, The Rise and Triumph of the Modern Self: Cultural Amnesia, Expressive Individualism, and the Road to Sexual Revolution (Wheaton: Crossway, 2020), 379–402.
794 ESV, Matthew 10:32–33.
795 ESV, Revelation 21:8.
796 Richard Baxter, The Reformed Pastor (1656; abridged ed., Edinburgh: Banner of Truth Trust, 1974), 102.
797 ESV, Proverbs 24:11–12.
798 Douglas Murray, The Madness of Crowds: Gender, Race and Identity (London: Bloomsbury Continuum, 2019), 267–295.
799 Nancy R. Pearcey, Total Truth: Liberating Christianity from Its Cultural Captivity (Wheaton: Crossway, 2005), 123–150.
800 ESV, Acts 4:29.
801 ESV, Amos 5:15.
802 ESV, Isaiah 62:6.
803 ESV, Acts 18:9.
804 ESV, 1 Corinthians 13:6.
805 Jonathan Edwards, A Treatise Concerning Religious Affections (1746; repr., Edinburgh: Banner of Truth Trust, 1986), 8, 17.
806 ESV, Ephesians 4:15.
807 Edwards, Religious Affections, 17.
808 ESV, Leviticus 19:17.
809 Carl R. Trueman, Strange New World: How Thinkers and Activists Redefined Identity and Sparked the Sexual Revolution (Wheaton: Crossway, 2022), 16–21.
810 ESV, Matthew 18:15.
811 Richard Baxter, The Reformed Pastor (1656; abridged ed., Edinburgh: Banner of Truth Trust, 1974), 46–48.
812 ESV, Galatians 4:16.
813 Greg Lukianoff and Jonathan Haidt, The Coddling of the American Mind: How Good Intentions and Bad Ideas Are Setting Up a Generation for Failure (New York: Penguin Press, 2018), 5, 9–10.
814 ESV, Luke 17:3.
815 Thomas Watson, The Doctrine of Repentance (1668; repr., Edinburgh: Banner of Truth Trust, 1987), 20, 24.
816 ESV, Proverbs 27:6.

817 John Owen, The Mortification of Sin in Believers (1656; repr., Edinburgh: Banner of Truth Trust, 1967), 9–10.

818 Gregory the Great, The Book of Pastoral Rule, trans. George Demacopoulos (Crestwood, NY: St. Vladimir's Seminary Press, 2007), 89–92.

819 ESV, Proverbs 27:5.

820 Samuel Rutherford, Letters of Samuel Rutherford, ed. Andrew Bonar (Edinburgh: Banner of Truth Trust, 1984), 89–91.

821 Watson, Doctrine of Repentance, 20, 24.

822 Richard Sibbes, The Bruised Reed (London, 1630; repr. Edinburgh: Banner of Truth Trust, 1998), 39–41.

823 Owen, Mortification of Sin, 9–10.

824 Paul Kingsnorth, "The Cross and the Machine," First Things, June 2021, accessed February 14, 2026, https://www.firstthings.com/article/2021/06/the-cross-and-the-machine.

825 Nancy R. Pearcey, Love Thy Body: Answering Hard Questions about Life and Sexuality (Grand Rapids: Baker Books, 2018), 51–86.

826 John MacArthur, The Master's Plan for the Church (Chicago: Moody Press, 1991), 43–46.

827 George Whitefield, Journals (London: Banner of Truth Trust, 1960), 216–218.

828 Lukianoff and Haidt, Coddling of the American Mind, 9–10.

829 Octavius Winslow, Personal Declension and Revival of Religion in the Soul (London: John F. Shaw, 1841; repr. Edinburgh: Banner of Truth Trust, 2002), 112–114.

830 ESV, Colossians 3:16.

831 Adrian Rogers, Believe in Miracles but Trust in Jesus (Wheaton, IL: Crossway, 1997), 67–69.

832 R. C. Sproul, The Holiness of God (Wheaton, IL: Tyndale House, 1985), 220–223.

833 John R. W. Stott, The Cross of Christ (Leicester: Inter-Varsity Press, 1986), 159–161.

834 ESV, Luke 17:3.

835 David Wilkerson, The Vision (Old Tappan, NJ: Fleming H. Revell, 1974), 98–101.

836 ESV, Revelation 3:19.

837 John Calvin, Institutes of the Christian Religion, ed. John T. McNeill, trans. Ford Lewis Battles (Philadelphia: Westminster Press, 1960), 1:108–112.

838 John C. Lennox, 2084: Artificial Intelligence and the Future of Humanity (Grand Rapids: Zondervan, 2020), 141–144.

839 ESV, Leviticus 19:17.

840 John Flavel, The Mystery of Providence (London, 1678; repr. Edinburgh: Banner of Truth Trust, 1963), 183–185.

841 ESV, 2 Timothy 4:2.

[842] Horatius Bonar, God's Way of Holiness (1864; repr., Edinburgh: Banner of Truth Trust, 1999), 38–41.

[843] Robert Murray M'Cheyne, Memoir and Remains of Robert Murray M'Cheyne, ed. Andrew Bonar (Edinburgh: Banner of Truth Trust, 1966), 151–153.

[844] ESV, 1 Kings 19:18.

[845] ESV, Romans 11:5.

[846] J. C. Ryle, Holiness: Its Nature, Hindrances, Difficulties, and Roots (1879; repr., Edinburgh: Banner of Truth Trust, 2014), 64–66.

[847] ESV, John 15:18.

[848] Athanasius of Alexandria, On the Incarnation, trans. John Behr (Yonkers: St. Vladimir's Seminary Press, 2011), 167–170.

[849] ESV, Acts 5:29.

[850] ESV, 2 Timothy 3:12.

[851] Eusebius of Caesarea, The History of the Church, trans. G. A. Williamson (London: Penguin Classics, 1989), 177–180.

[852] ESV, Proverbs 22:6.

[853] Francis A. Schaeffer, A Christian Manifesto (Westchester, IL: Crossway Books, 1981), 17–23.

[854] ESV, Proverbs 1:7.

[855] Voddie T. Baucham Jr., Family Driven Faith: Doing What It Takes to Raise Sons and Daughters Who Walk with God (Wheaton: Crossway, 2007), 21–24.

[856] ESV, Daniel 3:18.

[857] John Knox, The History of the Reformation of Religion in Scotland (1587; repr., Edinburgh: Banner of Truth Trust, 1982), 112–115.

[858] ESV, Romans 1:25.

[859] Ignatius of Antioch, Letter to the Romans, in The Apostolic Fathers, trans. Bart D. Ehrman (Cambridge: Harvard University Press, 2003), vol. 1, 269–273.

[860] ESV, Isaiah 5:20.

[861] Eric Metaxas, Bonhoeffer: Pastor, Martyr, Prophet, Spy (Nashville: Thomas Nelson, 2010), 361–366.

[862] ESV, Revelation 12:11.

[863] Corrie ten Boom with John and Elizabeth Sherrill, The Hiding Place (Grand Rapids: Revell, 1971), 180–210.

[864] ESV, 1 Corinthians 16:13.

[865] D. Martyn Lloyd-Jones, Preaching and Preachers (Grand Rapids: Zondervan, 1971), 53–56.

[866] ESV, Hebrews 13:14.

[867] John Bunyan, Grace Abounding to the Chief of Sinners (1666; repr., Edinburgh: Banner of Truth Trust, 1987), 121–124.

[868] ESV, Romans 12:2.

[869] A. W. Tozer, The Pursuit of God (Harrisburg: Christian Publications, 1948), 96–98.

[870] ESV, Ecclesiastes 8:5.

[871] ESV, Acts 4:20.

872 William Wilberforce, A Practical View of Christianity (1797; repr., Peabody, MA: Hendrickson, 1996), 67–70.

873 ESV, Philippians 4:5.

874 Rod Dreher, Live Not by Lies: A Manual for Christian Dissidents (New York: Sentinel, 2020), 19–22.

875 ESV, James 1:12.

876 Richard Wurmbrand, Tortured for Christ (London: Hodder & Stoughton, 1967; repr. Bartlesville, OK: Living Sacrifice Book Co., 1998), 72–76.

877 ESV, Ephesians 6:13.

878 ESV, 1 Corinthians 15:58.

879 Dietrich Bonhoeffer, Ethics, ed. Clifford J. Green, trans. Reinhard Krauss, Charles C. West, and Douglas W. Stott, Dietrich Bonhoeffer Works, vol. 6 (Minneapolis: Fortress Press, 2005), 37–40.

880 ESV, 2 Timothy 2:19.

881 Courtney Anderson, To the Golden Shore: The Life of Adoniram Judson (Boston: Little, Brown, 1956; repr. Valley Forge, PA: Judson Press, 1987), 341–344.

882 ESV, James 1:22.

883 Richard Wurmbrand, Tortured for Christ (London: Hodder & Stoughton, 1967; repr. Bartlesville, OK: Living Sacrifice Book Co., 1998), 15–18.

884 ESV, Revelation 14:12.

885 The Holy Bible: English Standard Version (Wheaton, IL: Crossway, 2016), Psalm 11:3.

886 ESV, Matthew 7:24–27.

887 ESV, 1 John 2:15.

888 ESV, James 4:4.

889 John Calvin, Institutes of the Christian Religion, ed. John T. McNeill, trans. Ford Lewis Battles (Philadelphia: Westminster Press, 1960), 1:108.

890 Augustine, City of God, trans. Henry Bettenson (London: Penguin Books, 2003), 632.

891 Augustine, City of God, 633.

892 Basil the Great, On Social Justice, trans. C. Paul Schroeder (Crestwood, NY: St. Vladimir's Seminary Press, 2009), 70.

893 Victor Davis Hanson, The Dying Citizen: How Progressive Elites, Tribalism, and Globalization Are Destroying the Idea of America (New York: Basic Books, 2021), 45.

894 Douglas Murray, The Strange Death of Europe: Immigration, Identity, Islam (London: Bloomsbury, 2017), 2.

895 ESV, Jeremiah 17:5.

896 Thomas Sowell, A Conflict of Visions: Ideological Origins of Political Struggles (New York: Basic Books, 2007), 112.

897 Jordan B. Peterson, 12 Rules for Life: An Antidote to Chaos (Toronto: Random House Canada, 2018), xxviii.

898 ESV, Psalm 146:3.

899 ESV, Isaiah 40:8.

900 ESV, Psalm 119:89.

901 ESV, Isaiah 28:16.

902 ESV, Haggai 2:6.

903 ESV, Hebrews 12:26–27.

904 Carl R. Trueman, The Rise and Triumph of the Modern Self: Cultural Amnesia, Expressive Individualism, and the Road to Sexual Revolution (Wheaton, IL: Crossway, 2020), 303.

905 ESV, Hebrews 12:28.

906 ESV, Daniel 2:44.

907 Nancy R. Pearcey, Total Truth: Liberating Christianity from Its Cultural Captivity (Wheaton, IL: Crossway, 2004), 20.

908 Pearcey, Total Truth, 372.

909 Trueman, Rise and Triumph of the Modern Self, 45.

910 Rod Dreher, Live Not by Lies: A Manual for Christian Dissidents (New York: Sentinel, 2020), xvii.

911 John MacArthur, Ashamed of the Gospel: When the Church Becomes Like the World (Wheaton, IL: Crossway, 1993), 31.

912 R. Albert Mohler Jr., The Gathering Storm: Secularism, Culture, and the Church (Nashville: Thomas Nelson, 2020), 12.

913 David Platt, Radical: Taking Back Your Faith from the American Dream (Colorado Springs: Multnomah, 2010), 3.

914 John Piper, Don't Waste Your Life (Wheaton, IL: Crossway, 2003), 46.

915 Voddie Baucham, Family Driven Faith: Doing What It Takes to Raise Sons and Daughters Who Walk with God (Wheaton, IL: Crossway, 2007), 17.

916 D. A. Carson, The Gagging of God: Christianity Confronts Pluralism (Grand Rapids: Zondervan, 1996), 388–392.

917 Platt, Radical, 162.

918 Mohler, Gathering Storm, 201.

919 ESV, Joshua 24:15.

920 ESV, Deuteronomy 6:5–7.

921 ESV, Judges 2:10.

922 Voddie Baucham, Family Driven Faith: Doing What It Takes to Raise Sons and Daughters Who Walk with God (Wheaton, IL: Crossway, 2007), 139.

923 Oswald Chambers, My Utmost for His Highest (New York: Dodd, Mead & Company, 1935), 8–10.

924 Jordan B. Peterson, 12 Rules for Life: An Antidote to Chaos (Toronto: Random House Canada, 2018), 96.

925 Chambers, My Utmost for His Highest, 8–10.

926 J. C. Ryle, The Duties of Parents (Edinburgh: Banner of Truth Trust, 1888; repr. 1993), 14–17.

927 Sinclair B. Ferguson, The Holy Spirit (Downers Grove, IL: InterVarsity Press, 1996), 172–175.

928 ESV, Psalm 78:5–7.

929 Jonathan Haidt and Greg Lukianoff, The Coddling of the American Mind: How Good Intentions and Bad Ideas Are Setting Up a Generation for Failure (New York: Penguin Press, 2018), 29–30.

930 Charles H. Spurgeon, Lectures to My Students (London: Passmore and Alabaster, 1875), 8–11.

931 Jonathan Edwards, Religious Affections, ed. John E. Smith, Works of Jonathan Edwards, vol. 2 (New Haven: Yale University Press, 1959), 197–201.

932 William Gurnall, The Christian in Complete Armour (London: Ralph Smith, 1655; repr. Edinburgh: Banner of Truth Trust, 1964), vol. 1, 112–115.

933 Rod Dreher, The Benedict Option: A Strategy for Christians in a Post-Christian Nation (New York: Sentinel, 2017), 148.

934 Douglas Wilson, Recovering the Lost Tools of Learning: An Approach to Distinctively Christian Education (Wheaton, IL: Crossway, 1991), 44–48.

935 Mark Dever, The Church: The Gospel Made Visible (Nashville: B&H Academic, 2012), 88–92.

936 ESV, Joshua 24:15.

937 ESV, Psalm 127:3–4.

938 Richard Baxter, A Christian Directory (London, 1673), chap. 10.

939 Robert Murray M'Cheyne, Memoir and Remains of Robert Murray M'Cheyne, ed. Andrew A. Bonar (Edinburgh: Banner of Truth Trust, 1844; repr. 1966), 154–157.

940 ESV, Deuteronomy 11:19.

941 Rosaria Butterfield, The Gospel Comes with a House Key: Practicing Radically Ordinary Hospitality in Our Post-Christian World (Wheaton, IL: Crossway, 2018), 13.

942 Butterfield, The Gospel Comes with a House Key, 35.

943 John R. W. Stott, The Cross of Christ (Leicester: Inter-Varsity Press, 1986), 281–284.

944 George Barna, Transforming Children into Spiritual Champions (Ventura, CA: Regal Books, 2003), 78.

945 Os Guinness, The Call: Finding and Fulfilling the Central Purpose of Your Life (Nashville: Thomas Nelson, 1998), 78–82.

946 ESV, Joel 1:3.

947 ESV, Romans 12:2.

948 ESV, 2 Timothy 3:15.

949 ESV, Malachi 2:15.

950 Alexander Strauch, Biblical Eldership: An Urgent Call to Restore Biblical Church Leadership, rev. ed. (Littleton, CO: Lewis & Roth, 1995), 222–226.

951 Kevin DeYoung, The Hole in Our Holiness: Filling the Gap between Gospel Passion and the Pursuit of Godliness (Wheaton, IL: Crossway, 2012), 94–98.

952 Sinclair B. Ferguson, The Holy Spirit (Downers Grove, IL: InterVarsity Press, 1996), 144–148.

953 ESV, Joshua 24:15.

954 ESV, Psalm 34:11.

955 ESV, Proverbs 22:6.

956 ESV, 1 Kings 10:23.

957 ESV, 1 Kings 11:4.

958 ESV, 2 Timothy 4:10.

959 Samuel Rutherford, Letters of Samuel Rutherford, ed. Andrew Bonar (Edinburgh: Banner of Truth Trust, 1664; repr. 1984), 298–301.

960 ESV, Matthew 6:24.

961 John Calvin, Institutes of the Christian Religion, ed. John T. McNeill, trans. Ford Lewis Battles (Philadelphia: Westminster Press, 1960), 1:108.

962 ESV, Matthew 15:8.

963 ESV, Judges 2:7, 10.

964 Adoniram Judson, quoted in Francis Wayland, A Memoir of the Life and Labors of the Rev. Adoniram Judson (Boston: Phillips, Sampson, 1853), vol. 1, 44–47.

965 ESV, Proverbs 14:34.

966 ESV, Psalm 11:3.

967 ESV, Matthew 7:24–27.

968 William Tyndale, The Obedience of a Christian Man (1528; repr. London: Penguin Books, 2000), 44–47.

969 ESV, Isaiah 40:8.

970 ESV, 2 Timothy 2:2.

971 ESV, Psalm 119:89.

972 ESV, Matthew 24:35.

973 ESV, 2 Kings 23:25.

974 A. W. Tozer, The Pursuit of God (Camp Hill, PA: Christian Publications, 1982), 7–8.

975 ESV, 1 Kings 18:21.

976 ESV, 2 Timothy 3:13–14.

977 ESV, Romans 11:4.

978 Francis A. Schaeffer, The Church at the End of the Twentieth Century (Downers Grove, IL: InterVarsity Press, 1970), 60.

979 ESV, Deuteronomy 6:7.

980 ESV, Ephesians 2:20.

981 John MacArthur, Ashamed of the Gospel: When the Church Becomes Like the World (Wheaton, IL: Crossway, 1993), 29–31.

982 ESV, 1 Corinthians 15:58.

983 A. W. Tozer, The Knowledge of the Holy (New York: Harper & Row, 1961), 1–6.

984 Owen, The Mortification of Sin, 33–36.

985 John Bunyan, Grace Abounding to the Chief of Sinners (Edinburgh: Banner of Truth Trust, 1666; repr. 1987), 14–18.

986 David Wilkerson, The Vision (New York: Pyramid Books, 1974), 112–115.

987 John Owen, The Mortification of Sin (Edinburgh: Banner of Truth Trust, 1656; repr. 2000), 33–36.

988 Thomas Watson, A Body of Divinity (Edinburgh: Banner of Truth Trust, 1692; repr. 1958), 22–25.

989 Douglas Murray, The Strange Death of Europe: Immigration, Identity, Islam (London: Bloomsbury, 2017), 2.

990 George Whitefield, Sermons of George Whitefield, ed. Lee Gatiss (Wheaton, IL: Crossway, 2012), 44–47.

991 Horatius Bonar, God's Way of Holiness (Edinburgh: Banner of Truth Trust, 1864; repr. 1999), 18–22.

992 Elisabeth Elliot, Through Gates of Splendor (Wheaton, IL: Tyndale House, 1957), 172.

993 Richard Sibbes, The Bruised Reed (Edinburgh: Banner of Truth Trust, 1630; repr. 1998), 88–92.

994 ESV, Psalm 145:4.

995 ESV, Psalm 102:18.

996 ESV, Joel 1:3.

997 ESV, Psalm 103:17.

998 ESV, Deuteronomy 7:9.

999 ESV, Proverbs 20:7.

1000 ESV, Proverbs 13:22.

1001 ESV, Exodus 34:7.

1002 ESV, Matthew 6:24.

1003 ESV, Joshua 24:15.

1004 ESV, Hebrews 11:4.

1005 ESV, Genesis 18:19.

1006 ESV, 2 Timothy 3:15.

1007 ESV, Psalm 78:7–8.

1008 ESV, Titus 2:7–8.

1009 ESV, 1 Corinthians 15:58.

1010 ESV, Revelation 14:13.

1011 ESV, 1 Timothy 4:16.

1012 ESV, Acts 2:39.

1013 ESV, Proverbs 22:6.

1014 ESV, Malachi 2:15.

1015 ESV, Psalm 112:1–2.